T0339450

Foundations and Practice of Research

Many of the issues on which meaningful research is founded are seldom discussed; for example, the role of everyday experience, diversity and coherence of meaning in the world, the meaningfulness and wider mandate of research, the very nature and validity of theoretical thought, and the deep presuppositions of philosophy and how they undermine the success of research. Such questions are material to the philosophies that guide research thinking in all fields, and since they cannot be satisfactorily addressed in a piecemeal fashion, this book employs the radically different philosophy of Herman Dooyeweerd to consider them together. Parts I and II discuss these issues theoretically and philosophically, while Part III discusses them practically, specifically the adventures that researchers across the world have had using Dooyeweerd's philosophy. *Foundations and Practice of Research* assembles a wide range of experiences of using Dooyeweerd's philosophy in research in the fields of mathematics, the natural sciences, the social sciences, the design sciences and the humanities. Case studies demonstrate how Dooyeweerd's philosophy has been found fruitful in most stages of research, and the philosophical discussion backs this up. This book challenges researchers to join the adventures, including suggestions of potential research that could be carried out, as well as questions still left unanswered.

Andrew Basden is Professor of Human Factors and Philosophy in Information Systems at the University of Salford, UK. He has been active in research for 40 of the past 50 years, informed by 12 years of professional practice.

Routledge Advances in Research Methods

For more information about this series, please visit: www.routledge.com/ Routledge-Advances-in-Research-Methods/book-series/RARM

Foundations and Practice of Research

Adventures with Dooyeweerd's Philosophy

Andrew Basden

Routledge
Taylor & Francis Group

NEW YORK AND LONDON

First published 2020
by Routledge
605 Third Avenue, New York, NY 10017

and by Routledge
2 Park Square, Milton Park, Abingdon, Oxon, OX14 4RN

First issued in paperback 2021

Routledge is an imprint of the Taylor & Francis Group, an informa business

© 2020 Taylor & Francis

The right of Andrew Basden to be identified as author of this work has been asserted by him in accordance with sections 77 and 78 of the Copyright, Designs and Patents Act 1988.

Publisher's Note
The publisher has gone to great lengths to ensure the quality of this reprint but points out that some imperfections in the original copies may be apparent.

Library of Congress Cataloging-in-Publication Data
A catalog record for this book has been requested

ISBN 13: 978-1-03-208692-7 (pbk)
ISBN 13: 978-1-138-72068-8 (hbk)

Composed on the Amiga 1200 with Protext and Pagestream.

Typeset in Sabon
by Apex CoVantage, LLC

To Richard Russell, who started the adventure, to Mike Winfield, who turned the adventure towards empirical research, and to Jesus Christ, who has made the adventure especially meaningful for me.

Contents

Figures

Tables

Foreword

How might we make the fullest sense of this world?

How might we derive the fullest meaning?

How does research philosophy help us know what we find?

There is a sophistication to the work of Dooyeweerd that enables ontological and epistemological plurality and richness. In plain: We can seek to get at more, and to explain more in more ways, but without ever needing to lose balance, to lose shape and to diminish either our rationality or our richer humanity.

Dooyeweerd wrote of the "*Gegenstand*" of the researcher, that he or she 'stands over against' their subject insofar as their analytical functioning allows and reaches. In other ways the researcher is retained within that world, differentiated only by a certain selective attitude to it. The watchfulness of the researcher is as much towards his or her own attitude as it is towards the research subject itself. Hence Dooyeweerd's philosophy leads the researcher to a humble finding rather than an arrogant knowing. It is a joy to approach this world of research. All of the world and how we might know it is ultimately facilitated by the modalities or 'aspects' of Dooyeweerd's work.

Discovering Andrew Basden's quiet passion for the work of Dooyeweerd reminded me of why I first came to the university. When I came to academia, I imagined that I was coming to a place of big ideas, of big debate, of openness and freedom of thought. Some still come as I came those years ago, seeking the profound and the biggest river of thought. I still find students like me, as young as I was then, looking, asking, open to the big encounter with an idea that envelops you as you uncover it. I hope these students are not too disappointed because much of the daily experience of university life is not like that. Much of our daily engagement is actually concerned with a sedimentary accumulation of knowledge, with a safety and a respectability in the face of one's peers, with the unsurprising and with the rote.

It was clear to me that Andrew had incubated a special interest in a bold subject. As I listened to him, one day in a classroom of Manchester Business School, I was taken back to the ideas and minds that first brought me into the university. I remember writing letters to Stafford Beer, for one, and reading Peter Checkland's book on the 148 bus. I had one friend who promised me that Michel Foucault would change my life, another who stuffed my bag with the works of Lewis Mumford and then another who shared Christopher Alexander, Maturana and Varela, and Douglas Hofstadter. We lived in a constant sway of debate. At that time, it might surprise you, but I was studying in a Department of Computer Science, albeit under the expansive tutelage of Brian Warboys, a professor of software engineering 'in the large' for whom the boundary between the university and 'real life' was not a wall but a catalyst and a calling.

So here, much later, was Andrew telling me about this philosopher called Herman Dooyeweerd, in whom he had been investing for many years, and that a book was in preparation. I was, at once, reminded of that rush of heady thinking that accompanies all the best days at university and the same sense of doors opening. The research philosophy that Dooyeweerd opens up is, as Andrew said in that Manchester classroom, "lifeworld oriented."

Peter Kawalek,
Professor,
Director of the Centre for Information Management,
Loughborough University, 2019

Preface

Why have I written this book? As I mention in Chapter 1, I have found a "pearl of great price", which is the radically interesting philosophy of Herman Dooyeweerd, and I believe it is worth researchers looking into—and then either rejecting or adopting and adapting it. This preface explains how it was that I came to find this pearl, and then why I wrote this particular book.

The first I heard of Dooyeweerd, with whose philosophy I have had many interesting and rewarding adventures, was not in my academic or professional work, but in my concern about *environmental sustainability* and responsibility.

I was bemused by the various warring factions in the *Green Movement*. Upon being presented with Dooyeweerd's aspects in the early 1990s, I suddenly realised that each faction was merely advocating a different aspect—the biotic aspect made sense of the "deep greens" who treat humanity as merely another species; the social aspect, those who emphasised communalism; the economic aspect, those working to green the economy; the pistic aspect, those emphasising the spiritual side; and so on. It struck me that a truly 'green' (environmentally responsible, sustainable) outlook is one that takes all the aspects seriously and elevates none above the others. Instead of warring, should not each accept humbly they are only one part of the picture?

All that occurred in a flash while, or shortly after, talking with *Richard Russell*. I was at a seminar on Christians in politics, and Richard was selling thought-provoking books, one of which I had recommended to participants (Marshall 1984). "Do you know the background to Paul Marshall's book?" Richard asked me, over coffee: It was the philosophy of the Dutch philosopher, Herman Dooyeweerd, of whom I had never heard. He then explained about Dooyeweerd's aspects, and immediately I saw its relevance, as above, to understanding sustainability and green thinking.

That was a paradigm shift for me, in my environmental activity. A similar paradigm shift occurred in my work.

Soon after meeting Richard, I realised that the very same aspects could help me understand the *use of information technology* (IT). I had worked a dozen years developing databases and expert systems in the medical profession, the chemical industry and the surveying profession, and was perplexed by the fact that though they would bring benefits in use, like lowered costs, they also caused problems, such as increased workloads and social pressure. On hearing of Dooyeweerd's aspects, I realised that the use of IT exhibits the same aspects, but this time as kinds of benefit or harm: for example, economic benefit versus social and psychological harm.

Dooyeweerd's aspects freed me from two major errors. Instead of trying to justify or damn something absolutely, I could recognise benefit alongside harm, but in different aspects. Instead of trying to 'balance' benefits against 'costs', perhaps assigning monetary values (can we really put a monetary value on a death?!), I could simply recognise the different aspects and then take responsibility for harmonising them in each situation. Moreover, aspects allow both benefit and harm in the same aspect.

In my academic work, I began to understand interdisciplinarity as interest in different aspects. I had learnt by this time that not only are Dooyeweerd's aspects irreducibly distinct but they form a harmony, the kind of harmony that is the ideal in interdisciplinary research and practice.

In the mid-1990s, one of my research students, *Mike Winfield*, began using Dooyeweerd's aspects in his research to elicit expert knowledge, and developed his *Multi-Aspectual Knowledge Elicitation* method (MAKE), described in §11–6.2. Mike's work showed me that Dooyeweerd's ideas could give us, not just an overview understanding of things, but also practical methods of analysis.

That was another paradigm shift for me. I began to expect Dooyeweerd's aspects to be practically useful in research and analysis, and began to recommend them to most of my then PhD students. Another of my then PhD students, Suzanne Kane, developed a method similar to Mike's (see §11–6.3), which showed clearly how 'ordinary people' could understand Dooyeweerd's aspects. Dooyeweerd's aspects are not esoteric—and Dooyeweerd offers a sound philosophic basis for this finding, in his notion of intuitive grasp (see §4–3.13).

In the late 1990s I explained the idea of an aspectual understanding of sustainability to Professor Peter Brandon and his then PhD student, Patrizia Lombardi. I remember walking around the university environs with Patrizia, pointing out the various aspects of unsustainability. Patrizia and Peter then took the idea and made it work in sustainability more effectively than I had until then managed to do in information technology. The result was groundbreaking research, developing a new paradigm in sustainability, discussed in §11–3.3.

I had begun to find other researchers who were interested in Dooyeweerd's philosophy, especially a group in north Sweden led by Prof. Donald de Raadt. In the mid-1990s they had joined with Dr. Sytse Strijbos, an engineer-philosopher at the Free University of Amsterdam, to found what became the Centre for Philosophy, Technology and Social Systems (CPTS). This was an annual working conference that we ran for 20 years, which gave researchers from across the globe a critical community in which to develop thought related to Dooyeweerd, systems theory, interdisciplinarity and development. After ten years we published a book (Strijbos & Basden 2006) with not only good papers but also comments from two 'critical friends', Gerald Midgley and Carl Mitcham. I learned two things through CPTS.

One was that Dooyeweerd's thinking could stand up well among mainstream thinkers. I had already been discovering this via the (socio-)critical information systems work in the UK, in which Habermas, Foucault and Bourdieu were usually cited. One of the 'fathers' of the information systems field, the late Prof. Heinz Klein, especially, saw value in Dooyeweerd alongside these, and, drawing on his ideas, I argued (Basden 2002) that Dooyeweerd could be seen as a thinker in the (socio-)critical theory line.

The other was a different kind of relationship between Christianity and mainstream ("secular") philosophical and scientific thinking. I am a committed Christian, and it is Jesus Christ who gives meaning to all I am and do. Early on I discovered that Dooyeweerd was also a deeply committed Christian. So were Sytse Strijbos and Donald de Raadt. Until then, I had known only three ways to relate Christian beliefs to mainstream thinking: (a) keep them separated, (b) Christian thinkers try to impose their doctrines on science, and (c) Christians acquiesce to scientific or philosophic theory, accepting it unquestioningly, either in the life of churches (e.g. business theories) or using philosophy to argue about God, religion or ethics. None of them satisfied me.

Through these colleagues and CPTS, I learned a fourth way in which Christian thought could engage positively and fruitfully with mainstream thinking in an attitude of mutual respect. In this approach, Christian thinking can offer insights (not doctrines) that can benefit mainstream thinking, rather than benefit or protect itself (see the example of Michael Faraday in §5–4.3). This approach finds its grounding in Dooyeweerd's philosophy. Dooyeweerd's deep philosophical investigations of the nature of theoretical thought showed that all thinking necessarily has a "religious" root (defined in §5–2.3), which needs to be made explicit. It so happened that the socio-critical thinkers had arrived at a similar conclusion, arguing the need to make explicit our basic ideological presuppositions. Dooyeweerd and they seemed to be travelling in similar directions.

Clear statement (not promotion) of fundamental religious presuppositions opens up dialogue. As far as I am aware, neither of the CPTS "critical friends" nor Heinz Klein professed any Christian faith, nor did some of those who took part in CPTS activity, yet they found discourse like that at CPTS immensely attractive. Indeed, since that time, I have found, paradoxically, that it is non-Christians more than Christians who find Dooyeweerd interesting.

This gave me both impetus and courage to publish, not in Reformational circles, which would be safe, but in mainstream circles. The problem was that since Dooyeweerd was unknown, each paper I wrote needed to include more detailed explanations of his thought than was necessary for known thinkers like Habermas, Heidegger or Aristotle. Also, my ideas of how Dooyeweerd can benefit my information systems field were patchy and disconnected.

So I decided I needed to write a book, in which I would try to bring my disparate ideas together, and which could also be referred to by myself and others, reducing the need for such repeated explanations. In that book, *Philosophical Frameworks for Understanding Information Systems* (Basden 2008a), I developed conceptual frameworks for understanding five main areas of concern in the information systems field. Two main advantages I discovered in Dooyeweerd were that (a) the frameworks his philosophy engendered were richer, deeper and yet more practical than most then available, and (b) he offers a way in which discourses in these five areas might meet, which until then (and even now) they very rarely did.

Two of the frameworks I then developed into an undergraduate course in human-computer interaction and a master course in information systems development. In the latter, especially, the students found Dooyeweerd's aspects of great value.

That work, however, contains only a few initial indications of how the Dooyeweerdian-grounded frameworks could engage with extant thinking. Over the next decade, and having settled my ideas into a coherent picture, I concentrated on trying to engage with extant discourses in the field of information systems. This resulted in *Foundations of Information Systems: Research and Practice* (Basden 2018a), which discusses how Dooyeweerd can enrich over 50 discourses in the information systems field.

It was during this period that my PhD supervision became more intense, with most of my students using Dooyeweerd in various ways. Together, we learned much about the utility and limitations of Dooyeweerd's philosophy in 'ordinary' research. Their work is discussed in Chapter 11, alongside that of others, to show actual experience of using Dooyeweerd's philosophy in research.

During this time, my understanding of Dooyeweerd sharpened up. For instance, Dooyeweerd's transcendental critique of theoretical thought (see Chapter 6) had always baffled me, but I began to see that it makes sense of the real situation of research in information systems, in which three main approaches had reigned supreme—positivist, interpretivist and socio-critical. They were seen as mutually incommensurable. Dooyeweerd's transcendental critique could explain this very well—but also could then suggest how they might become commensurable—so, in honour of Heinz Klein, who had been seeking *integration* among them, I worked out how Dooyeweerd's thought could provide what Heinz sought (Basden 2011a); see also §7-3.

Another idea that became increasingly important, was what in this book I call *"everyday experience"* (§1-3). I came to see that Dooyeweerd might be the best philosopher of everyday experience to emerge to date and to understand why this is so (see Chapter 2). One of my research students, Hawa Ahmad, was using Dooyeweerd to develop the notion of "down-to-earth" issues, which are the 'real-life' issues that affect users of information technology and which are seldom discussed in the literature. It was Dooyeweerd's aspects that enabled her to do so. Two more of my PhD students, Ghadah Khojah and Opeoluwa Aiyenitaju, took her idea and developed it further (see §11-7.3). Other research students, mentioned in Chapter 11, also developed similar ideas.

These were not students trained in philosophy. They were ordinary research-ers who found Dooyeweerd's philosophy very helpful in their research. For some reason, this work then seemed almost unique in the world, in that most others who were interested in Dooyeweerd focused on philosophic issues. Whilst I am interested in philosophic issues myself, my joy lies in its application—bringing benefit to the world. As I have watched the worldwide use of Dooyeweerd's ideas, I have seen them becoming more fruitful in a wide range of fields, in the mathematical, natural, human, social and societal sciences.

This is why this current book has emerged. The past 25 years since discover-ing Dooyeweerd have been an exciting adventure, in which we have together discovered the benefits, and some challenges, of using Dooyeweerd in research. Now at the end of my career, I wanted to assemble experiences of using Dooye-weerd so that others could learn and benefit therefrom, with experience and reflections together. My hope is that this current book will serve almost as a handbook for researchers who wish to continue the adventure.

Such a 'handbook' would need, of course, to set out what I see research is, which occurs in Chapter 1. It would need to explain and discuss Dooye-weerd's philosophy in sufficient breadth and depth to enable researchers to make use of it, which occurs in Parts I and II, and it should offer practical material, which is Part III.

Whereas in Basden (2008a) I took the usual line of explaining first why Dooyeweerd's philosophy differs from others, and then explaining his understanding of the world, including his aspects, in this book, I decided to approach it from the researcher's point of view. It so happens that the three main starting-points of Dooyeweerd's philosophy that make it so radi-cally different are ones that give flavour to research: respect for everyday experience, for diversity and coherence, and for meaning, especially what I call "meaningfulness". Dooyeweerd's philosophy is then explained in the context of that. Those are the chapters in Part I. Part II explains Dooye-weerd's deep investigation of the nature of theoretical thought, which, para-doxically, though reaching philosophically deeper and more profoundly than most other philosophers have done, yields ideas that are eminently practical, which enable researchers to see things in refreshingly new ways.

The role of Part III is to offer material for practical guidance of research. It contains what is possibly the first systematic explanation of Dooyeweerd's 15 aspects that is intended for academic reference. It discusses the real-life intricacies of the activity of research, including those hidden aspects that undermine or build it up. It then offers, in one very long chapter, a panoply of actual experience of using Dooyeweerd's philosophy in research.

Finally, in Part IV, the handbook calls upon researchers to join the adven-ture—but with their eyes wide open to criticisms that have been made of Dooyeweerd's ideas.

Andrew Basden,
Frodsham, UK,
2019

Acknowledgements

If this book is useful, most of the credit must go to those who have helped in its development and writing.

The whole adventure that it narrates would not have occurred had it not been for Rev. Richard Russell and Dr. Mike Winfield and the critical encouragement of colleagues like Prof. Heinz Klein, Prof. Donald de Raadt and Dr. Sytse Strijbos, as explained in the Preface.

The greatest credit, however, must go to my wife, Ruth, who, over many years has encouraged and supported me in this work, with love and kindness. She it was who, early on, patiently listened to my frustration and redirected me towards the needs of research rather than merely an explanation of Dooyeweerd's philosophy.

Much of the credit for the readability of this work goes to Dr. Stephen McGibbon who, with wisdom gleaned from years in management and his intense understanding of Dooyeweerd, provided the main thing an author needs: critical comments on the many places where the text did not make sense or was a hostage to fortune or might distract readers from the main issues. It was a boon that his interpretation of Dooyeweerd's philosophy differs from mine, so that he could challenge me to ensure that my ideas were properly explained or justified. Authors all too easily take for granted their own assumptions.

Stephen also provided continual encouragement for this project. So did Prof. Anita Mirijamdotter (Linnaeus University, Sweden) and Prof. Peter Brandon (University of Salford, UK), over the 25 years I have been working with Dooyeweerd.

I would like to thank my research students, as well as a few others with whom I worked, who are mentioned in this book, including Dr. Suzanne Kane, Dr. Kamaran Fathulla, Dr. Gareth Jones, Dr. Hawa Ahmad, Dr. Nick Breems, Dr. Sina Joneidy, Dr. Ghadah Khojah, Dr. Opeoluwa Aiyenitaju, Dr. Alex Kimani, Dr. Karen Swannack, Dr. Charmele Ayaduai, doctoral candidate Subrahmaniam Krishnan-Harihara, and erstwhile master's student Aisha Abuelma'atti (and Mike Winfield and Stephen McGibbon mentioned above), for their hard work, which demonstrated the utility of Dooyeweerd's philosophy in mainstream research, and for allowing me to use their work in this book.

Many others have helped with critical comments on draft chapters of the book, including Dr. Andrew Hartley, who devoted considerable effort to reading confusing texts and providing ways of clarifying them (as well as helping me properly understand his own research), Prof. Alaric Searle (Professor of European History, University of Salford, UK), who provided incisive comments that placed my writing in a wider context, especially of kinds of research outside my fields, Rev. Dr. David Lamb, who provided me with his work in sociolinguistics, Prof. Sue Halliday (University of Hertfordshire, UK) who forced me to clarify my attitude to Dooyeweerd, and Maurice Manktelow and Mark Surey (the UK Christian Academic Network), who challenged me with the question, "Is Dooyeweerd a solution looking for a problem?"

Finally, I would like to thank Nadia Hosseiny and Dr. Steve Bishop for help with proofreading.

1 Introduction

To Help You Read This Book

This book is about research. Not research in any one field—social sciences, psychology, chemistry, theology, mathematics—but research as research, across all fields. It is about the practical realities encountered in all kinds of research. It is about what lies at the foundations of these realities in all research fields, which are often taken for granted.

This book is about problems that challenge all fields, though manifested differently in each, many being hidden but which we feel intuitively.

Much has been written about research in this or that field, but little on research as such. Why? Is it because approaches that suit one field do not suit other fields and, moreover, because this unsuitability is presumed to be fundamental? Is it because researchers in different fields do not understand each other but divide into camps?

People may think that what is meaningful and rational in one field is meaningless in another—for example physical concepts and laws in physics are usually of little interest in social science, while social factors are usually excluded from physical theories. Yet my own fields of information systems and environmental sustainability are interdisciplinary to a degree and so have built in me an awareness of a wide range of issues as potentially important and of interest across all fields.

This chapter's sections are from the book title, in reverse order.

1–1. Adventures With Dooyeweerd's Philosophy

Why has this book appeared? For two reasons.

The motivational reason: As I have carried out my research, I have discovered a "pearl of great price", which I want to share. The "pearl" has proven not only beautiful but also valuable over the last 25 years and has made sense retrospectively of the 25 years before I discovered it. The pearl is Dooyeweerd's philosophy. I want people to examine it to decide for themselves what it is worth.

The intellectual and practical reason: Research is fascinating, and I have found Dooyeweerd's philosophy enriches it. Research is important, and I have found that Dooyeweerd's philosophy can make research more effective. Research areas are fragmented, and I have found Dooyeweerd's philosophy can provide some integration. Philosophy underlies research but often seems irrelevant, yet Dooyeweerd offers philosophy that approaches things in an eminently practical way. There are serious problems in philosophy, whether pre-modern, modern or postmodern, that I believe Dooyeweerd addresses, offering foundations that differ intrinsically from those offered by many philosophers. I have found Dooyeweerd's philosophy can also be used as a conceptual tool and provide guidance, especially in directing research into healthy directions.

Readers who have not read the Preface may find it helpful to do so here, because it outlines the chronology of my "adventures with Dooyeweerd's philosophy" and how the value of Dooyeweerd was opened up.

Throughout my life as a reflective practitioner and as researcher, I have felt, rather than crisply identified, problems. I have learned that such feelings often do indicate real, but hidden, issues, and that Dooyeweerd's philosophy in particular has helped me to crystallise them. It was the problem of *diversity in fields*, in both scholarship and practice, that initially led me to Dooyeweerd (see Preface). The first idea of his that I encountered was his suite of aspects, with which I could understand that diversity and see how it is meaningful as a symphonic harmony. I discovered that he allows us to approach research—and indeed everyday life—from a radically different perspective. For instance, Realism and Anti-realism, so long presumed to be in opposition, are but part of a more nuanced, diverse and yet cohering reality (see §6–1). Quantitative and qualitative research, so often separated, come together in Dooyeweerd (§6–3.4, §11–7).

This book recounts my adventures with Dooyeweerd's philosophy in several fields of research, especially information systems and sustainability, along with adventures some others have had.

Of course, I am biased; each treasures their own pearls and those pearls might not appeal to others. However, I wish to bequeath the pearl of Dooyeweerd to those who might value it. Though I lay out the benefits that I and others have found Dooyeweerd's philosophy can bring to research, this is not an apologia for it; Chapter 12 discusses criticisms of Dooyeweerd. I believe that Dooyeweerd's philosophy can bring genuine and unique benefit to research. I also believe there are limitations, but that these cannot be found merely by philosophic criticism, but only by seriously applying his philosophy. So this book is not a critical discussion of the philosophy as such, but an invitation to try the ideas out, so that they will be tested within research. Only then can real critical evaluation of Dooyeweerd's ideas begin.

Though Dooyeweerd's ideas are introduced and discussed in the book, readers are invited to *dwell* in them for a time, to see what issues emerge. It will turn out that issues emerge that are often overlooked or seem peripheral whereas Dooyeweerd makes them central. Thus readers might find this book useful, not only for their research but also for their teaching and their research supervision.

Who for? Researchers in any field—mathematics, physics, biology, psychology, linguistics, languages, philosophy, sociology, organisational sciences, economics and management, the arts, jurisprudence, ethics, theology, and many more. Though perhaps unreasonable according to C.P. Snow's *Two Cultures*, the modern idea of rationality-driven progress, or the postmodern questioning of grand narratives, I have found that Dooyeweerd offers basic understandings in each field, sufficient to be able to make sense within it and take an interest. Readers are assumed to know something about research but not necessarily philosophy.

This is not a book about philosophy as such, but what might be called "applied philosophy". As such, it includes an explanation of Dooyeweerd's philosophy that I hope will interest philosophical as well as scientific researchers. It may be seen as a handbook for researchers who wish to join the adventure.

- Part I shows the direction in which research with Dooyeweerd tends to head, respecting everyday pre-theoretical experience, diversity, coherence and meaningfulness, and it explains the historical context of Dooyeweerd's philosophy.
- Part II discusses the core of research, theoretical thought. It examines Dooyeweerd's transcendental critique of theoretical thought to draw out a deeper understanding of this than most philosophy offers, which, paradoxically, offers a very practical basis for understanding fields, discourses, paradigms, and ideas and can tackle thorny issues like progress.
- Part III furnishes researchers with practical tools and understanding to undertake research using Dooyeweerd. It recounts actual experience of using Dooyeweerd in research, by this author and others, which has surprised me by its extent.
- Part IV is a call to join the adventure with eyes wide open, so as to learn together what benefits Dooyeweerd might bring and where he is to be avoided.

1–2. Research

Research has been defined as "critical and exhaustive investigation or experimentation having for its aim the discovery of new facts and their correct interpretation" (Webster 1971, 1930) or "systematically finding out things thereby increasing our knowledge" (Saunders et al. 2012). Yet, in reality, research is beyond concise definition. Researchers have found a much wider range of things to be important; research is

> multi-disciplinary; an attitude to reality; developing ideas in exciting ways; triggering new ideas; a service to humanity; or a selfish occupation; curiosity about reality; highly diverse; a chore; stimulating; a joy; a great responsibility; or shirking responsibility; creative; puzzle-solving; fascinating; a way of life; a discipline; finding out and making sense; route to theoretical understanding; theoretical analysis and synthesis; deconstruction; construction; projects;

paper-writing; bid-writing; promotion of ideas; critical discourse; intellectual elitism; paradigm-shifts; a contributor to our bodies of knowledge; a mandate and calling; "Thinking God's thoughts after him" (Kepler); or the way humanity controls the world; humanity's ultimate freedom and dignity; the way to truth; or an irrelevant sham; making a name for ourselves; necessary path to an academic career; pleasing university management; a privileged occupation; robbing the world of resources; a great community; back-stabbing; collaboration; competitive self-interest; too much in silos; too often trivial; a job; a vision; a commitment; pressure; resilience and perseverance.

I do not agree with all those, yet all are meaningful as facets of research, and hence worthy of consideration in a book like this.

1–2.1   The Mandate of Research

Despite the intricate fluidity that is research, we need to at least understand something of its mandate, to differentiate it from other complex activities. Why is it good to research? During my research life, I have taken the core *mandate for research* to be *to offer theoretical findings to contribute to humanity's bodies of knowledge that enhance our understanding of the way reality works.* So have many others.

What are bodies of knowledge? In this book they are taken to be *collections of beliefs about the way reality works, which are general and on which it is reasonable to rely, which exhibit some kind of coherence, and which offer the potential of bringing good into the world.* The terms used, and the reasons for them, are explained later.

The following example, from my field of information systems, will be used as a case study throughout this book, along with examples drawn from other fields.

> Example: Davis' (1989) Technology Acceptance Model (TAM) is an established part of the body of knowledge of the information systems field. TAM was devised in its initial form, from theories of behaviour (the existing bodies of knowledge), to predict the degree of usage of information technology packages (then, email; today, others). Davis interviewed users of email to measure degrees of perceived usefulness and ease of use, and with this data analysed certain hypotheses. After TAM was published, it was widely adopted. Many researchers used it to investigate usage of other information systems in other contexts, which widened the community's understanding of factors that are relevant, so revised versions were produced, as well as a different model, which are more universally applicable. Now TAM and its variants are widely accepted as part of the body of knowledge about information systems. TAM represented a paradigm shift, because it brought together two factors that had previously been treated separately: usefulness and ease of use. Doing so brought this "good" into

the world, that the importance of both together, which many had felt intuitively, was now explicitly established. Chapters 3 and 7 explain TAM more.

In this book, bodies of knowledge are viewed more widely than elsewhere, such as Romme's (2016, 211) view of them as collections of "values, constructs, models, principles and instantiations", or as institutions, professions and regulations. The view here raises research and bodies of knowledge above personal, institutional or even national concern. Good research has always been trans-national and trans-individual.

The emphasis on the "good" that bodies of knowledge can bring is intended to transcend Foucault's (1977) idea that bodies of knowledge express, and are a means of, power and control. Two kinds of more general good (or corresponding harm) can inform our discussions: (a) in practice, by applying the theories, and (b) in academic life, by offering reliable theoretical foundations on which further research depends (e.g. axioms of mathematical theorems or sociological conceptual models).

Bodies of knowledge are amorphous, and their boundaries cannot be precisely identified; they include each other, relate to each other and interpenetrate each other. Bodies of knowledge occur, exist or pertain for various fields, such as arithmetic, physics, healthcare, history or theology. There are also bodies of knowledge within these, on prime numbers, quantum physics, paediatric healthcare, German history and Calvinistic theology, and, between these, on history of theology and theology of history. Bodies of knowledge should not be seen as *things* but rather as *Umwelten* (§4–3.5): environments within, and by reference to which, research and its application take place. Bodies of knowledge provide a meaning-context beyond the interests of the researchers or their institutions or communities.

Knowledge increases, advances. What does that mean, and is it desirable? Throughout history, theories have been built up but then overturned or abandoned, sometimes by 'better' theories but not always. Kuhn (1962) tackles this in *The Structure of Scientific Revolutions*, but his famous notion of paradigm is ambiguous. What is "better"? Dooyeweerd helps us understand paradigms and knowledge advance, as discussed in §8–2 and §7–2.

Does "mandate" sound, to some readers, too much like Lyotardian grand narratives? Lyotard's (1984) suspicions were rightly levelled against total views of a rationalistic, modernistic kind. So were Dooyeweerd's, and yet he still believed reality is meaningful. That is why mandate is important.

1–2.2 *Clarifying Concepts Used in This Book*

This section clarifies what terms relevant to research and bodies mean when used in this book.

> *Knowledge*: Either of specific facts or general understanding. Here, knowledge will usually refer to the latter.

Understanding: Generic knowledge, the answer to "Why?", either theoretical or pre-theoretical. Pre-theoretical understanding is often expressed in rules-of-thumb (heuristics) or common sense. Pre-theoretical understanding is respected, not disdained (Chapter 2).

Example: "Honey is a good remedy for coughs" has, for centuries, been pre-theoretical understanding in medical bodies of knowledge, deemed mere folklore, but while writing this book, research established a theoretical basis for it in biological theory.

Good research helps crystallise both understanding and limits of applicability.

Theoretical and pre-theoretical thought: See Chapters 2 and 6. Theoretical thought involves 'standing back' from reality; pre-theoretical thought involves proximal engagement in reality. Both include the activity of thinking and the ideas (knowledge) that emerge.

Findings: Suggestions that emerge from research, which contribute to theoretical understanding, or theory, generated by theoretical thought during research. Usually generated by analysis of collected data (§6–3.4).

Theory: "Beliefs about the way the reality works, which are general and on which it is reasonable to rely". The reason I did not use "theory" above is because I wanted to open up what constitutes that disputed concept, theory. That theories are *beliefs*, rather than "facts" or "truths", indicates the provisional nature of all knowledge and the active reliance on, or questioning of, knowledge when we use it. This is recognised not only by Dooyeweerd but also by Habermas, Foucault, Polanyi, Kuhn and others. Theories may be expressed as rules and principles that guide, models, maps and statements that explain or describe, or conceptual frameworks that situate, stimulate and influence the first two. Classifications may also be seen as theories.

Situation: That which is researched, not necessarily involving humans. Compare Dewey's (1938/1991) use of the term—except that I do not presume, as Dewey did, that 'inquiry' (how to get a grip on a situation) is always of an analytical nature. Action in a situation might be intuitive or even instinctive (see later) and is only analytical when studying it.

World: (a) The *reality* we study or think about, as set of situations studied by research. (b) As in Husserl, a body of knowledge, e.g. the world of physics, lifeworld. Depending on the field, the world comprises numbers, spaces, forces, plants, animals, ideas, constructions, utterances, relationships, resources, attitudes, beliefs and so on.

Reality: Some Anti-realist researchers might dislike reference to "reality", while many Realist researchers in natural sciences might rejoice. However, as explained in §6–1.1, I use "reality" in neither sense, seeing the stances and supposed opposition between Realism and

Anti-realism as misdirected. The world in its 'worldness', its 'otherness' to the researcher, are respected, but the researcher is also part of the world (reality) (§2–2).

The way reality works: The way reality (world) tends to function. In my research I have always treated reality as *faithful*, continuing to tend to work in certain ways irrespective of us, but not completely without us. As discussed in §4–3.8, I tend to see this in terms of deep laws that enable and govern functioning and wellbeing.

Works: Functioning, but also implying Good, as in "it works well" or "it doesn't work". There is no connotation of goal, defined end or power.

Fields: In the main, *science* refers to theoretical understanding of the way reality works in one of its aspects (not only the exact or natural sciences, but also human, social and societal areas of study). *Discipline* adds some normative intent and guidance. *Field* refers to either. Sub-fields are called *areas* of concern or interest.

Research: The discussions in this book are mainly about academic research, which seeks generic understanding, though much will be relevant also to professional research, which studies specific situations, and to research-and-development as long as the aim of development is greater understanding for all. The difference between *pure research* and *applied research* lies not in the type of research itself, but in what motivates it, and this is part of the everyday experience in which research is embedded (Lazarsfeld & Reitz 1970).

Researcher, *scientist* and *thinker* are treated largely as synonyms.

1–2.3 Some Requirements for Research

The activities of research should be designed to meet the requirements for generating findings that are worthy of potential inclusion in bodies of knowledge. Each field implies different requirements, which it is a purpose of this book to discuss, some of which are usually presupposed rather than discussed openly.

Generality: Findings are expected to be general rather than specific, so that they can apply across a range of previously unforeseen situations, not just to those studied, and can be applied by others than the original researchers. Generality opens the future to possibility. Generality usually takes the form of understanding ("Why it rains") rather than idiographic knowledge ("It rained here yesterday"), though facts like the Gravitational Constant or the populations of countries can also be generally relevant.

Reliance-worthiness: Findings should be those **on which it is reasonable to rely**. This replaces the commonly assumed criteria of truth or accuracy, for reasons discussed in §6–1.3. Reliance-worthiness takes different forms in the exact, natural and social sciences (see §8–1). It can be undermined by diverse factors discussed by others, including carelessness in carrying out research, too few or poorly selected samples (§7–1.2), inappropriate rationalities employed (§7–1.3), lack of reproducibility (§7–1.4), overlooking relevant issues because of over-narrow focus on certain aspects (§2–1.1) (example: overlooking trust and ethics in banking, resulting in the 2008 banking crisis), "interests" and power (§2–3.2), and dysfunctions like bias and cheating (§7–4.2).

Value: Findings should be those that can, potentially or actually, bring good into the world, whether practical or academic. Often, it is presumed that research can improve situations. Good to the world implies responsibility. This is preferred to the criterion of *relevance*, because we cannot foretell the relevance of general knowledge. The 'ocean of meaningfulness', within which research and its applications operate (§4–3.10), is vast and unexplored.

Dissemination: Contributing findings to bodies of knowledge implies dissemination, so that others may understand, critique, refine and apply them. Hence the edifice of journals, conferences and institutions. Sadly, bodies of knowledge are distorted because (1) Many topics are ignored because reviewers and editors opt for fashionable ones—and so do researchers who want to increase their publication rates. (2) Researchers often study the pathological rather than the healthy and multi-faceted (example: Foucault's dystopian idea of Panopticon has curtailed surveillance studies for decades (Lyon 2007)). (3) Reviewers don't understand and thus reject 'blue ocean' topics in favour of 'safe' ones. As Oliver Sacks (1973) once remarked,

I was struck by the irony, the paradox, of all this: when I had nothing much to say I could be published without difficulty; now I had something to say I was denied publication. [*Thanks to Peter Kawalek for drawing this to my attention.*]

Among all involved—researchers, community and institutions alike—self-critique and humility are important, and a sensitivity to ideas not usually considered.

Coherence/Harmony: In order to build a body, rather than ad hoc assortments, of knowledge, it should be understood how findings relate to existing knowledge, as relevant to some topic or aspect of reality. Harmony between findings and body is not uniformity but rather that of the symphony, where new themes arise from time to time, enriching the whole.

Originality: Research must generate new knowledge, not merely reformulate existing knowledge (unless that reformulation is itself new). The 'gold standard' is new paradigms or at least new ideas, but new interpretations and sources are more common. The empirical reality in all fields offers an inexhaustible supply of new sources, but they should be chosen carefully. Retesting existing findings *seems* unoriginal but in fact is valuable for testing *reproducibility*, which is a major challenge in some fields (§7–1.4).

Dignity of researched and researcher: Dignity of the world being studied and of the researcher. When people are being studied, they are treated as fully human. The researcher is not just a recorder or mirror, but a responsive-responsible formulator of useful findings.

These are the main requirements the discussions in this book will assume for research.

1–2.4   Research Content, Activity and Application

Three elements of research will be covered in this book, which may be conceptually distinguished but relate to each other in the real-life practice of research: research content, activity and application. Examples of each are included in the "Research is . . ." list earlier.

> *Research content*: The content of research includes its findings together with all the material from which findings are crafted—literature, conceptual models, data, analyses, assumptions, presuppositions, etc. Research content revolves around the research topic and *main research question* (which is the *research aim* expressed as the question(s) that the research answers).

Chapter 2 relates theoretical to pre-theoretical content, Chapter 3 discusses diversity and coherence, and Chapter 4 discusses the meaningfulness of content. Chapter 5 discusses the impact philosophy has on research content and why Dooyeweerd's philosophy is promising. Chapter 6 probes the nature of research data, analyses, presuppositions, etc., using Dooyeweerd's "transcendental critique of theoretical thought". This yields a useful notion (three-part Ground-Ideas, Chapter 7), which helps us understand issues like bias and with which we can more systematically discuss fields, discourses, paradigms, concepts and ideas (Chapter 8). Chapter 6 also contains a discussion of truth and facts. Chapter 11 discusses actual experience of using Dooyeweerd's philosophy in these kinds of research content.

> *Research activity*: The activities that go on in research to craft and disseminate findings. These include both the 'obvious' activities of theoretical thought like data collection and analysis, and the 'hidden' ones like back-stabbing versus collaboration. Both types affect the quality and nature of research content, but the 'hidden' ones are often more pernicious and poorly understood.

Research activity is especially discussed in Chapter 10, with emphasis on hidden aspects. Chapter 2 discusses the 'everyday' and pre-theoretical character of research activity that gives research its context. Chapter 3 emphasises its diversity and coherence. Chapter 4 offers a philosophical foundation for understanding research activity and Chapter 5, one particular hidden aspect: religious presuppositions. Chapter 6 deepens understanding of theoretical activity. Chapter 11 discusses stages in research, and actual experience of the activities of formulating areas of concern, critiquing paradigms, clarifying ideas and concepts, and methods of data collection and analysis.

> *Research application* refers to using the findings of research to bring benefit (or harm) to the world and as material for further research. The beneficial or harmful repercussions of research in the world can occur immediately, but they are also often indirect or long term, sometimes long after the originating researchers have passed away. If application is widespread (example: theories of communication encapsulated in social media), the good or harm is amplified. So, researchers potentially have an enormous *responsibility*, not only to abide by the accepted rules of "research ethics", not only to provide deliverables, but also to consider the possibility of indirect, long-term or widespread impact.

The importance of research application implies that we need to understand and discuss the wider context in which research is placed—*the world*. This is the discussion in Part I. Chapter 2 argues against the presupposition of detachment of research from the world in three ways. Chapter 3 examines the diversity and coherence of the reality within which research is embedded. Chapter 4 sets out the rich meaningfulness of the world. Chapter 5 then briefly discusses the philosophical world within which Dooyeweerd's philosophy operates and how the "immanence-standpoint" (§5–3) has exacerbated the detachment of research. Throughout the rest of the book, research application is occasionally discussed explicitly but more often assumed as an axiological attitude with which to research.

Research, content, activity and application should be considered together in *research strategy*, *research design* and *research planning*, which, in this book, occurs implicitly rather than explicitly, mostly in Chapters 10 and 11. In *action research* (Reason 2006), they are already fused together.

1–2.5   *Range of Fields*

Throughout our discussion, examples are drawn from many fields, with many from my own fields of information systems and sustainability.

Chapter 2 draws on examples from the fields of information systems development, anthropology, physics, finance and agriculture. Chapter 3 draws on examples from the fields of information systems use, mathematics, theology, quantum theory and trust. Chapter 5 draws on examples from the fields of sociology, information systems and Korean culture.

Chapter 6 draws on examples from the fields of information systems, mathematics and sociolinguistics. Chapter 7 draws on examples from the fields of sociolinguistics and theology, mathematics, physics, sustainability, psychology, information systems and sociology. Chapter 8 draws on examples from the fields of history, information systems, healthcare, theology, biology and quantum theory.

Chapter 10 draws on examples from the fields of information systems, physics, theology, psychology, software development and government policy on research. Chapter 11 draws on examples from the fields of statistics, sustainability, sustainability policy, politics, knowledge management, information systems, electrical engineering, healthcare records, cognition, computer procrastination, diagrammatology, e-government, information science, documentation, philosophy of trust, education, healthcare, discourse analysis and chemistry.

1–3. Practice

"Practice" in the book's title refers to both research activity and research application related to research content. "Practice" is defined by Webster (1971, 1780) as "the exercise of a profession" and "actual performance or application of knowledge, as opposed to mere possession of knowledge" and it often refers to developing a skill, but in this book it refers to more than these. "Practice" implies the realities, the real life of research, as distinct from theories or principles about it. This book, though applying philosophy and digging foundations, tries to tackle seriously the richness of these realities.

A number of terms and concepts, relevant to this, are used throughout our discussions to imply this full reality, deriving from various quarters. The concepts relate to each other as knots in a fishing net—pick up one and all the rest rise too. All will be mentioned where appropriate, but the main term—the picked-up knot—is *everyday experience*, along with *pre-theoretical*, and these will usually imply all the others.

> *Everyday life*: The total functioning, situation and being of people engaged in living, working, playing, etc. Example: using *Twitter* on a mobile phone while walking along.
>
> *Real life*: Everyday life, emphasising its complexity, richness and the unexpected, as in "Theoretically it's easy, but in real life it's frustrating".
>
> Everyday experience: Reality in its full actuality and meaning, as it actually happens, has happened or could happen, which de Certeau (1984, xi) calls "'ways of operating' or doing things", in its fullest extent, without neglecting any aspect thereof *a priori*. Everyday life is real life from the perspective of the experiencer, their experiencing and being experienced. Three common connotations of "everyday experience" do not apply in this book. (a) Beyond human experience, it extends to the realities of non-human activity. The everyday

experience of an asteroid, for example, will be its orbit, being warmed by the sun, the slow changes in its structure or mineral composition, and so on, but perhaps also of it being visited, sampled and photographed by a satellite. (b) Beyond appearances, everyday experience also includes reality which is behind and beneath them. (c) Unlike some writing, where "everyday" has connotations of being second-class, mundane, unworthy of our attention, here the everyday is respected for its richness and as part of the *foundation* of research (see Chapter 2), as that full reality from which data is abstracted for research.

Pre-theoretical attitude of thought or *Naïve attitude*: The attitude our thinking takes in most everyday life, when we accept it as given and engage therein. Contrasted with the *theoretical attitude of thought*, which involves 'standing-over-against' things around us (§2–1.1).

Down-to-earth issues: The kind of issues encountered in everyday life, which are important to those involved, 'on the ground' (Ahmad & Basden 2013). Example: clarity in health records. Contrasted with high-level issues, of interest to academia, management, etc., such as power relations, cost-effectiveness, and object-oriented design.

Tacit knowledge: Knowledge we possess which cannot (easily) be explained (Polanyi 1967), but on which we rely in everyday functioning (§2–4). Contrasted with explicit knowledge (§4–3.12).

Intuition: "the act or process of coming to direct knowledge without reasoning or inferring" (Webster 1971, 1187), with which it is contrasted. Everyday life involves a mixture of intuition with reasoning (see §4–3.12). Instinct, as direct psychical knowing, is but one component of intuition.

Common sense: The harmony of rationalities that we often employ in everyday life.

Lifeworld: Shared background understanding: emphasising the assumptions and tacit knowledge in everyday experience. Contrasted with the scientific worlds of e.g. physics. "The life-world is above all the province of practice, of action" (Schutz & Luckmann 1973, 18). Dooyeweerd helps expand the notion of lifeworld (§4–3.11.2).

We must give due respect to all of these if we are to properly understand research in its richness. As Chapter 2 shows, this everyday attitude pervades all three of research content, activity and application, but in different ways.

Note: In research content, it is the everyday experience of the people or situations being studied that is to be respected, and it must not be contaminated with the lifeworld assumptions of the researcher. To understand this can be challenging when the assumptions of the researcher and those being researched differ, as might be the case in history research and cross-cultural research.

What is called "research ethics" is rightly seen as concerning the everyday practice of research activity and application but is too often just a bolted-on check about safety and privacy. This book goes beyond this, to take account of the attitude and responsibility of researchers and appliers.

1-4. Foundations

"Foundations of research" employs a metaphor from the construction industry: the whole building is built upon foundations, rests upon foundations, gains its integrity from foundations—and the foundation remains unseen, except in its effects, perhaps when a building subsides. For good findings, on which it is reasonable to rely, good foundations are essential, and this is what Dooyeweerd offers.

1-4.1 Foundations of Research

The foundations upon which the content, activity and application of research are built, on which they rest, from which they gain their integrity, are presuppositions and assumptions made about the nature of the reality being researched, the nature of the research activity and the nature of application. (That foundations are dug into the earth might stretch the metaphor towards what Dooyeweerd calls standpoints; see §5–3).

> *Note on terminology: assumptions, presuppositions.* In this book, *assumptions* are about what is true ("I assume it will rain tomorrow") while *presuppositions* are about what is meaningful ("But you are in a desert, so your assumption is meaningless!"). Assumptions depend on presuppositions to make them meaningful. An *axiom* is an assumption expressed explicitly in a statement. Most assumptions and presuppositions otherwise are implicit. Dooyeweerd differentiates three levels of presupposition (§5–2).

Foundations tend to underpin a whole field or major areas of fields. They are often expressed in conceptual frameworks. For example, Basden (2008a, 2018a) conceptualises information systems use as three interwoven human engagements, each of which is multi-aspectual, and information systems development, as four interwoven responsibilities (outlined in §11–3.6). With a good foundational understanding, various challenges in the field can be understood and addressed, and new directions of research are given impetus.

Since fields and areas of research are diverse—information systems, chemistry, mathematics, theology, management studies, etc.—so too are the foundations that are appropriate to them. Some thinkers, however, seek single, unitary frameworks across multiple fields, such as systems theory or chaos theory. However, as discussed in Basden (2018b), systems theory can mislead or distort, and usually cannot be used without additional information that is germane to the field and its foundations.

Instead of relying on such theories, this book makes use of philosophy.

1–4.2   *Philosophy*

Strauss (2009) characterises philosophy as the "discipline of disciplines", because it can address issues across all fields—issues like diversity and coherence, being, process and values, theoretical thinking and rationality, which lie at the foundation of all fields of research. Though this book is not a book about philosophy, because it is about foundations of research it must employ philosophy to help us think about these foundations.

As Midgley (2000) argues, philosophy is important even for practice, to provide tools for critiquing and justifying practice, to define alternatives, etc., and philosophy also helps to lay conceptual foundations and stimulate unconventional ideas (Basden 2018a, 20).

But which philosophy? Social philosophers might not have much to say about the foundations of mathematics, the natural sciences or theology—except perhaps about the activity and application of their research seen as social functioning. To grossly oversimplify the history of philosophy: Most ancient Greek philosophers treated what we call research in terms of pure thinking; Scholastic philosophers treated research as in service of theology, the "queen of the sciences"; many pre-Kantian philosophers were highly influenced by the natural sciences and presumed research delivered firm truths about the world; Kant's "Copernican Revolution" reconceived research as sovereign consciousness interpreting the world; Husserl recognised the importance of shared background knowledge (lifeworld) for research; Heidegger submerged the individual in the world; Foucault argued for research as an exercise of power. Yet none of these seems to tackle the realities and fun and frustration of research—those things in the "Research is . . ." list earlier. Many philosophers seem limited to reacting to previous ideas or to certain aspects of research.

By contrast, I have found Dooyeweerd can offer a good philosophical understanding of real-life complexity and for critiquing and constructing foundations for research. So have others. This is the "pearl of great price" mentioned earlier. This book is an account of my adventures with Dooyeweerd's philosophy over 25 years, alongside some adventures of those others.

1–4.3   *Dooyeweerd and Philosophy*

In many fields, the traditional relationship between philosophy and scientific research constrains research in two ways. Firstly, to discuss "research philosophy", often in terms of research approach, has been a requirement in many fields, and researchers have felt constrained to opt for a few acknowledged streams of philosophy, even when they do not fit comfortably. As we shall see in §7–4.1, Dooyeweerd offers an escape route.

Secondly, philosophy is often broken down into *ontology* (about types of being that are meaningful to the research), *epistemology* (about ways of knowing that are relevant to the research) and *axiology* (about values and normativity). To Dooyeweerd, these three cannot so easily be separated, because he takes meaningfulness, rather than being, knowing or values, to be the foundation for all these. (Chapter 4 contains a philosophical discussion of this.)

Dooyeweerd believed that (Western) philosophy was in need of inner reformation, given its long history of dead-ends and antinomies. (His philosophical stream is known as "Reformational Philosophy" partly for this reason and partly because it grew out of Dutch Reformed thinking.) To Dooyeweerd, unlike some other Reformational thinkers, reformation should not be forced from the outside but developed from the inside, natural to the way philosophy is. As we shall see in Chapter 5, Dooyeweerd addresses philosophical and scientific questions from a very different direction than do most philosophers, and this means that research rooted in Dooyeweerd's philosophy takes on a different flavour and can accomplish different kinds of things.

What freed him to find the different direction was, I believe, his deep Christian faith. However, he does not impose Christian ideas to constrain philosophy but lets philosophy be philosophy, recognising that all thinkers bring beliefs, which should be declared. This is discussed especially in §5–4.3. Paradoxically, I have found that it is non-Christians who have found his views attractive. He does offer a few Christian ideas to help philosophy, but this contrasts with many Christian thinkers, who use philosophy in discussion of their doctrines; Dooyeweerd and they work in opposite directions.

I do not claim that Dooyeweerd is the only philosopher who can help us, only that he is worth considering seriously by researchers in all fields, even if they then reject him. The most useful portion of Dooyeweerd's philosophy is undoubtedly his suite of irreducibly distinct yet inter-related aspects, described in Chapters 3 and 9. Any philosophy that provides a suite like this might be useful for the purposes of this book, and Dooyeweerd disclaims all pretensions of absoluteness for his suite. However, Chapter 9 discusses why Dooyeweerd's suite can be trusted, and §4–3.13 reveals that it rests on philosophically sound foundations.

The challenge is that Dooyeweerd's philosophy and its potential is not widely known, so there is little in the way of external critique, which is what is needed. There is however a modicum of recognition. For instance, Paul Cliteur (1983) was disgusted that the jubilee issue of the *General Dutch Journal of Philosophy* omitted Dooyeweerd, and he tried to rectify this with an article that critically presented the uniqueness and importance of Dooyeweerd's ideas. This is remarkable because Cliteur, Professor of Philosophy at the Technical University of Delft, was a committed atheist and president of the Dutch Humanist League, and thus not in agreement with Dooyeweerd's own Christian principles.

This book is offered in an attempt to invite proper external critique and then use of Dooyeweerd's philosophy where it is appropriate.

The discussions herein express my own research-oriented perspective on Dooyeweerd, with which not all agree, and some issues Dooyeweerd discusses in depth do not appear here. Those issues become important from other perspectives, such as from philosophy or religious belief (for example, much of NC,II [identified in next section] contains numerous discussions about specific philosophical points raised by others), and readers should consult Dooyeweerd's own writings to tackle those. The material here should provide at least a skeleton understanding of them.

1–4.4 Resources

The main source of Dooyeweerd's ideas is his second *magnum opus*, *A New Critique of Theoretical Thought* (Dooyeweerd 1955), which henceforth will be designated as "**NC**". Its importance has been recognised by the Dutch National Library Archive as important Dutch literature and is available for free download from there.

> Volume I (philosophy, transcendental critique and history):
> "www.dbnl.org/tekst/dooy002newc05_01/"
> Volume II (aspects and epistemology):
> "www.dbnl.org/tekst/dooy002newc06_01/"
> Volume III (things, relationships and the state):
> "www.dbnl.org/tekst/dooy002newc07_01/"
> Volume IV (thematic index):
> "www.dbnl.org/tekst/dooy002newc08_01/"

Those works are highly philosophical and not always easy to understand. Several websites render Dooyeweerd's ideas in more understandable chunks, such as:

> http://dooy.info/ (The Dooyeweerd Pages, explaining and discussing Dooyeweerdian themes)
> https://jgfriesen.wordpress.com (Glenn Friesen's explanations and comments)
> www.allofliferedemmed.co.uk (Steve Bishop's valuable, growing collection of articles by Reformational thinkers)

Also, the range of publications about Dooyeweerd's philosophy in English is growing, with philosophically oriented ones like Clouser (2005), Strauss (2009), Marcel (2013a, 2013b) and Zuidervaart (2016), and with ones that apply his philosophy like Brandon & Lombardi (2005) (sustainability), Strijbos & Basden (2006) (systems), Verkerk et al. (2015) (technology), Chaplin (2011) (politics) as well as several of my own.

1–5. Guide for Readers

This is not a philosophy book, but a book that applies philosophy. It does not argue philosophical theories, after the rigorous manner of Analytical Philosophy, but rather explains and reflects on philosophical issues in research.

Occasionally, however, it strays over the border into philosophical arguments, (a) to summarise how Dooyeweerd exposes and perhaps addresses problems in the mainstream philosophies, usually in a way that can engage them, and (b) to indicate where philosophical development might be needed, such as where I disagree with Dooyeweerd's ideas.

1–5.1 The Structure of the Book

As mentioned earlier, the book has four parts, Part I looking at research in its wider context, Part II discussing theoretical thought itself, Part III offering practical guidance in research, based on experience, and Part IV calling researchers to join the adventures with Dooyeweerd's philosophy. The chapters, mentioned earlier, are listed here systematically to show the overall argument of the book.

The chapter topics are not necessarily in the order many would expect. Many textbooks, such as Saunders et al. (2012), discuss research philosophy early, and presume extant philosophies are unproblematic as a foundation for research; so just choose one. But if philosophy needs reformation, we need to understand its **starting-points**: presuppositions that are made in philosophy, about research and the world. Dooyeweerd's starting-points are different from those of most philosophy—everyday experience instead of theoretical thought, diversity and coherence instead of attempts to simplify, meaning instead of being or process, and dependence instead of self-dependence; these are explained and discussed in Part I. I have found these starting-points very friendly to research in many fields (see, for example, Basden (2018a)). Therefore, in Part I, to introduce these starting-points:

- Chapter 2 situates research in relation to everyday experience.
- Chapter 3 discusses diversity and coherence of research and the world.
- Chapter 4 discusses the importance of meaningfulness as a way of understanding the world, as well as research.
- Chapter 5 situates Dooyeweerd's philosophy in its historical and scholarly context and discusses the deep problems in philosophy.

That provides a background understanding of Dooyeweerd's approach to theoretical thought, the core of research. Whereas most discussions of research presuppose it, Dooyeweerd sees it as problematic and in need of critique. His discussion can rejuvenate our research. Therefore, in Part II:

- Chapter 6 introduces Dooyeweerd's critiques of theoretical thought and how they disclose three fundamental philosophical problems that must be tackled. It brings a fresh approach to the apparent conflict between Realism and Anti-realism, truth and post-truth.
- Chapter 7 discusses how clear understanding of these three philosophical problems, reinterpreted as a Ground-Idea, can help us understand

what is going on in research and how apparently incommensurable approaches may be integrated.

- Chapter 8 discusses fields, paradigms and concepts and ideas.

Part III offers material of more direct practical relevance to researchers:

- Chapter 9 contains an encyclopaedia of (my understanding of) Dooyeweerd's 15 aspects.
- Chapter 10 discusses the multi-aspectual activity that is research: the responsibility and possibilities that researchers have in each aspect.
- Chapter 11 discusses actual experience of using Dooyeweerd's philosophy in research, in most of its stages, including understanding the field, reviewing literature, conceptual frameworks, research methods, collecting data and analysing it.

In Part IV:

- Chapter 12 discusses criticisms of Dooyeweerd's philosophy, suggesting that critique from users is needed.
- Chapter 13 briefly concludes our discussion, outlining where Dooyeweerd can contribute, discussing the relevance of Dooyeweerd's philosophy to the situation we face today, and calling researchers to adopt Dooyeweerd's ideas.

1–5.2   Some Tips on Reading

Some characteristics of the writing in the following chapters will help readers in their understanding.

1. Recognising that much of this material will be new to readers, copious *cross-references* are offered for where readers might find explanations or elaborations of what they are reading. These cross-references *do not have to be followed*, except as indicated and if the reader wishes further elucidation. Think of the book as a large semantic net. Structure of cross references: e.g. §4–3.11.1 means Chapter 4, Section 3, Subsection 11, Subsubsection 1.
2. Likewise, text in *parentheses* may always be skipped on first reading.
3. *References* in the *present tense* are to material that has relevance as it stands, even if their sources are long dead (e.g. "Aristotle argues . . ."). When thinkers are mentioned in the *past tense*, the emphasis is on the development of their thought, whether in past or recent present (e.g. "Aristotle argued . . .").
4. Most *references to philosophy* are offered mainly for those who wish to consider research philosophically. Readers whose main interested is in research as such might usually, if they wish, *skip over them.*

5. Most *references to Dooyeweerd's ideas* (usually as "**NC**") are offered so that readers might, if they wish to, critically understand the interpretations of his ideas offered in this book, develop them and perhaps suggest alternatives. Criticism of Dooyeweerd's thought is found in Chapter 12.

6. *Reference to my own work* is of two types. When I use the first-person pronoun, I am inviting the reader to enter into dialogue with me. When I reference myself in the third person (for example as "Basden [1999] argues . . .") I treat myself as just an author like others, with whom I might or might not agree.

7. A *Note on terminology* explains how words and phrases are used *in this book*, sometimes in specialised or unusual ways. It might also resolve ambiguity or gather synonyms together. It is usually in narrower paragraphs with smaller font. When in normal text and paragraphs, it usually contains material that should be read. Notes on terminology are indexed.

8. A *Research opportunity* is a brief suggestion for research that could be carried out. The three-dozen suggestions are research I should like to do, but I doubt whether I will, so I invite readers to undertake the research in their own names. Very many other opportunities exist, of course.

9. Likewise, *examples* are inserted, often as narrower paragraphs, usually in a smaller font. Where these are in the main font, they contain material to be treated as main text.

10. Text emphasised in *italics* often indicates key concepts of the current section, so that readers may easily locate them. Those in bold indicate extra topics or important messages.

11. Because the discussions in this book are taken from many fields, I cannot rely on readers understanding the jargon of each field or its assumptions and presuppositions. Therefore, sometimes, the *style* of writing might be explanatory, perhaps more suited to a textbook, while the *content* should be that of an academic monograph.

12. Likewise, because some researchers today enter research from cultures where critical thinking is not habitual, some things are explained that those used to critical thinking take for granted.

13. *Acronyms* (IS, IT, TAM, etc.): Look a few paragraphs back for the explanation. I try to use acronyms only locally within chapters or sections, defining them shortly before use.

14. To some extent, the chapters may be read *in any order*, as long as readers are happy to follow the cross references, where they will find explanations for items they do not find clear.

Part I

Part I is about the nature, role and position of research in the wider world. These provide a suitable context in which to introduce Dooyeweerd's philosophy.

- Chapter 2 discusses the relationships between research and everyday experience, reviews how mainstream philosophies have treated everyday experience, and discusses how Dooyeweerd's view differs and how it can help research.
- Chapter 3 discusses the diversity and coherence of the world, of everyday experience and of research, reviews how mainstream philosophies have addressed these, introduces Dooyeweerd's suite of aspects and the relationships between aspects, and discusses how these are relevant to research.
- Chapter 4 shows how important meaningfulness is to research, discusses Dooyeweerd's radical understanding thereof and how it is the ground of being, functioning, value, etc., and discusses briefly how these apply in research.
- Chapter 5 discusses philosophy and its role in research, what Dooyeweerd saw as its deep problems, and how Dooyeweerd's philosophy relates to most other philosophies. It also suggests how philosophical boundaries may be crossed.

2   Research and Everyday Experience

How does research relate to everyday life and experience, theory to practice? Traditionally, they have been divorced from each other. I once came across the following in an introduction to philosophy related to research: "Given the difficulty of doing philosophy (i.e. escaping from the natural attitude which constantly seeks to reassert itself)" (Moran 2000, 146). I asked myself, What is wrong with the "natural attitude", from which Moran tries to escape? It is the attitude we adopt in everyday experience.

Has not Wenger (1998) deemed everyday experience worthy of study? Have not Bourdieu (1977) and de Certeau (1984) reflected on it philosophically? Did not Husserl (1954/1970) argue that all scientific thoughts are grounded in the natural understanding that is the lifeworld? Is not everyday practice the central motivation of American Pragmatism? Above all, does not application of research findings involve everyday experience? Yet Moran expresses a presupposition that has long been held throughout the history of philosophy, a belief about attitudes of thought

"In my opinion" and "I feel" rightly carry little weight in the theoretical arguments of research, yet are they completely irrelevant? Might they not indicate some underlying intuition that is asking to be made explicit? How do intuition and theoretical knowledge relate to each other, and why?

One of the things that most attracted me to Dooyeweerd, and still does, is that Dooyeweerd makes the natural attitude (he called it the "pre-theoretical attitude of thought") a starting-point for his whole approach to philosophy and science. We will find that it encompasses and enriches all these other views.

This chapter discusses everyday experience and the *pre-theoretical attitude of thought*, and their relationship with research—not only research application, not only research activity, but even research content. It examines three components of this relationship, about each of which a traditional presumption needs to be questioned: the relationship between researcher and the everyday world in Section 2–2 (traditional presumption of detached observer), between theoretical and pre-theoretical thinking in Section 2–3 (traditional presumption of neutrality and autonomy of theoretical thinking), and between theoretical and pre-theoretical knowledge in Section 2–4 (traditional presumption of superiority of theoretical knowledge). Section

2–5 reviews various discussions about everyday experience and introduces Dooyeweerd's fuller approach. Section 2–6 discusses its relevance to research. There we discuss research application, activity and content separately, but until then they are not differentiated.

2–1.   Some Preliminaries

Given the mandate of research as contributing understanding to our bodies of knowledge, on which it is reasonable to rely, what are the differences and the relationships between research and everyday experience, between theory and practice?

2–1.1   *Differences Between Research and Everyday Experience*

Some of the differences between research and everyday experience are readily seen in Table 2.1. The left-hand column contains a list of issues discussed in the academic research literature around information systems development (ISD); the right-hand column lists issues actually encountered during a particular ISD project, Elsie (Brandon et al. 1988). (The table comes from one in Basden (2010b), with a few minor amendments; readers need not read in detail.)

Table 2.1 Comparison of issues discussed and overlooked in ISD literature

Issues Addressed in ISD Literature	*Additional Issues Important in Elsie*
ISD methodology: linear v. iterative, and combining both; agile approaches	Bestowing credibility on project. Dignity of all team members.
Data models: procedural / declarative; E-R / Relational / O-O;	Team members given space to develop expertise.
Clarifying business problem: Hard v. soft v. critical systems thinking	Trustability: knowledge in IS will not let users down even in exceptional conditions
'Persistent Problems': Diversity to be reduced by organisation and specialisation Knowledge to be acquired and negotiated Structure to be perceived and established	Saleability: attract those who would benefit but do not yet realise they might. Ethics overrides sales maximisation. Diversity of knowledge to be encapsulated. Disclosing domain understanding by separating out problem-solving contextual knowledge.
Assumptions of ISD Approaches: Data as descriptive v. constitutive IS as technical v. social systems Humans: determined v. voluntaristic Technology as determining v. choice Organisations as structural v. interactional Epistemology as positivist v. anti-positivist	Trust and mutual respect in relationships with domain experts. Maintaining dignity of all who disagree with each other. 'Frills': features important in everyday use but not reported in academic papers. Attitude in team: willing to learn, to expend oneself on behalf of others. Users changing their minds as a source of valuable knowledge.

Issues Addressed in ISD Literature	Additional Issues Important in Elsie
Role of IS science as means to end v. interpretation	A listening attitude coupled with common sense, putting oneself in shoes of other.
Value of IS research: to assist organisations, communication, problem-solving, justice (interests), management (professionalism)	Criticality must be generous, not destructive. Importance of aiming for beneficial real-life use, not mere delivery/sale of IS. Giving domain knowledge its due; no cutting corners.
Research methodology: case studies, conceptual development, formal analysis, technical development, action research	Unexpected and indirect repercussions of use. Build so stakeholders can discover their own ways of working. Paradox: loss of power welcomed.

I had been involved in this project as part of a dozen years outwith academia, developing information systems in the health sector, chemical industry and surveying profession. The project was undertaken before I had discovered Dooyeweerd, and the rest of Basden (2010b) discusses how Dooyeweerd could (retrospectively) make sense of the difference between research and actual experience in ISD.

Perusing the lists reveals a wider diversity of kinds of issues meaningful in the realities of IS development than in discourses within the academic research communities. There is also a difference in the types of issue meaningful in each. Both types involve concepts, but the (theoretical) concepts that emerge from research are more abstract. They have been set in relationship to each other, especially by a "versus" relationship, and by grouping. Models and classifications (categories, taxonomies) have been constructed; these are two manifestations of theory (generic knowledge on which it is reasonable to rely, §1–2.2), a third manifestation being general rules. The everyday issues are more specific, often concern action, and are more normative in nature (e.g. "must be": what ought to be done). Relationships among them are not very often specified.

What is it to be theoretical? What does being theoretical entail? Anticipating Dooyeweerd's in-depth discussion of that (Chapter 6), we can say that the *theoretical attitude of thought* involves abstraction of data that is meaningful to the research. Abstraction is a standing back from the world, in what Dooyeweerd calls a *Gegenstand* relationship, in order to conceptualise selected aspects thereof. In the *pre-theoretical attitude* that characterises everyday experience, we engage with the world, and do so in a wide range of aspects. Sometimes we are just acting and sometimes we are thinking, conceptualising and reasoning, but in a less abstract way than in the theoretical attitude. Clouser (2005) calls these higher and lower abstraction. In lower abstraction, we are aware of things we encounter and of their properties (e.g. this rose is red and beautiful but diseased), whereas in the higher abstraction of the theoretical attitude, we abstract away from the things to the kinds of properties themselves (e.g. redness, beauty or disease).

In my fields of information systems and sustainability, I have always found that Dooyeweerd has helped me recognise both the diverse realities of every-day experience throughout my research and the nature of abstraction and engagement that characterise them. The recognition is often more as an attitude than as a formal conceptual method. Respect for everyday experi-ence has made me aware of issues from the 'real world' that are sometimes overlooked during research. Others have found similarly. Eriksson (2001) used Dooyeweerd's understanding of diversity of everyday experience, as expressed in his suite of 15 aspects (§3–2.1), to investigate the failure of a stock control system in a vegetable wholesaler. He found that, whereas most of Dooyeweerd's aspects were relevant to the real life of this business, the stock control system, which encapsulated an economic model (theory) of stock control, obliterated many of them, and especially the social aspect, and this obliteration was the reason for failure.

The nature and implications of abstraction are discussed in Chapter 6; the concern of this chapter is how theoretical and pre-theoretical thought, as operative in research and everyday experience, relate to each other, so that we can understand research in the context of the everyday.

2–1.2   Relationships Between Research and Everyday Experience

The relationship between research and everyday life has at least three com-ponents that are conceptually different.

- The relationship between researcher and world. Is the researcher (observer, thinker) detached from the world or a participant in it?
- The relationship between theoretical and pre-theoretical thinking. Is theoretical thinking a neutral kind of thinking, which has authority compared with pre-theoretical thinking?
- The relationship between theoretical and pre-theoretical knowledge. Is theoretical knowledge superior to pre-theoretical, intuitive, everyday knowledge?

The three align, if you like, with subject, functioning and generated object. Each presupposes the others, and they are closely intertwined in practice, working together at the roots of the sciences and philosophy. The presumed superiority of theoretical knowledge depends on the neutrality of theoretical thinking, and both appeal to those who think a detached researcher is more trustworthy. Detached researcher and neutrality of theoretical thinking are ideals which, it is assumed, we should work towards, but increasingly this is being questioned, not only whether they are ideal but whether they are even possible.

In much early Greek thought, and in much modern thinking, detachment of thinker, neutrality of theoretical thinking and superiority of theoretical knowledge have been presupposed, but, in ancient Hebrew Wisdom literature and by some philosophers discussed below, these presuppositions have been questioned. Dooyeweerd also questions them. His questioning is, however, more penetrating and more useful in research than that of most others. He explores roots in a way that many of the extant discussions have not; in fact, several thinkers end up where Dooyeweerd begins, so his ideas might fruitfully inform extant thinking. Sadly, to date, Dooyeweerd's ideas have been largely isolated from the rest.

Dooyeweerd calls the combined presumptions the "absolutization of theoretical thought" (NC,I, 13), referring to giving theoretical thought overmuch importance so that it obliterates the pre-theoretical, and "autonomy of theoretic thought" (NC,I, 35), which refers to presuming that it is free from constraints, self-sufficient, and neither needing nor influenced by pre-theoretical thought. Whereas Dooyeweerd mixes all three relationships together, it is useful to understand each separately. So, each occupies a different section, with a similar structure. The nature of the relationship is discussed, then whether what is presumed about theoretical thought is either possible or desirable, and Dooyeweerd's view is briefly noted in the context of other philosophy. Drawing these together emphasises the importance of pre-theoretical thought and everyday experience as a context in which research should be understood and undertaken.

> *Note on terminology: everyday.* To summarise §1–3, "everyday experience" in this book (a) is used alongside "pre-theoretical", which refers to an attitude in which we engage with reality, (b) refers to full reality, "real life" as opposed to a narrowed-down experience, (c) refers not just to humans but to non-humans too, (d) has no negative connotations but is respected for its reality and richness. Dooyeweerd seldom uses the word "everyday", but instead "pre-theoretical" and "naïve". ("Naïve", used by philosophers to refer to everyday experience, has no negative connotation, whereas "naive" without umlaut does.) In this book, these will be used almost synonymously with "everyday", though "pre-theoretical" more to qualify thought and "everyday" more for experience. Everyday experience includes theoretical activity within it, rather than being opposed to it, and all research has an everyday experience of its own.
>
> *Note on terminology: theoretical.* Here, "theoretical" refers to an attitude of standing back from reality in order to understand it (in some aspect(s)). "Theoretical thought" will usually refer to the core of research, the activities and output of research most directly concerned with its theoretical mandate, but sometimes will be used synonymously with the whole of research. The latter seems to be how Dooyeweerd uses the term, including the extra-logical and even

communal activity. "Reasoning" will mainly refer to theoretical activity, and "logic" to a more abstract version of reasoning.

2–2.   The Researcher-World Relationships: Detached or Participant Observer?

What is the relationship that thinkers or researchers have with the world they are studying? Two possibilities have been discussed: detachment or engagement. The so-called *detached observer* thinks about the world without affecting the world being thought out. This detachment has been crystallised by Descartes' *cogito* ("I think"). By contrast, following Heidegger's idea of being-in-the-world, the *participant observer*, the engaged thinker, is embedded and active in the world being thought about so that each affects the other. This section discusses both.

2–2.1   Is Detached Observer Possible?

Throughout most of its history, Western philosophy has largely presupposed the possibility of the detached observer, but over the last century its possibility has been questioned.

Of course, the premier questioner is Heidegger, who argued for being-in-the-world. On the face of it, he allows no detachment at all, but if one digs deeper, and especially in his later work, we find something more nuanced: the task of thinking is "unconcealment". However, let us get closer to actual research.

Researcher detachment is obviously not possible in action research in business or technology, nor practice-as-research in the arts, in which researchers are involved in the situation being researched and, as they produce findings, those are used to improve the situation.

Yet, even in 'ordinary' research, Polanyi (1962/1974, vii) exclaims,

> I start by rejecting the ideal of scientific detachment. In the exact sciences this false ideal is perhaps harmless, for it is in fact disregarded there by scientists. But we shall see that it exercises a destructive influence in biology, psychology and sociology, and falsifies our whole outlook far beyond the domain of science.

There are reasons why full detachment is not possible. Dysfunction in research activity, which can include carelessness, mistakes and researcher bias or prejudices, precludes detachment of one kind. The activity of research precludes another kind, by affecting what is being researched (Heisenberg's Uncertainly Principle in physics, the Hawthorne Effect in the human sciences (Roethlisberger & Dickson 1939)). In the human sciences, the style and wording of interview questions can change the results obtained. In the social sciences and humanities, it is recognised that the cultural attitudes and beliefs of the researcher can affect the outcome of research, often unseen.

Statistical analysis of well-chosen samples can iron out individual biases— but is not this influenced by what the researcher's academic culture presumes to be meaningful? In qualitative research, is not the selection of groupings during analysis likewise influenced by what is deemed meaningful?

In research that involves introspection, researcher detachment would seem impossible since, as Hume argued, introspecting a mental state tends to alter the state. Countering this, Nisbett & Wilson (1977) claim that "there may be little or no direct introspective access to higher order cognitive processes", suggesting that even in introspection the observer is detached from what they observe of themselves. These, however, have not been properly tested (it might be untestable (White 1987)) and have been too readily accepted by the psychology community (Johansson et al. 2006).

Pragmatism's view is similarly complex. The researcher is "participant" in the situations being researched and yet does not enter them. Dewey sees our relationship with "situation" as confrontation. Knowing is seen as inquiry rather than engagement. All imply some detachment.

From this summary overview (fuller treatment continues throughout this book), it seems that some kind of detachment is happening but also some non-detachment at the same time. How do we understand this?

2–2.2   *Is Detached Observer Desirable?*

Assuming researcher detachment is possible, is it desirable? Why or why not?

Examples of several practical benefits (the everyday experience of research) of detachment are offered by Confluence (2012), some when observing internal mental states (detachment prevents the researcher's thoughts, feelings, emotions, etc. becoming their master), some when observing an external scene (detachment offers a bigger picture and more appropriate judgments). Detachment helps us generalise from the specific situations we study.

Despite such benefits of detachment, embeddedness in and engagement with the world is important in the responsibility of researchers, during both activity and application of research. This is "research ethics" (discussed later). The detached researcher finds it difficult to assume responsibility for what occurs because of their research—the repercussions of their findings being applied. Repercussions from research findings are especially important when applied widely—as, for example, in incorporation of psychological theories into mobile technology (Basden 2018a, 264–5, 289–92).

Questions of detachment and engagement pertain to research content too. This is obvious in sociology, anthropology and ethnography, where the detached observer is criticised as being insensitive to what is meaningful to those being researched, but Polanyi (1962/1974) develops the theme for the "exact" and natural sciences as well.

Pike (1954/1967) introduced the *etic-emic distinction* as an expression of detached-engaged when studying linguistic behaviours, and it has become useful where it is important to understand cultural issues as intuitively as possible. When using the etic approach, the researcher emphasises what *they* consider important, 'outside' the situation, whereas the emic approach, from 'inside' the situation, is more sensitive to what *those being researched* find meaningful. Yet the emic approach can mislead researchers when they are too involved to be impartial (Kottak 2006).

However, real research is not as simple as this distinction implies, mixing etic and emic. The early pioneer of *participant observation*, Malinowski, believed the goal of the anthropologist is to "grasp the native's point of view, his relation to life, to realise his vision of his world" (Malinowski 1922, 25). So,

> To study the institutions, customs, and codes or to study the behaviour and mentality without the subjective desire of feeling by what these people live, of realising the substance of their happiness is, in my opinion, to miss the greatest reward which we can hope to obtain from the study of man.

Therefore, the researcher first becomes part of (what is called) the "local" or "native" situation being researched, such as by living therein, hoping to imbibe cultural assumptions, norms, habits, etc. so that the researcher no longer interprets through the lens of their own culture.

Yet, in his discussion of the Kula Ring transactions (pp. 82–5), do we not find him taking a detached view? He says (pp. 83–4),

> They have no knowledge of the total *outline* of any of their social structure. . . . Not even the most intelligent native has any clear idea of the Kula as a big, organised social construction, still less of its sociological function and implications. . . . the Ethnographer has to construct the picture of the big institution, very much as the physicist constructs his theory from the experimental data.

Is not Malinowski imposing his theoretical notion of "big institution"? He justifies this by saying, "it is necessary to clear the ground when approaching any economic subject." To Malinowski, "economic" is meaningful, yet if one reads his account, to the "natives" the transactions are more social than economic, with social standing being more important than exchange of useful goods.

Should Malinowski have imposed "economic" on social and the big-institution category which the "natives" do not find meaningful? On what grounds is it valid to the researcher to introduce meaningfulness that transcends the researched? This raises the question, what is the origin of meaningfulness? From where does meaningfulness arise that is valid to both researcher and researched, such that it yields findings on which it is reasonable to rely? Neither researcher detachment nor researcher non-detachment, in dogmatic form, can address that question, since one makes the researcher the sovereign determiner of what is meaningful and the other denies the researcher any role in understanding meaningfulness.

In all these—and what is found in anthropology is found in most human sciences—it seems that both detachment and non-detachment offer benefits; how do we understand this?

2-2.3   *Dooyeweerd's View of the Researcher-World Relationship*

Dooyeweerd rejects both the possibility and the desirability of the detached observer, and yet he recognises the validity of a kind of detachment. As explained in Chapter 4, he treats reality, at its root, as meaningfulness (which enables being, process, norms, etc.) Using a metaphor introduced in §4–3.10, researcher and the researched situations 'dwell' and 'swim' in the same 'ocean' of meaningfulness; this is the origin of meaningfulness for both researcher and researched. It is an important feature in Dooyeweerd's understanding of theoretical thought (§6–3). (Note: this 'ocean' of meaningfulness is not the same as individual *meanings* of words, objects, etc., which are seen as 'picked out' by us; see §4–3.11.1.)

This 'ocean' of meaningfulness is engaged non-detachment of researcher in the world; the valid element of detachment is understood as the researcher, still ontically within and part of the world, adopting a certain *attitude* to the world. This is what has been called the *"theoretical attitude of thought"*. Chapter 6 will reveal this as the researcher 'standing over against' the world (*Gegenstand*), abstracting selected aspects thereof as data (for example, mainly physical concepts in materials science, social concepts in sociology, a mixture in anthropology). The aspects selected are those relevant to the topic of the research. (This echoes Husserl's two modes of the "I" who thinks, the natural attitude and the "constitutive" attitude of generating theoretical ideas.)

The selection is necessary because of the diversity of meaningfulness (discussed in Chapter 3); *aspects* are ways in which the world is meaningful and may be seen as broad kinds of properties and laws (Clouser 2005). However, from the pre-theoretical perspective, the things from which data are abstracted exhibit many aspects, actually or potentially, and so each abstracted concept brings with it unbidden meaningfulness of other aspects. This is discussed in Chapter 4, and in Part III, we will see aspects lend themselves very nicely to categorisation.

This can resolve tensions around detachment and engagement mentioned above in Pragmatism, introspective research, participant observation, action research and etic-emic mixing. Concerning the Malinowski problem, for instance, it can be valid for the researcher to introduce aspects of which the researched might not be aware (the "big-institution" concept is meaningful in the economic and juridical aspects alongside the social)—as long as this is done with an attitude of respect, as fellow-'swimmer' in the same 'ocean' of meaningfulness, rather than as authority. If the researcher is to do so, they cannot bring their own experience to bear without self-critique. It also makes the converse valid, for the "natives" to introduce new meaningfulness to researchers, of which the latter is unaware. Dooyeweerd believes this idea of meaningfulness applies not only to anthropology and social sciences but even to the natural sciences and mathematics. Understanding how and why this can be so requires the next few chapters.

I have found this view bears rich fruit for research. It provides a philosophical basis for responsibility towards planet and ecosystems, cross-cultural research, a broader research ethic, inter-field cooperation and interdisciplinary research, fresh understanding of paradigms, clarification of concepts and sensitivity to everyday experience in data collection and analysis. Many of these are met again in later chapters.

The *Gegenstand* attitude brings us to the relationship between theoretical and pre-theoretical thinking.

2–3. The Relationship Between Theoretical and Pre-Theoretical Thinking

Theoretical thinking has been presumed to be, in principle, neutral and "objective", whereas pre-theoretical thinking, which accommodates various kinds like feeling, alluding or believing, is presumed biased and too "subjective" to be reliable as a generator of good quality knowledge. To guide thinking, Aristotle developed term-based logic and Chryssipus, propositional logic, which logics have become central to theoretical thinking, with most arguments based on them. They do not, however, satisfactorily embrace the entirety of theoretical thinking, and this section discusses how it always relates to pre-theoretical (everyday) thinking.

Theoretical thinking, while an activity, is also an *attitude of thought*, which differs from the pre-theoretical attitude. (See Chapter 6.)

2–3.1   *Is Neutral Theoretical Thinking Desirable?*

Polanyi (1962/1974, 4) sets out some supposed benefits of theoretical thinking. It is not (in principle) "led astray by my personal illusions" or biases, preferences, etc., so is neutral (objective) with respect to the researcher. It constructs theory "without regard to one's normal [everyday] approach to experience", not limited by idiographic circumstances, personal or group preferences, and is thus neutral with respect to the researched situations. It commends its findings (theories) equally to all, and thus can be appropriate for inclusion in bodies of knowledge. A theory, when set down, is a general 'map' of the world, and is thus neutral with respect to those applying its output.

This seems to bestow authority on theoretical thinking, for interpretation and argumentation in every field, which is not accorded to pre-theoretical thinking.

Yet, does it make theoretical thought truly authoritative? There may be other criteria. To Pragmatism, utility is the most important criterion, for instance.

As will be argued more fully in Chapter 6, theoretical thought narrows down our thinking. It consists in abstracting selected aspects of the world ("focal aspects") for study and ignoring others; physicists select physical phenomena to abstract and ignore social; sociologists, largely, the reverse. This narrows the view, which reduces the reliance-worthiness of findings because, in principle, every aspect has some relevance. The selection of aspects itself is influenced by accepted presuppositions, which never can be neutral.

By contrast, the "natural", pre-theoretical attitude ignores no aspects, in principle. It is more engaged and so can obtain a more sensitive, *emic* view. It can also accommodate a range of criteria beyond those of Polanyi and Pragmatism. Hence, though less precise than theoretical thinking, it gains authority from its breadth of view.

So, both theoretical and pre-theoretical thinking offer complementary benefits. How can they work together to yield all benefits?

2–3.2 Is Neutral Theoretical Thinking Possible?

The neutrality or authority of theoretical thought relates to how well it can deliver knowledge on which it is reasonable to rely; that is, effectively, "truth". Is it possible? This relates to the tension between rigour and relevance (e.g. Lee 1999).

Several philosophers have argued that theoretical thought can never be neutral, even if desirable. The following summarises the fuller discussion on truth in §6–1. Kant's "Copernican Revolution", which made the thinking ego sovereign, implies that theoretical thought will always be subjective. Husserl argues that the meaning of all scientific concepts is based on a pre-theoretical background knowledge (lifeworld), which comes from everyday experience and is not grounded in logic. Habermas (1972) argues that theoretical thinking and discourse is influenced by what he calls human interests, which are "basic orientations" that precede theoretical thinking. Most of the criticisms levelled at Habermas since then do not affect this. Foucault argues that power (political or personal authority) determines what is accepted within rational discourse and what constitutes good knowledge.

Philosophers of science offer different reasons why theoretical thinking is not neutral. Kuhn (1962) argues that theories are determined by paradigms, which are beliefs and commitments by a scientific community about the nature of the world, meaningful issues and how problems may be solved (see §8–2), and are chosen pre-theoretically. Paradigms are similar to Lakatos' research programmes (core sets of beliefs and assumptions retained and protected by tacit agreement), and Feyerabend's worldviews ("a collection of beliefs, attitudes, and assumptions that involves the whole person, . . . and imposes itself with a power far greater than the power of facts and fact-related theories") (Lakatos & Musgrave 1970).

Polanyi's (1962/1974) *Personal Knowledge* makes a powerful argument why theoretical thinking cannot be neutral. He first argues against objectivism in physics (though accepts objective truth), that physicists have been motivated by more than truth-seeking, then discusses probability, order and skills in other sciences, examines tacit knowing, and then proposes personal knowledge as "an alternative ideal for knowledge" (p. vii).

Non-neutrality in physics is brilliantly illustrated in Polanyi's (1962/1974, 11–14) exposure of what really happened when Einstein developed his theory of special relativity. Scientists, who are popularly expected to abandon their theories when faced with contrary evidence, are (p. 13)

> "wont to look down from the pinnacle of their intellectual humility upon the rest of dogmatic mankind."

They had so readily accepted Einstein's theory that they refused to listen to contrary evidence. Something else goes on here, which Polanyi touches upon: the quest for intellectual satisfaction.

These (and others) all build, with their separate parts, a picture of the impossibility of complete neutrality in theoretical thinking, Habermas and Foucault from the social sciences, and Husserl, Kuhn and Polanyi from the natural and mathematical sciences too. Yet the picture is fragmented. Each view raises questions—about the grounds on which Husserl's lifeworld, Habermas' basic orientations, Foucault's power, Kuhn's paradigms and Polanyi's personal knowledge all stand, and how each relates to others.

Dooyeweerd suggests that the presupposition of full neutrality is a mirage, and that truth is other than even most of these thinkers have presupposed (§6–4). By taking a completely different approach, we can obtain benefits sought for both theoretical and pre-theoretical thought.

2–3.3   Dooyeweerd's View of Theoretical and Pre-Theoretical Thinking

"Over twenty years before Michael Polanyi's important book *Personal Knowledge* made its appearance in 1958," Hart (1985) points out, "Dooyeweerd forcefully advanced the conviction that knowledge, including theoretical knowledge, is personal." He also remarks,

> Michael Polanyi's theory of the scientist's indwelling in his framework of commitment, Jürgen Habermas's theory of the role of human interest in science, Gerald Radnitzky's theory of steering fields internal to science, and Thomas Kuhn's theory of the role of paradigms in the natural sciences are all prefigured in the way Dooyeweerd worked out his theory. He not only saw the problems connected with belief in rational autonomy very early, but he also was one of the first to formulate a comprehensive theory to deal with these problems.
>
> (Hart 1985, 145)

Dooyeweerd begins with the idea of researchers as embedded in the world, trying to understand what enables us to understand, like fish (assuming they can think) trying to understand water and the entire ocean. His argument, expanded in Chapter 6, is that theoretical thinking inescapably depends on pre-theoretical choices or attitudes at three points. They may be summarised for research as:

- *Diversity of world.* Researchers pre-theoretically select focal aspects of the world to abstract. This yields data—which ignores non-focal aspect(s).
- *Rationalities.* To generate findings from data, researchers employ selected rationalities, yet there is no overarching rationality, so how they work together is our (pre-theoretical) responsibility.
- *Wider meaningfulness.* The research community critiques findings (e.g. by peer review) but do so by reference to wider meaningfulness and ultimately to a presupposed origin of meaningfulness. Agreement on the origin of meaningfulness is related to deepest beliefs of the society.

Kant addresses rationalities. Husserl addresses diversity and rationalities. Habermas and Foucault address wider meaningfulness, as does Polanyi. Kuhn's paradigms arise from wider meaningfulness but express what the community accepts about world and rationalities. Dooyeweerd addresses all three. We shall see in coming chapters how the ideas of each may be affirmed, critiqued and enriched by Dooyeweerd.

To overcome the narrowness of theoretical thinking focusing on selected aspects, may we not simply ensure that we include all aspects as focal? Dooyeweerd argues that even this is not possible. Not only would it be combinatorially challenging, but, more fundamentally, we would need to (a) identify all the aspects (what he calls "*totality of meaning*" (NC,I, 5) and (b) understand the relationships among aspects. To do this is the mandate of philosophy. However, Dooyeweerd argues, philosophy exhibits all the weaknesses and strengths of theoretical thought, for the same three reasons, though in different form (see §6–3 and NC,I, 22–68).

To address this diversity and coherence of meaningfulness (see Chapters 3 and 4 for Dooyeweerd's views) requires taking a stance on the totality (of meaningfulness), and Dooyeweerd shows that philosophy has been prevented from doing so by its "Immanence-Standpoint" (§5–3). What Dooyeweerd does is not to solve the problem, but to expose the philosophical issues that need to be addressed if we are to do so.

What we can say at this point, concerning the relationship between research and everyday experience, is that right from the start (NC,I, 12), Dooyeweerd is adamant that the "thinking self" is a full human being, not just a rational engine.

> Philosophical thinking [and all theoretical thinking] is an actual activity; and only at the expense of this very actuality . . . can it be abstracted from the thinking self.
>
> (NC,I, 5)

Theoretical thinking is not some purely abstract activity that runs according to mechanical rules but is a fully human activity, embedded in everyday experience and exhibiting its own everyday character. Dooyeweerd understands all human activity as functioning in a diversity of aspects (§4–3.8.2), so "our analytical function of thought is embedded in cosmic time itself" (NC,II, 473) (for "cosmic time" see §4–3.14).

The supposed benefits of theoretical thought are not achieved by pursuing an illusory neutrality but by facing up to the diverse aspects of the everyday experience of research. To do this, we must understand diversity and coherence (Chapter 3), meaningfulness (Chapter 4), and how to theoretically separate and reintegrate them (Chapter 6), as well as the nature of religious presuppositions (Chapter 5). Later it will be seen that Dooyeweerd's ideas can enrich the ideas of these thinkers.

> *Important note*: Henceforth, our discussion will include both pre-theoretical and theoretical portions. Theoretical discussion is expected in a book like this, but, as mentioned earlier, cannot *a priori* be presumed valid, since theoretical thought depends on, and must ultimately defer to, pre-theoretical experience. However, we include both insofar as we anticipate the discussion of the nature and validity of theoretical thought in Chapter 6.

2–4.   The Value of Theoretical and Pre-Theoretical Knowledge

Theoretical knowledge has been presumed to be more valuable to our bodies of knowledge than pre-theoretical or everyday knowledge, such as *intuition*. (Theoretical knowledge is not restricted to formal theories, but is also expressed in models, rules, etc., §1–2.2)

What makes theoretical knowledge important is that it constitutes precise, explicit, general understanding of the way reality works and thus contributes to humanity's bodies of knowledge. Pre-theoretical knowledge is neither so explicit nor precise nor general but is more holistic, recognising a wider diversity of meaningfulness.

Both are important. In everyday life, we rely mostly on pre-theoretical knowledge (though tools embody theoretical knowledge; see §6–3.3, §7–1.2.3). Theoretical knowledge is used in business, engineering, finance and elsewhere as a means to achieve our chosen ends. Example: The CAMELS rating system expresses a theory that capital, assets, management, earnings, liquidity and sensitivity to risk are all necessary and together sufficient for sound banking, and, being objectively measurable, is used to evaluate, and set strategy in, banks. Theoretical knowledge is also used in academia as axioms from which to build new knowledge.

Yet in both professional and academic life, pre-theoretical knowledge is also important and we ignore it at our peril. For example, CAMELS was not sufficient to prevent the 2008 banking crisis, which resulted from several 'human' factors like vision, fear or greed that motivated the formation of banking systems (Calomiris & Haber 2014). The reason is that "Monetary theory . . . cannot avoid a relation to reality, which in other economic theory is sometimes missing. It belongs to monetary history, in a way that economic theory does not always belong to economic history" (Hicks 1967, 156). Such "reality" is what we are calling everyday experience (§2–1.2).

Polanyi (1967) introduced *The Tacit Dimension. Tacit knowledge* is that which we have but cannot or do not make explicit, including muscular knowledge in sport, long-practised skills, knowledge of using language or operating socially, etc. It is important in both everyday experience and when we use theoretical knowledge in practice. It is also important when we generate theoretical knowledge (research). Husserl (1954/1970) introduced the *lifeworld*, which is shared background knowledge, a kind of social tacit knowledge. Husserl argues that all science depends on the lifeworld to give meaning to scientific concepts. Both lifeworld and tacit knowledge are manifestations of pre-theoretical knowledge, and in both the use and the generation of theoretical knowledge, pre-theoretical knowledge is important.

> *Research opportunity: tacit knowledge and lifeworld.* The relationship between tacit knowledge and lifeworld has not been adequately explored—but §4–3.12 provides a basis.

Thus, in both research application and content, and we well see also in activity, theoretical knowledge depends on pre-theoretical. Pre-theoretical knowledge relates to the whole and provides context and grounds for theoretical knowledge, a conclusion that parallels those concerning the researcher-world relationship and that between theoretical and pre-theoretical thinking. This implies that we need to understand both theoretical and pre-theoretical knowledge together, not separately, and understand their relationship.

Dooyeweerd sees theoretical and pre-theoretical as intimately linked, agreeing with Bourdieu (1977) that "practical knowledge" precedes theoretical knowledge, but goes further, as outlined in §6–3. The challenge we face is that philosophy, for most of its history, has shown little interest in pre-theoretical everyday experience, even denigrating it. So has much science. Only relatively recently has philosophy addressed it seriously.

This examination of the three relationships between research and everyday experience implies that theoretical thought should be a critical problem for philosophy, not presupposed, and that we should respect everyday experience. Dooyeweerd did just that. The next section reviews briefly how philosophy has treated everyday experience and pre-theoretical thought, to place Dooyeweerd's understanding of them in context.

2–5.   Understanding Everyday, Pre-Theoretical Experience

It has been argued that neither the detached observer, the neutrality of theoretical thinking, nor the supremacy of theoretical knowledge is universally desirable nor possible. Each brings some benefits but so do their pre-theoretical, everyday counterparts. In all three, we need to understand theoretical and pre-theoretical together. Two characteristics of the pre-theoretical and everyday have emerged: *embeddedness* and *diversity*.

Though much has been written about the theoretical (especially in literature on epistemology), far less has been written on the pre-theoretical, and that only relatively recently. Until then, most philosophy has deemed everyday experience unworthy of interest, for several reasons. This section reviews a variety of philosophical discussions about everyday experience and pre-theoretical thought and places Dooyeweerd's views in perspective. Three ways of according respect to everyday experience are discussed: as something to study, as something to appeal to, and as a starting-point.

2–5.1   Interest in Everyday Experience

Philosophical interest in everyday experience awakened a couple of centuries ago, with different philosophers addressing different facets.

As it emerged gradually from a preoccupation with the theoretical, initial interest was in pre-theoretical knowledge and rationality (intuition). Reid emphasised intuitive judgments, reacting against the scientism of Hume, etc., and devised principles of common sense, which express deep assumptions and presuppositions we hold while discussing. Important to him were empirical evidence, the fallibility of our theories, and cross-cultural understanding.

Bergson argued for the importance of intuition but has a rather limited view of intuition as sensory and bodily in nature. Husserl criticised Kant for not taking pre-theoretical diversity seriously (NC,II, 569–570) and drew attention to the pre-theoretical lifeworld (§2–3.2, §6–1.2), but it was Schutz & Luckmann (1973) who made the lifeworld an object for study. Habermas developed the idea of lifeworld, emphasising its meaningfulness and normativity, through the lens of communicative action.

Pragmatism emphasises everyday practice as a worthy topic for philosophy, yet most of its discourse is around utility, as expressed for instance in "Consider the practical effects of the objects of your conception. Then, your conception of those effects is the whole of your conception of the object" (Peirce 1878). The tendency of Pragmatism's emphasis on utility is to ignore, for example, fun, faith or fairness, which, if acknowledged at all, are reduced to mere types of utility.

Later interest turned to everyday life itself, for example, Bourdieu's (1977) *Outline of a Theory of Practice*. This sees everyday experience as social life, and Bourdieu interprets the theoretical attitude of the researcher as "domination". His everyday experience is *habitus*, the mix of past engagements in the social world that influences life now.

De Certeau's (1984) *The Practice of Everyday Life* wants "everyday practices, 'ways of operating' or doing things, [to] no longer appear as merely the obscure background of social activity" (p. xi) (which occurs in Husserl) and to understand "the logic of unselfconscious thought" (p. xv). Recognising the challenge of discourse on the "non-discursive activity" that is everyday life (p. 61), he aims, not to discuss this, but to make discussion possible. He criticises Foucault for being selective in the issues discussed and offering no basis for coherence with the other issues. He criticises Bourdieu's "dogmatic" "aggressive seduction" and "dogmatic" "violently imposed truths" of the "fetish of the *habitus*" (pp. 59–60). His answer—as his writing—is aesthetic. He argues for employing the arts in the quest to understand the everyday and focuses on the aesthetic aspect of the everyday.

Not surprisingly, after centuries of neglect, many philosophers have been emphasising the *importance* of intuition and the everyday, but to be fully useful in research there needs to be an understanding of their *nature*. Discussion of their nature, where it occurs, has tended inexorably towards seeing them through the lens of just one of their aspects: Pragmatism towards Functionalism, Bergson towards biology, Husserl towards analysis, Foucault towards power, Bourdieu towards signification and domination, and de Certeau towards aesthetics.

As we will see in Chapters 3 and 4, Dooyeweerd can offer a fuller view. He understands everyday experience as functioning simultaneously in all aspects (ways of being meaningful), intuition as multi-aspectual ways of knowing, and theoretical thought as a *Gegenstand* attitude within the analytic aspect. He also throws light on the problem philosophy has had with everyday experience; philosophy has fundamentally misunderstood the nature of everyday experience because of its "Immanence-Standpoint" (§5–3.1).

2–5.2   Appealing to Everyday Experience

All research appeals to everyday experience, in the form of "situations" (§1–2.2), when obtaining data, even though this may be limited to focal aspects (§2–3.1). "Situations" is Dewey's word adopted here but, whereas Dewey emphasises inquiry into situations, Dooyeweerd wants the situations to speak to us, to "present themselves" to us.

A broader appeal is made to everyday experience when new paradigms are introduced. Anticipating discussion in §8–2, new paradigms draw attention to aspects previously overlooked, and evidence from the multiple aspects that everyday experience offers is accumulated in support. Everyday examples ease understanding and acceptance of new ideas, such as Einstein's sitting-on-a-train introduction to the Theory of Special Relativity, whereas Noether's lack of reference to everyday experience when introducing her Physical Symmetry Theory might have impeded its acceptance.

Everyday experience inexorably reveals its importance within theoretical thinking, even though what is happening is not usually recognised explicitly. It just happens, inescapably. Dooyeweerd, however, makes this explicit, for instance when discussing philosophy's misunderstanding of being.

> To all of these speculative misunderstandings [made by philosophers] naïve experience implicitly takes exception by persisting in its pre-theoretical conception of things, events and social relationships.
>
> (NC,III, 28)

He makes it even more explicit in his transcendental critique of theoretical thought (Chapter 6). The problem in most philosophy's appeal, however, is that it, too, tends to focus on single aspects. Recognising this, Dooyeweerd tried to take all aspects (full "totality of meaning") into account when developing and arguing his ideas. We will find this important, especially in our discussions of the practice of research in Part III.

2–5.3   Starting With Everyday Experience

Most philosophers presume that we may apply theoretical thought to understanding the pre-theoretical. It is a trap. Example: Though Bhaskar (2012) has "everyday" in the book title, it is seldom mentioned in the text and not in its index. He begins his discussion of Critical Realism with the scientific enterprise of finding out about reality theoretically. Dooyeweerd specifically criticises Critical Realism for theorising everyday experience (NC,III, 44–47).

Likewise, though the Pragmatists held that experience is what needs to be explained and experience is the ultimate test, they presumed theoretical thought for the explaining and the testing.

To Bourdieu (1990), by contrast, practice precedes theoretical knowledge— however, he does not question whether theory itself is sufficient to understand everyday practice.

Even de Certeau (1984) begins by declaring (p. xi) that his goal

> will be achieved if everyday practices, 'ways of operating' or doing things, no longer appear as merely the obscure background of social activity, and if a body of theoretical questions, methods, categories, and perspectives, by penetrating this obscurity, make it possible to articulate them.

The first objective is admirable, but the second shows he will rely on theoretical apparatus in order to understand the everyday.

All these thinkers presuppose theoretical thought as their starting-point even if understanding the everyday is their goal.

Dooyeweerd reverses this. Taking the pre-theoretical attitude of thought as his starting-point, the opening words of his *magnum opus* are "If I consider reality as it is given in the naïve pre-theoretical experience" (NC,I, 3). In the pages that follow, he first argues that we need to understand what makes theoretical thought (hence, research) possible from a pre-theoretical standpoint, and only then may we employ theory to understand the pre-theoretical. (His theoretical understanding of everyday experience is as multi-aspectual functioning, §4–3.8.2.) (Arguably, Foucault also makes everyday experience his starting-point, in his genealogy of knowledge, but his 'everyday experience' is narrowly confined to power.)

Unfortunately, adequate philosophical tools for starting from the pre-theoretical attitude were just not available, so Dooyeweerd had to forge his own. He uses immanent and transcendental critiques of theoretical thought, outlined in Chapters 5 and 6, which went deeper than most thinkers had done, to understand the fundamental conditions that make theoretical thought possible.

Dooyeweerd can then bring fresh insight to understanding how theoretical thought relates to pre-theoretical, research to everyday experience, in research application, activity and content.

2–6. Everyday Experience and Research

This final section discusses how the Dooyeweerdian understanding of research in the context of everyday experience might enrich and critique research— first its application, then its activity and finally its content or output.

Dooyeweerd's stance is no romantic reaction against earlier denigration of the everyday, nor an uncritical 'naive realism', but a strongly critical, philosophical position, which (a) respects everyday experience, not only as a topic of interest or source of information, but as a starting-point, and (b) meets the challenges posed by the three research-everyday relationships. Dooyeweerd sees theoretical thought as a *Gegenstand* attitude always within the context of the pre-theoretical and dependent on it. In all three relationships, both characteristics of everyday experience are important, embeddedness and diversity. They are usually inseparable since being embedded in the everyday exposes research to diversity.

As mentioned earlier our discussion will include both pre-theoretical and theoretical portions.

2–6.1   *The Everyday Experience of Applying Research*

How might we understand the application of research findings (bodies of theoretical knowledge)? Application of research findings occurs in "real life", and hence should be treated as everyday experience.

Today, most overt application of research findings occurs in professional, rather than private, life. Findings are applied to achieve defined goals, often to enhance economic performance or reputation. Even Pragmatism largely presupposes this. Is not this the "Rationalization of Society", which Habermas (1986) discusses? "Systems" of mechanical-rational rules have "colonized" the lifeworld of meanings and norms and suppressed them. Yet, argues Geertsema (1992), drawing on Dooyeweerd, meanings and norms are not entirely lost. Are not the theories expressed in "mechanical" rules meaningful in some way?

Dooyeweerd offers a more nuanced understanding of application of theory, in which the pre-theoretical is inescapable.

> The naïve attitude cannot be destroyed by scientific thought. Its plastic horizon can only be opened and enlarged by the practical results of scientific research. . . . To mention only some examples: telegraph, telephone, trains, aviation, the technical application of gas, electricity
> (NC,III, 31)

... and we might add computers, the Internet and mobile phones. Though the products of theoretical thought, they "belong to the *opened* temporal reality of modern human experience and are not theoretical abstractions" (*ibid.*, emphasis in original) (see also §4–3.8.3). How these become part of our everyday experience has been discussed by Polanyi (1967) in a more detailed way than we find in Dooyeweerd.

The reality is more complex than the rationalisation view allows. Rational motivations (economic, etc.) are by no means the only ones. The practice of application is often more confused than merely fulfilling a motivation or achieving a goal, by such things as confused objectives, technical failures, miscommunication, personal rivalries, limited time, personal or organisational style, legal restrictions, self-protection or hidden agendas.

Extending beyond rationalisation is recognised in Lazarsfeld & Reitz's (1970) classic theory of application: A client has a problem (maybe as yet unclarified) for which a researcher can offer solutions (and possibly clarification). This relationship operates at both "rational" and "social" levels, the rational being about the problem itself and "social" about all other factors.

The main criticism this has received to date is by Adorno and others, for ignoring social structure and power relations. This is partly unfair since Lazarsfeld & Reitz include these among "social" issues, but the criticism is valid if we wish them to be differentiated from the amorphous mess of "social" issues. However, anticipating our discussion of diversity in Chapter 3, we might go further than Adorno, to question why only power and structures should be differentiated. Should not the whole diversity of "social" issues be understood?

Each research finding tends to be meaningful in one main, focal aspect (§2–3.1) and hence is limited in scope compared with the diverse "totality of meaning" that is everyday experience.

I have found that Dooyeweerd's understanding of the relationship between theoretical and pre-theoretical (Chapter 6) offers a foundation for understanding the balanced, holistic application of research findings in everyday life, whether embodied in technical artefacts or not. His understanding of diversity of meaningfulness and his suite of aspects (Chapters 3 and 9) offer us a framework by which the diversity of issues in application can be explored and discussed—and in which the "rational" is not opposed to, but integrated with, "social" issues of all kinds.

> Example: Farming today follows many theories, encapsulated in the equipment used, principles that guide, rules to follow, etc. Jan Huygens, of Eemlandhoeve Farm in the Netherlands, when I visited it some years ago and as far as I know still does, ran his farm according to Dooyeweerd's understanding of diversity of meaning. It follows the principles of organic farming (biotic-organic aspect), community involvement (social aspect), frugality (economic aspect), good communication (lingual aspect), the Christian faith (pistic aspect), and other aspects.

We will see that Dooyeweerd finds a coherence among the aspects (§3–2.4) and so no one aspect need dominate the others and all aspects are given their due.

Conventionally, "successful" and "responsible" application are seen as different things, success measured by limited, explicit goal-criteria and responsibility being limited to "ethics". Anticipating our discussion in §4–3.7 and §4–3.8.2, Dooyeweerd urges us to see both the same way, as innately normative issues. Each aspect offers a different norm (good, evil) by which both success and responsibility may be defined and evaluated. True success merges with true responsibility, both covering the entire "totality of meaningfulness". To realize that *eudaemonic* vision, however, requires all that is discussed hereafter.

2–6.2   Research Activity as Everyday Experience

The activity of research has, at its core, the analytical-theoretical activities of obtaining data from the world, reasoning about it to generate new knowledge and then offering it to the community for critique and refinement. These activities are not just logical processes but, as in application, involve many more aspects of human functioning. For example, obtaining data via interviews requires not just an ability to communicate but also planning, politeness and participation (plus several not starting with 'p'!). Dissemination requires many authoring and presentation skills, but also such things as honesty and openness to criticism. Even reasoning about data involves not only logic but care and patience, plus research ethics by which information from human participants is protected. Such things are the everyday activity of research. In-depth discussion of them continues in Chapter 10.

2–6.3   Everyday Experience in Research Content

Research content exhibits an everyday character in two ways, within its field and across fields.

Within its field, while research validly focuses on core aspects that are meaningful to the field (see §2–3.1 and §6–3.3) and that give the finding its primary meaningfulness, other aspects become important. Theories of language eventually must take sociality into account; conversely, sociologists need to take language into account, along with justice, ethics, belief, etc. (see the discussion of secondary aspects in §8–1.3). This is so even in the mathematical and natural sciences (§6–1.1). Dooyeweerd argues that even "religious" presuppositions play an inescapable role in theory (§6–3).

Especially within fields of human or social behaviour, it is advisable to ensure that the entirety of the everyday experience of those studied is sought. As Chapter 11 will show, research is enriched by an intuitive awareness of all the aspects encountered in everyday experience. Dooyeweerd's theory echoes Polanyi's idea of personal knowledge, Habermas' idea of interests, Husserl's idea of lifeworld, etc., mentioned earlier, but I have found his perspective both broader and deeper, and also more systematic and serviceable in practice; so have others.

Recognising it is embedded in a "totality of meaningfulness" along with all other fields, each field should reach out to others. This, of course, is especially important in interdisciplinary research, discussed in §8–1.4.

When too much emphasis is placed on a field's core aspect, there is a danger of reductionism. For example, when the economist Frank Knight in 1924 wrote,

> Since economics deals with human beings, the problems of its scientific treatment involves fundamental problems of the relations between man and his world. From a rational or scientific point of view, all practically real problems are problems in economics. The problem of life is to utilize resources 'economically,' to make them go as far as possible in the production of desired results. The general theory of economics is therefore simply the rationale of life,
>
> (Knight 1924/2009, 97)

he was reducing life to its economic aspect, and claiming for economics more than is appropriate. Though human life does depend on utilisation of resources, that does not exhaust the meaningfulness or purpose of life.

These considerations should lead to humility in research, both within and between fields, at two levels. Researchers should avoid claiming more than is justified, in relation to their field. No field should elevate itself to encroach on others, as Knight seems to be doing above—though his other writings might be less arrogant. (Though these norms and expectations are widely known, they are 'hidden' aspects of research activity and, as discussed in §10–4, Dooyeweerd's philosophy provides a foundation for discussion.)

2–7.   Conclusions

To summarise, we have seen that research cannot be divorced from everyday experience but is a distinct kind of activity within it. The researcher cannot be detached from the world, and yet takes a theoretical attitude of standing over against the world, which Dooyeweerd calls "*Gegenstand*". Theoretical thinking depends on pre-theoretical (intuition) and hence can never be neutral; in the *Gegenstand* attitude, it abstracts aspects for study that are selected pre-theoretically. This gives theoretical thinking a specific role and authority but within the different role and authority of pre-theoretical thinking. Theoretical knowledge has value as general, precise and explicit, but always within the context of pre-theoretical knowledge (tacit knowledge, lifeworld), which has value as holistic. All these relationships affect research content, activity and application.

Dooyeweerd may be one of the best philosophers of everyday life yet to emerge, and this might partly explain why his philosophy is becoming useful in research. The relationships between research and everyday experience, and the embeddedness and diversity thereof, can be understood well by Dooyeweerd's ideas of 'oceanic' meaningfulness (see §4–3.10).

From now on, "everyday experience" and "pre-theoretical" come with connotations of the full diverse totality of meaningfulness, contrasting with the limited-aspect view of theoretical thought. This diversity of meaningfulness is discussed in Chapter 3.

3   Diversity and Coherence

As argued in Chapter 2, research needs to be understood in relation to every-day experience because it is embedded within it, the theoretical within the pre-theoretical, and everyday experience is diverse in meaningfulness. In this chapter we investigate *diversity* and its counterpart, *coherence*.

Referring to everyday experience, as recommended in §2–5.2, consider the following vignette (whether as actuality, as online virtuality or as metaphor):

> Early in the morning, you walk along the street. You are enjoying the sight of the sun rising into a blue sky among a few wisps of cloud, think-ing over a puzzle that your eldest child set before you. Suddenly, you trip over a raised paving stone and regain your balance, momentarily grumbling about 'the council' who *ought* to have maintained the pave-ment, and forget your puzzle. Your thoughts switch to the reason for walking: to buy bread.

In this short vignette we have morning, place, perambulation, sight, sun, sky and clouds, colour, enjoyment, puzzle-solving, reasoning, family, interruption, physical impact, falling, muscular exertion, grumbling, local authorities, "ought", forgetting, purchasing, food. Most of these cannot be reduced to any of the others, without losing their meaningfulness. Food is a purchased product but, *qua* food, must also be seen as sustenance. Enjoy-ment of sun is more than colour. There are diverse ways in which things can be meaningful. All are needed to understand this situation. (What meaning-fulness is, is discussed in Chapter 4.)

Yet there is coherence in this diversity, such as why we are out walking (to buy bread), with a context of the street, the morning, the family, the jurisdic-tion of the council, and so on.

Now consider research, with the vignette as allegory; the research jour-ney, enjoying thoughts rising clearly in a theoretical view, solving research conundrums, unexpected problems, complaints, authorities, rights, redi-rected investigations, need of resources. Research has an everyday "real life" that is highly diverse, and it all coheres around *why* we are undertaking the research, including in its context. Research activity is diverse and coherent, and so are research content and application.

This chapter is about diversity and about coherence in and of this diversity, often known under the ambiguous term "complexity".

A reason I have found Dooyeweerd useful in my research is that he gives diversity and coherence greater respect than most. Whereas many philosophers and scientists have tried to reduce this diversity (e.g. Occam's razor), while others assume diversity is so vast that we need not consider it, Dooyeweerd refuses to do either. Instead, he faces its complexity head-on, treating coherence and diversity as a starting-point (along with everyday experience), not just as a topic to theorise. Exploring their nature, he proposes conceptual tools for tackling them in both research and everyday life.

Section 3–1 briefly overviews how various philosophies have dealt with diversity, before introducing Dooyeweerd's view. Section 3–2 introduces Dooyeweerd's suite of aspects as the main conceptual tool he offers us for navigating complexities and explains his understanding of the relationships among aspects, which express their coherence. This chapter then discusses how Dooyeweerd's understanding relates to research activity (§3–3), research application (§3–4), and research content (§3–5).

3–1.   A Philosophical Look at Diversity and Coherence

We find not only a diversity of particulars (bread1, bread2, etc.) but also a diversity of universals (breadness, beauty, blueness, physicalness, responsibleness, etc.). That is Plato's theory of Forms or Ideas. Forms include things like blueness, redness, beauty, greatness, tableness, circleness, straightness. In a magnificent achievement, Plato argued extensively for the reality and importance of Forms, discussing how they relate to instances, are ideals, are beyond space and time, etc., though he recognised the notion was not without its flaws.

It seems to offer insights into diversity and coherence, but one question remains: What is the basis of the diversity of Forms themselves? Why is there blueness, redness, tableness, beauty? Why are blueness and redness more akin than they are to tableness or to greatness or circleness? It is the question underlying all classifications, like Maslow's (1943) hierarchy of needs, Hartmann's (1952) strata or Bunge's (1979) systems genera (see Table 9.1). We will discover later, especially in Chapter 11, how understanding such differences helps in research.

Complexity Theory offers insights into the nature of disorder and order but, likewise, does not address that question.

Some systems thinking tries to account for diversity by the doctrine of emergence. Somehow, properties that we recognise as life emerge from properties that we recognise as physico-chemical. But, as discussed later in §3–2.4.4, on what basis may we recognise such kinds of properties? That is not a question about the processes (mental, logical) by which we recognise them, but about why it is valid, for example, to call certain complex mixes of chemical reactions "digestion" (a life-meaningful function). What right do we have to think of certain impure chemical mixtures as bread?

Dewey's *philosopher's fallacy* is that we presume conceptual differences like mental-physical or individual-communal, yet such differences arise from tackling different types of problem. Our first understanding of even such basic diversity comes from pre-theoretical, everyday experience. Yet on what basis may we recognise diversity in everyday experience? Dewey merely shifts, not addresses, the problem.

Dooyeweerd, in taking both everyday experience and diversity and coherence as starting-points, addresses the problem directly. He explores them with respect rather than trying to reduce them, but does so critically, without allowing undue proliferation. After the first words of his *magnum opus*, quoted previously, "If I consider reality as it is given in the naïve pre-theoretical experience" (NC,I, 3), he continues,

> and confront it with a theoretical analysis, through which reality appears to split up into various modal aspects, then the first thing that strikes me, is the original *indissoluble interrelation* among these aspects . . . A[n] indissoluble inner coherence binds the numerical to the spatial aspect, the latter to the aspect of mathematical movement, the aspect of movement to that of physical energy, which itself is the necessary basis of the aspect of organic life. The aspect of organic life has an inner connection with that of psychical feeling, the latter refers in its logical anticipation . . . to the analytical-logical aspect. This in turn is connected with the historical, the linguistic, the aspect of social intercourse, the economic, the aesthetic, the jural, the moral aspects and that of faith (emphasis in original).

Then,

> In this inter-modal cosmic coherence no single aspect stands by itself; every-one refers within and beyond itself to all the others.

Here is both diversity and coherence, diversity, in that these "various modal aspects" are irreducibly distinct modes in which things can exist or function, and coherence, in that each aspect inherently depends on or refers to others.

3–2.   Dooyeweerd's Aspects

Dooyeweerd refers to "modal aspects" (NC,I, 3), and this is perhaps the portion of his philosophy that is most widely used in research and practice alike (as the rest of this book attests). This section introduces Dooyeweerd's concept of modal aspects (from now on, just "aspects").

3–2.1   *An Initial Look at Diversity*

Our everyday experience and our research activity exhibit multiple aspects. Dooyeweerd identifies 15 (as in the quotation above). He never precisely defined them (for reasons; see §4–3.13) and he called them by various names.

In this book we will try to be more systematic. Table 3.1 introduces the names of aspects as they will be used in this book (Column 1), some of which differ from those in the excerpt above. Each aspect is a "meaning kernel" or "nucleus" (NC,II, 75), which Column 2 tries to express in words—though these should be treated as approximations and understood intuitively, since kernels can never be fully expressed in words (§4–3.13). Column 3 gives examples of how elements of the earlier vignette are meaningful in each aspect, and Column 4, examples of various issues in research activity.

Dooyeweerd's understanding of the aesthetic aspect seems to cover two things, hence "/". Dooyeweerd used "pistic" (from Greek *pistis*, actual faith "of the common people" (NC,I, 177), vision, commitment) to name this aspect, to differentiate it from mere opinion (NC,II, 309) or even creeds. It is the name used throughout this book.

Table 3.1 Dooyeweerd's 15 aspects and diversity: examples from the vignette and of research activity

Aspect	Kernel	... of Vignette	... of Activity of Research
Quantitative	Amount		Measure
Spatial	Continuous extension	Sun in sky, among clouds	Arrange
Kinematic	Movement	Walk, Rising	Change, progress
Physical	Energy	Sun, clouds, Shoe hits stone	Power cuts, overheating
Organic / Biotic	Life	Food	Health of researchers
Psychic / Sensitive	Feeling, response	Seeing, Stumbling, Forgetting	Sensing data
Analytic	Distinction	Changed line of thought	Think
Formative	Construction, achievement	Puzzle, Purpose	Solve puzzles, plan, innovate
Lingual	Symbolic signification	Grumbling	Discuss, write, disseminate
Social	Relationships, organisations	Family	Cooperate or compete
Economic	Frugality	Purchase	Manage project resources
Aesthetic	Harmony / enjoyment	Enjoying	Integrate / Enjoy or not
Juridical	Due, justice, appropriateness	Council responsibilities	Treat justly: people, topics
Ethical / Attitudinal	Self-giving love	Grumbling	Help others, be generous
Pistic / Faith	Belief, commitment		Rely, assume, presuppose

This table is neither definitive nor complete. Refer to it for approximate understanding of aspects, and to Chapter 9 for elaboration of each aspect, continually, while reading this book. The purpose of this chapter is to explain and illustrate several things about Dooyeweerd's suite of aspects and his understanding of what aspects are, sufficient to show their relevance for research in the chapters that follow. In line with the message of Chapter 2, I recommend that readers approach our discussion seeking intuitive more than precise understanding of the kernels.

Dooyeweerd holds that all things and functionings in concrete reality exhibit all aspects, though in various ways to be discussed later. My Windsor chair exhibits not only the psychic aspect of comfort but also the physical (weight-bearing), social (that it belonged to my father), aesthetic (its rustic beauty), and so on. Research quality similarly exhibits all aspects: pistic (believability), juridical (accuracy), aesthetic (harmony, interest), analytic (clarity) and other aspects.

> *Important note*: Dooyeweerd stresses (NC,II, 556) that his suite of aspects, or any other, is no final truth but merely a best guess. At any time, new aspects might emerge that were not understood before. It is, however, probably the best available so far. See the discussion of the suite's validity (reliability) in §9–3.

3–2.2   Aspects as Modes

Each aspect is a sphere of meaningfulness, a way in which reality can be meaningful. The diversity of everyday experience is a diversity of meaningfulness (as intimated in Chapter 2). Dooyeweerd argues that it is this which gives rise to diversity of things, norms, functionings, etc., and that aspects are their modes. (It may be noticed that Column 3 above refers to things, mostly nouns, while Column 4 refers to activities, verbs.) How these arise from these spheres of meaningfulness is explained fully in Chapter 4; the following gives readers a summary overview:

- **Modes of being.** Types of thing may be defined by aspects; examples: plants are organic, poems, aesthetic. Many things are multi-levelled (multi-aspectual), example: plants are also physical, poems, also lingual.
- **Rationalities.** Each aspect is a different way of making sense; examples: $2 + 5 = 5 + 2$ (quantitative sense), "give and it shall be given to you" (ethical sense). No rationality is superior to others; there is no overall rationality.
- **Modes of functioning.** Human activity may be seen as multi-aspectual function; examples: writing this is lingual functioning, but also social functioning in trying to suit a particular readership, and economic functioning in trying not to waste words.

- Along with this are distinct **kinds of repercussion** that arise from modes of functioning. Examples: physical causality, logical entailment, juridical retribution.
- **Kinds of possibility.** Each aspect makes future functioning possible; examples: a video contains the possibility of being liked or disliked (aesthetic possibility), watched by many or few (quantitative possibility), profitable or loss-making (economic possibility).
- **Distinct norms.** In each aspect from the organic onwards we can differentiate good from evil, desirable from undesirable; examples: health and disease (organic), generosity and meanness (ethical).

Situations, which involve a complex of things, norms, activity, possibilities, etc., may thus be analysed by looking at aspects within them. This can assist research data collection and analysis.

That aspects undergird so much is why many have found Dooyeweerd's aspects widely and almost universally useful in research and practice. See Part III especially.

3–2.3 *Irreducibility of Aspects*

The reason diversity may be addressed by reference to aspects is that aspects are irreducible to each other. This aspectual irreducibility Dooyeweerd calls "sphere sovereignty".

Aspectual irreducibility implies that every aspect is important, in principle, so that if we ignore aspects then we prevent a full understanding of situations and things. Throughout this book occur many examples of where problems have arisen because aspects were ignored.

Dooyeweerd's aspects are not, in themselves, classifications or categorizations, but, because of their fundamental irreducibility, they may be used to form good *categories* with fewer errors. Example: Dahlbom & Mathiassen's (1993, 135) three types of information quality—functional, aesthetic and symbolic—relate to the formative, aesthetic and lingual aspects. As shown in Section 9–3, many categorizations may be seen as subsets of Dooyeweerd's suite of aspects. However, Dooyeweerd warned (1997, 154), "Sphere-sovereignty does not yield a watertight compartment or mechanical division among the areas of life."

Reductionism refuses to recognise diversity, in several ways (Clouser 2005), with two being most detrimental. (a) One aspect is treated as the only important one, leading us to ignore others; as in technological determinism (see Basden (2018a, 173, 286)) or treating economics as the "rationale of life" (Knight 1924/2009, 97). (b) One aspect is presumed to be self-explanatory and able to explain all others; for example, trying to explain everything in terms of power, language, psychology, evolution or chemistry. Reductionism undermines incentive to explore diversity, because it presupposes other aspects are meaningless. Desire to escape reductionism might be tacit recognition of reality's innate diversity. *Dualism*, as well as *monism*, can be reductionistic, in reducing the diversity to just two aspects; Dooyeweerd's answer is pluralistic.

But are not aspects just a 15-way reductionism that still constrains? I do not believe so. (a) His immanent analysis, over millennia and across many fields, has not revealed any other aspects. (b) As mentioned above, Dooyeweerd expressly forbids us to consider his, or any other suite of aspects, as a final truth (NC,II, 556). (c) Dooyeweerd's aspects are not alternatives to each other but all apply simultaneously, giving a rich meaningfulness to everything (§3–2.4.1).

It is for these reasons that, though never treating them as 'the truth', we rely on Dooyeweerd's suite of aspects heavily throughout this book. If readers prefer to substitute another suite of aspects, they are free to do so.

3–2.4   Inter-Aspect Coherence

Giving too much emphasis to the irreducibility of aspects can lead to fragmented views. Though irreducible to each other in their meaningfulness, there is a cohering harmony among aspects, which Dooyeweerd calls "sphere universality" (NC,II, 331) and "the integral coherence of cosmic time" (NC,I, 34). This coherence is inherent in the aspects, whether we recognise it or not. Four coherences are discussed: simultaneity, non-conflict, analogy and dependency.

3–2.4.1   Aspectual Simultaneity

Simultaneity of aspects refers to the multi-aspectual nature of things (§4–3.3) and activities (§4–3.8.2). They cohere in individual things and also in their types. Looking through my bunch of keys, I notice the gleam on the metal of one, then select another with which to open my door. Discovering it bent and will not work, I hammer it back into shape, and then it works. (Thanks to Gareth Jones for this example.) My keys exhibit several aspects simultaneously. The main aspect is that of the purpose of keys, a juridical one (rightful access). A spatial aspect (shape) is important, a physical (the metal must not bend), and an aspect of distinctness (each must be unique). The gleam suggests an aesthetic aspect. All this is what being-a-key entails.

3–2.4.2   No Conflict Among Aspects

"Being virtuous jeopardises economic success!", as expressed in Mandeville's *Fable of the Bees*, presupposes conflict between the ethical and economic aspects. Dooyeweerd held (NC,II, 3) that there is no conflict among aspects. All contribute to the full actualization of others (see the *Shalom Principle*, §4–3.7). Indeed, experience shows that, long term, ethical businesses last longer (Collins & Porras 1998). Any apparent conflict arises, argued

Dooyeweerd (NC,II, 334ff), from foundational problems in philosophy itself, discussed in Chapter 5.

(To be fair, Mandeville's fable was against *absolutising* virtuosity rather than virtuosity as such.)

3–2.4.3   *Inter-Aspect Analogy*

Each aspect contains echoes of all the others. For example, causality is physical but logical implication and historical bringing-about resemble this (Geertsema 2002). See Dooyeweerd's own account of many analogies (NC,II, 118ff).

Inter-aspect analogy is not to be confused with the concrete analogies that we make between things, such as metaphors; rather it is what enables metaphors to 'work'.

Inter-aspect analogy can be useful in research to stimulate fresh ideas. Too much reliance on analogy, however, can mislead because the laws of one aspect (for aspectual law; see §4–3.8) cannot be reduced to those of another. Example: The organic metaphors of growth, health and survival have been unquestioningly applied to businesses and nations, but some argue that this has led economics astray (Pilling 2018). With powerful metaphors it is too easy to forget this.

Somewhere, Dooyeweerd makes an interesting observation that it is because each aspect contains within it echoes of the others that reductionism sometimes seems to work, or at least yield fruitful results. It is because, when we reduce to one aspect, that aspect still echoes the others that we are ignoring. The results of such study are likely to be thin and unsustainable over the long term, but they can still be useful. For example, useful insights in economics emerged from the organic metaphor of growth and health, but some argue it has kept us from fully opening up the economic aspect of environmental stewardship (see §4–3.8.3).

3–2.4.4   *Inter-Aspect Dependency*

Each aspect depends on other aspects, both earlier and later (NC,III, 91), but differently in the two directions. *Foundational dependency* (or *retrocipatory dependency*) means that functioning in an aspect depends on good functioning in an earlier aspect. The earlier aspects provide a substratum or foundation, as in Hartmann's notion of lower strata 'bearing' higher ones.

> Example: Good social activity depends on good lingual functioning (talking, writing), which depends on good formative and analytic functioning (structuring, clarity).

Transcendental dependency (or *anticipatory dependency* (NC,III, 108)) works in the opposite direction. If aspect Y depends foundationally on aspect X, then aspect X anticipates (and lets us anticipate!) aspect Y.

Example: Irrational numbers (quantitative) antecipate spatiality. The lingual aspect antecipates the social; lingual functioning would be very limited (e.g. to setting up reminders for ourselves) if not used in communication with others.

Note on terminology: antecipate, anticipate. Dooyeweerd used "anticipate" but, following Strauss (2009), "antecipate" is used here since "ante" means "before". "Anticipate" is used for human expectation.

Sometimes, antecipation and retrocipation form a cycle. For example, that conversation alters our social relationships is a lingual-social antecipation, and that social relationships and structures affect our language is a social-lingual retrocipation. This is important to understanding social media and is recognised in Critical Discourse Analysis.

A common mistake is to conflate *dependency* with *reducibility*. For example, believability of research (pistic) depends on accuracy (juridical), but neither can be reduced to the other.

Supervenience and **emergence** (see §3–1) may be understood in terms of Dooyeweerd's antecipatory and foundational dependency: properties meaningful in the later aspect supervene on (emerge from) those of the earlier (e.g. life supervenes on chemistry). In saying life emerges from chemistry, do we not already have an intuition of what is meaningful in the organic aspect and 'smuggle' in that meaning? Klapwijk (2008) discusses emergence from a Dooyeweerdian perspective, to which several authors responded in the 2011 issue of *Philosophia Reformata.*

Research opportunity: emergence. Might Dooyeweerd's suite of aspects help emergence theorists understand what meanings they are already presuming?

3–2.4.5   The Order of Aspects

Retrocipatory and antecipatory dependency expresses an order among aspects, which is fundamental. Dooyeweerd called it "the order of *cosmic time*" (NC,I, 29, emphasis in original). One of the very few diagrams that Dooyeweerd devised, reproduced in Figure 3.1, shows each aspect as a kernel

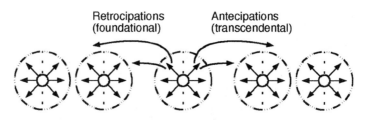

Figure 3.1 Spheres of meaningfulness in sequence

with a constellation of meaning, half of which antecipates later aspects and half of which retrocipates earlier ones.

> *Note on terminology: later, earlier aspects.* Dooyeweerd refers to aspects as 'later' and 'earlier', not 'higher' and 'lower', because they are all equally important.

The order does not depend on subjective interpretation—though our *knowledge of* the order does. Example: Sentience (psychic aspect) depends foundationally on organic functioning, which depends in turn on chemistry and physics, whether we know it or not. At the time of Dooyeweerd, most philosophy had never posed the problem of this order (NC,II, 49) (though systems thinking might now have done so); he spent Volume II discussing it.

The *terminal aspects*, quantitative and pistic, lack retrocipation and antecipation respectively (NC,II, 52–54). The pistic aspect influences retrocipatorily our functioning in all other aspects; that is why beliefs, commitments, assumptions and presuppositions are so important in research.

3–3. Diversity and Coherence of Research Activity

Too often, unfortunately, research fails. Some research generates worthless findings, some exceeds its deadlines or budget, some expects too much of researchers so that their families or their work-life balance suffer, some is riven with personal rivalries, some is vexed by hidden agendas. With increasing globalisation of research, cultural problems abound.

This signals the diversity that is research activity. As mentioned in Chapter 2, Dooyeweerd believes the researcher (thinker) is fully human, not just a rational engine—and humanness is no departure from the ideal. Increasingly, Dooyeweerd's insights are being echoed by others. It is wise to view research as a multi-aspectual, fully human activity.

The question "How can we improve our research?" is often addressed by means of reaction. The problem of missed deadlines and budgets has been tackled by a reaction against the exploratory nature of research into a more managerial approach, increasing pressure on researchers. The problem of worthless findings is exemplified by mid-20th-century adoption of positivistic methods in the social sciences, the results of which could not be trusted to include all relevant factors, especially 'subjective' ones. In reaction, interpretivist approaches became popular, which are sensitive to such factors—though not to social structures, so socio-critical approaches became popular. Section 7–3.1 explains more.

Such reactions are often driven either by pet ideas or by dualistic ground-motives (§5–2.2). These see one pole as the problem and the opposing pole as the solution. The main dualistic ground-motive currently in force, the Nature-Freedom ground-motive, opposes control/determination/law to freedom. Positivist approaches (problem) align with the Nature pole, so the answer, it is believed, lies in the Freedom pole (to which interpretivism aligns). Missed deadlines are believed to result from researchers having too much freedom (problem); so the solution is managerial control.

Reaction rarely improves research because, while perhaps overcoming one perceived problem temporarily, it usually generates others, unforeseen.

Dooyeweerd's view of research as a fully human activity, which in Chapter 2 was characterised as the everyday experience of research, implies multiple aspects simultaneously. Aspectual irreducibility (§3–2.3) and coherence (§3–2.4) implies that every aspect is important; this is the diversity of research activity.

With this view (and anticipating our discussion of aspectual normativity in §4–3.7) we can understand the failures listed earlier as dysfunction in several aspects:

- Worthless findings: analytic, lingual;
- Deadlines, budgets: economic;
- Undue suffering of families: juridical;
- Work-life balance: aesthetic;
- Rivalries: ethical, pistic;
- Hidden agendas: pistic;
- Cultural: social, pistic.

Instead of reaction, this approach suggests that research may be improved by rectifying dysfunction in each diverse aspect of research activity. Research activity may be planned by attending to the good each aspect can bring.

Research activity shows two coherences. One is the non-conflict among aspects (§3–2.4.2), all working together simultaneously (§3–2.4.1). Understanding this can help guide research activity. Another is around the primary aspects of research activity, the analytic and lingual, which together make the mandate of research meaningful. The analytic is the primary aspect of theoretical thought (*Gegenstand*) along with the lingual, of dissemination into bodies of knowledge.

Chapter 10 is devoted to discussion of each aspect of research activity from a practical perspective. Along with 'obvious' aspectual issues like dissemination, it draws attention to 'hidden' issues like rivalries.

3–4. Diversity and Coherence of Research Application

When research findings are applied, repercussions may reasonably be expected. If we see research application as "real life" (§2–6.1), it exhibits multi-aspectual diversity in the way research activity does.

Functioning in multiple aspects implies diverse kinds of repercussion (§4–3.8). Usually, repercussions in the focal aspects of the research are expected, planned for and discussed (e.g. efficiency, emancipation), but alongside these is a myriad of repercussions in other aspects, which are often unexpected and might beget 'collateral damage'. Some are indirect, by behaviour of other people, and many are long term.

Example: Applying Fishbein & Ajzen's (1975) Theory of Reasoned Action in business might embrace logicality (analytic aspect), but it might also jeopardise social relations because it ignores social aspects (Terry et al. 1993, 255).

Repercussions and possibilities in applying research may be beneficial and/ or detrimental. Understanding the innate normativity in the aspects (§4–3.7) can help us think about and discuss them—including issues of power and social structures. Also, aspectual antecipatory dependency can help stimulate ideas about new application possibilities.

Like research activity, research application shows two coherences. One is coherence among the aspects themselves (§3–2.4), particularly inter-aspect dependency, by which a repercussion meaningful in one aspect reinforces that in another. Since dependency can both antecipate and retrocipate, self-reinforcing loops can occur, which for example can affect communities (§11–3.3).

Another coherence of application is that research findings should harmonise both with the *world* in its diversity, which feels the repercussions of research, and with the *bodies of knowledge* to which research contributes. This involves every aspect, not only the analytic and lingual (of theory-making and dissemination), but also others, such as pistic coherence involving beliefs that prevail in the community of thought/practice about the meaning-context the body of knowledge offers and how it might expand; §6–3.5 discusses this further.

This brief discussion suggests that Dooyeweerd's suite of aspects offers a foundation for understanding, exploring and even managing the diversity and coherence of research application.

3–5. Diversity and Coherence in Research Content (Theories)

Research content concerns the theoretical output of research, rather than its activity. We look at diversity and coherence *of* fields and diversity and coherence *inside* fields: data, concepts and findings. A major theme throughout them all reiterates that, because of the irreducible distinctness of aspects, the researcher should, in general, consider each and every one, omitting none.

3–5.1 Diversity and Coherence of Research Fields

We have many sciences and disciplines—physics, chemistry, materials science, biochemistry, and biology within the natural sciences; human sciences, including psychology of various kinds, sociology, economics, and also linguistics and semiotics; design sciences, engineering of various kinds and technical topics; humanities and the arts, jurisprudence, ethics, and theology; and mathematical sciences. That is their diversity. How do they relate to each other, especially in interdisciplinary research? That is their coherence.

Dooyeweerd suggests that each main scientific area tends to focus on one sphere of meaningfulness, one aspect of the world: physics, chemistry and materials on the physical aspect, life sciences on the organic-biotic aspect, psychology on the psychic aspect, and so on (see §8–1.2). "Focus on" for sciences usually means studying laws that enable the world of the core aspect to function and, for disciplines, being guided primarily by the norms of the aspect or the possibilities that aspect offers (see §4–3.7, §4–3.8, especially about what "law" means). (The "world of a core aspect" is approximately a Husserlian "world".)

The focus of fields on aspects is actually more nuanced than this, with each taking account of neighbouring aspects; see §8–1.3.

Some fields (sciences, disciplines) cross aspectual boundaries, such as biochemistry and sociolinguistics, which take a couple of aspects as focal, and interdisciplinary fields, which take several aspects as focal. So aspectual coherence becomes very important.

- *Aspectual simultaneity* accounts for the possibility and validity of interdisciplinary research. Boden (1999) gives the example of artificial intelligence, which includes cognitive science, computer science, linguistics, mathematics, etc.—analytic, formative, lingual, quantitative aspects respectively.
- *Aspectual non-conflict* gives hope that fields interested in different aspects might work towards a common goal.
- *Inter-aspect dependency* explains how each field might relate to others conceptually. For example, the laws of the formative aspect, which Basden (2008a) argues is the focus of computer science, depend foundationally on those of the analytic and psychic aspects, and antecipatorily on those of the lingual aspect, which in AI refers to content of computerised information.
- *Inter-aspect analogy* can stimulate fresh ways of thinking. This is one of the thrills of interdisciplinary research.

See Section 8–1 for a fuller discussion of all fields and interdisciplinary research. See also Chapter 2 of Strauss (2009).

3–5.2   Diversity and Coherence of Data Collected in Research

Most discussion of data collection revolves around collection methods or sources of data (in the human sciences, data comes via questionnaires, interviews, data mining or study of texts, videos, etc.; in the natural sciences, via experiment, field studies, observations, etc.; and in the mathematical sciences, via thought experiments, imagination, computer search, etc.).

The question asked here is different: What kinds of data are appropriate to collect in each field, and why? Some of the answers that Dooyeweerd leads us to might be surprising.

As has already been mentioned and is set on a firmer foundation in §4–3.8.2, the world (the situations we study), in its full reality, functions in every aspect simultaneously. So, every aspect is relevant in general and in principle. However, this is qualified by a focal aspect (§2–3.1) and the context of the research, around which the research coheres, usually relating to several other aspects.

In the physical sciences, the physical is the focal aspect, so data of the physical world are collected. The "other aspects" are those that the physical aspect depends on foundationally (§3–2.4.4), the kinematic, spatial and quantitative; so data about movements, locations and quantities are collected. In the life sciences, the focal aspect is the organic-biotic and the other aspects are the physical to quantitative. In animal and behaviourist psychology, the psychic-sensory is the focal aspect, but data are also collected about bodily functions, materials, etc. (organic-biotic to quantitative aspects).

Sometimes, later aspects might be relevant. For example, if a horse is injured during a race, then the formative aspect of driving the horse to achieve something for human purposes is likely to be relevant. There is a difference, however, because of Dooyeweerd's unconventional subject-object notion, which is explained in §4–3.9. The focal psychic aspect is that in which the horse functions as subject rather than object, but in the formative aspect, s/he functions as object of human functioning in the formative aspect, which exerts retrocipatory influence on the psychical behaviour of the horse and the organic behaviour of its body.

Humans, however, can function in every aspect as subject. This implies that any aspect might be focal (primary) when researching human or social behaviour. The research coheres around this. Which aspect(s) is/are focal depends on the purpose or scope of the research. The most important data collected will be that meaningful in this/these aspect(s), but other data will be collected from earlier aspects on which it depends foundationally, and later aspects that exert retrocipatory influence.

The diversity and coherence of research content may be illustrated by research into the use of email in offices. Davis' (1989) *Technology Acceptance Model* (TAM) arose from the question of what leads people to actually use information technology (IT); see §1–2.1. It is one of the seminal papers of the field and will be used as an example later on. Drawing on behaviour theory, Davis composed a model (Figure 3.2) and converted it into hypotheses, which he tested by surveying users of email, to obtain data from the everyday experience of users (§2–5.2). He concluded that two main constructs determined amount of use: perceived usefulness and perceived ease of use. To measure these, however, required careful selection of relevant "external variables", from which questions were compiled for the survey. These are shown in Table 3.2, which also indicates the aspects that make each variable meaningful.

We can see some diversity here, in that the following aspects are meaningful: formative, economic, lingual, psychic, quantitative, juridical, ethical. The *coherence* is the focal formative aspect of use of software.

In fact, the aspectual diversity of information systems use is wider than Davis expected in his study. His model was taken up and tested in other contexts, mandatory rather than voluntary use, social and hedonic rather than professional purposes and personal rather than organisational use, greatly extending the range of external variables. Yousafzai et al. (2007) collected

Table 3.2 External variables by which Davis measures perceived usefulness and ease of use

TAM external variables	Aspects
Quality of Work	Formative, ethical
Control over Work	Formative, formative
Work More Quickly	Formative, economic
Critical to My Job	Formative, formative
Increase Productivity	Quantitative, formative
Job Performance	Formative, formative
Accomplish More Work	Formative, quantitative
Effectiveness	Formative
Makes Job Easier	Formative, psychic
Useful	Formative
Cumbersome	Formative
Ease of Learning	Formative, lingual
Frustrating	Psychic
Controllable	Formative
Rigid & inflexible	Juridical, formative
Ease of Remembering	Psycyic
Mental Effort	Psychic, formative
Understandable	Lingual
Effort to Be Skillful	Formative, formative
Easy to Use	Formative, formative

over 80 of them, including such things as "navigation", "sex", "gender", "social presence", "competitive environment", and "perceived enjoyment".

The full set is shown in Table 7.1 and covers nearly every aspect, showing that the *diversity* of what is meaningful, in the supposedly simple concepts of (perceived) usefulness and ease of use, is enormous.

What this shows is that, in many research fields, a wide diversity of issues is potentially relevant. If aspects are ignored during data collection (rather than thoughtfully excluded), relevant issues might be overlooked, ending up with partial, misleading findings and theory. This is likely to extend the period of critique and refinement of the theory until all relevant aspects are included; with Davis, this took a decade and still continues, with several versions and new models. Chapter 11 discusses practical methods of data collection with Dooyeweerd's aspects.

Research opportunity: model refinement. Review models and their periods of critique and refinement and investigate the gradual inclusion of wider aspects.

3–5.3 *Diversity and Coherence Within Concepts*

Each concept used in science, Husserl argued, depends for its meaningfulness on the pre-theoretical lifeworld. This is readily seen in the case of trust, a concept important in business, commerce, finance, the Internet, etc. Stephen McGibbon's (2018) extensive survey of literature found every aspect of trust discussed, as direct functioning (e.g. ethical self-giving, pistic reliance), indirect functioning (e.g. communication) or analogy (e.g. physical force). The coherence of all these, he argues, is the ethical aspect: real trust, of all kinds, necessarily involves the self-giving attitude of vulnerability to being let down. All other aspects cohere around that. Some of the complex research methods he used are discussed in §11–4.4 and §11–7.5.

We might expect trust to be multi-aspectual, but so are even physical concepts. The concept of *entropy* is defined as "the amount of energy in a system not available for doing work" (Webster 1971, I, 759). This contains the following aspects:

- "amount"—quantitative;
- "energy"—physical (mass), kinematic (velocity-squared);
- "in a system"—analytic (a closed system distinct from its environment), physical-kinematic (thermodynamically);
- "not available"—economic;
- "for doing work"—formative, but depends on kind of work, which is physical.

(Now I see why I found entropy difficult to understand during physics classes: later aspects!)

Almost all concepts we employ are multi-aspectual in their meaningfulness— even in mathematics (see §6–1.1)—and can only be understood if we understand aspects.

> *Research opportunity: lifeworld.* Might this give shape to Husserl's idea of lifeworld, insofar as our grasp of aspect kernels is intuitive (see §4–3.13, §4–3.10)?

3–5.4 *Diversity and Coherence in Research Findings/Theories*

Since a research finding (theory) relates issues to each other, we need to say something about the diversity and coherence that is these relationships. Relationships often express a rationality, which is different in each aspect (§4–3.6), and each aspect enables a distinct kind of relationship (§4–3.8.4).

Davis' (1989) Technology Acceptance Model is depicted in Figure 3.2. Each arrow shows a 'causality' relationship, a "leading-to", which Davis took as a hypothesis to be tested statistically by his survey using questions described above (§3–5.2).

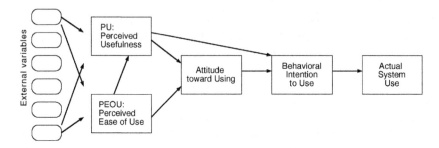

Figure 3.2 Davis' initial Technology Acceptance Model

Each "leading-to" relationship exhibits several aspects, for example for "perceived usefulness increases intention to use":

- perception-leads-to-intention: psychic;
- usefulness-leads-to-use: formative;
- increase: quantitative.

Since all TAM's relationships and variables are meaningful in the same three aspects, TAM feels harmonious. Delone & McLean's (1992) model of information systems success felt less harmonious. It included two kinds of relationship: mixing formative leading-to with analytic association. (On being criticised, they produced a new version with only the leading-to.)

This, however, raises the question of when multiple kinds of relationship might be valid, especially during interdisciplinary research. If we understand the problem in aspectual terms, then it may be valid to include several relationship types as long as inter-aspect harmony of meaningfulness is explicitly discussed and managed.

3–6. Conclusion

We have discussed the diversity and coherence inherent in research activity, application and content. Dooyeweerd's understanding of diversity is as aspects (spheres of meaningfulness), which also cohere. This chapter has shown how Dooyeweerd's suite of 15 aspects can help us understand and manage research failure, unexpected repercussions of research application, harmonisation with bodies of knowledge, the plethora of fields and of kinds of data collected, the hidden complexity within theoretical concepts and the harmony of theoretical models. These, and other issues, will be expanded throughout this book.

Aspects have been treated as distinct yet related ways in which things may be meaningful, but we have not yet understood meaningfulness. That is discussed in the next chapter.

4   Meaning in Research and Reality, and an Overview of Dooyeweerd's Understanding of Reality

This chapter is about meaning—about meaning as such, as a cross-field philosophical notion rather than meanings from a psychological, linguistic, sociological, theological or any other perspective.

Meaning of this kind is very important in research. In the previous three chapters, we have discussed:

- the meaningfulness of research as such in the wider world (its mandate), the meaningfulness of fields, and the purpose of projects, that of each facet of what research is;
- aspects as spheres of meaning, and their irreducibility and harmony;
- the diverse meanings encountered in pre-theoretical everyday experience and the lifeworld, the rich meaningfulness of things;
- relevance, focal meanings in research and unbidden meanings arising from other aspects;
- what is meaningful to the researcher and to those being researched (Malinowski and his "natives"); what is meaningful to the research community and the surrounding culture, presuppositions;
- the common 'ocean of meaningfulness' in which they all 'swim' together, the diversity and harmony of meaningfulness as a whole, the totality of possible ways of being meaningful;
- the meaning-complexity of concepts and variables within research;
- loss of meaning in reductionism;
- smuggling meaning into emergence;
- and the meaning of life.

Meaning pervades research and everyday experience alike, surrounding, enabling, guiding them and making them worthwhile, often unseen. Meaninglessness leaves us bereft. In everything, meaning is presupposed. Dooyeweerd's third starting-point is expressed in one of his most famous statements:

> *Meaning* is the *being* of all that has been *created*, and the nature even of our selfhood.
>
> (NC,I, 4, emphasis in original)

After some preliminaries, this chapter offers an overview of how philosophy has addressed meaning. Section 4–3 then sketches out Dooyeweerd's understanding of meaning. Since meaning (or rather, meaningfulness) is one of Dooyeweerd's starting-points and is the philosophical notion from which his ontology, epistemology and axiology all emerge, it is a lengthy section, somewhat encyclopaedic in style (to provide reference material) rather than philosophically discursive. What this implies for research application, activity and content is then briefly discussed, as a preparation for later chapters.

4–1.   Types of Meaning

Given the prevalence of meaning, it is surprising how seldom the word "meaning" occurs in the indexes of philosophy books, as though it is not a topic of philosophical interest—not even in Merleau-Ponty's (1962) *Phenomenology of Perception*, even though the word appears throughout his text. In his text, "meaning" seems to refer to more than one thing.

Indeed, throughout philosophy, and in everyday life, the word "meaning" seems to mean at least five different things. Differentiating these five here is merely to assist clarity and is based on intuition; a tentative justification is presented later.

- *Signification-meaning*, the meaning carried by words, utterances, etc., for example, "red", "red rose" or "Prune that red rose carefully." Often, this is what philosophy refers to when it uses the term "meaning".
- *Interpretation-meaning*, the meaning we assign when we interpret something, e.g. a group of scattered feathers to mean a bird was killed, or a dot as the pupil of an eye, the top of the letter "i", the end of a sentence and so on (Merleau-Ponty's "perception meaning"), in which a perceiving subject perceives an object (dot, feathers) and interprets it.
- *Attribution-meaning*, the meaning we attribute to things, such as the vase my grandmother gave me. Attribution-meaning is often linked to utility, purpose or memory.
- *Life-meaning* (*meaning of life*), as in "What is the meaning of my life (or career, etc.)?" Identity is similar to this.
- *Meaningfulness*, similar to life-meaning, but the idea that things are meaningful whether or not we signify, interpret or attribute, and whether or not a human life is involved. Meaningfulness applies to all temporal reality (e.g. animals, habitats, planets). In everyday language, words like "value", "importance" and "significance" are often used to denote or connote meaningfulness. For example, in "reality has a value in itself that is independent of its usefulness for humankind", Jochemsen (2006, 98) is referring to meaningfulness.
- There may be others.

Interpretation- and attribution-meanings arise from a subject giving meaning to objects, but in interpretation-meaning the meaning takes more account of the objects rather than the subject. Signification-meanings arise from subjects generating objects to express their intended meaning(s). Life-meaning is the subject seeking meaning for themselves from beyond themselves, possibly in society or world, and is often what constitutes *identity*. Meaningfulness offers meaning to both subjects and objects but ultimately transcends (refers beyond) both, and beyond past, present and future. It is the only type of meaning that does not presuppose a subject. Section 4–3.11 discusses how the first four types are rooted in (depend on and presuppose) meaningfulness.

> *Note on terminology: meaning.* As far as possible, "meaning" will only be used to signify all types generically, without differentiation. Otherwise the five terms will be used. This excepts, of course, quotations from other authors. The first four types may properly be called "meanings" rather than "meaning".

So, meaningfulness is the most fundamental. For this reason, it is meaningfulness that is discussed most in this chapter. There are two other reasons: meaningfulness pervades research, and meaningfulness has been least discussed by philosophers. Almost everywhere Dooyeweerd uses the word "meaning" (thousands of times), he seems to be referring to meaningfulness.

4–2.   Treatment of Meaning in Philosophy

This section is about how philosophy has treated meaning, especially meaningfulness, and may be postponed to read later if preferred.

Philosophy has seldom discussed meaning, as such, especially not meaningfulness. In the absence of any authoritative overview of how philosophy treats meaning, the following oversimplified account, from which much has been omitted, must suffice. As far as I know, the overall picture that emerges is accurate.

Most Greek philosophers were interested in being and behaviour more than meaning as such. Aristotle, however, recognised meaning indirectly in his theory of the causes of behaviour. Alongside "material", "formal" and "efficient" causes, he proposed "final cause", as a for-the-sake-of-which something occurs, like a magnet pulling all towards it. However, Aristotle reduced this mainly to Matter striving towards Form (NC,I, 25–6), and *Scholasticism* reinterpreted this in eschatological terms. As discussed in §5–2.4, these views rob us of diversity.

Life-meaning was discussed in Greek thought as "which final ends a person ought to realize in order to have a life that matters" (Stanford 2013a). Usually, "matters" refers to one of life's aspects, such as goodness, health, happiness or virtue. To many Scholastic thinkers, meaning is associated with either soul or God, and life-meaning is constituted in fulfilling God's purposes (Stanford 2013b). More recently,

> it is only in the last 50 years or so that something approaching a distinct field on the meaning of life has been established in Anglo-American

philosophy, and it is only in the last 30 years that debate with real depth has appeared.

(Stanford 2013b)

Life-meaning is treated as "a certain property that is desirable for its own sake", like coherence, intelligibility, inspiring awe, devotion or love, transcending animal nature, or transcending one's own life to connect with organic unity, whereas maintaining an exact number of hairs on one's head (Stanford 2013a), for example, is meaningless. All these views, however, presuppose a basis for identifying virtues, God's purposes or innate desirability. Do they imply that animals as such are meaningless—and why or why not?

Kant mentions meaning a number of times in his *Critique of Practical Reason*, but he nowhere defines nor discusses it, merely employing it intuitively. From the way he uses it, meaning seems to be something innately valuable and closely linked with the Good, which he discusses at length. He sought a theory of Good that transcends mere personal interests or pleasures—thereby, perhaps, beginning to distinguish meaningfulness from the first four types of meaning. His *Critique of Judgment* discusses aesthetic and teleological judgment. The latter is akin to meaningfulness, which Kant calls "purpose". Kant discusses several levels of purpose, up to the "final purpose" of the entire Creation (nature and humanity together), which, he concludes (Kant 1790/1987, 344, K454), is humanity itself in its moral being. (Is this not the ultimate Humanism?) But on what basis do we decide what "moral being" is, except by reference beyond even this? Also, in an era when humanity threatens nature with plastics, deforestation and climate change, how can Kant's view be valid?

Pragmatism started out as a criterion of meaning, and then became a whole epistemology with wide-ranging implications for all philosophy. What Dewey called Immediate Empiricism wants to "give a place to meaning and value instead of explaining them away as subjective additions to a world of whizzing atoms". Dewey's answer to the philosopher's fallacy (§3–1), that conceptual differences arise from tackling different types of problem, presupposes distinct ways of being meaningful to differentiate problem-types.

Peirce's theory of signs starts by trying to understand signification-meaning in terms of the triad of sign, object and interpretant (mental activity). He then noted that the interpretant itself is meaningful and suggested interpretants are themselves signs, with their attendant interpretants, and so on, infinitely, and ended up by saying "all is sign." This moves near to what we call meaningfulness, but Peirce did not explore it.

Phenomenology began to recognise that meaning cannot be sidelined, and seeks to understand the meanings that things have in our experience, including the relationship between meanings (Moran 2000, 101). Husserl discussed meaning twice, first as the content of the object of thinking (Husserl 1913/1950, 167) (interpretation-meaning, attribution-meaning, signification-meaning), second as *lifeworld* (Husserl 1954/1970). He argued that the meanings of concepts in science, on which the truth of scientific findings rests, themselves rest on shared background meanings that constitute the lifeworld, and these are pre-theoretical. For example, "the practical art of surveying" is a "meaning-fundament" for the science of geometry (p. 48). Husserl's lifeworld seems similar to our meaningfulness, but, perhaps because of his immanence-standpoint, he presumed the lifeworld may be understood an accumulation of signification- and other meanings. Husserl often confused different types of meanings (NC,II, 225n).

In Heidegger's discourse on *Being and Time* (1927/1962), we find meaning plays important parts, under various guises. He understood being, not as substance (as had been presupposed since Aristotle), but as relationships with, and situatedness in, the world. Being is being-in-the-world, and the being of *Dasein* (a being for whom their own existence is a concern, usually human or perhaps organic) is 'care' or concern-with. *Dasein* has "concernful" dealings in the world and with objects-in-the-world (pp. 95–6, H.66), which are "manifold ways", "split up into definite ways of Being-in" such as "producing . . . attending . . . looking after . . . giving up"—and there are corresponding "deficient" ways like "neglecting, renouncing" (p. 83, H.56–7).

That care is ontically prior to attitudes and situations, as a "primordial structural totality" (p. 193), suggests tacit recognition of a transcending meaningfulness and its diversity. Yet, in trying to explain how *Dasein*'s "care" arises, he presupposed the world is meaningless. His answer, that *Dasein*'s "wholeness", totality or meaningfulness is realized only at its "end", its death, makes his "a philosophy of death", as Dooyeweerd wryly notes (NC,II, 24). As such, it is not very helpful in research, where meaningfulness is here-and-now.

In his later writings, we still finding Heidegger reaching for a transcending meaningfulness. His discussions of poetry (Heidegger 1971) and technology (1977) suggest this; meaningfulness transcends both, enabling poetry to be, and being what it is the role of technology to reveal. Similarly, "the task of thinking" (Heidegger 1972) is "unconcealment", which presupposes a transcending meaningfulness to be revealed.

Merleau-Ponty (1962), in discussing perception, frequently mentions meaning, though presupposed rather than much discussed. As "sense", he mixes it up with sensation. As with most philosophers mentioned earlier, he locates meaning in the subject, while seeming to reach for meaningfulness.

Several philosophers took a Linguistic Turn, calling on the sciences of linguistics and semiotics to understand the world. They began with signification-meaning but most gradually moved towards meaningfulness. To Gadamer, meaning is not an object that can be found by examination, but is inevitable, whether one is engaging with a text, artwork or experience, and we always come with pre-understandings. To discern meaning external to the thinker requires a hermeneutic cycle (our understanding of the whole helps us understand each part, which builds up the former). Yet, around what does the cycle revolve, and how does interpretation take into account the interpreters' often-conflicting cultural attachments (Shklar 1986)?

Derrida argued that texts do not stand alone but refer to each other (intertextuality), the individual semantic unit gaining its meaning by "*différance*" from others—but what makes *différance* possible, if not meaningfulness that transcends both?

Ricoeur argued that meaning is an engagement of a self with an other. "The purpose of all interpretation is to conquer a remoteness, a distance . . . By overcoming this distance, . . . the exegete can appropriate [the text's] meaning to himself: foreign, he makes it familiar, that is, he makes it his own" (Ricoeur 1974, 16–17). Meaning is thus not seen as something generated by author and given to reader, nor as generated by reader from material supplied by author, but as something that binds author and reader together.

Linguistic Turn thinkers began to realise that meaning extends beyond signification-meaning to the whole of life and reality. Gadamer saw meaning as a stream in which we move, Derrida declared that "all is text" and Ricoeur, that "text" is anything other than self—a meaningful world. Derrida's deconstruction is an "unravelling of meaning" and, to Ricoeur, philosophy is a hermeneutic concerned with meaning and its aim is to recover and restore meaning. These strongly indicate an interest in meaningfulness.

Yet what Dooyeweerd calls "Humanistic philosophy" presupposes that meaning is generated *ex nihilo* (from nothing) by a (usually human) subject and would not allow any consideration of a meaningfulness that transcends the subject or intersubjective group thereof. Some posit that meaningfulness accumulates as a 'sedimentation' from intersubjective interactions, for example, Habermas' (1987) explanation of the lifeworld arising from communicative action. Yet this merely postpones, not meets, the challenge. What is meaningfulness that transcends the social milieu?

There is, however, one tributary of philosophy that takes seriously the possibility that meaningfulness transcends the subject and social milieu. An early trickle thereof is Aristotle's "final cause", which was taken up by Liebniz. Another is Bergson's (1908, 95) "*elan originel*", an initial impetus in a particular direction from which reality developed thereafter. Physical reality is propelled towards free sensorimotor actions and then eventually towards human intellect and consciousness (Bergson 1911/1998).

More radically, however, Polanyi & Prosch (1975) suggest that we *dwell* in meaning. This is meaningfulness that transcends subjects. They develop their argument fairly systematically from within the scientific realms of physics, chemistry and biology and the humanities of arts, music, poetry and myth, rather than philosophy. Meaning gives a 'gradient' to reality. Echoing Bergson, they argue that evolution exhibits a gradient towards biology, which gives rise to a "panorama of meaningful achievements" (p. 173), but they do so more profoundly and go beyond the natural sciences into the humanities. From observations of tacit knowledge, they recognise that pre-theoretical knowledge arises from "profound acts of indwelling", as do joint meaning and unrevealed meanings, and the possibility of mutual understanding between people (the other-minds problem).

Dooyeweerd's view resembles Polanyi & Prosch's but comes from philosophy rather than the sciences. If we *dwell* in meaning(fulness) then meaning(fulness) is our starting-point, rather than something to neglect (as largely in earlier philosophy) or to explain as constructed *ex nihilo*. Not only can Dooyeweerd's view meet various philosophical challenges mentioned earlier (see §4–3.11), but I have found it particularly helpful in my various areas of research, to stimulate fresh perspectives (see Chapter 11). The next section draws together much of what Dooyeweerd wrote about meaning, with how he used it in his philosophy, to provide a systematic understanding of Dooyeweerd's approach.

4–3. Meaningfulness as the Foundation for Ontology, Epistemology and Axiology

That the words "meaning", "meaningful", etc. occur 3,077 times in Dooyeweerd's *New Critique* (NC) demonstrates its importance in Dooyeweerd's philosophy. Dooyeweerd's understanding of meaning differs radically from that of most philosophy (with the possible exception of Polanyi).

To Dooyeweerd, reality is meaning, indeed, almost a synonym for reality (Dooyeweerd 1999, Appendix). Everything is meaningful in a deeper way than is ordinarily assumed. The major implications this has for research are discussed in §4–4 and throughout the rest of this book.

Sadly, Dooyeweerd did not systematically discuss meaning, but he refers to it intuitively as though we all understand it. Nor did those who follow him in Reformational Philosophy. It may be that the notion can only be fully understood intuitively (van der Hoeven 1978), but if Dooyeweerd's philosophy is to be employed in mainstream research, as he urges in NC (I, viii), then his novel idea of meaning needs and deserves clear elaboration and discussion.

As van der Hoeven (1978) remarks, whereas most philosophers use "meaning" semantically, Dooyeweerd stays closer to its use in "ordinary life" as meaningfulness that transcends semantics, as in the meaning of life or history (van der Hoeven does not distinguish life-meaning from meaningfulness). (This may be a manifestation of Dooyeweerd's respect for everyday life; Chapter 2.) In almost all places where Dooyeweerd uses the word "meaning", he seems to be referring to *meaningfulness* rather than the four meanings (Basden 2019), which will be shown later (§4–3.11) to derive from meaningfulness and presuppose it. So, this section is mainly about meaningfulness and explains how meaningfulness resonates around most chambers of Dooyeweerd's philosophy. As I understand Dooyeweerd,

It is meaningfulness that makes everything possible
—anything at all, of any kind.
And meaningfulness is the coherence of all the aspects.

The material here, drawn from a longer version (Basden 2019), to which readers are referred, has links added to other philosophic thought and to some philosophical implications for how to understand things and activities. The section explains more than critically discusses; critical discussion has yet to occur and depends on clear explanation.

4–3.1   *Diversity and Coherence of Meaning*

It was suggested in Chapter 3 that the diversity we experience in the pre-theoretical attitude is a diversity of meaningfulness. This is because, even though the diversity we most immediately experience is of things and activities, accounting for diversity of things (or activities) does not work well. Accounting for diversity of individual things proves extremely difficult because of the interminable variety of factors that shape things. Accounting for diversity of types of thing, however, is also problematic, because most things are of multiple and changeable types.

Dooyeweerd proposes, instead, that *irreducible diversity is most fundamentally of meaningfulness* rather than of, for instance, types of thing. This might echo Heidegger's (1927/1962, 83, H.56–7) multiplicity of kinds of "concern" or "care", insofar as they are meaning. Starting with this belief that there are irreducibly distinct ways of being meaningful, Dooyeweerd explored meaningfulness and delineated 15 aspects, listed in §3–2.1. As we shall see, this works as an account of the diversity of things, activities, rationalities and good.

Coherence is partly inherent within things, as simultaneously exhibiting (being meaningful in) all aspects, and this is made possible by the inter-aspect coherence described in §3–2.4 (simultaneity non-conflict, dependency and analogy). There is, however, a deeper coherence: It is characteristic of all meaning, that *meaning refers beyond* and expresses dependence (NC,I, 4). Meaning:

> cannot exist by itself, but supposes an [*arché*], an *origin which creates meaning*. All meaning is *from, through*, and *to* an origin.
>
> (NC,I, 8–9, emphasis in original)

This is obvious in the case of signification-meaning, in that the signification necessarily refers to a signifier and a signified (c.f. Peirce), and likewise for interpretation-, attribution- and life-meanings, but meaningfulness also has a referential character, in two ways.

(a) In similar vein, meaningfulness as a whole refers beyond itself to a 'signifier', which is 'divine', to use Clouser's (2005) word. By "divine", he means that which is self-dependent, on which all else depends. Meaningfulness implies dependency, non-absoluteness, relativity to an *origin of meaningfulness*. (For deeper discussion of the notion of divinity, see §5–3.2, Clouser (2005) and *NC* (I, 8–9).)

(b) The kernel meaningfulness of "every aspect refers beyond itself to all the others" (NC,I, 3) to be an "inter-modal coherence of all the aspects of the temporal world" (NC,I, 4). The meaningfulness of each aspect is enriched by inter-aspect dependency, analogy and non-conflict with others, discussed in §3–2.4. Dooyeweerd's phrases "coherence of meaning(fulness)" and "fullness of meaning" will signify all aspects together.

4–3.2   Aspects: Spheres of Meaningfulness

What are the coherently diverse aspects listed in §3–2.1? Dooyeweerd uses "aspect" more or less in its ordinary sense as a way of viewing things—as in architecture, where the south and east aspects of a building differ. (In so-called Aspect-Oriented Programming, which arose without any awareness of Dooyeweerd's ideas, aspects are "cross-cutting concerns", and Black & Harman (2006) have suggested that Dooyeweerd's aspects offer a good foundation for AOP.)

However, several statements give a more precise understanding required for philosophy. Aspects are "modal speciality of meaning" (NC,I, 7), ways in which things can be meaningful. We will consider speciality, then modality.

Aspects are, first, distinct kernels or nuclei of meaningfulness (NC,II, 75), around which is a constellation of meaning. Aspects may be called *spheres of meaningfulness*, though Dooyeweerd never uses that term. Figure 4.1 shows these for the lingual aspect. Chapter 9 shows them for every aspect, and should be referred to understand each of Dooyeweerd's aspects.

The kernel meaningfulness of an aspect may be grasped by intuition (§4–3.13) but never fully expressed in words or theoretical models. This is the challenge that physicist Feynman et al. (1964) recognised: How can we explain what energy actually is? We might get near it, however, especially if we triangulate from several concepts we know, and those used in this work are fairly close. To understand a meaning-kernel theoretically requires understanding how it relates to other aspects (dependencies, analogies).

Despite this, aspects offer a particularly good basis for categorisation/classification, because of their fundamental irreducibility of kernel meaningfulness, e.g. distinguishing physical from organic, psychological from social. See

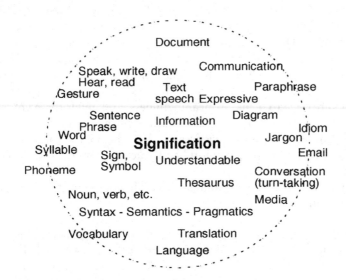

Figure 4.1 The lingual aspect, with its kernel and constellation

also §3–2.3. Aspectual categorisation has been useful in research (§11–2.4, §11–7.3.7). Aspects are more than categories, however. Henderson (1994, 37–8) quotes Dooyeweerd as explaining,

> I enjoyed going for walks in the dunes in the evening. During one of these walks in the dunes I received an insight (*ingeving*) that the diverse modes of experience, which were dependent upon the various aspects of reality, had a modal character and that there had to be a structure of the modal aspects in which their coherence is reflected. The discovery of what I called 'the modal aspects of our experience horizon' was the point of connection.

Aspects are "modalities of meaning" (NC,I, 4)—and modes of being, functioning, possibility, relating, good (and evil) and knowing. These modalities occupy the rest of this section.

4–3.3   *Meaningfulness as the Modes of Being*

Both Heidegger and Dooyeweerd reject the substance presupposition, deriving from Aristotle, but they seek different answers. Substance presupposes *being-in-itself*. Heidegger argues that all being is *being-in-the-world* of other beings. Dooyeweerd argues *being-as-meaningfulness*:

> *Meaning* is the *being* of all that has been *created*, and the nature even of our selfhood.
>
> (NC,I, 4, emphasis in original)

Dooyeweerd's short statement deeply influenced all my research, teaching and practice, shifting its focus away from being and process toward meaningfulness. Things are insofar as they mean. I have found it very fruitful to take all being and process to be, at root, meaningfulness. Strictly, Dooyeweerd allows for being that is not meaningfulness (including God, being-in-itself and being-in-the-world), but his whole philosophy speaks to those who are open to being-as-meaningfulness, and, in his three volumes of *NC*, he argues that treating being as in-itself or in-the-world has, and always will, stifle philosophy and the sciences and lead them into dead-ends. I have found his idea very freeing, insightful and practical, and the rest of this section explains how and why.

All being and process as meaningfulness: How can this be? Dooyeweerd gives an example:

> A bird's nest is not a 'thing in itself', which *has* a specific meaning in the bird's life. It has *as such* no existence apart from this meaning.
>
> (NC,III, 108, emphasis in original)

That is, the nest does not exist as a pile of sticks to which bird-attribution-meaning is added, but its very existence *qua* nest is its organic meaningfulness of reproduction. Meaningfulness is prior to being. (See below for attribution-meaning, etc., being borne by things.)

This "as such no existence apart from this meaning" is obvious for things generated by sentient agents (nests, pens, poems, policies), because we can identify subject-operated processes that create them (meaningful, respectively, in the organic, lingual, aesthetic and juridical aspects). However, Dooyeweerd intended it to apply in every aspect. The pebble exists *qua* pebble because of the physical mode of being, which is a sphere of meaningfulness that makes possible physico-chemical bonds. Seven exists *qua* seven (its seven-ness), by the quantitative mode of being, in which seven is forever less than eight and more than six.

Philosophically, how can we have being that is not a mode of being, a way in which existence is possible?—physical being, social being, numerical being, etc. Being is not possible prior to modes of being. Each "way in which" is an aspect of meaningfulness. Being is different in each aspect, and Basden (2008a) calls each being-in-an-aspect an *aspectual being*.

However, actual things (including activities, processes, situations and stuff) are *multi-aspectual beings*, simultaneously several things from different aspects—a coherence of aspectual beings. The nest is an organic-biotic nest, but also a physical pile: it exhibits both organic and physical aspects (and also quantitative, spatial, kinematic). The poem is both an aesthetic and lingual thing (work of art, piece of writing), as well social, formative and psychic, and other things. This helps researchers understand things at multiple levels, and also hybrid things.

Dooyeweerd's treatise on being and types of thing (NC,III) expounds this for many kinds of thing. It begins, however, with the challenge of becoming and change. How can Dooyeweerd account for his book being the same book though its pages get torn, and yet it ceases to be when consumed in fire (NC,III, 3)? As shown below, this multi-aspectual understanding of being helps answer that: a tear changes its physical aspectual being, but not in its main, lingual one, whereas being burnt up makes its lingual aspectual being impossible. To understand this fully, we need to understand types (next subsection) and functioning (§4–3.8), which are other philosophical fruits of understanding being as meaningfulness.

> *Research opportunity: Heidegger.* How Dooyeweerd might enrich Heidegger's ideas has yet to be adequately discussed.

4–3.4 Types and Identity

Dooyeweerd wanted to understand being without substance, partly because he believed the idea of substance prevents us understanding types and identity properly. Dooyeweerd leads up to the bird's nest, with

> For it is really impossible to ascribe their typical nature to an independent substance. Their very nature is meaning, realized in a structural subject-object relation. A bird's nest is not a 'thing in itself', which *has* a

specific meaning in the bird's life. It has *as such* no existence apart from this meaning.

(NC,III, 108, emphasis in original)

The type, Nest, is to be understood via its meaningfulness, which is primarily organic. The type, Sign, is to be understood via its primarily lingual meaningfulness; Pebble, via its physical meaningfulness; Poem, via its aesthetic aspect, and so on.

Dooyeweerd understood types in terms of profiles of aspects, which he called *structure of individuality* (or *type law* (Clouser 2005)), in which aspects play various roles. What Dooyeweerd calls a thing's *qualifying aspect* is that which most determines its internal structure, its *founding aspect*, that which accounts for its coming-into-being, and its *leading aspect*, that which guides it (Clouser 2005, 267). Usually one aspect most defines the type, and other aspects define sub-types and so on. For example:

- Plant: organic
- Symbol or Utterance: lingual
  - Symbol: lingual-analytic (distinctness)
  - Utterance: lingual-formative (structure)
- Institution: social
  - Church: social-pistic
  - Business: social-economic
  - Club: social-social
    - Sports club: social-social-aesthetic (leisure)
    - Book club: social-social-lingual

Notice how sometimes an aspect occurs twice.

Thus, *identity* derives from meaningfulness. Whether it is always hierarchical as this suggests, I doubt; our discussion does not assume so. The human being, Dooyeweerd says, is not qualified by any single aspect in the way these things are, but always displays multiple, fluid identity (as mother, artist, wife, etc.).

Multiple classification is thus possible, each way according to one aspect.

Obviously, many types of thing would not fit into a single constellation, such as depicted in Figure 4.1. In fact, the idea of constellation, though useful initially, should probably be replaced by the notion of network, with links to multiple aspects.

4–3.5 Structural Relationships

Functional relationships, which occur when we function in the world, are discussed in §4–3.8.4. *Structural relationships*, discussed here, pertain to the structure of things, as part of their individuality structures.

The best-known structural relationship is *part-whole* (system-subsystem). In Praxiteles' marble sculpture, *Hermes and Dionysus* (NC,III, 110), the relationship between limbs and body is part-whole, but it does not seem right to say that the limbs are part of the piece of marble, and especially not that calcium carbonate molecules of which the marble is composed are parts of the limbs of Hermes. Nor does it seem right to say a football team is part of a city.

These are relationships between wholes, which Dooyeweerd calls "*enkapsis*", borrowed from biology. He identified five types of *enkaptic relationship*, and there may be others. Basden (2018a) supplies examples from information technology (IT).

- *Foundational enkapsis* is that which occurs between meaningful wholes and the same thing viewed from a different aspect, such as the sculpture and the block of marble from which it is made—and between a computer memory chip, a byte and the character it is interpreted to implement.
- *Subject-object enkapsis* is exhibited by a hermit crab and its shell—and by person-using-computer.
- *Symbiotic enkapsis* is exhibited by clover and its nitrogen-fixing bacteria—and between IT use scenarios that reinforce each other.
- *Territorial enkapsis* is the relationship between, for example, a city and its university, orchestra or football team—and between an organization and its website.
- *Correlative enkapsis* is the relationship that exists between a forest and its denizens (trees, fungi, insects, etc.)—and between computers and the Internet or us and society.

A relationship is part-whole only when the part is qualified by the same aspect as the whole; parts have no meaning as parts without reference to the whole (Clouser 2005, 287), for example limb-body (organic part-whole) and molecules-marble (physical part-whole). Enkaptic relationships are between wholes, which can be qualified by different aspects, and form an *enkaptic structural whole*. (Dooyeweerd argues that the substance conception is intrinsically contradictory, using the example of the structure of cells (NC,III, 767), and shows how the idea of enkapsis overcomes the contradiction.)

Correlative enkapsis is particularly important, as the circular relationship between an *Umwelt* (environment) and its denizens—just as a forest exists by virtue of its trees, insects, fungi, etc., which are themselves maintained by the forest. Giddens' structuration relationship between structure and agency is another example. Though usually meaningful in the same aspect, it is not a part-whole relationship. An *Umwelt* is not static, nor is it pre-determined in its shape (NC,III, 648).

Basden (2018a, 299–303) discusses the notion of enkapsis in some depth, including how it requires research.

4–3.6 *Meaning and Rationality*

Meaningfulness defines ways of making sense or, correspondingly, nonsense. Each aspect gives us a distinct kind of rationality. Linking rationality to mistakes, Winch (1958, 99) notes fundamentally different kinds: "How does a mistake in engineering differ relevantly from that of the entrepreneur? And is the entrepreneur's mistake really comparable at all to the performance of a magical rite?" We might see these as involving rationalities of the formative, economic and pistic aspects, and they differ fundamentally from each other and from those of the quantitative, organic-biotic, analytic and juridical aspects.

Strauss (1984) makes a useful distinction between contradiction, which is nonsense within an aspect, and antinomy, which is nonsense involving different aspects. It is important in research to know which aspect's rationality is in play.

To Dooyeweerd, there is no single, overarching rationality, but all aspects contribute to rationality as an orchestral harmony, which is important in theoretical thought (§6–3.4). What is usually called "logic" turns out to be just one rationality among the others, that of the analytic aspect. Interestingly, the Stanford Encyclopedia of Philosophy has no entry on "Rationality", though it has one on "Instrumental Rationality". This is one of four kinds of rationality defined by Weber. Under it things make sense according to the formative aspect of achievement, means-end, etc. Weber's belief-value and affectual and habituation rationalities are meaningful in the pistic, the psychic and arguably the analytic aspects respectively.

Dooyeweerd's aspects can help to prevent *category mistakes* in our thinking, in which one category of thing is presented as belonging to another category. Ryle (1949) introduced the idea with examples like "She came home in a flood of tears and in a sedan chair" (p. 23). We can understand clearly why this is a category error when we recognise that "in" has different signification-meanings, psychic for floods of tears and spatial for the chair. Category mistakes can be avoided by careful attention to aspectual kernel meaningfulness.

Any attempt to explain one aspect's meaningfulness in terms of others results in antinomy (deep paradox). Example: Zeno's Paradox of Achilles unable to beat the tortoise is explained as an attempt to reduce kinematic meaningfulness to spatial (NC,II, 45–6, 103). Every possible reduction of one aspect to another yields antinomies.

> *Research opportunity: paradoxes.* Investigate whether Zen koans may be understood by aspects and vice versa. Example: "Clap with one hand" is social and organic.

4–3.7 Meaning, Value and Good

Meaningfulness implies value and *good*. Ways of being valuable and good (axiology) presuppose meaningfulness. This is hinted at in life-meaning and is echoed in Habermas' (1987) observation that the lifeworld is characterised by meaningfulness and normativity.

Philosophy seems not to have adequately discussed the relationship between meaningfulness and value or good; the Stanford Encyclopedia of Philosophy (Stanford 2016) page on Value Theory not mentioning "meaning". Nor does

Dooyeweerd discuss the relationship systematically. Yet Dooyeweerd, and others, seem to presuppose that meaningfulness is good, good is meaningful, and each aspect in a different way.

So we are left to express it ourselves, as attempted in Basden (2019) with an intuitive argument that calls for fuller philosophical treatment. That it is meaningful to signify (lingual activity) or save (economic activity), for example, suggests that signifying and saving make a contribution to reality. Even physical causality and numeric discreteness make contributions. Without such contributions, our intuitions tell us, reality would not work so well. Thus these contributions are good, each in a different way (according to its aspect). Each is needed for the others to work well too (inter-aspect dependency). For example, without lingual good activity, social good would be difficult to achieve. Thus each aspect introduces a different kind of *responsibility*.

For most aspects there is a corresponding *evil*, which undermines or jeopardises the working-well of reality. Like good, evil and harm are rooted in meaningfulness (c.f. Heidegger's differentiating good from "deficient" concern). Table 4.1 suggests examples of good and evil, benefit and harm, that are meaningful in each aspect, offering a rich axiological perspective.

> *Research opportunity: axiology.* Philosophically explore how good relates to meaningfulness.

When taken together, in coherence, all the varied good might constitute virtue and all the benefits, what is meant by the Hebrew word *shalom*, the Arabic *salaam*, the Greek *eudaemonia* and the recent *flourishing*. This is not just personal but situational and contextual too. Basden (2008a) proposes a "Shalom Principle", which states that for full success or good, we must be working well in all aspects, and that dysfunction in any aspect can undermine the whole. However, to understand this concrete coming-into-being of good as benefit, we must first understand law, functioning and repercussion.

4–3.8 Law, Functioning and Repercussion

So far, all is rather static. How do we account for dynamic activity, change or becoming as well as being? Previous chapters have sometimes referred to "functioning" or activity in an aspect. Functioning and activity are, like being, made possible (enabled) by aspects, and without meaningfulness there would be neither; each aspect is a *mode of functioning*.

What follows in the rest of this section is a systematic interpretation of how I have understood Dooyeweerd's views; it may be awry, but I have found it useful in research (and it might stimulate philosophical discussion).

4–3.8.1 Law: The Possibility of Functioning and Repercussion

To Dooyeweerd, meaningfulness implies, and is presupposed by, law. Law is that manifestation of meaningfulness which makes *functioning* (changing, becoming) possible (NC,I, 102–106); meaningfulness without (functional) law is static. Each sphere of meaningfulness (aspect) is also a sphere of law (a term that Dooyeweerd used) and offers fundamental laws to guide and enable a variety of modes of functioning—laws of arithmetic, gravity, non-contradiction, sociality, etc.

> *Note on terminology: law.* We will call this "aspectual law", to differentiate it from humanly constructed laws, regulations or social norms that guide our lives as *ought*. Dooyeweerd was clear: the entire law, or *nomos*, must not be conceived in juridical terms like "ought" (NC,I, 93).

Aspectual law is like promise:

```
WHEN Fa THEN Ga.
```

or conversely,

```
WHEN Da THEN Ha.
```

where `Fa` is functioning and `Da` is dysfunction in an aspect, `a`, and `Ga` is a repercussion that is good according to that same aspect, `a`, and `Ha` is the correspondingly harmful repercussion.

Good and harm are different in each aspect, as shown in Table 4.1, which includes examples in each aspect of F, G, D and H. Readers might wish to refer to these examples from the rest of this book.

In the first four aspects there is only good (as understood in §4–3.7) and no dysfunction (as far as we know). From the kinematic onwards, functioning involves dynamic change, but in the quantitative and spatial aspect it feels more like having a property. Timescale of repercussions lengthens with the aspects from zero, to decades for full societal pistic outcomes.

Functioning-then-repercussions echoes causality, and we may see it, in each aspect, as its analogy of physical causality (inter-aspect analogy, §3–2.4.3)—for example historical 'cause-and-effect' is formative functioning-then-repercussion. The functioning-then-repercussions relationship is different in each aspect, for example physical force causes mass to accelerate, voluntary vulnerability (ethical aspect) engenders openness in others. The good-evil differentiation depends, not on (inter)subjective perspectives but on the inherent meaningfulness of each aspect (§4–3.7).

Aspectual law both enables and guides. Functioning is a responsible response to aspectual law, which is not determined (except in the mathematical aspects). The "THEN" indicates a tendency with latitude, which we experience as *freedom* and indeterminacy. (Physical 'freedom' occurs mainly at the quantum size-range.)

> *Research opportunity: nature of freedom.* Thus freedom is revealed to be not one amorphous unitary phenomenon, but different in each aspect; explore this philosophically.

Table 4.1 Functioning, dysfunction and corresponding repercussions typical of each aspect

Aspect	Functioning	Dysfunction	Repercussions	
			Good	Harmful
Quantit'ive	Amount as given		Reliable sequence	
Spatial	Simultaneity Continuity		Continuous extension	
Kinematic	Movement		Change (non-stasis)	
Physical	Force, causality		Persistence	
Organic/ Biotic	Feeding, reproduction	Starvation, suffocation	Vitality, survival	Disease, extinction
Psychic/ Sensitive	Interaction	Insensitivity	Emotional and sensory vitality	Sensory, emotional deprivation
Analytic	Distinction	Conflation	Conceptual clarity	Confusion
Formative	Working, planning, constructing	Laziness, destroying	Achievement, construction	Lost opportunities, destruction
Lingual	Expressing, signification	Deceiving	Information	Misinformation
Social	Relating, befriending	Disdaining, hating	Friendship, amplified activity	Working against each other
Economic	Frugality	Squandering	Prosperity	Waste, poverty
Aesthetic	Harmonizing	Fragmentation, narrowing	Integrality, interest, fun	Fragmentation, boredom
Juridical	Giving due, responsibility	Irresponsibility	Justice	Injustice
Ethical/ Attitudinal	Self-giving love, vulnerability, trust	Selfishness, self-protection	Culture of goodwill	Competitive, harsh culture
Pistic/Faith	Belief, courage, commitment	Idolatry, disloyalty	High morale in society	Loss of meaning, morale

Idolatry: Treating something non-absolute as absolute

If I understand Dooyeweerd aright, owing to irreducibility of meaningfulness, the laws of one aspect cannot be reduced to those of another. There is no "WHEN Fa THEN Gb." So, for example, justice (juridical) does not ensure the good (ethical), though it provides a foundation for it via inter-aspect dependency. There is no inter-aspect 'causality'.

Yet we see, for example, oppression (juridical dysfunction) leading to poverty and starvation (economic, organic harm). How can this be? See multi-aspectual functioning in the next subsection.

The coherence of all law-spheres (aspects) is what Dooyeweerd calls the **law-side** of reality, in that it is the entire system of laws that govern (enable and guide) reality. Taken together, aspectual laws can guide us towards bringing about good, or *shalom* (§4–3.7). (He also includes type laws, §4–3.4, therein, but I question that.) Correlating with the law-side is what he calls the **fact-side**, or **subject-side** (or subject-object-side), which is all that actually exists and occurs. (Law-side and subject-side might be equivalent to the Real and the Actual in Critical Realism.)

Aspectual law may thus be seen as *law-side possibility* (or *aspectual possibility*) of activity or occurrence with repercussion (a generator of time: §4–3.14). Whereas square circles are meaningful in the spatial aspect (and thus may be thought about), they transgress its laws and thus are fundamentally impossible. There is also *fact-side possibility*, which takes account of the actual situation in which we find ourselves (e.g. Bismarck's "Politics is the art of the possible"). It is made possible by law-side possibility.

4–3.8.2   Multi-Aspectual Functioning

All activity, especially human activity, is *multi-aspectual functioning*, in which we function in every aspect simultaneously (§3–2.4.1).

> *Note on terminology: functioning.* In this book, I tend to use "functioning" to imply a single aspect and "activity" to imply multi-aspectual functioning.

Examples: In our activity of writing, we function primarily in the lingual aspect of signifying via words, but simultaneously with it, we function in the formative aspect of shaping thoughts, the analytic aspect of choosing what to say, the psychic aspect of seeing and motor control, the social aspect of recognising this is for readers, the juridical aspect of trying to do justice to the topic and to readers, the pistic aspect of believing (or not) what we write, and so on. In our thinking, the primary functioning is analytic, but we also believe and depend (pistic), form our thoughts (formative), our nerve cells function organically, and so on.

Multi-aspectual functioning is to activity what multi-level being is to things (§4–3.3). *Everyday experience* is multi-aspectual functioning. We are usually unaware of distinct aspectual functioning until we step back and think about it. It helps to address two conundrums.

1. This helps us understand how some changes leave a thing intact, while other changes do not. For example, a book fulfils a primary lingual function but functions in all aspects, including physical paper, spatial pattern, being-seen, being-owned, etc. (Basden & Burke 2004). The tearing of Dooyeweerd's book (NC,III, 3), *qua* book, does not affect its lingual function, despite changes in its physical functioning. Burning it, however, makes its lingual function impossible.
2. We can explain apparent cross-aspect repercussions. In Chapter 3's opening vignette, it appears that the physically raised stone caused many things to happen. In fact, it is you, functioning in each aspect that brought them about: (a) psychically in righting yourself,

(b) analytically in changing your line of thought, (c) formatively in returning to your original purpose, (d) ethically in adopting a grumbling attitude, (e) lingually in expressing the grumble. Had you not done so, all that would have happened is that you would have fallen.

This is the coherence that is *aspectual simultaneity* discussed in §3–2.4.1. It has implications for research and the apparently frustrating unpredictability of behaviour of people (and animals), who should be recognised not as passive reacters but as responsive in every aspect.

> *Research opportunity: prediction.* Might systematic consideration of all aspects help us understand human responses and behaviour better?

4–3.8.3 Society, Progress and Meaningfulness

The coherence of aspects (law-side) governs not just individual activity but social and societal too. The juridical, ethical and pistic aspects are particularly important for society in that, being post-aesthetic, their laws are holistic. Though individuals can be just/unjust, self-giving/-seeking or faithful/faithless, these aspects find their fullest expression in structures of justice/oppression, attitudes that pervade society and prevailing shared beliefs, assumptions, etc. (Basden (2018a, 298) links them with Giddens' Structuration Theory.) Unlike some social science perspectives, Dooyeweerd does not allow us to separate these aspects from those that govern individual functioning, but all work together.

Dooyeweerd's theory of progress or history, which impinges on research as advancing knowledge, is based on a combination of aspectual possibility and functioning. Each aspect is opened up by meaningfulness from later aspects (e.g. justice as mercy). In addition, humanity has the mandate and capability to open up the innate possibility in each of the aspects, to release its aspectual good into the world. This may be called *"aspectual opening"*. For example, the potential the analytic aspect affords is opened up in logic and science, that of the formative aspect, in techniques and technology, that of the lingual aspect, in writing, drawing, film, and information technology, and so on. Aspectual opening and progress is the foundation of the *mandate of research* and is discussed in NC (I, 29; II, 181ff.) and, as advancing knowledge, in §7–2.

Dooyeweerd also discusses the idea that progress also necessarily involves differentiation of society's structures. This has been severely criticised (§12–1.8) and does not seem necessary to understand knowledge advance.

4–3.8.4 Meaningful Properties and Functional Relationships

I have found it useful to understand properties and relationships in terms of aspects. When something functions in any aspect it will exhibit properties that are meaningful in that aspect. Properties are another way of saying "X

Table 4.2 Example properties and relationships that are meaningful in each aspect

Aspect	Example relationship(s)	Example properties
Quantitative	Greater than	Many, prime
Spatial	Near to, inside	Small, spherical
Kinematic	Follows	Fast, diverging
Physical	Causes	Hard, cold, solid
Organic/Biotic	Feeds on	Healthy, fertile
Psychic/Sensitive	Stimulates-responds	Hungry, visible
Analytic	Similar to, Implies	Clear, unique, contradictory
Formative	Produces	Well-constructed, planned
Lingual	Describes, Suggests	Tortuous, well-argued
Social	Associates with	Friendly, alone
Economic	Consumes	Cheap, wasteful
Aesthetic	Enjoys	Integrated, enjoyable
Juridical	Rewards, punishes	Unjust, inappropriate
Ethical/Attitudinal	Loves	Generous
Pistic/Faith	Commits to, Believes	Certain, loyal, courageous

functions in aspect Y". To say a plant, animal or person is healthy is to say they function well in the organic-biotic aspect. Example properties in each aspect are shown in Column 2 of Table 4.2.

Clouser (2005) ties properties even more closely to aspects, in defining aspects as "basic kinds of properties and laws"—but that makes aspects derivative on properties, whereas I believe the reverse.

Column 3 of the table shows examples of functional relationships meaningful in each aspect. These are relationships that arise from and within aspectual functioning, not the structural relationships discussed earlier in §4–3.5. Functional relationships between entities are multi-aspectual. What is the relationship between Wordsworth and the poem, *Daffodils*? Are there not aesthetic, lingual, formative and juridical relationships, in created-by, written-by, composed-by and copyright-of? These relationships result from Wordsworth's functioning in each of these aspects.

4–3.9   *Subject and Object in Terms of Meaningfulness and Law*

Dooyeweerd offers a radically different understanding of subject and object, by relating both to aspectual law, argued in depth in *NC* (II, 366–413). Subjectness as agency is constituted in being subject to aspectual law—thus merging the two English-language meanings of "subject". Whereas in most philosophy, "'Object' is identified . . . with that to which our mental activity in thought or volition is directed" (p. 367), restricting the subject-object relationship to a limited range of aspects, to Dooyeweerd, subject-object functioning is possible in any aspect.

For example, whereas Descartes' subject is usually assumed to be human or sentient, Dooyeweerd offers a more nuanced view: anything can function as *subject* in a given aspect when it responds to its laws. So a pebble is a physical *subject*, not physical object.

An entity functions as *object* when its aspectual functioning occurs because some other subject is functioning in that aspect. So my pen is a lingual object, wielded by me as lingual subject when I write. There are two types of object (NC,II, 369): In my writing, my pen is a *prior object*, existing before I write. The sentences I write are *generated objects*, generated by my functioning. Dooyeweerd sees objectness not as a passive but as a responsive role: an object "allows" itself to act as object (hence book "being-seen" above).

Often, especially when intentionality is involved (in which we direct our functioning towards an object), another aspect is important in addition to the one in which we function. I call it a *target aspect*. For example, when we utter the word "red", we function in the lingual aspect and target the psychic aspect, in which redness is meaningful.

Dooyeweerd suggests that:

- non-living material functions as subject only in quantitative to physical aspects;
- plants, only in quantitative to organic-biotic;
- animals, only in quantitative to psychic;
- humans in all aspects.

All may function as object in all aspects (minerals, trees, animals and people can all be economic objects).

In Dooyeweerd's scheme, whether something is subject or object is not within the thing in itself, but in the role it takes in response to the laws of each aspect. This bears interesting philosophical fruit, which Basden (2018a, 136–9) capitalises upon. (a) The subject-object relationship is not Cartesian distance but is intimate engagement of subject and object functioning together in an aspect. This echoes Heidegger's being-in-the-world and also Polanyi's (1967) proximality, the object as 'part of' the subject. (b) It allows *subject-subject relationships* as well as subject-object. Subject-subject relating in an aspect may be the basis for interaction in that aspect. (c) Inter-entity functional relationships can be subject-subject and subject-object simultaneously in different aspects. A person-pen relationship is subject-object in the lingual aspect (writing) but subject-subject in the physical (equal-and-opposite forces). Person-person relationships might be subject-subject in the social aspect but subject-object in the economic (e.g. officer-soldier). (d) The innate normativity of aspects implies no subject-subject or subject-object relationship can be devoid of normative considerations, and (e) no aspect can be excluded from the relationship. That someone is an employee is no excuse for injustice (juridical), being taken advantage of (ethical) or demeaned (pistic).

In short, subject and object are defined by meaningfulness rather than by being: as relationships made meaningful by the various aspects of a situation.

4–3.10   *Prior Meaningfulness and the Metaphor of Ocean*

As discussed earlier, being presupposes meaningfulness, and functioning, its corresponding aspectual law. So, as Strauss (2009, 393) puts it, "modal aspects are seen as the *a priori ontic conditions* making possible the many-sided existence of concrete (natural and social) entities". Meaningfulness is prior, but in what way? Dooyeweerd did not clarify this, but four versions may be found in the literature.

1. An intersubjectively shared *lifeworld* supplies meaningfulness prior to the activity of social beings. However, is not meaningfulness prior to the lifeworld itself? Does not the lifeworld-forming activity itself make several presuppositions (Schutz & Luckmann 1973)? It is meaningfulness prior to the lifeworld that concerns Dooyeweerd.

2. Aristotle's *final cause*, as fixed point of meaningfulness, pulls reality towards it, matter pulled towards form (NC,I, 25–6)—pulled towards something that is foreign to its nature. To Dooyeweerd, however, meaningfulness is inherent in existence, not foreign to it.

3. Bergson's (1908, 95) *elan originel* is a prior meaningfulness that propels physical reality in a certain direction, towards free sensorimotor actions and then eventually towards human intellect and consciousness.

With both Aristotle and Bergson, I get a feeling of a separation between meaningfulness and reality and a narrowing-down of it to singular points, whereas in Dooyeweerd I get a feeling of warmth, intimacy, richness, and a widening out as each of the aspects is opened up (in §4–3.8.2, §4–3.9, §3–2.3, §4–3.8.3 respectively). Separation of meaningfulness from reality is something that Dooyeweerd criticises in what he calls immanence-philosophy (§5–3.1).

4. Polanyi & Prosch's (1975) *indwelling* suggests that meaning(fulness) surrounds us and pervades us, and within it we are comfortable. This seems closest to what Dooyeweerd had in mind, in "We have been fitted into this coherence of meaning with all our modal functions" (NC,I, 4).

This is Dooyeweerd's third starting-point. If meaningfulness surrounds us, this links it closely with his other two starting-points, in that "indwelling" is also characteristic of the pre-theoretical attitude of thought, and what surrounds us is diverse. This is depicted in Figure 4.2, where solid lines indicate subject-functioning in various aspects and dotted lines, object-functioning.

A metaphor suggests itself, that of an *ocean of meaningfulness*. Just as fish swim and exist in the ocean, which is what enables them to swim and to be fish, constituted (physically) of ocean water and its constituents, so we 'swim' and exist in the ocean of meaningfulness, which enables all our functioning (§4–3.8), and of which our very being is constituted (§4–3.3). ("We" here refers to all, not just humans.)

The development of reality is not circumscribed in the way Bergson and Aristotle suggest, towards Aristotelian form or a Bergsonian consciousness, but within and towards a rich panoply of actualized meaningfulness.

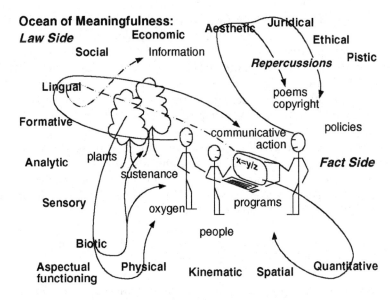

Figure 4.2 Functioning and being in the ocean of meaningfulness

> *Note on terminology: meaningfulness.* Dooyeweerd himself did not employ the metaphor of *ocean of meaningfulness*, referring to it as *law-side* (§4–3.8.1). Since the two terms denote the same thing (law derives from meaningfulness) and "law" has unhelpful connotations of determinism (natural sciences) and constraints and power-structures (social sciences), I usually refer to "ocean of meaningfulness" except where lawfulness is important.

4–3.11   Towards a Model of Meaning

This lets us understand more clearly the types of meaning outlined in §4–1. It has not been discussed by Dooyeweerd but is an implication of the above.

4–3.11.1   The Proposed Model

The first four types of meaning distinguished in Section 4–1 may be understood in terms of aspectual functioning with target aspects:

- *Signification-meaning* involves functioning in the lingual aspect, targeting another aspect, which is its semantic content (e.g. writing or reading "red" or "beauty": targeting psychic or aesthetic meaningfulness).
- *Interpretation-meaning* involves functioning in the analytic aspect, targeting other aspect(s). Scattered feathers might be interpreted

(analytic functioning) as bird-kill (targeting organic meaningfulness) and perhaps also poaching (formative and juridical meaningfulness).

- *Attribution-meaning* is the target meaningfulness of the functioning that is attributing meaning. Example: My grandmother's vase has social and organic-biotic meaningfulness to me (relationship, ancestry), in addition to the aesthetic beauty that others might appreciate. The functioning that is meaning-attribution is often in the formative aspect, especially when purpose is involved, but may be in others.
- *Life-meaning* often involves functioning in the ethical aspect, of wanting to give good, and the pistic, of reaching for an Ultimate. The target aspect is the type of good or Ultimate sought, such as having discovered (analytic target), invented (formative), entertained (aesthetic) or served (ethical), or fulfilling God's plans (see §4–2).

Attribution- and life-meanings are often linked with value, which is accounted for by the inherent good of aspects.

Meaningfulness is not a functioning as the other types of meaning are, but rather it makes them possible (law-side). In both their functioning and targeting they presuppose meaningfulness. Signification-meanings may be said to 'parcel up', and interpretation-meanings and attribution-meanings to 'pick out', targeted 'pieces of meaningfulness'. These 'pieces', though primarily meaningful in a main aspect(s), as earlier, are actually meaningful in all aspects. Examples: The word "red" is a piece of primarily psychic meaningfulness but it also carries juridical connotations of a stop sign and perhaps of danger. Example: McGibbon (2018, 305) finds three aspects in the concept, *Creator*—pistic (Divine), formative (creating) and ethical (invoking trust)—none of which are connotations.

Actual, fact-side experience, including the lifeworld, may perhaps be seen as an accumulation of such parcelled-up and picked-out 'pieces of meaningfulness'.

On one hand, these meanings differ for each person, especially in their target aspects. This is made even more complex by the fact that most targeting involves multiple aspects (example: redness as both psychic and juridical, earlier). Dooyeweerd discusses these differences and what various aspectual terms might imply in *NC* (II, 55–74).

On the other hand, it is the same for all. Since all share the same 'ocean' of meaningfulness, the same law-spheres, because all are enabled by it to exist and occur, then a degree of mutual understanding is in principle possible, despite differences. In particular, this gives hope for the possibility of participant observation (§2–2.2) and of cross-cultural understanding (§4–4.2). This mutual understanding is intuitive rather than theoretical (§4–3.12).

Research opportunity: meaning. This model of meaning has yet to be critically developed and refined.

4–3.11.2   Application to Philosophy

> *Research opportunity: philosophy of meaning.* The following contains sugges-
> tions for how the Dooyeweerdian understanding of meaning(fulness) might
> affirm, critique and enrich extant philosophical ideas.

The distinction between 'pieces of meaningfulness' and the 'ocean of meaningfulness' itself, and awareness of the aspectual diversity and coherence
of both, might enrich extant philosophical discourses around meaning and
provide new foundations for critique and affirmation. The following outlines
some Dooyeweerdian comments on philosophers mentioned earlier, which
may be developed.

Might Aristotle's *final cause* and Bergson's *elan originel*, which appear
to be singular points of meaningfulness separated from reality (§4–3.10),
be enriched by the multi-aspectual idea of ocean of meaningfulness? Heidegger's world (of being-in-the-world) might be conceived as 'ocean' of
beings, but closer examination suggests that some of it is actually an 'ocean'
of *meaningfulness*, despite his dogma that the world is meaningless. Might
Heidegger's idea that *Dasein* ascribes meaning to things be enriched, and perhaps freed from its preoccupation with death, by differentiating attribution-
meaning and life-meaning from meaningfulness and capitalising on the idea
of meaningfulness?

Husserl's *lifeworld* may now be understood as having two sides, a fact-
side, which is the community's accumulated experiences (signification-,
interpretation- and attribution-meanings), alongside a *law-side lifeworld*
('ocean' of meaningfulness), which makes it all possible, and which we grasp
intuitively because we 'swim' therein. Might the normativity of aspects offer
a foundation for Habermas' (1987) observation of meaningfulness and normativity characterising the lifeworld? Does Foucault's argument that power
inescapably pervades all echo our 'ocean of meaningfulness', especially its
societal aspects (§4–3.10, §4–3.8.3)?

Might we see Peirce and the Linguistic Turn philosophers initially focusing on signification-meaning, widening to interpretation-meaning but then
reaching for meaningfulness? Might not Gadamer's "stream" in which we
move, Peirce's "all is sign" and Derrida's "all is text" all benefit from a
Dooyeweerdian understanding of meaning? May we view Gadamer's hermeneutic cycle (metaphorically) as revolving, not mechanically around a self-
sufficient 'centre' in the void, but fluidly within an ocean of meaningfulness
(see §5–3.3)? Is Ricoeur's author-reader binding like a rope, or something
more fluid within which both live, function and exist? Might some ambiguities in Polanyi's tacit knowledge be resolved (see §4–3.12, §11–3.5)?

Fresh perspectives might be offered to *(socio)linguistics* and any field
involved with *texts*. May we understand texts (including what interviewees
say) as not just pieces of information that the researcher must sift, select and
interpret, but (to use our metaphors) as 'parcelled up' pieces from the ocean

of meaningfulness, in which both writer and reader (interviewee and interviewer) swim? And, moreover, as multi-aspectual pieces of meaningfulness? If so, then text and context are no longer separated, in need of recoupling, as is widely presupposed, but both are enabled by this same 'ocean'. Then, when interviewees are encouraged to express (or authors express) what they find meaningful in each aspect, then not only text, but context and structures will be available to the researcher via aspectual analysis. This is demonstrated in Chapter 11.

Discussions over what is a document, which began in the 1930s but still evoke much confusion, may be clarified, as discussed in §11–4.3, and why stones in museums and landscapes must be seen metaphorically as 'texts'. *Texts* are objects in lingual functioning, whereas '*texts*' are objects in functioning in other aspects where the lingual analogy within those aspects (§3–2.4.3) is relevant.

4–3.12   Meaningfulness and Knowing the World

Dooyeweerd offers useful perspectives on knowing and knowledge, as a combination of knowing both the fact-side and knowing the law-side (§4–3.8.1)—both the actual world around us and the aspects (law-spheres) that enable it. How we know each is fundamentally different, however. Knowing the fact-side involves subject-object functioning with things we are coming to know, and is the topic of this subsection; knowing the law-side aspects is discussed in §4–3.13.

As discussed in Chapter 2, most philosophers have presupposed that the best knowledge is theoretical, but Dooyeweerd situates theoretical knowing within pre-theoretical. Theoretical knowing is discussed in Chapter 6; here, pre-theoretical knowing is discussed.

Two things at least have brought to light long-held assumptions about ways we know the world. One is Polanyi's (1967) drawing attention to *tacit knowledge*, distinguished from the conventionally assumed *explicit knowledge*, by "We know more than we can tell." Tacit knowledge includes bodily knowledge (e.g. how we cycle) and skills. Polanyi's perspective has been broadened to include "tacit knowledge in organisations" (Baumard 1999; Nonaka & Takeuchi 1995). There is disagreement over whether (organisational) tacit knowledge can be made explicit. With a similar dichotomy feminist writers like Adam (1998) stress that knowing involves not just propositional knowledge ("masculine"), but also embodied, holistic and caring knowledge ("feminine").

Both those views tend to be dichotomous. Dooyeweerd, if I understand him aright, makes a more nuanced view possible, with each aspect offering a different way (aspect) of knowing, with knowing as a whole seen as multi-aspectual functioning. In each aspect, knowing is functioning that leaves a residue in the knower, as an aspectual repercussion. This residue is knowledge. Table 4.3 shows what each way of knowing might be; it is based on information from http://dooy.info/knowing.html and used with kind permission of The Dooyeweerd Pages.

Table 4.3 Aspects as ways of knowing

Aspect	Ways of knowing	Tacit/ Explicit
Quantitative Spatial Kinematic		
Physical	(Persistent change of physical state caused by functioning in the physical aspect).	Tacit 1
Organic/ Biotic	• E.g. plant roots 'know' where water is, growing towards it. • Muscles grow with exercise. • Nerve cells grow and establish synapses.	Tacit 1
Psychic/ Sensitive	• Receiving stimuli and holding a memory of them. • Recognition of a pattern (seen or heard). • Instinct.	Tacit 1
Analytic	• Being aware. • Holding concepts, 'facts' and categories. • Theoretical knowing. • Knowing how to reason and theorize.	Explicit 1 Tacit 1/2
Formative	• Skills (knowing how to do things). • 'Knowing my way around.'	Tacit 2
Lingual	• 'Pieces of meaningfulness' set down in symbolic form. • Discourse, debate that disseminates knowledge. • Books, libaries, data bases.	Explicit 2
Social	• Agreement. • Shared cultural knowledge, assumptions; Lifeworld. • Networks of knowledge.	Tacit 3
Economic	• Understanding limits on our knowledge e.g. assumptions.	Tacit 3
Aesthetic	• Sense of the whole, of harmony. • Art helping us understand reality. • Wisdom as all types of knowing together.	Tacit 3
Juridical	• A sense of the aptness of things. • Proportion and a sense of 'perspective'.	Tacit 3
Ethical/ Attitudinal	• Complete 'entering in' with the other (Bergson) requires self-giving. • Buber's I-Thou relationship	Tacit 3
Pistic/Faith	• Certainty • Assumptions (about what is so). • Presuppositions (about what is meaningful). • Commitment (to a belief); prejudice.	Tacit 3

In this view, tacit and explicit, "feminine" and "masculine", are seen no longer as opposites but as irreducibly distinct aspects. Feminine and masculine aspects are discussed in Basden (2008a, 175, 325–6). Column 3 of the table suggests two types of explicit and three of tacit knowing. Analytic knowing is explicit because the knower (thinker) stands back from the world to conceptualise it (§2–1, §6–3.2). Lingual knowing is explicit because it externalises signified 'pieces of meaningfulness'. As will be discussed in Chapter 6, theoretical knowing is a special form of analytic explicit knowing.

Tacit knowing might differ according to how its aspect relates to these two aspects by inter-aspect dependency (§3–2.4.4). Tacit-1 knowing is pre-analytic, so probably can be neither conceptualised nor expressed because it depends on neither (e.g. muscular and sensory-motor knowing, as discussed by Polanyi). Tacit-2 knowing is post-analytic but pre-lingual, unlikely to be explainable but might be conceptualisable within each individual. This may be seen in well-learned skills like kneading bread (Nonaka & Takeuchi 1995, 63), a type to which Polanyi also refers. Tacit-3 knowing is post-lingual. Since post-lingual functioning usually involves lingual functioning, Tacit-3 knowledge may be expressible in principle. This includes social expectations and unspoken rules (Nonaka & Takeuchi 1995, 63) and tacit knowledge in organizations is (Baumard 1999).

> *Research opportunity: tacit knowledge.* Table 4.3 has been drawn up by asking "What might be reasonably deemed knowledge or knowing in each aspect?" It is neither exhaustive nor based on any scientific study but rather offers examples to stimulate researchers (a) to think differently about knowledge in their own fields, (b) to draw together existing, scientific investigations into knowing and extend them across all aspects. Alex Kimani (2017) has made a start, using these ideas in the field of knowledge management.

Kant claimed that we cannot know the *Ding an sich*, thing-in-itself, noumenon, but only phenomena that appear to us. This led to a presupposition that the world 'resists' being known. Dooyeweerd disagrees. Since knower, known and knowing all occur and exist because of prior-surrounding 'ocean' of meaningfulness, the world is 'friendly' to our knowing it. It is friendly to our pre-theoretical knowing, but does resist our theoretical knowing, for reasons inherent in the nature of theoretical knowing itself, which are discussed in Chapter 6.

We may now understand *intuition*, as the coherence (harmony) of all aspectual knowings, the residues in the knower of multi-aspectual functioning. Bergson's discussion of psychical intuition, contrasted with analytical thought, might contribute to this wider picture, but Dooyeweerd maintained that they cannot be divorced from each other and intuition involves more than psychic knowing (NC,II, 480). In fact, three accounts of what is often called intuition may be found in Dooyeweerd:

- multi-aspectual ways of knowing the *fact-side*, discussed here;
- an intuitive grasp of *law-side* aspectual meaning, discussed next;
- the immediate experience of *self*, discussed in §4–3.14.

Because of the common 'ocean' of meaningfulness, intuition can be expected to be shared at least to some extent (including across cultures).

4–3.13   Knowing Meaningfulness Itself: Delineating the Aspects

How might fish understand the ocean that enables them to exist and function? How might we know the aspects, that 'ocean' of meaningfulness (lawside), by which all, including ourselves, exist and function?

Whereas with things in the world we stand in subject-object relationships, law-side aspects cannot be objects themselves, since it is they which make objectness possible (§4–3.9). They cannot be known in the same way. Instead, we know aspects by functioning therein. This gives us a deep **intuitive grasp** of the meaningfulness that each aspect makes possible, which is not always easy to explicate.

This is a challenge faced not only by Dooyeweerd, but by every compiler of an ontology. To properly delineate aspects calls for what Dooyeweerd called a *Special Theory of Modal Spheres*, but he never completed it. However, he devised a number of principles, which he outlines, discusses and demonstrates in his *General Theory of Modal Spheres* (NC,II, Part I).

- Diversity. The diversity of meaningfulness encountered in pre-theoretical experience should be critically respected.
- Intuition. Begin with intuition of aspect kernels derived from pre-theoretical experience, sensitively but critically reflecting on insights of thinkers throughout the ages. Examples: space, energy, justice.
- Concepts. Discuss concepts that are directly meaningful in an aspect but not in others, differentiating them from aspectual analogies (example: physical causality, from historical repercussion (NC,II, 77)). Dooyeweerd did this by considering subject-object relationships in each aspect.
- Aspectual opening. Discuss how one aspect opens up fuller meaningfulness of another (§4–3.8.3). This offers insights into the dependency-order of aspects. Example: social opens up meaningfulness of lingual.
- Method of antinomy. "[S]ystematically examine the antinomies arising from the theoretical violation of the modal boundaries of meaning" (NC,II, 46). Example: Zeno's Paradox.
- Express aspectual meaningfulness. The term(s) we choose to designate a meaning-kernel "must be able immediately to evoke the intuition of the ultimate irreducible nucleus of the modal aspect of experience concerned" (NC,II, 129).

I have also found it useful to ask, "What Good does this aspect contribute that is not offered by any other?" and Zuidervaart (2016) suggests other principles, listed in Basden (2019).

This is a kind of hermeneutic cycle, with growing understanding of each aspect interplaying with growing understanding of the entire suite. Dooyeweerd demonstrated these principles especially in regard to the mathematical aspects, those of natural science and the juridical aspect, with briefer discussion of other aspects.

Though the *aspects as such* are not socially constructed (NC,II, 429), being that which makes social construction possible, Dooyeweerd recognises that our theoretical *knowledge of aspects* involves social construction. He clearly warns:

> In fact the system of the law-spheres designed by us can never lay claim to material completion. A more penetrating examination may at any time bring new modal aspects of reality to the light not yet perceived before. And the discovery of new law-spheres will always require a revision and further development of our modal analyses. Theoretical thought has never finished its task. Any one who thinks he has devised a philosophical system that can be adopted unchanged by all later generations, shows his absolute lack of insight into the dependence of all theoretical thought on historical development.
>
> (NC,II, 556)

Research opportunity: aspects. A full *Special Theory of Modal Spheres* "is still unbroken ground" (NC,II, 77)—and it still seems to be.

4–3.14   Meaning, Time and Self

Dooyeweerd's notions of time and self are grounded in meaning but, since I have not found them useful in research and Dooyeweerd's discussion of them is unclear, I offer only the briefest explanation.

In his argument for why the Being of *Dasein* is a philosophical problem that had not previously been addressed, Heidegger (1927/1962, H.§10) argues the need to go beyond biology, psychology and anthropology. *Dasein* is being that is concerned about its own being—which is true of the human ego or self. Dooyeweerd agrees. In fact, the self functions in many more aspects than these and to understand its full, integral functioning requires taking them all into account: multi-aspectual functioning. Dooyeweerd goes beyond Heidegger, in arguing that the self cannot be understood theoretically: it cannot be reduced to merely the total of its aspectual functionings or constrained within time. In its "heart", the self is supra-temporal, transcending both functioning and time—but not transcend meaningfulness: "*Meaning* is . . . the nature even of our selfhood" (NC,I, 4).

Bergson argues that feelings of time (*duree*) cannot be reduced to "clock" time. Dooyeweerd goes much further, arguing that time is different in every aspect, and none can be reduced to others: physical and psychical time as in Bergson, also analytic time (antecedent-consequent), formative time (historical impact), juridical time (retribution), and so on. He speaks of *cosmic time*, but never explains it; my understanding is that it is the coherence of all aspectual times, which are the functioning-then-repercussions in each aspect (§4–3.8); time is not like railway lines down which we travel but something that fact-side reality generates as it functions in each aspect, a synonym for actuality—an African rather than Western view.

Dooyeweerd's views are discussed in *The Dooyeweerd Pages* on:

```
http://dooy.info/self.html
http://dooy.info/time.html
```

which includes a table of each aspectual time.

4–4.   Potential Relevance for Research

The previous section clarified what meanings and meaningfulness are and how they are the foundation for all reality, both law-side and fact-side. Just as the ocean is prior to fish, enabling them to be and occur, and surrounds and pervades them, so meaningfulness is prior to being and functioning, enabling, surrounding and pervading them. For research, this offers us radically new ways of understanding things, types, law, possibility, functioning, properties, normativity, the coherence of multi-aspectual being and functioning, and time. This section offers indications of how research application, activity and content may be interpreted in the light of these ideas.

4–4.1   *Meaningfulness and Research Application*

Application of research findings (theories) places research in the context of the wider world, in both practice and scholarship (§1–2.4). Application may be conceptualised as multi-aspectual functioning of the applier (§4–3.8.2), with each aspect-functioning targeting specific aspects (§4–3.9). Application in professional and academic contexts tends to focus on the core aspect(s) of the theory, but in both cases, and even more in non-professional applications, other aspects are also important.

Example: In applying the CAMELS rating system in the field of banking, which theorises six measures of bank soundness, the main aspects are economic and quantitative (resources expressed as quantities). There is also a tacitly assumed lingual element, in that the resources, such as assets, are mainly symbolised as currency. Application of CAMELS seemed to work for many years to ensure banks were sound, but the banking crisis of 2008 prompted wider assessment of other aspects of bank functioning that had been overlooked. These are revealed by examining the history (formative functioning) and motivational roots (pistic functioning) of banking, comparing countries where the crisis was more and less pronounced.

The banks of Germany, England and the USA, for instance, countries hit by the crisis, were set up with motivations of commitment to political ends, specifically to facilitate war and national prestige (Germany, England) and with populist ends (USA), whereas the banking system of Canada, which remained relatively sound, was set up along old Scottish lines to facilitate genuine trade and commerce among the people (Calomiris & Haber 2014). In addition, the USA banking system was fragmented with flawed payment systems, leading to the development of security markets and shadow banking (Bordo et al. 2015). (Thanks to Charmele Ayadurai for example.)

Aspectually, we may see the Canadian-Scottish motivation as proper economic functioning, whereas the other three involved pistic and aesthetic primary dysfunctions and pistic, juridical and social secondary dysfunction. The primary pistic dysfunction lies in absolutising something that should not be absolutised, namely pride, war and populism, which are pistic, juridical and social secondary dysfunctions. The aesthetic dysfunction is fragmentation, resulting from populism. A deeper study reveals contributions from yet other aspects.

Notice the indirect as well as direct nature of aspectual repercussions. The original Scottish banks were founded 1695–1746, based on what was understood at that time (theories about life and resources in the light of the Scottish Reformation), the original Canadian banks were founded by Scots, and yet the original motivation has repercussions today.

If aspects offer norms for *shalom*, as Dooyeweerd believed, then the possible direct and indirect repercussions of research findings are a matter of importance, not just intellectual reputation or curiosity. This implies *responsibility* on researchers and their communities to consider all possible repercussions. Of course, full prediction of repercussions, especially long term and indirect, is impossible, but Dooyeweerd's idea, of aspects as modes of functioning that have repercussions, offers a useful conceptual tool for systematic analysis. A concern I have kept in mind during my research is our responsibility for nature and planet. The recent OECD report (OECD 2018) predicts that global raw materials consumption will nearly double by 2060, doubling environmental pressure that we see in 2018. Use of metals and minerals consumption will increase faster. Insofar as this results from research (e.g. in digital electronics), this is a responsibility that we researchers should take seriously.

4-4.2 *Meaningfulness and Research Activity*

Research activity is discussed in Chapter 10; the following prepares philosophical foundations for that.

The meaningfulness *of* research activity is to generate research content, anticipating application, to ensure their highest quality. But what is the meaningfulness *within* research activity?

The most obvious meaningfulness *within* is that of each research task or process which, put together, constitute the entire activity of research. Research is typically carried out in projects, where tasks are clearly distinguished, each with a different purpose (meaningfulness in relation to the project). These may be seen as qualified by different aspects, such as planning (formative), team-building (social), managing (economic), literature (lingual), conceptualising (analytic), data collection (lingual), analysis (analytic) and dissemination (lingual). Success of research may be seen as multi-aspectual *shalom* (§4–3.7). However, each of these tasks is itself multi-aspectual activity, the success of which depends on functioning well in all their aspects.

This multi-aspectuality within multi-aspectuality explains why research—and all human activity—is complex. Many of the aspects, especially the later ones, are often taken for granted, overlooked or even ignored, yet their functioning-then-repercussion laws still hold and take effect. Many of the activity aspects are, therefore, hidden, but should be deliberately considered, even if a deliberate decision is made that they are not relevant.

Chapter 10 discusses each aspect of research activity in turn, to offer researchers help with this complexity, with emphasis on hidden issues. It is based on the *Shalom Principle* (§4–3.7) that every aspect can contribute something of value to the whole research, and dysfunction in any aspect jeopardises its success, sometimes in unexpected ways.

Relationships between colleagues, with things and people being researched, and with various stakeholders may be understood as subject-subject relationships in each aspect. Subject-object relationships occur in each aspect, with prior objects like equipment, tools, literature, situations, etc. and with generated objects like constructed equipment, conceptual models, data, findings, reports, papers—as well as friendships made during research.

In §2–2.2, the problems of researcher-world detachment were discussed. It may be that the only sound philosophical foundation for research engagement is the idea of 'ocean' of meaningfulness. The researcher is, in effect, a meaning-giver, not just a meaning-recorder, and it is only shared meaningfulness that transcends both researcher and world, which enables the researcher to truly understand instead of imposing their own meanings. This enables barriers of class and background to be surmounted and is especially important in **cross-cultural research**. The validity of researchers like Malinowski discerning meaningfulness that the "natives" ignore (§2–2), and vice versa, lies in their awareness of different aspects.

> *Research opportunity: researcher-world relationship.* The above suggestion should be worked out conceptually and empirically, using this chapter as guide.

That aspects not only define distinct ways of being meaningful but also types of good provides a philosophical foundation for research ethics and, more widely, good practice in research. See §10–4.

4–4.3 Meaning and Research Content

Dooyeweerd implies that the main mandate of science is to build humanity's understanding of the law-side, the laws of each aspect and their inter-aspect dependencies (e.g. the laws of physics, which depend on those of kinematics, spatiality and quantity). Since the rationalities and laws of each aspect are mutually irreducible, each major science focuses its investigation on the laws of one aspect. This will be used in Chapter 8 to discuss the differences and commonalities between fields of research.

Earlier, it was said that our immediate experience is of things and activities. We can now understand that as experiencing the fact-side directly, and the law-side only indirectly via the fact-side. Research content is knowledge of, or information about, both the fact-side and law-side. Data is collected during research that relates to the fact-side; general findings generated are fallible expressions of theoretical beliefs about the law-side. All the discussion of meaningfulness and what emerges from it, outlined in Section 4–3, is relevant to this, and is discussed elsewhere as follows.

- Aspects of the world govern research data: §6–3.3, §7–1.2.
- Irreducibility of meaningfulness (aspects) helps clarify concepts, especially regarding things, types and identity: §11–4.
- Dooyeweerd's aspects help in clarifying and disclosing amorphous and tacit knowledge: §11–6, §11–7.
- Rationalities govern reasoning about data: §6–3.4, §7–1.3.
- Research content includes normativity and values as well as description and explanation: §11–3.7
- Meaningfulness and aspects provide basis for categorisation and classification: §11–4.
- Rigid definitions may be escaped by recognising the multi-aspectual (multi-level) nature of things: §11–4.3.
- Cut the Gordian Knot of problematic issues: §10–1.3.
- Research fields focus of meaningfulness: Chapters 8, 11.
- Paradigms shifts recognise new aspects: §8–2.2.
- Wider meaningfulness establishes findings: §6–3.5.

4–5.   Conclusion

Dooyeweerd offers a radically different perspective on reality, including research, in which meaningfulness, rather than being or process, is fundamental. Meaningfulness is the "*a priori* ontic condition" (Strauss 2009) for all reality. Metaphorically, meaningfulness is an 'ocean' in which all reality 'swims' and exists.

In particular, this chapter has strengthened the notion of aspects, as modalities or spheres of meaningfulness and corresponding law. As such, aspects are the possible modes of being, types of being, rationality, good/evil, functioning, repercussions, properties, relationships, subjects and objects, and knowing, whether tacit or explicit. It is in this chapter that most of Dooyeweerd's positive philosophical understanding of the world has been discussed. This has been presented reasonably systematically (because Dooyeweerd did not), so that it can be referred to throughout the rest of the book and in researchers' publications.

(Some Reformational philosophers disagree with some points of this interpretation of Dooyeweerd's understanding of meaning, meaningfulness, and what derives therefrom. The interpretation is one that has proven useful in research. This, and the longer discussion of Dooyeweerd's understanding of meaning in Basden (2019), are being placed in public for critical discussion and use.)

Some implications for research application, activity and content have been discussed, in preparation for the coming discussions. For example, that meaningfulness is a unifying context for all three implies that ontology, epistemology and axiology are no longer separate issues.

The next chapter discusses philosophy and its role in research, to help us understand why Dooyeweerd developed in the radical way he did. Then Part II discusses theoretical thought that forms the core of research. It may be noticed that little has been said about truth; to understand truth, we need to understand the nature of theoretical thought first, in Chapter 6.

5   Research and Philosophy

Why is philosophy important in research? Why is what some call "research philosophy" important? On what basis may we judge the philosophies available? Why is Dooyeweerd's philosophy important among the others? Those are the questions discussed in this chapter. Readers who are not interested in these questions may skip it and return later.

Since this is not a book on philosophy but on research, no overview of philosophies is attempted. Instead, the eras and movements of philosophy over the centuries, their basic types and tendencies, are discussed to account for why Dooyeweerd's rather different approach might be relevant. For fuller coverage, read Dooyeweerd himself, who, in *NC*, discusses the ideas of 14 ancient Greek philosophers, 14 Scholastic, 3 Reformational, 14 Renaissance, 25 19th-century and 34 20th-century philosophers, along with scores of legal theorists, political theorists and many in the sciences.

Section 5–1 outlines three roles philosophy plays in research, to which reference will be made later. Section 5–2 discusses two kinds of presupposition that lie at the roots of research, which philosophy enables us to discuss: worldviews and ground-motives. Ground-motives offer a historical account of philosophic thought, and explain why philosophical debates are so often fruitless. Section 5–3 discusses a third, deeper, kind of presupposition, standpoints, which explains why Dooyeweerd's starting-points are philosophically important and radical. Section 5–4 sets Dooyeweerd's philosophy among others, as a philosophy rooted in Christian faith in an unusual way, and Section 5–5 suggests how to cross boundaries between philosophies of different kinds. This chapter ends Part I of this book.

5–1.   Roles of Philosophy in Research

In their widely used work on *Research Methods for Business Students*, Saunders et al. (2012, 128–9) explain,

> The research philosophy you adopt can be thought of as your assumptions about the way you view the world. These assumptions will underpin your research strategy and the method you choose as part of that strategy.

Researchers ground their research in a philosophy, knowingly or not. They should philosophically reflect on the assumptions they make and be able to defend them. In much research, though, especially in the natural sciences, research philosophy is tacitly assumed rather than made explicit, except perhaps during discussions around paradigms, such as the nature of quantum physics. Even when research philosophy is explicitly discussed, many researchers merely select a standard philosophy, without critical analysis thereof. This section discusses the roles philosophy can play in research.

5–1.1   Ontology, Epistemology and Axiology

Traditionally ontology, epistemology and axiology are three main branches of philosophy. They study, respectively, what there is, how we know what there is, and what is good and evil, including the value and norms of studying. Researchers are encouraged to think about all three as foundations for their research, usually separately.

In Dooyeweerd, however, ontology, epistemology and axiology intermingle and have a common root in meaningfulness. As we saw in Chapter 4, what there is and how it functions, ways of knowing and making sense, and what is good all alike derive from meaningfulness, and Dooyeweerd, in his suite of aspects, offers a very useful, irreducibly diverse ontology, epistemology and axiology.

Not only philosophically, but in real-life research too, the three depend on each other. Epistemology presupposes an ontology of knowledge and axiology of knowing. To be rooted in reality rather than speculation, ontology requires epistemology. Axiology accounts for why research is valuable and also for what constitutes good ontology and epistemology (standards).

In this book I follow Dooyeweerd, mingling them together. Because this book is about research rather than philosophy, a more useful division is the roles philosophy plays in research: philosophy as approach, as foundation and as source of conceptual tools.

5–1.2   Philosophy as Approach

In its role as approach, philosophy provides a broad view of the world (ontology), of how to get to know it (epistemology), of what is right in research and what to avoid, and sometimes of how to behave in the world (axiology) together. When Saunders et al. (2012), in their famous "research onion", include Positivism, Realism, Interpretivism, and Pragmatism as research philosophies, they are offering four such overall approaches. Into the research onion others have added: Functionalist, Interpretive, Radical Humanist, Radical Structuralist "sociological paradigms" from Burrell & Morgan (1979), and Objectivism and Constructivism.

The suffix "-ism" indicates a belief and commitment. Table 5.1 shows the ontological, epistemological and axiological commitments for six examples of these -*isms*. In Column 5 it also lists mainstream philosophers cited by those operating within the -*ism*.

Table 5.1 The philosophical beliefs of various -isms

-ism	World	How to know	Avoid	Behaving	Philosophies
		- From Saunders et al. (2012) -			
Positivism	Objective facts	Prizing facts from studied situations	Opinions, beliefs	(Ignored)	Kant Logical positivism
Realism	Things (and laws)	Observing, experimenting	Opinions, beliefs	(Ignored)	Pre-Kantian
Interpretivism	Interpretations	Harmonizing interpretations	Constraints	(Ignored)	Phenomenology, Hermeneutics
Pragmatism	Human practice	Observing, surveying	Irrelevance	Functional purpose	Peirce, James, Dewey
		- From Burrell & Morgan (1979) -			
Radical Structuralism	Society structures (classes)	Prizing out facts	Status quo	Oppression of classes	Marx
Radical Humanism (Socio-critical approach)	Society structures	Challenging assumptions	Status quo, assumptions	Oppression, power	Frankfurt School, Foucault

Which "-ism", or philosophy-as-approach, should the researcher choose? Many of them seem incommensurable with some of the others, so how do we relate them to each other and to our research? "In the debate among philosophical schools," remarks Dooyeweerd (NC,I, 37), "one receives the impression that they are reasoning at cross-purposes, because they are not able to find a way to penetrate to each other's true starting-points." These starting-points, by which each might appreciate the others, Dooyeweerd continues, are "masked by the dogma concerning the autonomy of theoretic thought" (§2–1.2). As we shall see below, most "-isms" arise by reaction against others, so how far can we trust them? The problem "touches the empirical sciences as well as philosophy, since both imply the theoretical attitude of thought."

Dooyeweerd is useful to us because, in offering non-traditional starting-points, he sought something deeper than the difference between philosophies, something common to all—not a 'meta-philosophy' but an exposing of presuppositions that lie at the root of each "-ism" as approach. Exposing these is made easier by Dooyeweerd's starting-points of everyday experience and the humanness of all philosophers, and in diverse, coherent meaningfulness, as discussed in the previous chapters.

Wisely, Saunders et al. warn that no "-ism" they cite should be seen as better than others—each suits a particular kind of situation—and that researchers should not be bound by a philosophy. However, does that encourage mere pick-and-mix? Researchers need deeper understanding in order to make proper choices.

Philosophies and paradigms determine what the researcher can 'see' as meaningful. Phenomenology (and Gadamer and Dooyeweerd) has used the metaphor of *horizon*: however high we stand, we can see things as far as the horizon but not beyond. The horizon of Radical Structuralism and Humanism, for example, extends to structures of society, power and the evil of oppression, and seldom further. A similar metaphor is that of the *lens*, through which researchers see the world and focus on it, and fail to see other things.

So if the philosophy that informs research prevents the full diversity of reality being 'seen', it might distort its findings. This occurs in an example discussed by Basden (2008a, 163–4), where Foucault, used as a lens, resulted in generosity being seen as its very opposite, "leveraging power".

I have sometimes found Dooyeweerd's philosophy can offer an approach to research in its own right, but usually I prefer to use it to affirm, critique and enrich extant approaches. This can be done via his aspects and ideas presented in Chapter 7 in the context of Dooyeweerd's starting-points. So, when trying to understand other research or theory, I find myself asking, "On which aspects does it focus as meaningful? Which does it ignore? Are the ones it ignores important?" This has helped me avoid endless debates about the classification of things or processes.

5-1.3   *Philosophy as Foundation*

Philosophy-as-approach concerns presuppositions; philosophy-as-foundation comes from philosophy's positive understanding of the world/reality in the light of its presuppositions. Philosophy-as-foundation can help researchers explore and understand the nature of things with which they are concerned. In physics, Aristotle and Liebniz are referred to, because physicists find themselves reflecting philosophically on the nature of space, movement, time, causality and fields, and to Analytic Philosophy regarding clarity of argumentation. In the life sciences, there is occasional reference to general philosophers who have struggled to understand what life and organism are: Deleuze and Plato in Kelty's 2018) discussion of robot "life", or Kant and Liebniz in Demares & Wolfe's (2017) discussion of organism. In design science, researchers reflect philosophically on the nature of design, referring e.g. to Dewey. Radical Structuralism, above, uses Marx to understand society.

Philosophy may also be employed to create foundational conceptual frameworks in a field, based on which theories may be formulated and which research programmes and projects may be devised. In the life sciences, the Gaia Hypothesis, which treats the whole planet as though it were an organism, is referred to as a "philosophy" (e.g. Dutreuil 2014), though strictly it is a framework for understanding ecology.

In the field of information systems, Mingers & Willcocks (2004) collect several authors who discussed their philosophies and philosophical social theories and show how they can help the field of information systems—Functionalism, Phenomenology and Heidegger, Hermeneutics, Adorno, Habermas, Foucault, Structuration Theory, Social Shaping, Critical Realism and Complexity Theory.

Example: Introna & Ilharco (2004) use Phenomenology and Heidegger to understand what (computer) screens are. They conclude that screens are not just outputs from computers, but that "screen *qua* screen reveals itself as already ontological agreement" (p. 84). The agreement is not over the information content that the screen presents, but is over the function of screens as a "form of life". Screens show themselves, call for our attention, attract us, make us look at them, and hide themselves, because of the "already agreement" about the screen. Screens conceal and spread meaning because of "already agreement". This offers a framework for understanding screens and their nature.

However, it is perhaps not specific enough to be useful to formulate research projects (except very abstract ones). The phrase "already agreement" occurs eight times in a single concluding paragraph. Does this indicate a supreme importance to Introna & Ilharco? "Already agreement" seems not unlike the Dooyeweerdian notion of prior meaningfulness translated into intersubjective functioning. If it is, then Introna & Ilharco end up where Dooyeweerd begins (as his starting-point); their discussion of what is "already agreed" about screens feels like an aspectual analysis (c.f. §11–4).

Often, it seems, Dooyeweerd's starting-points, of everyday experience, diversity and coherence, and 'oceanic' meaningfulness are where many contemporary thinkers are currently arriving. If so, then Dooyeweerd could open up their thought, in ways we discuss, especially in Chapter 11.

Basden (2008a, 2018a) uses Dooyeweerd's philosophy to formulate conceptual frameworks for understanding five areas of interest in the field of information systems (IS) (§11–3.6). In particular, the framework for understanding IS features, like screens, as objects existing and functioning with the users in the same 'ocean' of meaningfulness, affirms Introna & Ilharco's idea but makes it more precise and enriches it (Basden 2018a, Chapter 7). With it we can explore both the affordance and appropriateness of attracting, presenting, concealing, spreading, etc. of screens in each aspect. Basden finds Dooyeweerd's philosophy to be richer and more fruitful than many others are.

5–1.4   *Philosophy as Source of Conceptual Tools and Methods*

Philosophy can be a source of conceptual tools for research—categorisations, models, methods, etc. As with philosophy-as-foundation, this relies on the way philosophy understands the world. For example, Husserl developed the method of phenomenological reduction, which was followed by Introna & Ilharco (2004). Hermeneutic philosophy has been appealed to in the fields of philology, literature and exegetics to assist interpretation of texts. Heidegger and Gadamer developed the methods of the hermeneutic cycle.

In the field of knowledge representation (once a subset of artificial intelligence), "ontologies" need to be constructed: beliefs about the types of thing (including activities) that need to be reasoned about in computer programs, expressed in computer language.

In the early days, for example, the expert system, MYCIN (Shortliffe 1976), which diagnoses bacterial infections, did so with a programmed ontology of types of bacteria, types of symptom, types of dysfunction and types of relationship between them. Such ontologies were constructed from experience in the various fields, probably implicitly influenced by pragmatic philosophy. In many cases, the expert systems using these ontologies were of good quality. Later, Wand & Weber (1995) sought to define a knowledge representation ontology based on philosophical ontology rather than field experience. They chose Bunge's (1977) "furniture of the world". The Bunge-Wand-Weber ontology aroused considerable intellectual interest, but it is not clear that it ever resulted in good quality expert or information systems— maybe because Bunge deliberately excluded certain aspects because of a religious adherence to materialism (see §5–2.4; Basden (2008a, 295)).

The contribution of Dooyeweerd's philosophy as a source of conceptual tools is discussed in Part III.

5–2.   Presuppositions: Worldviews and Ground-Motives

In these three roles, especially in our approaches to research, philosophy acts at a deep level, providing or influencing the presuppositions which the researcher and their community make. Somewhat like axioms or assumptions, presuppositions lie at the start of our thinking, but whereas axioms and assumptions are about what is *true* or given, presuppositions are about what is *meaningful*. (Example: The assumption "It might rain tomorrow" is not meaningful if we are in a desert.) As such, they steer research and its surrounding discourse, and also philosophy and the thought of society, into particular directions.

Presuppositions are usually deeply hidden, taken for granted, but Dooyeweerd discusses at least three kinds or levels of presupposition: *worldviews*, *ground-motives* and *standpoints*. Today, "worldview" is often used loosely for all three, but since each influences thought in different ways, they need to be differentiated. Unfortunately, Dooyeweerd does not give a clear picture of the relationship between them, perhaps because the history of philosophy is tangled, but here I try to clarify them. Some might disagree with my interpretation of Dooyeweerd, but I have found it useful in research. This section discusses worldviews and ground-motives; Section 5–3 discusses standpoints.

5–2.1   Worldviews

A worldview ("life- and world-view") is a community's beliefs about reality and how to understand and act in it. Dooyeweerd discusses worldviews at length, including the views of Dilthey, Rickert, etc. (NC,I, 115–64). Many worldviews elevate one aspect, allowing us to view the world from that aspect. For example, materialism elevates the physical aspect, or Rickert's types; intellectualism, aestheticism, mysticism, moralism, eroticism and theism elevate respectively the analytic, aesthetic, pistic, ethical, psychic and pistic aspects.

Worldviews define our approach in research. They are often about which aspects are important. We will see, in §8–2.2, that this is also what a paradigm does—though in the academic context, whereas worldviews are general. In research, worldviews/-isms/paradigms can 'generate' theories. What Burrell & Morgan (1979) call "sociological paradigms" (Interpretive, Functionalist, Radical Structuralist and Radical Humanist) are worldviews in our sense. These offer

> very basic meta-theoretical assumptions which underwrite the frame of reference, mode of theorising and *modus operandi* of the social theorists who operate within them . . . which separate a group of theorists in a very fundamental way from theorists located in other paradigms.
>
> (p. 23)

The assumptions are about "alternative views of reality which lie outside [the paradigm's] boundaries and which may not necessarily even be recognised as existing". (§8–2 offers a more nuanced view on paradigms.)

Many such worldviews tend towards reductionism. Rickert's eudemonistic worldview, however, might be seen as embracing several aspects (c.f. *shalom*, §4–3.7), as might Kuyper's Calvinistic worldview (NC,I, 157).

The diversity of worldviews may thus be enumerated, but how do we understand their historical development, one from another? Dooyeweerd offers insights into this with his notion of ground-motives.

5–2.2   Ground-Motives

A *ground-motive* is a "spiritual driving force that acts as the absolutely central mainspring of human society", which is "spiritual" and "central" in that it "not only places an indelible stamp on the culture, science, and social structure of a given period but determines profoundly one's whole world view" (Dooyeweerd 1979, 9). Ground-motives thus offer a meaning-context in which to critique and generate worldviews; if we are dissatisfied with existing worldviews, our ground-motive tells us what is wrong with them and where to seek alternatives. Ground-motives define the *totality of meaningfulness*, which defines what thinkers take to be foundations of reality and are usually so deeply presupposed as to be taken as obvious truths.

Philosophies have developed by historical processes, as thinkers have encountered new challenges within their own cultural milieu. Western philosophy may be said to have begun 2,500 years ago with Greek and Hebrew thought, with input from philosophies of India and China. Western philosophy is sometimes divided into three main eras: Classical (2500 to 1500 years ago), Mediaeval (1500 to 500 years ago) and Modern (500 years ago to today). Dooyeweerd's discussion in *NC* (I, 15–206) shows that thinking during each era has been dominated by a different ground-motive, three of which are dialectical (dualistic) in nature, with input from one that is non-dialectical. The following summarises them; a full account may be found in Dooyeweerd (1979).

The Classical era was dominated by the *Greek Form-Matter ground-motive* (FMGM) (NC,I, 15–22). It sees the foundations of reality as form and matter, usually with one treated as superior to the other. We can see its influence in dualities like mind versus brain, soul versus body, reasoning versus sensing and passion, works-with-mind versus works-with-hand, online versus 'bricks-and-mortar', and at the root of various philosophical positions like materialism. Its influence stretches right into the present times.

During this period, Hebrew thinking was influenced by the non-dialectical, pluralistic (multi-aspectual) *Biblical ground-motive of Creation, Fall, Redemption* (CFR) (NC,I, 28–39). It sees reality as created by a Divine Origin ('God') that transcends it and emphasises wisdom. Its influence is found more in everyday life than in academic life; attempts to work out a theoretical approach based on it have been few, with Dooyeweerd being the foremost to date (see later).

The *Scholastic Nature-Grace ground-motive* (NGGM) (NC,I, 111–149) arose from synthesis of FMGM and CFR. It finds the foundations of reality in nature and supernature, the mundane and the sacred, usually with one seen as superior. We can see its influence in dualities like reason v. faith, secular v. sacred, State v. Church, public affairs v. private beliefs, atheist v.

religious. It sparked two reactions, the Reformation and the Renaissance; from the Renaissance the next ground-motive emerged. It is still influential in much Christian thinking.

The *Humanistic Nature-Freedom ground-motive* (NFGM) (NC,I, 148–206) sees the foundations of reality in determinism versus freedom, where freedom is the presumed human ability to interpret or choose. It generates two opposing ideals in philosophy, which Dooyeweerd calls "science ideal" v. "personality ideal". It is the Nature-Freedom ground-motive that exerts most influence today, taking many forms:

*   mechanistic physical processes v. 'free' human thinking, choosing or acting;
*   Cartesian human subject v. passive object;
*   being v. morality (Hume);
*   Kant's "Copernican Revolution";
*   subjective opinions v. objective 'facts', subjectivism v. objectivism;
*   essentialism v. social construction;
*   Positivism v. Interpretivism;
*   authoritarian control v. human freedom;
*   free agency v. controlling social structures;
*   management-by-control v. management-by-facilitation;
*   free behaviour v. constraining norms/laws;
*   nature v. human;
*   the presumed division between natural science and the humanities;
*   and so on.

The historical emergence of the ground-motives is shown in Figure 5.1, with a tiny selection of representative philosophers, much simplified (for example the link from FMGM to NFGM is not shown). The cross represents the start of Christianity. The dotted arrow, explained in §5–5, indicates that the CFR ground-motive is the one which inspired and guided Dooyeweerd in working out his philosophy as set out in the previous chapters (a few others were influenced too).

These ground-motives are not unique to Dooyeweerd, being recognised also by Vollenhoven (1950), Heidegger (1971), Habermas (2002) and others. Dooyeweerd, however, provides a penetrating discussion of them and how they relate to each other, in terms of their presuppositions about the nature of reality. This allowed him critical distance from all three dialectical ground-motives, so as to transparently discuss their problems; see §5–2.4.

Dooyeweerd did allow for other ground-motives, mentioning that of the Zoroastrian religion (Dooyeweerd 1979, 112). Today, there seems to be a dialectical tension between individual and society; this might be an expression of the Nature-Freedom ground-motive or might be a new ground-motive emerging from it, but it is too soon to say.

Choi (2000) has undertaken a similar exercise, tracing four Korean ground-motives: Shamanism, Buddhism, Confucianism and Christianity.

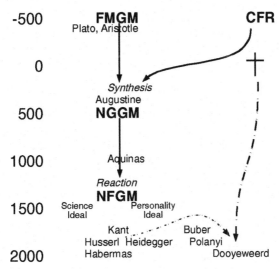

Figure 5.1 Development of ground-motives of Western thought

Korean Shamanism's ground-motive is of *Hananim* (high heaven) and nature, leading to problems of superstition. Korean Buddhism's ground-motive is *Kyo-Son* (doctrine-meditation versus scholarship-practice), leading to social irresponsibility. Both are less dialectical than Western ground-motives. Korean Confucianism's ground-motive is *I-Ki* (indispensable universal principle versus material force), which became highly dialectical and led to class problems and denial of rights and dignity. Protestant Christianity arrived when these three ground-motives were weak and corrupt and many Korean people found it addressed their problems, and moreover it sided with the people against the colonial aggressors, so it was taken up widely, but Choi does not crisply identify its elements. He suggests that Dooyeweerd's dialectical idea is over-simple.

Note: Later, we introduce Dooyeweerd's notion of Ground-Idea; this is not the same as ground-motive.

5–2.3   *Ground-Motives as Presuppositions Not Truths*

Ground-motives are not truths, but presuppositions that abstract away from everyday experience. It is not a truth but a presupposition of philosophers, for instance, that freedom and determinism are mutually exclusive. As Chesterton (1908, 35) put it, "The ordinary man has always believed that there was such a thing as fate, but such a thing as free will also." Choi (2000) found Korean Shamanism and Buddhism less dialectical than he expected. Even the Nature-Freedom ground-motive takes various forms, listed earlier, and the differences between them calls for finer-grain understanding.

Ground-motives operate more deeply than logic and reason, pre-theoretically determining what we deem reasonable, and they involve commitment and belief, adherence and rejection, similar to those found in religions and ideologies. For this reason Dooyeweerd characterises ground-motives as "religious".

> *Note on terminology: religion.* By **religion**, Dooyeweerd does not mean creeds or rituals, nor even belief in God, but defines it in a philosophically relevant way as "the innate impulse of human selfhood to direct itself toward . . . [an] absolute Origin of all temporal diversity of meaning" (NC,I, 57). Religion is deep belief or commitment that motivates and directs what we do or think, including what we presuppose and, in research, operating within paradigms.

Most philosophies have disguised their religious commitments as theoretical axioms (NC,I, 70). The entrenched conflicts between intellectual camps like Positivism and Interpretivism, and such things as mutual disdain, may be explained by the religious-ideological nature of ground-motives. For example, Basden (2018a, 147–8) sees three dialectical ground-motives in the interminable debates in artificial intelligence: three computer-human human debates occur, grounded in matter-form, nature-supernature and determined-free, and all continue fruitlessly unresolved and unresolvable. Basden offers an alternative grounded in Dooyeweerd.

To Dooyeweerd, religion differs from pistic functioning because he brings in the human self (see §4–3.14), but I find them closely related, especially from my experience of the Nature-Freedom ground-motive in the information systems field. However, Clouser (2005) helpfully differentiates ordinary from religious believing, in that the latter concerns what is ultimately self-dependent and on which all else depends.

5–2.4   Differences Between Dialectical and Pluralist Ground-Motives

Pluralist and dialectical ground-motives differ in the way they account for diversity and coherence, and also good and evil. Ground-motives constitute the totality of meaningfulness that society acknowledges.

Dooyeweerd argues (NC,I, 15–206) that dialectical ground-motives have undermined theoretical thought, especially philosophy, for example generating dilemmas that are "falsely posed" (NC,I, 24), thereby leading us into blind alleys and fruitless debates.

Dialectical ground-motives impart an oppositional character to both the sciences and philosophy, imposing a claim that the totality has only two alternatives (effectively, a two-aspect suite) so, if one pole is seen as problematic, the opposite pole is the only (main) meaningful solution offered. Obvious examples may be found in economics (Marxism, Capitalism) and research approaches (Positivism, post-positivism). Burrell & Morgan (1979) separate out their sociological paradigms (§5–2.2) by the interaction of two polarisations, subjective-objective and consensus-conflict. The former obviously manifests Nature-freedom. Consensus-conflict might also manifest Nature-freedom in that they link consensus with regulation in Radical Structuralism and conflict with freedom in Radical Humanism. As discussed in §11–3.1, even mathematics is affected by this ground-motive, in both its methods and its interpretation.

A more nuanced analysis is offered by Eriksson (2003). In his discussion of systems thinking, he argues that hard systems thinking (HST) aligns with the Nature pole and soft systems thinking (SST) with the freedom pole. Critical systems thinking (CST) was introduced by Jackson (1991) as an antidote to SST, which he criticised as ignoring the difference between oppression and emancipation and the social structures that generate them. However, since emancipation involves both human freedom and juridical structures that emancipate, which constrain people's behaviour, Eriksson argues that CST is trying to bridge the divide it presupposes and is thus doomed to failure. This is echoed by Wilson (1997), who, in commenting on "emancipatory information systems development", argues that this can end up on the paradox (antinomy) of "enforced emancipation".

In addition, dialectical ground-motives cut reality in half and urge us to emphasise one half and ignore the other as either worthless or to be explained away. They close down diversity. Example: Bunge (1979, 257) curiously omits psychical systems from his ontological framework of systems genera, with the explanation, "We might have distinguished a system genus between biosystems and sociosystems, namely psychosystems. We have refrained from doing so from fear of encouraging the myth of disembodied minds." This "fear"—hardly valid in philosophy!—is driven by the Form-Matter ground-motive and his religious adherence to the matter pole as a materialist.

Under the Scholastic Nature-grace ground-motive, mediaeval scholarship made theology the queen of the sciences, which focused on e.g. proofs of God's existence. Now this is reversed within the Nature-grace ground-motive, and religious thought is excluded from most scholarship. As a result, it is difficult to do justice to faith *qua* faith, without reducing it to psychology or sociology. For example, the field of sustainability has forfeited valuable insights that come from specific "pistic systems" like Christianity or Judaism, because while it recognises some of the influence of faith, it lumps all faiths together (Basden 2017).

The pluralistic CFR ground-motive, which motivated and informed Dooyeweerd in working out his philosophy, can ameliorate these problems because, if a worldview/paradigm centres on one aspect, the ground-motive offers multiple alternatives and it encourages consideration of them all (§3–5). The original view and all alternatives are seen as alongside them in a diversity that is mutually coherent. This enables apparently incommensurable approaches to be understood as within a wider philosophical context, as exemplified in §7–3.1 for positivist, interpretivist and socio-critical approaches. This employs aspects rather than ground-motives to analyse what is meaningful in each approach, as suggested by Basden (1999) (which also discusses Hegel's notion of dialectic), and results in a more nuanced approach that provides extra insight, even into variants of the socio-critical approach (see §10–1.2). Basden (2018a, 297–9) argues that Giddens' Structuration Theory, which tries to overcome the structure-agency dichotomy, might be fruitful because it is an aspectual rather than dialectical approach.

Incommensurability is thus revealed as not intrinsic to the approaches but an artefact of viewing them through the lens of a dialectical ground-motive—a "religious" act. So is the antinomy revealed by Eriksson and Wilson above in so-called emancipatory approaches. Dooyeweerd escapes such artefacts and gives hope of overcoming both by directing our attention to aspects that make things meaningful.

5–3.   Presuppositions: Standpoints

Similar philosophical themes crop up repeatedly in different eras (Levi 1975, 248). Aquinas, Berkeley and Kierkegaard all saw philosophy as a means of dispelling the errors of Materialism or Rationalism. Pythagoras, Descartes and Russell grounded everything in quantitative concepts and deductive methods. Plato, Hobbes and Mill explored political and social issues. The Milesians, Bacon and Whitehead tried to make philosophy resemble more the generalizations of physical science rather than those of religion or sociology.

Ground-motives do not alter the fundamental kinds of issues that are the domain of philosophy, but only the ways they are addressed. What governs which philosophical issues are actually addressed is the deeper kind of presupposition that Dooyeweerd calls *standpoints*. From the way he uses the idea (never defined), it seems to be the collection of starting-points of a philosophy.

As seen in the three previous chapters, part of Dooyeweerd's standpoint is that pre-theoretical experience, diversity, coherence, and meaningfulness are all important as starting-points and, as we shall see in §5–4, Dooyeweerd treats these as depending on Something that transcends temporal reality. By contrast, what he calls the *immanence-standpoint* makes philosophic thought (or theoretical thought) its starting-point (NC,I, 14); theoretical thought is presumed "autonomous", self-dependent, neither needing nor influenced by pre-theoretical (§2–1.2, §2–5.3). The immanence-standpoint has pervaded philosophy since the start, but in different ways:

> The age-old development of immanence-philosophy displays the most divergent nuances. It varies from metaphysical rationalism to modern logical positivism and the irrationalist philosophy of life. It is disclosed also in the form of modern existentialism. The latter has broken with the Cartesian (rationalistic) 'cogito' as Archimedean point and has replaced it by existential thought, conceived of in an immanent subjectivistic historical sense.
>
> (NC,I, 13)

(Archimedean point: a self-dependent idea on which all other ideas rest—metaphor from the solid pivot on which Archimedes claimed to be able to lift the world with a long enough lever. Dooyeweerd later stopped using the notion.)

5–3.1   *Problems Resulting From the Immanence-Standpoint*

Dooyeweerd argues (NC,I, 12–21) that philosophy has been deeply mis-led by the immanence-standpoint. To summarise Dooyeweerd's arguments, immanence philosophies:

- have *divorced meaningfulness from reality* (NC,II, 25, 26), thus lacking motivation to properly understand meaningfulness (§4–2), and so philosophy has presupposed "It exists", "It occurs" or, post-Kant, "I encounter it" to be the most fundamental statements we can make about anything, but the immanence-standpoint hides the question "In what ways?" (§4–3.3);
- consequently, have not properly addressed the *structure of things* as encountered in everyday experience (NC,III, 167), as multi-level beings (§4–3.3), which generates interminable debates about essence—though since Dooyeweerd passed away, some systems thinking has tried to understand multiple levels;
- have prevented a truly sensitive approach to *understanding everyday experience*, instead, always forcing us to take one sphere of meaningful-ness as our point of reference for all the others (NC,I, 15) (§2–5.1);
- have *absolutised* specific aspects or types of thing (NC,III, 169), thereby generating competing and conflicting "-isms" and *reductionism* (NC,I, 46, 169) (§3–2.3, §5–1.2);
- have not adequately discussed the coherence or *relationships between the aspects* (NC,II, 49), thus undermining genuine interdisciplinary research (§8–1.4);
- have presupposed a dialectical idea of what is meaningful (hence the *dialectical ground-motives*, §5–2) which led philosophy into fruitless conflicts;
- have posited the problem of *concept formation* incorrectly (NC,II, 50), which restricts our understanding of truth (see §6–1.3).

These problems entangle research when it encounters meaning(fulness), complex things, everyday experience, multiple aspects, inter-aspect relation-ships and multiple views and as it handles concepts. It was because Dooye-weerd experienced this while researching his field of jurisprudence (see below) that he sought a different standpoint and starting-points.

5–3.2   *Alternative Standpoints*

Dooyeweerd believed that philosophy would benefit from adopting a dif-ferent standpoint, to overcome its deepest problems, and discusses one alternative.

Clouser (2005) offers a more extensive understanding. He interprets Dooyeweerd's idea of standpoint as a "divinity belief", in which something is treated as divine. The "Divine" is that which is treated as self-dependent, on which all else depends. The Divine need not be personal, and might refer to an aspect to which all else is reduced; in materialism the physical aspect is divine in this sense, and to the Pythagoreans, number is divine. He defines "Creation" or the non-divine as that which is dependent on the Divine. It is usually all of temporal reality, and that about which we can think, but in Clouser the dependence need not be temporal. (Note: "Creation" should not be confused with fundamentalist Creationism, which Clouser argues is incompatible with Dooyeweerd's thought.)

Clouser (2005) differentiates divinity beliefs according to their view of the relationship between the Divine and the non-divine (Creation), suggesting there are 14 possible ones, of which he discusses three (p. 43). The three views are:

- The Pagan divinity-belief presupposes the self-dependent Divine is a subset of, and is to be sought within, the Creation—that is, within what we can think about. This is Dooyeweerd's *immanence-standpoint*. In philosophy or science governed by this view, the Divine is often a fundamental principle that is sought within temporal reality, as that which explains all else. Examples: the laws of mathematics, those of physics, or those of social construction. To most immanence-philosophy, theoretical thought is divine in this sense, as are Being or Process.
- The Eastern divinity-belief presupposes the Creation is within, and part of, the Divine. Dooyeweerd does not discuss this option, but Choi (2000) does.
- The Biblical divinity-belief (a transcendence standpoint) presupposes the Creation is separate from but unbreakably dependent on the Divine.

"Our claim," wrote Clouser (2005, 342), "is not that all theories are produced or forced on us by some divinity belief . . . The claim is that the nature of a theory's postulates is always *interpreted* in the light of what is presupposed as divine" (emphasis in original).

5–3.3 *Towards a Different Standpoint*

Dooyeweerd adopted the third divinity-belief for his standpoint. This might have been partly because of his Christian beliefs, but I believe it was mainly because of the problems of the immanence-standpoint. It is not a theological but a philosophical exercise.

Rather than compartmentalise the Divine as the Scholastic ground-motive tends to, ignore the Divine as the Humanist ground-motive tends to, or divinise some part or aspect of temporal reality as the immanence-standpoint tends to, Dooyeweerd took seriously the philosophical challenge the Divine poses. The idea that all temporal reality might be created demands philosophical consideration. Though I have yet to properly understand it, there is a resonance between Dooyeweerd's standpoint and starting-points: createdness can imply prior the philosophical importance of meaningfulness, diversity, coherence and even the importance of the fullness of reality ("everyday experience", §1–3).

This provides a vantage point from which Dooyeweerd (and we) can notice things that immanence-thinking takes for granted. It was what 'allowed' and encouraged Dooyeweerd to critically explore mainstream philosophies, rather than react against them or accept them without question. It can also, via his starting-points, begin to speak to some of the problems the immanence-standpoint generates.

For example, the theory of *hermeneutic cycle* states that our understanding of detail builds up our understanding of the whole, which informs our understanding of the detail. Originally describing processes of understanding texts, it has been extended to understanding the world. But it has been criticised (Shklar 1986). Where does the centre of the circle lie: with the interpreter or in an "organizing principle" of interpretation? How do we take into account the analysts' cultural attachments? The immanence-standpoint makes it difficult to answer such questions because it divorces meaning from reality. If meaning is merely generated *ex nihilo* by sovereign subjectivity (§4–2), the hermeneutic cycle remains (metaphorically) a lonely gyroscope spinning in the void, allowing no external input.

However, if, from Dooyeweerd's starting-points, we may view the cycle as revolving, not mechanically around a self-sufficient 'centre' in the void, but fluidly within a surrounding ocean of meaningfulness (§4–3.10), then external input is allowed, as something from elsewhere in the 'ocean'. Such a perspective does not undermine the insights of the hermeneutic cycle, but enriches them.

Another example: Regarding *dialectical ground-motives*, it seems the three dualistic ground-motives began as dualities, not necessarily in opposition. They may be seen, from Dooyeweerd's perspective, as two (sets of) aspects: form and matter, as analytic-aesthetic and physical-organic-psychic aspects, nature and grace, as pistic-ethical and earlier aspects, and nature and freedom, as physical and analytic-formative aspects, for example. It is the immanence-standpoint, which refuses to consider the possibility of given spheres of meaningfulness, that forces the dualities into opposition.

> *Research opportunity: ground-motives.* Reinterpret the three Western dialectical ground-motives and those of Korean thought (Choi 2000), as emphasising groups of aspects.

In such ways (still to be philosophically developed) problems of the immanence-standpoint might be fruitfully addressed. When we feel constrained by one or more of the problems listed earlier, we have the right to question the immanence-tandpoint, and Dooyeweerd offers the means to tackle it.

From a Foucauldian perspective, however, we may ask: Did Dooyeweerd manufacture the above problems and his starting-points *in order to* oppose the immanence-standpoint (as many Christian thinkers oppose Humanism, and vice versa), or did his starting-points highlight for him problems most of us take for granted *and lead him to* understand a common root that he called the immanence-standpoint? I believe the latter, because he struggled long within the immanence-standpoint, as we discuss below. However, once he had glimpsed the root of the problem, this enabled him, cyclically, to clarify the problems he was having and the starting-points that meant they are problematic.

The fundamental problems of the immanence-standpoint do not mean that we should ignore all that has emerged from most thinkers. (Moreover, some of Buber's and Polanyi's thought might also be seen as influenced by a transcendence standpoint similar to Dooyeweerd's.) Dooyeweerd argued that it is not the insights themselves that are problematic, but the ways they are worked out under its influence. Because every thinker has stand-point and ground-motive presuppositions (as argued in Chapter 6), these should be openly declared and exposed to critique. (Socio-critical, "Radical Humanist", thinkers agree with Dooyeweerd on this.) He did this himself: he declared himself as a "Christian" philosopher but in a new, non-Scholastic, non-Humanistic way.

5–4.   The Development of Dooyeweerd's Philosophy

Herman Dooyeweerd (1894–1977) initially studied law and went into poli-tics as the research director of the Anti-Revolutionary Party in the Nether-lands during the 1920s. Becoming Professor of Jurisprudence at the Vrije Universiteit, Amsterdam, he investigated philosophy, initially as it relates to law but then more generally, and wrote his first *magnum opus*, *De Wijsbe-geerte der Wetsidee* in 1935–6. His second, *A New Critique of Theoretical Thought*, written in 1955–1958, which updates his first, is the main source for this book, and is referred to as "NC". For full accounts of the develop-ment of Dooyeweerd's thought, see Henderson (1994) and Verburg (2015).

5–4.1   *Struggles With the Immanence-Standpoint*

Dooyeweerd spent years within the immanence-standpoint, struggling against the problems listed earlier, which seemed to prevent him from find-ing satisfactory answers.

The reason he moved into philosophy was that he realised questions like "What is law (jurisprudence)?" and "On what basis is it valid?" are philo-sophical questions. As he examined (what we would call) paradigms in law, he realised that their differences arose from their underlying philosophies (Verburg 2015, 31–3). He was perplexed that they did not, and could not, dialogue with each other, and realised that philosophy itself exhibits deep-rooted problems. In jurisprudence, issues of everyday experience, diversity, coherence and meaningfulness will have been important from the start, and he gradually came to see that the inability to address them properly might have a common root, the *immanence-standpoint*, which he concluded is "apostasy from full self-hood" (Verburg 2015, 192). He discovered this affects all disciplines, not just jurisprudence, from mathematics and physics to sociology and theology.

His "great turning-point" was "the discovery of the religious root of thought itself" (NC,I, v) (in the sense defined earlier), in that all philosophies have (hidden) religious roots. So he concluded it is philosophically valid for him to explore how a non-immanence-standpoint, arising from Christian beliefs, might contribute to philosophy, as long as he approached the task correctly.

Traditional Christian thinking concerns itself with proofs of God, etc. and/or tends to impose its doctrines onto philosophical or scientific bodies of knowledge (NC,II, 40); Dooyeweerd believed one is impossible, the other improper, in principle. Traditional Christian and mainstream thinking diverged by mutual consent to the two poles of the Scholastic ground-motive. In place of the immanence-standpoint, he believed that a non-Scholastic Christian perspective can offer insights to philosophy that are not available elsewhere, which would be of benefit to philosophy *as philosophy* (whichever philosophy it happens to be).

He believed that Christian philosophy then available was not in a position to provide such insights, so he found himself trying to formulate a "Christian philosophy" that could offer insights that are germane to philosophy as philosophy and which can be offered without any hidden agenda of imposition. Philosophy is not the handmaiden of theology!

(He saw his criticism of the immanence-standpoint as "self-criticism, as a case which the Christian thinker pleads *with himself*" (NC,I, viii, emphasis in original).)

In his main work, *NC*, three motivations can be detected:

1. to address the deep problems in philosophy, especially those arising from the immanence-standpoint and dialectical ground-motives;
2. to critically examine what is meant by "Christian" philosophy and what shape such a philosophy should take (and why what has traditionally been called "Christian philosophy" will not suffice);
3. to find a way whereby philosophies may engage with each other, especially how (his version of) Christian philosophy can engage with mainstream and other philosophies in a way that is proper to philosophy as such.

It is the first and partly the third that are the most important in this book. In *NC*, sadly, these motivations are tangled together, so I try to untangle them throughout this work.

5-4.2   Seeking a "Christian" Philosophy

Dooyeweerd's kind of "Christian" thought differs radically from traditional Christian thinking, which was rooted in the Nature-grace ground-motive.

What seems to be Heidegger's (1927/1962, 74) criticism of Christianity is actually of that ground-motive alongside the Greek Form-Matter ground-motive. Since Dooyeweerd distanced himself from both, Heidegger's criticisms do not apply.

Raised in Dutch Calvinism (Basden (2008a) detects some Celtic influence), Dooyeweerd was inspired by the statesman Abraham Kuyper, who worked for fruitful, critical dialogue. What Dooyeweerd believed to be truly Christian was something that is philosophically faithful to the idea of createdness as portrayed in the Bible. The roots of Dooyeweerd's philosophical idea of aspects, which he developed with Dirk Vollenhoven, may be found in Kuyper's contention that each sphere of society (e.g. family, business, state, church) should be free from domination by others. Table 5.2 compares briefly the Scholastic and Dooyeweerdian tendencies and some implications of the latter for research.

Dooyeweerd's philosophy has also been called "Cosmonomic Philosophy", "Philosophy of the Law Idea", "Reformational Philosophy", "Calvinistic Philosophy", the "Amsterdam Philosophy", and sometimes as "Christian Philosophy". This should not be misunderstood as being driven by Christian

Table 5.2 Differences between Scholastic and Dooyeweerdian tendencies (a somewhat simplified caricature)

Scholastic tendency	Dooyeweerdian tendency	Implications for Research
Theology is "queen of sciences" (sciences serve theology).	Theology is science of the pistic aspect alongside other sciences.	Recognise theology's proper role; benefit from its insights.
Philosophy directed towards theological issues, e.g. proof of God.	Philosophy and theology have different roles.	Each field should operate by its own rationality, not that of others; philosophy should treat all fields as equally meaningful.
Sciences to support religious doctrines; hostility to those that do not seem to, e.g. Evolution.	Seek genuine dialogue with mainstream thought, even where it seems to contradict religious doctrine.	Listen, try to understand where the opponent is 'coming from' and where they want to get to, and why. Do not try to defend doctrines (whether sacred or secular).
Scientific knowledge of 'secular' fields may be acquiesced to, because it is of little ultimate interest.	All knowledge, whatever field, needs to be critically examined for its presuppositions.	Be always sensitive to presuppositions, publish and discuss them.
Religious doctrines dominate.	Religious beliefs should be acknowledged and taken seriously as such, but not allowed to dominate.	Do not reduce religious belief to psychology, sociology, etc. but recognise and respect them as they are rather than as Scholastic or Humanist thought might distort them.

theology or anti-secular reaction, nor as requiring personal Christian commitment in those who adopt it, as we now discuss.

5–4.3   *Fresh Insights for Research*

To Dooyeweerd, the role of a Christian (or any non-mainstream) philosophy is to be alongside others to bring fresh insights for the benefit of philosophy and the wider world. Basden (2008b) calls this "Abrahamic blessing": the role of Christian philosophy is to bring blessing to the world. (This contrasts with three other possible relationships between a religion and philosophy that are mentioned in the Preface, of mutual isolation, of domination or of utilisation.)

That Christian thinking might bring fresh insights is illustrated by Michael Faraday's idea that magnetism is a force rather than particles. Faraday was freed to consider forces by his strong Biblical beliefs, whereas materialists refused consider anything other than material explanations (Russell 2000). However, nobody suggests that only Christian believers may use or theorise about magnetism as a force. Likewise, Dooyeweerd's exploration of the diversity and coherence of meaningfulness and law in everyday experience was 'released' by his Christian beliefs and rejection of an immanence-standpoint, yet it does not preclude those with different religious beliefs from benefiting. Paradoxically, my experience has been that Hindus, Muslims and Humanists appreciate Dooyeweerd's ideas more than Christians do (Basden 2018a, 366).

Dooyeweerd was not arrogant, but he was courageous enough to state what he believed and honest enough to work it out philosophically, while openly acknowledging his religious roots. Despite and because of his radically different standpoint, his philosophy is able to engage with most others—over 100 in his *New Critique.*

It may be that another, non-Christian, philosophy might achieve similar or better results than can Dooyeweerd, though I see none on the horizon yet. I refrain from taking sides; what I want to do in this book is to open up experience of using Dooyeweerd's philosophy in research to critical scrutiny and use. It has so far proven very fruitful to Christians and non-Christians alike.

It is now the responsibility of mainstream researchers and philosophers, not to reject this out of hand (which paradoxically might demonstrate Dooyeweerd is correct), but to engage with such ideas philosophically and as scientific researchers. The acclaim by the Humanist, P.B. Cliteur, has already been cited (§1–4.3).

5–5.   Crossing Research Philosophy Boundaries

During research, we must engage with theories and philosophical foundations already extant in the field, some of which seem deeply incommensurable with others, for example Descartes versus Heidegger, Positivism versus Interpretivism and, especially, Dooyeweerd's standpoint versus the immanence-standpoint. How can there be dialogue across such divides?

Dooyeweerd believed there can be, if all participants transparently expose their presuppositions (ground-motives and standpoints) for scrutiny. Laying them alongside each other can facilitate mutual understanding and even respect. He argues that even though there might be an antithesis in stand-point or ground-motive, there need not be an antithesis in the employment of philosophical thinking (NC,I, 120ff.). That is why philosophy must always be undertaken in ways that are proper to philosophy itself, not to theology or sociology, etc.

Being able to cross philosophical boundaries is primarily a matter of atti-tude, not rationality or technique (if you wish, in terms of Dooyeweerd's aspects, it is pistic and ethical functioning more than analytic or formative). Among incommensurable philosophies, *antagonism* or *conflict* are prevalent attitudes, which manifests itself either in passion or denigration or in over-much theoretical effort being directed to intellectual warfare. An alternative attitude is *acquiescence* or *compliance*, in which portions of other thought are adopted without question, being deemed beneath question. One can find examples of both in traditional 'Christian' thought, with antagonism exercised by creationists against evolutionists and liberals against tradition-alists, alongside unquestioning acquiescence to capitalist business theories or socialist social agendas. Common to both attitudes is the tendency to misunderstand the other.

Dooyeweerd wanted—and demonstrated—a third attitude, of *critical conversation*, in which each participant recognises the meaningfulness or validity of aspects important to the others, but in which all expose presup-positions, admit to them and understand the impact that these have. This opens up the possibility of mutual enrichment, even if not agreement, that is based on understanding.

> If a critique is to bear fruit, it must begin by placing itself on the point of departure of the theory it proposes to judge; otherwise, people wind up talking past one another. Naturally, one can always say: 'My standpoint is not the same as that of this writer,' but nothing is gained by doing that. One does not overcome the opposed point of departure by doing that. A critique is only fruitful when it begins by entering into the line of thought of the writer being considered; when with complete honesty it draws the necessary conclusions from the writer's epistemological premises; and when, having pointed out what is unsatisfactory in those conclusions, it clarifies what is untenable in the writer's point of departure.
>
> (Dooyeweerd, cited in Verburg 2015, 23)

This attitude of critical engagement is taken in this book. Critical conver-sation, I have found, can operate at two levels. At the broader, *macro*, level, Dooyeweerd explored the nature of theoretical thought itself (Chapter 6) and proposed a way by which we can understand the pre-theoretical (including

Table 5.3 Some thinkers whose ideas echo Dooyeweerd's

Thinker	Similarity	Difference	Section
Kant	Importance of human thinker	Thinking as multi-aspectual functioning, including pistic as well as analytic	§2-2 §3-8
Kant	Transcendental critique of theoretical thought	Deeper: theoretical attitude not just processes	§6-3
Husserl	Intuition; lifeworld; Input to thought not restricted to senses	Law-side as well as subject-side of intuition and lifeworld.	§2-4 §4-3.11
Heidegger	Being is dependent, especially on what surrounds it.	Surrounded by meaningfulness not just other beings; world is meaningful	§4-2 §4-3.3
Linguistic turn	Meaning	Differentiates meanings from meaningfulness, with meaningfulness as 'ocean'	§4-3.10 §4-3.11
Foucault, Habermas	Theoretical thought not neutral	Non-neutrality is not only from power nor interests but is, most deeply, religious in nature	§2-3 §5-2.3 §6-3
Polanyi, Foucault,	Dwell in meaning, Power pervades	Deeper philosophical foundation	§4-3.10

religious) choices that each philosophy makes (Chapter 7), so we may compare them and more clearly understand areas of agreement and disagreement. At the detailed, *micro*, level, I have found a practical approach useful, to listen, affirm, critique and enrich ("LACE", which is discussed in §10–1).

As already discussed, some of Dooyeweerd's ideas echo some of those of Kant, Husserl, Heidegger and the Linguistic Turn in philosophy, but with a new twist. He treated their ideas as genuine insights, which are often a corrective to previous thought that had become problematic, and which usefully 'open up' overlooked aspects (§4–3.8.3). Yet they were unable to reach their full potential, and we can now see this is because of restrictions imposed by the immanence-standpoint and/or dualistic ground-motives. Table 5.3 summarises some of them, showing similarities with these thinkers and the new twist (Foucault, Habermas, and Polanyi post-date Dooyeweerd). Most are discussed in Part II.

What Dooyeweerd did was not to develop his ideas *from* these insights but rather to see parallels with his own thought and *critically benefit because of* them.

5–6. Conclusion

This chapter has discussed how philosophy is important in research—as approach, foundation and source of tools. It summarises Dooyeweerd's reasons why philosophy needs to be questioned rather than accepted as given, because of three kinds of presupposition, worldviews, ground-motives and standpoints. Dooyeweerd argues that the latter two especially have led philosophy astray into unfruitfulness. This explains why Dooyeweerd's starting-points discussed in the previous three chapters (everyday experience, diversity-coherence and meaningfulness) are important philosophically, as well as practically, and can overcome various problems. I have found that the ground-motive and standpoint Dooyeweerd adopted have imparted a richer attitude in research. The chapter has also discussed how to engage with those of different standpoint or ground-motive.

It is too early to know for certain whether Dooyeweerd's standpoint and ground-motive are indeed useful in research, because wider experience is needed. Experiences so far, which are presented as "adventures with Dooyeweerd" and recounted in Chapter 11, are promising and exciting, and invite more. Before they begin an adventure, researchers need to understand the nature of theoretical thought at the centre of their research from a Dooyeweerdian perspective. That is the purpose of Part II. In Part III, practical issues are discussed.

Part II

Part II is about theoretical thought that is at the heart of research, and Dooyeweerd's critical understanding thereof.

- Chapter 6 introduces the problem of truth, and then outlines Dooyeweerd's critique of theoretical thought, in which he identified three transcendental problems about the necessary and universal conditions that make theoretical thought possible.
- Chapter 7 explains Dooyeweerd's notion of the three-part Ground-Idea, which derives from his transcendental problems, and shows how it can address the challenging issues of advance in knowledge, incommensurability of approaches and discourses, inappropriate philosophies and bias in research.
- Chapter 8 employs the notion of Ground-Idea to distinguish between fields, resolve ambiguities in the notion of paradigm and suggest how concepts and ideas may be clarified.

6   On Theoretical Knowledge and Research

If the role of research is to contribute theoretical understanding to humanity's bodies of knowledge, then we need to know what "theoretical" and "understanding" and "knowledge" are, especially when these are supposed to be generic and reliance-worthy (§1–2.1). This chapter elaborates these issues, first raised in Chapter 1, in the light of our situating research as a whole in the context of pre-theoretical everyday experience, of diversity and coherence, of the prior nature of meaningfulness and of the inescapability of philosophical presuppositions (Chapters 2, 3, 4, 5). This chapter contains an exposition of Dooyeweerd's exploration of the nature of theoretical thought, which I have reinterpreted to be relevant to research.

6–1.   The Challenge of Truth

In order that it is reasonable to rely on them, knowledge or theories should be true rather than false or misleading. But what is truth?

Webster's 1975 definition of research, with which Section 1–2 begins, includes "facts" and "correct interpretation", in an attempt to differentiate truth from falsehood. Yet the idea of facts and correctness has been contested since 1975, partly because it has been misapplied in the natural sciences, but especially because a reaction against "facts" occurred in the social sciences. Puddefoot (1999, 70) expresses this reaction against "facts" as "the modernist impersonal objective view of knowledge",

> that the facts are the facts and that is all there is to it; that the way the world is commands assent; that we are not responsible for what we treat as reality because reality is reality; that we are not responsible for what we treat as truth because truth is truth; that if you do not see things the way my tribe sees things, there must be something wrong with you.

The problem, he makes clear, drawing on Polanyi, is not the ontic status of facts or otherwise, but that fact-ness has been used in a bullying, totalitarian way, with "foot-stamping" by those with power.

But this does not do away with fact-ness, or truth. Dooyeweerd would suggest that Puddefoot's problems with "facts" lie not in the aspect to do with delineating facts, the analytic aspect, but in other aspects, in which the above behaviour is dysfunction: totalitarian or bullying use of facts, and the abrogation of responsibility, are ethical and juridical dysfunctioning. In this section, and in §6–4, we try to understand fact-ness or truth in a way that makes sense in all fields.

6–1.1   *Realism and Anti-Realism: Is There Generic Truth?*

Historically there have been two main positions on generic knowledge, which we will call Realism and Anti-realism, about which much has been written. In some fields, Realism is known as objectivism, essentialism or naturalism. Anti-realism takes several forms: subjectivism, relativism, nominalism, constructivism and others. A comprehensive understanding of these two camps, and the differences among the 'isms', is not appropriate here, partly because there are many nuances in each; a brief résumé must suffice.

They differ on their view of generic knowledge, especially beliefs about law and possibility (§4–3.8.1). Realism holds that such beliefs can be true (or false) and that true ones hold regardless of whether we know, believe or disbelieve them; Anti-realism holds that such beliefs are constructed by us.

Realism sees research as discovering laws and the possibilities they offer; Anti-realism sees research as constructing laws. To gain findings on which it is reasonable to rely, Realism assumes we can measure the world "as it is" and test hypotheses about it; Anti-realism focuses on minimising bias or poor argument or method. In practice, much research does both.

In the social sciences over the past century, there has been a movement from Realism to Anti-realism. Initially the methods of the natural sciences were employed, such as hypothesis-testing, but it became clear that the world is too complex for this, and in any case much social reality, such as kinds of institutions, is constructed socially (hence Berger & Luckmann's (1967) classic *The Social Construction of Reality*).

In the natural sciences and especially mathematics, many believe there is a generic reality that holds true regardless of human belief or construction, and so assume a Realist stance. Yet the situation is more complex. Penelope Maddy (Maddy 2009) describes how she found even in mathematics the picture is more complicated. She moved from Anti-realism to Realism then to naturalism. Initially, she adopted the Anti-realist position that mathematical truth is whatever derives from the accepted axioms of set theory. But how have we come to those axioms, and could there be others yet to be accepted? So she moved to a Realist position that allowed for mathematical truths that do not depend on current acceptance, employing the Quine-Putnam indispensability argument that mathematical objects play an indispensable role in our best physical theories. She discovered, however, that this was not the way physicists and mathematicians actually worked, so she then became concerned with on what grounds might new axioms be validly sought. This position she calls "naturalism".

After a period of accepting the basis of debates, she began to question their presuppositions, trying to build "from the ground up" and "on its own terms" (Maddy 2007), starting from commonsense perception. She began to recognise the centrality of human activity in mathematical logic. The approach at which she arrived, called "Second Philosophy", strongly echoes Dooyeweerd's approach as outlined in Part I: starting with everyday experience, questioning presuppositions, and recognising the full humanness of the researcher. In taking account of physical reality (with some biological and psychological too), we may see antecipatory inter-aspect coherence. Sadly, perhaps, what Maddy does at this stage is to define her position in terms of rejecting Descartes, not realising there are deeper problems, which Dooyeweerd discussed (Chapter 5).

Her experience—which is not untypical—suggests that the Realism-Antirealism divide is not absolute. That is what Dooyeweerd believed, and he offers a deeper understanding of theoretical thought, in which insights of both might meet. We will now look briefly at various positions on truth, to prepare us for understanding Dooyeweerd's own position.

6–1.2 About Truth

"Truth" is not an easy concept and is understood differently by different philosophical systems: speculative-metaphysical Realism, Kantianism, Phenomenology, Foucauldian philosophy, Critical Realism, Pragmatism and Dooyeweerd. Dooyeweerd (NC,II, 566–9) provides a useful discussion of the foundations of the first three, which we draw upon here to offer a contextualising simplified overview.

In the views Dooyeweerd's discusses, truth is an *adequatio* (adequacy) relationship between knowledge and what the knowledge is about, but each case differs in what the relationship is between and how truth is possible (or guaranteed). Various terms are used instead of *"adequatio"*, including *"convientiena"*, "correspondence", "accordance", "agreement", etc.

In (pre-Kantian) speculative-metaphysical *Realism*, truth is agreement between thought and being (*"adequatio intellectus et rei"*). To generate truthful new knowledge, the world (being) presents itself to thought via the senses, forming images of the world, from which thought (reason) synthesises truthful new knowledge. The guarantee of truth of this new knowledge is that our sensing and our synthesising are carried out properly. This seemed reasonable for research in the natural sciences, because the presupposition was that we can measure the natural world objectively. But it contained within it the battle between rationalism and empiricism about whether senses or reason are primary.

Kant sought to bridge this divide. Realism had not sufficiently opened up the nature of (theoretical) thought, so Kant emphasised the central importance of the thinking ego. This "Copernican revolution" shifts the 'centre' of theoretical knowing from the world to the ego or *consciousness*).

All we have, Kant believed, is sense data. The thinking ego can never have direct access to the *"Ding an sich"* (thing in itself, *noumenon*) but only to sensory impressions of it (*phenomena*). This presupposes a "Kantian gulf" between thought and thing, also called "transcendental subjectivism", or "transcendental idealism" (in which knowledge is composed of ideas). Theoretical thinking is possible, Kant believed, because of the data-synthesising activity of the thinker. Its guarantee of truth is that the data-synthesising activity is *a priori* (built-in, innate) in human thinking. Truth is then the correspondence between *a priori* human knowledge and objects as a whole. Dooyeweerd pointed out (NC,II, 569) a deep antinomy in Kant, in that "His epistemology works with unclarified presuppositions [of an objectivist kind] which do not agree with his transcendental subjectivism."

Husserl recognised this flaw in Kant, thinking him not radical enough. Kant had failed to make the hidden dimensions of consciousness accessible to immediate experience; Husserl argued that all scientific concepts gain their meaning only from the *lifeworld*, that "anonymous" pool of shared background knowledge that informs our everyday experience. Husserl also questioned the nature of the data that thinkers use: it comes not just via sensing but also from immediate "eidetic intuition" (p. 125). (Compare Thomas Reid.)

Husserl distinguished two types of truth (1954/1970, 124)—"objective truth," founded in theoretical thinking and logic, and "truth in pre- and extra-scientific life", which "has its ultimate and deepest source of verification in experience" including "self-evidences". He tried to work out what a "science of the lifeworld" (p. 123) might be like. The problem he faced, however, was that he accepted the validity of Kant's assertion that we can never know the noumenon but only phenomena. He tried to work out a phenomenological method by which appearances and "symbolic meanings" or "biases" could be peeled away by several steps of "*epoché*", of setting aside various things, including the natural, naïve validities that are accepted in ordinary life, of validities already in effect (p. 135), the aims of "objective science", and the idea that theories are truths (most of which chime with the position taken here).

He sought a method and found clues to it in what he called phenomenological reduction, but (arguably) never found what he sought—probably because he restricted himself to an immanence-standpoint.

Is such a peeling away possible? *Foucault* is one who believed not, insofar as what is accepted or allowed as true is dictated by power, and each society has its "regime of truth", which exclude things by prohibition, by rejection and by declaring it false. Likewise, *Habermas* (1972) argued that knowledge is determined by pre-theoretical interests. However, we might ask whether Foucault is too fixated on power (Baudrillard 1977/2007), and even if he is not, what makes power possible?

From the perspective of *Critical Realism*, Bhaskar (1975) undertakes transcendental analyses of experience, to argue for the ontic reality of what is being studied, and of "experimental activity", to argue that this is structured and that causal laws are real and not just products of patterns. However, he does not expose the transcendental conditions that make theoretical truth possible. As with Kant and Realism, he limits himself to theoretical thought and to sensory input, and his "experience" is not everyday experience but that from which scientists obtain their data. This criticism of Critical Realism was also noted by Dooyeweerd (NC,III, 44–7; Basden 2018a, 52).

Pragmatism is similar to Realism, acknowledging an external reality that must be coped with in practice. Its *adequatio* of thought is with whether the knowledge is useful-to-believe in practice. Truth has a "cash-value"; "Truth HAPPENS to an idea" (James 1907, emphasis in original). This implies some normative value of what is beneficial versus detrimental, but Pragmatism offers little to help decide what "useful" means.

6–1.3　Dooyeweerd's Critique of Truth

Early in his development, Dooyeweerd thought himself a Critical Realist, but his examination of truth (NC,II, 566–9) caused him to distance himself therefrom (Henderson 1994, 179). He cannot be called either Realist or Anti-realist, for three reasons, related to his three starting-points. First, pre-theoretical experience takes both things and laws to be both real and malleable, and Dooyeweerd respects this rather than trying to explain it away. However, he opens up the question, "In what way real?" Second, truth/reality is diverse: something can be true/real in one way but not in another. Third, he controversially states (NC,IV, 248) "There is no such thing as truth in itself"—not even "2 × 2 = 4" (NC,II, 572). The key phrase is "in itself". He believed that there is truth, but that truth is never "in itself". By "truth in itself" Dooyeweerd refers to treating a belief as isolated from all other meaning and thus denying the referential mutual inter-dependency of all reality (§4–3.1).

Dooyeweerd agrees with both Realisms and Pragmatism that there is a reality which we engage, with Kant on the central importance of the human ego in thinking (including philosophising), with Husserl and Reid that data comes from more than the senses and that intuition is important, with Foucault and Habermas on the non-neutrality of theoretical thinking and the resulting knowledge, and with Pragmatism about the importance of usefulness and normativity. However, he has criticisms of all of them, which derive from his starting-points:

1. Most *limit themselves to theoretical knowledge*. As indicated in Chapter 2, Dooyeweerd wants to embrace pre-theoretical knowledge too, and believes that there is truth therein. (Husserl's lifeworld might be seen as pre-theoretical knowledge.)
2. Because of this, most *inadequately understand pre-theoretical everyday experience*, especially Kant and probably Husserl (and Bhaskar), and consequently even their understanding of theoretical knowledge must be suspect (NC,II, 568).
3. Most, especially Realisms, *presuppose the detached thinker* (§2–2). Dooyeweerd held that the thinker, philosopher, scientist, researcher is part of the world being researched.
4. Realism, Kant and Bhaskar *limit data to the senses* (NC,II, 431). To Dooyeweerd, data for research may come directly from multiple aspects,

not just the psychic-sensitive, as we function in all aspects with an intuitive grasp of their meaningfulness (§4–3.13). Example: Input data for sociological research about relationships or communities comes from direct intuitive grasp of social meaningfulness.

5. Husserl, despite speaking of distinct "worlds", presupposes a *single totality of truth* to which they all belong. Dooyeweerd criticises this (NC,II, 570) and, though there is a totality of *meaning*, different aspects imply different truths. That what counts as truth in sociology, mathematics, physics, aesthetics and theology are so radically different lends support to Dooyeweerd.

6. Realism *presupposes being-in-itself*. So does Kant, in his notion of *noumenon* (though I believe that a Dooyeweerdian account could be given of this). Husserl treats *phenomena* as "in-itself", and Foucault treats power as "in-itself". "In-itself" is the core of the immanence-standpoint, that which is self-dependent, taking different forms in the different philosophies. Dooyeweerd argues, as we saw in §4–3.3, that no being is "in-itself", but is grounded in meaningfulness, which refers beyond itself (§4–3.1), ultimately to the Divine "In-Itself" ("I AM"). We may hear echoes of this in Husserl's introduction of the lifeworld (1954/1970, Section 29), which Dooyeweerd missed, but Husserl seems not to have developed them and prefers to see the lifeworld as fundamentally "given".

7. Pragmatism *narrows down* normativity to mere functional purpose (formative aspect), whereas Dooyeweerd sees diverse normativities.

Dooyeweerd argues (NC,II, 571) that the nature ("*a priori* structure") of truth cannot be understood by limiting it to truth of theoretical knowledge (nor, we might add, of pragmatic purpose), and, in his subsequent pages, that we must take into account the entire "horizon of human experience . . . in its full richness". He argues for what he calls a "perspective structure of truth" (NC,II, 565, 571): that truth always refers to a perspective; perspectives arise from ways of being meaningful. Dooyeweerd's view of truth is discussed later, because it depends on his understanding of theoretical thought.

This is why, in this book, the criterion of truth of research findings is replaced by "on which it is reasonable to rely", and that reasonableness depends on aspectual perspective (§4–3.6).

6–2.   On the Non-Neutrality of Theoretical Thought

Section 2–3 reviews several nearly recent thinkers who have all argued that theoretical thought is not neutral. Twenty years before them, Dooyeweerd argued likewise that theoretical thought never has been neutral and never can be neutral. His critical analyses of this actually went deeper than most recent ones. Dooyeweerd employed both immanent critique, to show it "never has been" neutral, and transcendental critique, to show it "never can be", which we discuss below.

We must, however, make very clear the terms we use, with the following *Note on terminology: immanent, transcendent, transcendental*:

- *Immanent critique* is critique of existing ideas 'from the inside', seeking to understand them in their own terms, especially in what they see as meaningful, or to be problematic in previous thought. Immanent critique was carried out by Habermas, Dooyeweerd and others. It is often used to understand historical movement ("never/always has been").
- *Transcendent critique* is likewise critique of existing ideas but, by contrast, 'from the outside', ignoring what is meaningful to the ideas being critiqued. It is sometimes used as a weapon in battles like that between Marxism and Capitalism. Consequently it is usually a flawed type of critique. Dooyeweerd avoided it.
- *Transcendental critique* (note "al") aims to expose the "transcendental" (universal, necessary) conditions that make something possible (Clouser 2005). Employed by Kant, Husserl, Bhaskar, Dooyeweerd and others. It is used to understand "must always/never could be". Very different from *transcendent* critique (NC,I, 37).
- *Immanence-standpoint* is not a critique but a deep presupposition of philosophy and has nothing to do with immanent critique, which is an activity. It refers to a standpoint in which philosophy presupposes that the most fundamental principle ("divine") is to be found within temporal reality. See §5–3.
- *Transcendence standpoint* is not a critique, but a deep presupposition that the most fundamental principle cannot be found in temporal reality but transcends it.

Whereas some thinkers employ transcendental critique, and some employ immanent critique, Dooyeweerd employs both, in a way that I find deeper and more comprehensive than most. Not only do Dooyeweerd's critiques show that theoretical knowledge can never be neutral, but from them emerges a very useful notion that is helpful in research (elaborated in Chapters 7, 8).

6–2.1 Dooyeweerd's Immanent Critique of Theoretical Thought

Dooyeweerd wrote hundreds of pages on the history of theoretical thought (NC,I,II; Dooyeweerd 1979), mainly in Europe, with some in other cultures, making an immanent critique of over a hundred philosophers and many other thinkers through the past 2,500 years (see list at start of Chapter 5). A notable lack in Dooyeweerd's discussion is American Pragmatism, so I try to include some on that—and of course thinkers who post-dated him. Choi (2000) has undertaken a similar immanent critique of Korean thought, to disclose the ground-motives that have directed it through the centuries.

> *Research opportunity: analysis of recent philosophers*. Dooyeweerdian immanent critique of later thinkers would be a useful exercise, but is beyond the scope of this book.

Reading original texts of thinkers, Dooyeweerd tried to expose presuppositions on which their thought is based, which, he argues, often undermine the thinkers' intentions. An overall picture emerges that theoretical thought has never been neutral, never autonomous of the thinker's pre-theoretical experience and especially its religious root (as defined in §5–2.3). This, he argues, makes the immanence-standpoint untenable.

> Immanence-philosophy in all its nuances stands or falls with the dogma of the autonomy of theoretical thought. . . . Not only traditional metaphysics, but also Kantian epistemology, modern phenomenology and phenomenological ontology in the style of Nicolai Hartmann continued in this respect to be involved in a theoretical dogmatism.
>
> (NC,I, 28)

It presumes, rather than critically examines, the possibility and value of theoretical thought as autonomous, absolutely authoritative and neutral. Dooyeweerd's discussion reveals the problems listed in §5–3.1 that result from the immanence-standpoint: never adequately addressing meaningfulness or pre-theoretical, everyday experience, tending to develop by swinging between poles of dialectical ground-motives, fostering 'isms' that elevate one aspect to which other aspects are reduced (e.g. analytical for rationalism (NC,I, 46)), which result in antinomies like Zeno's paradox (Achilles and tortoise).

These problems will not be addressed, let alone solved, Dooyeweerd believed, unless we recognise the deep religious (in Dooyeweerd's sense) root of theoretical thought. Geertsema suggests (2000, 85), "The main aim of his philosophy has always been to show how the religious starting-point controls philosophical and scientific thought, both in relation to Humanistic and Scholastic thinking and in relation to his own Reformational conviction." As indicated in §5–5, recognising religious standpoints has far-reaching and liberating consequences, enabling dialogue and opening doors onto many new fruitful avenues of research. These emerge from Dooyeweerd's transcendental critiques.

6–2.2   Dooyeweerd's Transcendental Critiques of Theoretical Thought

Dooyeweerd, however,

> is not satisfied with an argument that shows that in fact philosophy always has been influenced by religious convictions.
>
> (Geertsema 2000, 99)

Rather,

> He wants to show that it cannot be otherwise, because it is part of the nature of philosophy or theoretical thought. For that reason he called his critical analysis a transcendental critique.

"Neither Kant, the founder of the so-called critical transcendental philosophy," Dooyeweerd (1999, 6) remarks,

> nor Edmund Husserl, the founder of modern phenomenology, who called his phenomenological philosophy 'the most radical critique of knowledge', have made the theoretical attitude of thought into a critical problem. Both of them started from the autonomy of theoretical thinking as an axiom which needs no further justification.

Neither went deep enough, so Dooyeweerd accepted the challenge of doing so, undertaking two transcendental critiques to lay bare the fundamental conditions that make theoretical thought possible. He saw his critique as "resuming" Kant's project (NC,I, 36). Kant and others had asked right questions, but insufficient questions, and not gone deep enough in their critique.

The first transcendental critique (NC,I, 22–33), explained in Kalsbeek (1975) and discussed in Chaplin (2011) and Basden (2008a), does not much concern us because it was restricted to philosophy, and criticisms that were made of it led Dooyeweerd to a second, fuller transcendental critique (NC,I, 34). (The first critique depends on the notion of Archimedean point, a fixed point from which to leverage arguments, but not everyone agrees with the idea and I don't find it necessary in research.)

6–3. Dooyeweerd's Second Transcendental Critique of Theoretical Thought

Out of Dooyeweerd's second transcendental critique of theoretical thought comes an understanding of theoretical thought that Dooyeweerd intended to apply to scientific as well as philosophical thought. I have found it highly serviceable across many fields of research.

Dooyeweerd argues (NC,I, 4–60) that theoretical thought challenges us with three transcendental problems, which must necessarily be addressed by any attempt to understand foundations, defend them and enable discourse between approaches. Unfortunately, Dooyeweerd's main exposition of them is rambling and not easy to understand. This has led to criticisms (see §12–1.11), but none undermine Dooyeweerd's basic idea.

In NC,I, 4–60, he develops the ideas in relation to philosophy, but later (NC,III, 168) he applies them to a scientific field in sociology. Combining them, taking note of their differences, and also taking account of his lengthy discussion of "the epistemological problem" (NC,II, 427–598), I have reinterpreted Dooyeweerd's transcendental critique in the context of research as it is carried out across many fields.

Other attempts to explain Dooyeweerd's transcendental critique are available, which readers might prefer. Clouser (2005) and Strauss (2009) give it an analytical twist. Geertsema (2000) reinterprets it hermeneutically. Chaplin (2011) interprets it in the light of Christian thinking about the state.

6–3.1   *Preparing to Understand the Transcendental Problems*

Before outlining Dooyeweerd's "transcendental problems", we should understand how they might be approached.

1. Dooyeweerd is discussing theoretical thinking *in its completeness*, not merely the research project that generates findings but, more widely, its entire mandate of contributing good theoretical understanding to humanity's bodies of knowledge.
2. This is both *individual and communal activity* (NC,I, 59), which must include not only the individual's findings but also the community's critical debate about, and refinement of, their findings.
3. Dooyeweerd sees knowledge and theories as *beliefs* rather than "facts".
4. As stated in Chapter 2, Dooyeweerd refused to de-personalize theoretical thought; it must always be understood in relation to the *human being of the researcher*.
5. The researcher or thinker is no *detached observer* but is always part of the reality that is being studied (§2–2). The researcher and researched situations share the same prior meaningfulness (§4–3.10).
6. We should *expect diversity and coherence* in the meaningfulness encountered during research (Chapter 3).

These resonate with the approach to research outlined in previous chapters: transcendental critique is never absolute but always relative to one's starting-points.

6–3.2   *The Starting Question*

In an earlier article, Dooyeweerd (1947) actually posed four transcendental questions. In NC, the first is bound up with the second. Here we make it a question that starts things off:

> What is the difference between theoretical and pre-theoretical attitudes of thought?

Dooyeweerd's answer, alluded to in §2–5 as embeddedness and diversity was that, whereas "naïve experience has an integral vision of the whole" (NC,I, 84), theoretical thought involves abstraction from the world. In the pre-theoretical attitude of everyday experience we engage with reality in intimate subject-object functioning in each aspect (§4–3.9). This includes the "analytical subject-object relationship", where we make distinctions; not all analytic functioning is theoretical.

However, in the theoretical attitude, we function in the analytic aspect in a different way, standing back from reality, over against it, in a "*Gegenstand*" relationship, an "antithetic attitude" (NC,I, 41). In this attitude we abstract from the studied situation. Dooyeweerd's *Gegenstand* echoes Kant's insight that we do not study the "*Ding an sich*", Bhaskar's distinction between the Actual and the Empirical, and Polanyi's (1962/1974, 4) statement, "A theory is other than myself".

Clouser (2005) offers a more nuanced view, with an extra level of abstraction:

• distinguishing entities from their background, in everyday experience (this red rose);
• *lower abstraction*: distinguishing properties of entities from the entities themselves (this rose is red);
• *higher abstraction*: abstracting properties away from entities altogether (redness as such).

That research involves abstraction from situations under study applies, whatever field. Even anthropological research, which sees itself as studying everyday experience, finds itself abstracting. This leads us to the first transcendental problem: What do we abstract?

6–3.3   First Transcendental Problem (TP1), Abstraction: Thinker and Diversity of World

In full:

> What do we abstract in the antithetic attitude of theoretic thought from the structures of empirical reality as these structures are given in naïve experience? And how is this abstraction possible?
>
> (NC,I, 41)

Dooyeweerd's answer (NC,I, 38–45) is that we abstract aspects—ways in which situations are meaningful. This forms corresponding concepts that are the *data* from which research derives its *findings*. On this basis, Dooyeweerd explains Kant's "theoretical analysis". Research in each field abstracts a different *core aspect* (or "*focal aspect*" using Polanyi's terminology). It is different for each field: physical aspect for physics and materials science, lingual for linguistics. Table 8.1 offers more examples.

Note: There are *two* separations involved in this *Gegenstand* abstraction,

• separation of thinker standing over against the world;
• separation of the focal aspect from others, pulling it out of its coherence therewith.

Theoretical thought tries to sever an aspect from the coherence of meaningfulness. Poetically, Dooyeweerd describes this as reality being "set asunder" (NC,I, 34), so theoretical thought "is met with resistance" (NC,I, 38). It implies that theoretical thought can never lead to truth that can be fully relied on, because it will always yield at best partial understanding. This is the first reason why theoretical thought can never be neutral or absolute: the researcher chooses their focal aspect(s) pre-theoretically.

We might expect this problem in the human sciences, but Maddy found that even in mathematics she had to refer beyond the obviously relevant quantitative aspect to the physical and others, to adequately understand "mathematical truth" (§6–1.1).

The reason we can abstract aspects is that we already have an intuitive grasp of aspectual meaningfulness exhibited in the studied situations (NC,I, 50; II, 566–8). Example: Economists study costs and currencies, and gain their data about these from newsfeeds, reports, etc. by reading (lingual functioning) and then directly intuiting, from what they read, concepts that are meaningful in their focal aspect, the economic.

Kant, along with Aristotle, Russell and Bhaskar, seemed not to understand this, instead positing that all data comes *only through sensory* input and is somehow deduced therefrom. Dooyeweerd criticises this idea as a "functionalistic view of empirical reality" (NC,II, 431, 536ff; III, 25), arguing that data can come directly from intuition in *every aspect*, with sensory as only one, which seems closer to what researchers actually experience. Husserl, James and Dewey likewise understood the diversity of data sources. However, Husserl's account of the intuiting is via the lifeworld, which he presupposed is fact-side lifeworld, while Dooyeweerd allowed for a law-side lifeworld too (§4–3.11.2)—our intuitive grasp of aspectual meaningfulness (§4–3.13).

This does not, however, preclude the use of material or conceptual instruments (tools) in the collecting of data—telescopes, measuring equipment or conceptual models like wave-particle duality, Giddens' Structuration Theory or the hermeneutic cycle. Though such tools embody the results of theoretical thought, when using them it is by aspectual intuition that researchers recognise what is relevant (meaningful). See §7–1.2.3 for discussion.

6–3.4   Second Transcendental Problem (TP2), Reuniting That Which Was Set Asunder: Rationalities and Responsibility

Aspects are "set asunder" by *Gegenstand* abstraction, but in reality they are intertwined (coherence of meaningfulness, §4–3.1). To forge a good, full understanding of reality we must reunite them (NC,I, 45–52). Without it, we limit ourselves to thin, one-dimensional findings (knowledge) on which it is not reasonable to rely. This reuniting is Dooyeweerd's account of what Kant called "theoretical synthesis" by which new knowledge is generated. Dooyeweerd poses the second transcendental question:

> From what standpoint can we reunite synthetically the logical and the non-logical aspects of experience which were set apart in opposition to each other in the theoretical antithesis?
>
> (NC,I, 45)

(Note: As I understand Dooyeweerd, "logical aspect" here refers to the analytic functioning in standing-against the world, and "non-logical aspects", to its target aspects that are abstracted. The stood-against target can actually include the logical (analytic) aspect itself. See §12–1.11.)

In *philosophy*, this question concerns holistic coherence of meaningfulness (how the aspects relate to each other). In *research in the sciences*, where new knowledge (findings) is derived from data by reasoning, this reuniting is a question of harmonising the rationalities employed therein. As discussed in §4–3.6, each aspect yields a different rationality, irreducible to others, and there is no one overarching rationality—which is why different fields argue differently to generate new knowledge. Whereas Kant was interested in the process of reasoning, Dooyeweerd is more deeply concerned with the grounds for believing we can make sense of reality theoretically.

When generating findings from physical data, we employ physical rationality, alongside kinematic, spatial and quantitative on which the physical aspect depends. In economics, we employ economic, social, lingual, etc. rationalities. In both cases, we might also employ rationalities of later aspects that retrocipatively affect what we are studying. In addition, alongside such aspectual rationalities germane to our field, we employ aspectual rationalities of the analysis method itself, of the quantitative aspect in quantitative research and of the analytic in qualitative research. When interpreting data from interviews, we employ rationalities of the lingual and social aspects. In design research, we employ rationality of the formative aspect (for example about overcoming errors). It is by employing various rationalities together that findings are generated. See the example in §7–1.3.

This raises a version of the question above:

> On what grounds may multiple rationalities be harmonised to generate findings, if they are irreducible to each other?

Dooyeweerd's argument is not entirely clear, but I understand it as follows. We must harness the rationalities in ways that do not yield antinomies, category errors, irrelevances or unwarranted reductions. Since there is no overriding rationality to which appeal may be made (§4–3.6),

- it is the *responsibility of the thinker* to harmonise rationalities, and
- it is *intuition* that enables us to exercise this responsibility.

Regarding the first, exercising this responsibility is part of the full humanity of the thinker (multi-aspectual functioning, §4–3.8.2), including the pistic functioning of believing and committing. Regarding the second, what makes this possible is the fact that each aspect fundamentally coheres with the others (§3–2.4) and that we function with an intuitive grasp of the meaningfulness of each aspect and how they cohere (§4–3.13). It is this intuition that allows us to link the aspects of our experience together (NC,II, 478). Since our harmonisation operates intuitively, we are usually not aware how many rationalities are involved.

Example: Lamb (2014) discusses the use of sociolinguistics in analysing ancient texts (specifically the Gospel and Letters of John in the New Testament). Malina (1985) had argued that the Johannine community was an "antisociety" orientated against its Jewish roots, on the grounds that it used an "antilanguage", as defined by Halliday (1976) in terms of relexicalisation, overlexicalisation, etc. Others (Peterson, Neyrey, Thatcher) argue similarly but with different views of anti-language. Lamb finds flaws in their arguments based on lingual and social rationalities interwoven. For example, Halliday uses "overlexicalization" for a plethora of words for the same thing; Thatcher, for inclusion of new meanings for existing words; and Malina, for a collection of words for different things. It is the rationality of the lingual aspect that makes this problematic. Social arguments include, for example, that whereas these authors treat the Jewish culture as dominant (in relation to Johannine), in fact it is "itself in a subordinate position in wider society" (Lamb 2014, 124). An example of harmonising the two rationalities may be found in statements that link the two, such as "which intentionally uses common vocabulary [lingual rationality] *but* investing it with a disguising exterior to befuddle enemies [social rationality]" (Lamb 2014, 126, emphasis added), which relies on an intuitive understanding of social-lingual inter-dependency (§3–2.4) and whether it implies such a link. Lamb's research is discussed further in §7–1.5.

That example is a critique using rationalities, which will be developed further in §7–1.3. Critique of paradigms goes deeper, concerning such things as the motivations of researchers; for example, why were Malina, etc., keen to argue for an anti-society, and why does Lamb argue against them? This is addressed in Dooyeweerd's third transcendental problem.

6–3.5   Third Transcendental Problem (TP3), Grounds of Critical Self-Reflection: Origin of Meaning

How do we fulfil our responsibility to harmonise the irreducibly distinct rationalities (or, in philosophy, to reunite that which was set asunder)? On what basis may our findings, which emerge from this, be judged as appropriate contributions to bodies of knowledge? Power and interests inevitably operate, as Foucault and Habermas argue, but is it appropriate to just acquiesce to them? Dooyeweerd acknowledges these but poses a deeper question, which incidentally helps us understand these in context.

In philosophy, the challenge is to understand the full, diverse, coherent humanity of the researcher ("Philosopher, know thyself" (NC,I, 5)). Dooyeweerd puts his third transcendental problem in terms of a question about critical self-reflection:

How is this critical self-reflection, this concentric direction of theoretical thought to the I-ness, possible, and what is its true character?

(NC,I, 52)

For an answer, Dooyeweerd argues that the self cannot be grasped theoretically (§4–3.14), but we may understand its multi-aspectual functioning (for which Chapter 10 paints a picture). Accordingly, Dooyeweerd argues (NC,I, 52–68), we end up referring to an "origin of meaning." (Since meaningfulness is what Dooyeweerd meant by "meaning" (§4–1) we call it "*origin of meaningfulness*".)

However, in research, I do not find myself necessarily reflecting on myself. Critical self-reflection takes the form of critique of my own findings, not just in terms of their rationalities, but in terms of my full multi-aspectual functioning as a human being—including such things as my motivations (pistic functioning). So, in research, this transcendental problem takes a different form. Dooyeweerd applies it to philosophical sociology, with the different question,

Where do they find their radical unity and totality of meaning, or in other words, from which starting-point can we grasp them in the theoretical view of totality?

(NC,III, 168)

Both questions concern the totality of meaningfulness, which in this book I call "wider meaningfulness" of research. (Dooyeweerd links this with Kant's transcendental unity of apperception.)

Consider the following critical conversation carried out in the literature about a research finding, F:

Critic 1: "Finding F fails to consider factor X."

Critic 2, "The author has not analysed correctly, and should employ rationality R."

Rejoinder: "But X is not relevant, because Y. Rationality R is inappropriate because S."

Critic 3: "But S/Y are inappropriate in this field, because of T." (About paradigms)

Rejoinder: "But T is the current paradigm and is not appropriate; what is being suggested is a new paradigm U." (Paradigm shift)

Critic 4: "But the U must be resisted (or welcomed) because of O."

The first two criticisms relate to transcendental problems TP1 and TP2, but the others relate to wider meaningfulness. Both Critic 3 and its rejoinder refer to the wider meaningfulness that two paradigms, T and U, supply (see §8–2.2). Critic 4, wanting to critique the paradigms, refers to an ultimate origin of meaning, O.

(With such discourse, the findings are refined and enter the body of knowledge, as general and reasonably reliable beliefs. Discussion of wider meaningfulness is best done through open debate in a community of thought and practice, which may be why Dooyeweerd recognised that this activity is "supra-individual" (NC,I, 59). It is on, or because of, this third transcendental requirement that the whole edifice of theoretical activity has been built, from Socratic debate and the *agora*, to today's conferences, journals, books, institutions, peer reviewing, etc.)

The origin of meaning(fulness) is usually the prevailing ground-motive.

6–3.6   Ground-Motives as Origins of Meaning

Though Dooyeweerd is not entirely clear on this, the origin of meaning is usually the ground-motive, which is the community's presupposition about the totality of meaningfulness, by reference to which alternative paradigms are offered (§5–2.2) and such things as intellectual motivations may be understood. The ground-motives that Dooyeweerd discussed are outlined in §5–2.2, three of which are dialectical and generate conflicts.

Ground-motives seldom enter debates explicitly but rather are the soil in which debates germinate and grow. When the origin of meaning is a dialectical ground-motive, the alternative is sought in the opposite pole.

> Example: The dialogue about whether the Johannine writings are the product of an antisociety may partly be seen as motivated by the Nature-grace (secular-sacred) ground-motive, which still exerts influence in Christian circles, within which this debate takes place. As is discussed in §7–1.5, those who propose antisociety might be reacting against the sacred pole, which treats those writings as unquestionable divine revelation, seeking secular explanations for their content. Lamb is seeking to counter that.

Whereas dialectical ground-motives offer only two ways of being meaningful (freedom, determination for the Humanistic ground-motive), Dooyeweerd's ground-motive (§5–2.4), can offer multiple ways (aspects). In his transcendental critique of theoretical thought in philosophical sociology (NC,III, 168), Dooyeweerd's origin of meaning (the Biblical ground-motive) led him to reject all totalising or reductionist views of society that are based on any single aspectual view (such as family or state), because sociology needs a basis on which to relate to the "totality of meaning". Basden (2018a) likewise argues that Dooyeweerd's approach offers the artificial intelligence community a more fruitful basis for debate. In the Johannine dialogue, Lamb's actual motivation seems a little more than merely resisting secularisation; he wishes to put lingual and social aspects in their proper place in the discourse; see §7–1.5.

> *Research opportunity: ground-motives.* Investigate the benefits or problems of transplanting extant theories from dualistic to Dooyeweerd's pluralistic ground-motive.

6–3.7 Summary

Dooyeweerd went further than other contemporary thinkers who agree that theoretical thought is neither autonomous nor neutral, by revealing transcendentally at least three places where non-neutrality is located:

- TP1: in choice of what it is meaningful to think about;
- TP2: in responsibility for harmonising mutually irreducible rationalities during theoretical synthesis;
- TP3: in reference to a presumed origin of meaning during critique.

These are three ways in which meaningfulness plays a role in research, and they are developed further in Chapter 7.

In these three ways, theoretical thought, whether scientific research or philosophy, is treated as within everyday experience, rather than standing over it in judgment. Theoretical thought is never autonomous, always-already limited and non-neutral, inherently narrowing and distorting whatever we think about, even though it might provide genuine generic insight. This leads to a different understanding of truth.

(Some critiques of Dooyeweerd's transcendental critique are found in Chapter 12.)

6–4. Dooyeweerd's Perspective on Truth

Truth is much more than an adequacy of theoretical knowledge. To Keats, addressing the Grecian urn, "Beauty is Truth, and Truth, Beauty". Dooyeweerd notes that in everyday experience the word "truth" denotes action and fulfilment of what is proper (examples: "You are a true friend"; "The arrow flies true"). Truth as action is recognised by Pragmatism. Dooyeweerd also notes (NC,II, 571–2) that, in the Bible, "truth" connotes steadfastness, certainty, reliability. All these widen the notion of truth beyond the verity of a belief or statement, and most are important in our bodies of knowledge, to which research contributes its findings.

In discussing truth of knowledge, Dooyeweerd differentiates truth as experienced in the pre-theoretical and theoretical attitudes of thought. (So does Husserl (1954/1970, 124–7), though arguably not as richly.) Truth in pre-theoretical experience is more general:

> According to its transcendental a priori dimension truth is: [1] the accordance between [2] the subjective a priori knowledge [2a] enclosed by the temporal horizon, [2b] as expressed in a priori judgments, and [3] the a priori structural laws of human experience [3a] within this temporal horizon. The latter is open (as to its law- and subject-sides) to the light of the transcendent Truth [4] . . . [5].
>
> (NC,II, 573, numbers added; original was all in italics)

We may notice the following. Dooyeweerd, like other philosophers, sees truth of knowledge as an *adequatio* relationship [1] and, like Kant and

Husserl, he recognises the importance of the activity of a knowing-subject [2] and of *a priori* judgments [2b]. But the adequacy of knowledge is not related to being or phenomena but to "a priori structural laws" [3], by which he means what I have called aspectual law (§4–3.8), i.e. to the meaningfulness or "perspective" offered by an aspect. For example, Dooyeweerd made the surprising statement that "2 × 2 = 4 becomes an untruth, if the law-conformable state of affairs, expressed in it, is detached from the temporal world-order" (NC,II, 572). The "law-conformable state of affairs" is the quantitative aspect, and the "temporal world-order" is the law-side comprising all aspects in their coherence, or the "temporal horizon" [3a]. Dooyeweerd links truth, ultimately, to the Divine (NC,II, 572) as Truth, the self-dependent origin of meaning [4].

(Note. The [5] omitted above reads ". . . in Christ." Even though I share Dooyeweerd's religious faith in Christ, I have yet to understand philosophically why the Truth is linked with Christ, whom Dooyeweerd believed and I believe to be the fully human, fully divine Messiah, rather than with the Divine in general. I wonder whether this insertion of Christ is part of his second motivation, in §5–4.1, to define a Christian philosophy, and do not yet understand how it fulfils his first and third motivations, with which this book is concerned. For that reason, I have separated it out to here, so that readers may process it.)

This definition takes knowing, knower and known to be all enabled and dwelling in the same 'ocean of meaningfulness'. It is the ocean that enables reality (which Realism emphasises) and knowing (which Anti-realism emphasises), and the two cannot be separated (§4–3.10, §4–3.12). So neither Dooyeweerd nor I enter the battle between Realism and Anti-realism, whatever form it takes.

For theoretical truth, Dooyeweerd gives a more specialised definition, which has several (numbered) portions (I break them into lines):

"the correspondence of

[1] the subjective a priori meaning-synthesis
[2] as to its intentional meaning with
[3] the modal structure of the 'Gegenstand' of theoretical thought.
[4] This synthesis is actual in our a priori theoretical insight,
[5] and is expressed in theoretical a priori judgments.
[6] The modal 'Gegenstand' is included in its all-sided inter-modal coherence
[7] within the temporal horizon.
[8] This coherence exists both in the foundational and in the transcendental direction of time
[9] and is dependent on the transcendent fulness of the meaning of Truth."
(NC,II, 575, original all in italics)

"This somewhat lengthy description is indispensable," remarks Dooyeweerd, "if we do not wish to omit a single moment in the transcendental structure of theoretical truth." Dooyeweerd follows this with a lengthy discourse (pp. 575–82). For research, we may note:

[1] is the importance of the knower (Kant), and [2], of intentionality (Husserl).

[3] is the multi-aspectual nature of that against which our theoretical thought stands (*Gegenstand*) (§6–3.3). [4] and [5]: theoretical synthesising of data involves aspectual rationalities ("a priori judgments") (§6–3.4). [6]: That, against which our thinking stands (*Gegenstand*), is multi-aspectual, so, for truth, its entire panoply of aspects must be recognised.

[7] refers to all that could possibly be meaningful, given the entire set of law-side aspects (possibly affirming Husserl's recognition of 'worlds' if each 'world' revolves around one main aspect). This makes it important to consider not only the aspect at the core of a science but other, neighbouring, aspects, as discussed in §8–1.3. This is why Maddy found she needed to refer to the physical and other aspects too (§6–1.1) to find mathematical truth. In theoretical thought, though we abstract an aspect out of its coherence, for purposes of study and data-synthesising, we need to keep its coherence with all other aspects actively in mind; an example is given later.

[8] emphasises that truth, even when relative to one aspect, needs to take all aspects into account, both those before it (on which it depends foundationally) and those later than it (which infuse extra meaningfulness).

[9] emphasises that truth is never absolute but always dependent on a transcendent "fullness of meaning," which makes truth possible (see §4–3.1). Truth relates ultimately to what we treat as divine.

We will see the importance of [7] and [8] in understanding fields (§8–1) and paradigms that introduce previously overlooked aspects (§8–2.2). The importance of the other parts becomes clear in Part III.

6–5. Conclusion

Thinkers have long pretended that theoretical thought is neutral (autonomous, absolute), whereas in reality it is not. Dooyeweerd's immanent critique, supported by those of Habermas, Foucault, etc., revealed that it never has been. In an era that still clung to this pretension, Dooyeweerd's transcendental critique

> wages a merciless war against the masking of supra-theoretical prejudices as theoretical axioms which are *forced* upon the opponent on penalty of his being viewed as an outsider in philosophical matters. In other words, it aims its attack against the *dogmatic exclusivism* of the schools, all of which fancy themselves to possess the monopoly on philosophical truth.
>
> (NC,I, 70, emphasis in original)

His critique discloses three fundamental ways in which theoretical thought is never neutral, to do with diversity, unity and totality of meaningfulness. In research, these three transcendental issues take the form of:

- pre-theoretical selection of aspects to abstract as data to study;
- pre-theoretical responsibility for harmonising rationalities by which new knowledge (findings) is generated from the data;
- pre-theoretical/religious appeal to wider meaningfulness and, ultimately, to an origin of meaningfulness, during critique of findings.

These are three ways in which theoretical thought at the core of research refers to the 'ocean' of meaningfulness, in which it takes place.

Not only do these support Dooyeweerd's *deconstruction* of the presuppositions and pretensions about theoretical thought imposed by the immanence-standpoint, they enable *construction* of a clearer understanding of research. With this, we can understand advance in knowledge, can open up dialogue between incommensurable "-isms", free researchers from straitjackets imposed by inappropriate research philosophies, and understand bias, which will be discussed in Chapter 7, and understand fields, paradigms, ideas and concepts, discussed in Chapter 8.

7 Ground-Ideas

How Philosophies Work

Dooyeweerd's second transcendental critique, which was presented in §6–3, identifies three fundamental problems related to theoretical thought. They concern three roles that meaningfulness plays in theoretical thought and, together, form what Dooyeweerd called a *Ground-Idea* (NC,I, 68–79):

- *world and its diversity*: aspects of world/reality that are abstracted as data;
- *coherence/unity*: especially, in research, of rationalities applied to data to generate new theoretical knowledge;
- *totality of meaningfulness*: what the community presupposes as origin of, or wider, meaningfulness.

Ground-Ideas are useful in research because they give us a systematic way of uncovering philosophical presuppositions that lie at the foundation of research. Using a computer science simile, the three elements are like metadata for philosophy that underlies research.

Note: *Ground-Ideas* are not the same as *ground-motives* discussed in Chapter 5; they are 'grounding', foundational, in different ways. Ground-motives often provide the third Ground-Idea element (§6–3.6).

This chapter examines Dooyeweerd's notion of three-part Ground-Idea in relation to research (§7–1), to address various challenges, of advances in knowledge (§7–2), dialogue (§7–3), research philosophy and research bias (§7–4). Use of the Ground-Idea notion continues in Chapter 8.

7–1. Dooyeweerd's Notion of Three-Part Ground-Idea

The three elements of Ground-Ideas—diversity, coherence and totality—take different forms in sciences and philosophy. Whereas philosophy concerns itself with the breadth of diversity and coherence of meaningfulness (NC,I, 4), science is orientated towards single aspects and explores them in depth.

7–1.1 Ground-Ideas of Philosophy

When applied to philosophy, the three Ground-Idea elements boil down to the way philosophy addresses diversity, coherence and totality. Each philosophical stream or school has a different combination of presuppositions about these, which influences the formulation of every philosophic problem (NC,I, 22ff).

Dooyeweerd summarises the Ground-Ideas of various philosophical streams, including Thomistic metaphysics (NC,I, 71–3), Husserl's Phenomenology (pp. 73–4), Marburg neo-Kantianism (pp. 74–6), Litt's dialectical logic (pp. 75–6) and the Greek, Parmenides (pp. 79–82). For example, Husserl supposes he can "pass beyond" the diversity of meaningfulness by logical formalizing, trying to understand "The whole is more than the sum of its parts" (coherence) in purely logical-mathematical terms (totality). Nevertheless, Dooyeweerd recognises later, at least Husserl recognises diversity more than Kant does (§6–1.2) (NC,II, 569–70).

This exemplifies a more general tendency among philosophic thinkers, of raising an issue and then trying to work it out, either accounting for it or, seeing it as problematic, trying to solve it. Husserl recognises diversity in the world (the issue he believes Kant had overlooked, §6–1.2), accounts for it via his notion of lifeworld, but then sees this diversity as a problem for science and tries to solve the problem by appealing to the power of logic—a move that Dooyeweerd criticises. Why does he appeal to logic to do so? Because he adopts the immanence-standpoint, which has never really welcomed diversity (§5–3.1) and has always presupposed the absolute sufficiency of logic (theoretical thinking, §2–1.2, §2–3.3).

I find it useful, when critiquing theoretical thought, to differentiate identification of issues previously overlooked from attempts to work them out. Issue-identification is often helpful, ultimately fuelled by the nature of reality and can be affirmed, while working-out is often more influenced by the immanence-standpoint and dialectical ground-motives, and should be critiqued. Such differentiation helps me pursue LACE (Listen-Affirm-Critique-Enrich, §5–5, §10–1) cleanly, and Dooyeweerd's notion of Ground-Idea is very helpful. As §7–3 shows, revealing the Ground-Ideas of philosophies can open the door to dialogue between them and break down their "dogmatic exclusivism" (NC,I, 70).

Whether Dooyeweerd's proposal is of universal validity is yet to be properly tested; Choi (2000) finds it difficult to apply to some Korean thought, though I do not think that he has fully explored all possibilities. My experience is that it is useful in scientific research, but there the three elements take more focused forms than in philosophy. We examine each in turn.

7–1.2   *Diversity of World*

The first transcendental problem (§6–3.3) is about what we abstract as meaningful when we take a theoretical attitude, and Dooyeweerd's answer was *aspects*. Abstraction of focal aspects yields data as conceptualised 'pieces of meaningfulness' (§4–3.11.1).

To understand this helps us address three challenges researchers face. (1) On what basis may we differentiate fields and areas of research and tackle boundary issues? (2) On what basis is it valid to accept types of data, or to restrict what we accept? (3) On what grounds may we judge the use of instruments in research—hardware, software or conceptual? The first will be discussed in Chapter 8, the other two here.

7-1.2.1 Data From the World

The idea of aspects of world offers fresh insights on data collection in research.

Functioning in the analytic aspect, we target (§4–3.9) certain *focal aspects* that are meaningful to us as researchers—physical things for physicists, social, for sociologists, and perhaps several aspects in interdisciplinary research and anthropology—and form concepts of aspectual beings (§4–3.3) we see in the world. See Section 11–7 for examples of analysing interview transcripts.

In most sciences, by focusing on certain aspects, we ignore others—in the physical sciences we ignore e.g. social issues (Suppe 1972). Narrow selection of what is meaningful as data can be a source of unreliability in the content of research. Issues that are relevant may be overlooked, often because they are meaningful in aspects other than the focal aspect(s). Later research might uncover them, but that takes much time.

Example: From the information systems (IS) field, with which I am familiar, I am using Davis' (1989) *Technology Acceptance Model* (TAM) to illustrate several points in several chapters. As discussed in §3–5.2, Davis sought to understand what factors lead people to accept and use, rather than reject and ignore, information technology (IT). Using the hypothesis-testing approach, he constructed a model from various theories of human behaviour (Figure 3.2 in §3–5.4) and tested it by surveying users of IT and, from the data collected, showed it was statistically reliable. It became a widely referenced model, but then had to be improved.

As discussed in §3–5.2, the external variables that Davis employed in his original study are almost all meaningful in the formative aspect and another aspect (which varies), and then other studies in different contexts of use found many more external variables meaningful. Yousafzai et al. (2007) collected over 80 of them. To provide some semblance of order, they sorted them into four categories: "Organizational", "Personal", "System" (i.e. technological), and "Other" characteristics. This categorisation shows three problems. (a) It gives little insight into the nature of the diversity of characteristics of the usage situation that are meaningful to users (see §11–7.3). (b) That many variables are found in the "Other" category suggests there are some meaningful categories still to be elucidated. (c) Their classification is heterogeneous, composed from two dualities, socio-technical and personal-organisational.

What I have found is that Dooyeweerd's aspects can offer a much better way to categorise the issues, which is finer-grain, shows why "other" characteristics are meaningful, and is homogeneous. It reunites issues seen as similar in everyday experience (e.g. support) which had been separated in the original categories. Table 7.1 shows the variables by aspect and by the original categories; see Basden (2018a) for fuller discussion.

Table 7.1 The diversity of external variables of TAM

Aspect	Organisational	Info. System	Personal	Other
Quantitative				
Spatial				
Kinematic		Navigation		
Physical				
Organic / Biotic			Age, gender	
Psychic / Sensitive		Interface, Response time	Personality	
Analytic		Perceived complexity, Visibility	Awareness, Cognitive absorption	Task characteristics
Formative	Internal computing training, Peer usage, Training, Transitional support	Convenience, Objective usability, Perceived risk, Screen design, Trialability	Educational level, Experience, Personal innovativeness, Self-efficacy, Skills & knowledge	External computing training, Facilitating conditions
Lingual		Information quality, Output quality, Result demonstrability, Terminology	Computer literacy	Argument for change
Social	Image, End-user support, Internal comp. support, Management support, Organisational support, Organisational structure	Social presence	Involvement, Perceived developer's responsiveness, Role with technology	Cultural affinity, External comp. support, Situational normality, Social influence, Social pressure, Vendor's cooperation

Aspect			
Economic	Accessibility, Access cost, Response time	Perceived resources, Tenure in workforce	
Aesthetic	Compatibility, Media style, Perceived attractiveness	Perceived enjoyment Perceived playfulness	
Juridical	Relevance with job, Confirmation mechanism, Perceived s/w correctness, Accuracy, System quality, Web security		Subjective norms, Task technology fit
Ethical / Attitudinal	Competitive environment	Computer attitude, Voluntariness, Trust	
Pistic / Faith	Group's innovativeness norm, Job insecurity, Peer influence, Organisational use	Perceived importance, Reliability	Computer anxiety, Intrinsic motivation, Shopping orientation

The refinement of TAM has taken 20 years to gradually rediscover how each aspect is relevant, in an ad hoc way. If Davis had taken account of every aspect in his original model, might it have shortened the refinement period?

7–1.2.2   On Sources of Data

More generally, considering the aspects that are abstracted can untangle concerns over the sources of data.

One of these is, when is it appropriate to use fictional accounts as data for research? Studying fiction as literary work is valid in the field of literary studies, but can it ever be valid to provide data in sociology? Vallone (2018) studies people's reactions to human sizes (miniaturism, gigantism, obesity). Along with data from real-life cases, she includes input data from literary works, including fiction. Had her study been primarily of the actual sizes or psychology of small or large people (spatial, psychical aspects), then fictional accounts from literature would have been inappropriate, because they express the authors' beliefs, which might depart from reality. However, it is valid in her study because it is not of human sizes as such, nor of health nor even psychological issues, but of the social aspect of agreement and expectations about size (agreement: §9–1.10).

Another concern is a constraining influence that has come down from philosophy. The presumption that data for research comes from the senses (§6–3.3) and from this we deduce meaningful findings does not describe adequately the actual experience of researchers. Opinions in literature are not *deduced* from eye-patterns of the reader. Economists do not *deduce* items like costs or inflation from their sensory impressions, but directly intuit them from what they observe, hear or read. Rather, the reader *functions intuitively* in multiple aspects, psychically to see them, lingually to treat them as content, analytically to distinguish relevant from irrelevant content, and in the target focal aspect to understand that relevance. Our data comes to us directly via these intuitive aspectual functionings. Even physicists directly intuit items of physical meaningfulness, rather than deduce them from sensory impressions.

The element of world aspects offers a clear understanding of this diversity of data sources.

7–1.2.3   Secondary Data and Use of Instruments

This can throw fresh light on the conventional difference between primary and *secondary data*. Secondary data are data originally collected for some other primary purpose and are often documentary in form, either written or pictorial (Saunders et al. 2012). For example, the historian, the economist and even medics might all study the same newsreel feed. How is this possible? If Dooyeweerd is correct, though data might be meaningful in a primary aspect, it still exhibits all other aspects (§3–2.4.1, §4–3.8.2), which we might here call "secondary". So, sometimes hidden away, in all data, is the potential to be meaningful in other ways, to be data for other kinds of research. The newsreel from a war front shows human decisions, which might be of interest to the historian; use of resources, of interest to the economist; injuries, death and disease, which might be of interest to medics, and many other aspects. This multi-aspectuality is capitalised on in §11–7.2 to find hidden meanings.

Because it studies the past, *research in history* relies heavily on secondary sources. See, for example, Searle's (2005) discussion of the Tolsdorff trials, which shows, from sundry sources, the multi-aspectual 'everyday' factors that affected those trials, beyond juridical logic. This poses a challenge: On what basis may we properly understand the past (*cross-era research*)? Dooyeweerd's distinction between law- and fact-side realities (§4–3.8) is useful and, though the fact-side in which the researcher operates (cultural, religious, economic, technological context) might differ markedly from those of the past, the law-side—the 'ocean' of meaningfulness (§4–3.10)—remains the same. At the deep level of spheres of meaningfulness, what is meaningful to those studied is similarly meaningful in basic ways to the researcher, and vice versa, even though some of that meaningfulness might not have been opened up in the past. This suggests that aspectual analysis of texts, like that discussed in §11–7.2, might assist cross-era and cross-cultural research in history.

Dooyeweerd recognises the use of tools or *instruments in research*, whether hardware like microscopes or conceptual like theoretical models (NC,III, 31). Today, we might add computer software, such as analysis packages or *Twitter*. Though the instruments themselves are products of earlier theoretical thought, they have become part of the everyday experience of the activity that is research (c.f. §2–6.1).

Theoretical models, like ontological taxonomies, models and prior theories, enable researchers to 'see' things that would not have been 'visible' otherwise, acting as the 'lens' through which the world is seen. The instrument intensifies an aspect. This can be problematic when this is other than, or narrower than, the proper focal aspect of the research.

Example: In testing his model (Figure 3.2), Davis (1989) used several extant theories to 'see' the world of IT use, by providing concepts to look for. These include Self-Efficacy Theory, Adoption of Innovations, Theory of Reasoned Action, the Cost-Benefit Paradigm, etc. They intensified psychical and formative aspects and some analytic and economic. As a result, Davis' original model proved too aspectually narrow to cope with many kinds of IT use (§7–1.2.1) and, because of the intense focus on the formative aspect, his study is limited to voluntary use and not to mandatory use, which is meaningful in the social aspect of agreement; see §7–1.4.

Similarly, mathematical models are widely used in physics. Since the physical aspect depends foundationally on the mathematical aspects, they are relevant, but if over-emphasised without regard for physical meaningfulness, there is a danger of distortion: "The current emphasis on mathematics has gone too far" (Bohm & Peat 1987, 7).

7–1.3   Coherence of Rationalities

The second transcendental problem (§6–3.4) concerns reuniting the aspects that were "set asunder" during abstraction (NC,I, 45). *In philosophy*, this concerns the general unity or coherence of meaningfulness: how the aspects inter-relate, which the immanence-standpoint obscures (§5–3.1).

In the sciences, it concerns the harmonising of rationalities, by which we make sense of the data to generate new knowledge, i.e. findings (§6–3.4). Recall that rationality (sense-making) differs in each aspect (§4–3.6). Reference to aspects and their dependency, analogy and other relationships (§3–2.4) can assist harmonisation of rationalities.

It is obvious that rationalities must be harmonised in interdisciplinary research—that of each cooperating discipline. But even in single-focus research, multiple rationalities manifest themselves in at least five ways:

- the central rationality of the focal aspect(s) being studied;
- rationalities of the aspects those depend on;
- rationalities of data collection;
- rationalities of analysis method;
- rationalities of situating the research (contributions, recommendations).

It is from this mix of rationalities that the findings are generated from the data.

Example: Davis (1989) used questionnaires with Likert-scale questions to obtain data, analysing it by quantitative means. We may detect a number of rationalities involved.

- Build a list of factors related to PEOU, PU (Figure 3.2): formative and psychical rationalities, along with multiple aspects of the everyday life of users as secondary.
- Word these as questions: lingual rationality.
- After pilot study, decide that certain external variables were similar to others and hence could be combined: analytic.
- Rank them by importance: quantitative rationality.
- In main study, assess the importance of each ranked external variable to PEOU and PU, for example comparing Critical to My Job 0.87, Quality of Work 0.80: quantitative.
- In deciding the importance of such differences, the wise researcher takes into account the everyday experience of the situations of use . . .: multiple aspects;
- . . . and the aspects of the activity of answering questions (for example those with an axe to grind might answer Critical to My Job more strongly: pistic rationality).
- Cronbach's Alpha was used to measure internal consistency: quantitative with juridical rationality (the results ought to be consistent).
- Taking the professional context into account (e.g. Work More Quickly since time is a limited resource in work): economic rationality.

At least eight rationalities are involved in what seems, at first sight, to be a simple piece of hypothesis-testing. Dooyeweerd argues the poverty of Russell's approach which reduces all rationalities to the mathematical and analytic (NC,III, 24–6). In the natural sciences, perhaps, fewer rationalities might be involved, but they usually include at least the quantitative, analytic, physical and those it depends on.

Since (§6–3.4, §4–3.6) no rationality can be derived from others, and there is no overriding rationality by which harmonisation may be judged or ensured, researchers need to be aware of which rationalities they employ and of their responsibility in employing them.

Research opportunity: research rationalities. Very few discuss research rationalities explicitly. Study which are used in research and how researchers use them appropriately and inappropriately.

7–1.4   Wider Meaningfulness and Origin of Meaning

As discussed in §6–3.5, Dooyeweerd's third transcendental problem, concerning the grounds for critical self-reflection, directs us to wider meaningfulness and the origin of meaning. Whereas in philosophy the origin of meaning is that "spiritual mainspring", the ground-motive (§5–2.2), my experience has been that aspects play an important part in the sciences (§5–2.4).

In philosophy, critical self-reflection might include "Philosopher, know thyself", but in the sciences this is not introspective reflection of one's own self but rather critical reflection on the part that human selves (both researcher and researched) play in generating findings. This is recognised in Klein & Myers' (1999) principles 3 and 7 for interpretive research, which urge researchers to question both the effect of the researcher and what the researched say.

The wider meaningfulness, which involves all aspects, is what most fundamentally motivates the research, circumscribes the debates about research findings (example in §6–3.5) and provides the basis for critical discussion of research findings. A worked example, of analysing motivations by aspect, is given in §11–2.2 and §11–7.2, where two examples of wider aspects are discussed, from psychology and information systems.

One major issue in critique of research findings is *reproducibility*. Only if findings can be reproduced is it reasonable to rely on them. In psychology, less than half of findings are reproducible (Open Science Collaboration (OSC) 2015), casting doubt even on some widely relied upon theories in psychology, neuroscience and medicine. Why is reproducibility so low? The OSC discusses one reason in *research activity*, a pistic functioning (desire for innovation rather than verification), but ignores others.

Research opportunity: reproducibility. Dooyeweerd's aspects of research activity (Table 3.1, Chapter 10) might enable us to reveal others, such as the ethical dysfunction that is rivalry, and as follows.

But is there also a problem with *research content*? Reproducibility requires similar functioning under similar conditions, but what constitutes "similar"? Dooyeweerd's philosophy helps to tease this out. The focal aspects in psychology and medicine are the organic, psychic and analytic, functioning in which may be affected (a) foundationally by physical and organic conditions and (b) retrocipatively by functioning in the eight post-analytic aspects (§3–2.4). Taking into account the various ways that later aspects affect the focal aspects can be important in discussing reproducibility. Whereas in animals the effect of the later aspects is largely object-functioning (§4–3.9) and hence passive, in humans it is subject-functioning and therefore active and likely to be more unpredictable. So human psychology is likely to be more variable and varying, hence less reproducible.

In information systems, since we are always concerned with human functioning in later aspects, and not just their retrocipatory effect, reproducibility, fundamentally, cannot be an ideal. So critical discussion takes a different form, exemplified by the reception of Davis' (1989) *Technology Acceptance Model*. Initially, TAM was critically discussed by testing it with different kinds of information system, in different situations, and with different external variables (world aspects); see §7–1.2.1. Then the debate widened. TAM was criticised for assuming voluntary use of information technology and for ignoring major demographic information about IT users, such as age and gender, and other models emerged, including new versions of TAM. These criticisms are valid because of wider meaningfulness—beyond TAM's focal formative-psychical aspects (§7–1.2). Much organisational use of IT is mandatory (social aspect), not voluntary. Current research culture expects demographic factors to be included (organic aspect). Indeed, as Table 7.1 shows, nearly every aspect is relevant; a multi-aspectual approach to wider meaningfulness relocates research findings in everyday experience.

Another effect of wider meaningfulness is that TAM is ignored, rejected or used as a counter-example in much interpretivist research as being positivistic in approach. There is little logical reason for such rejection; it is motivated "religiously" (§5–2.3) by the Nature-Freedom ground-motive which, as discussed in §6–3.6, serves as origin of meaningfulness that informs the community that the remedy for (positivistic) constraint is (interpretivistic) freedom. Adopting Dooyeweerd's multi-aspectual ground-motive can integrate positivistic and interpretivistic approaches (see §7–3 below), so we may accept TAM (though we might question TAM's over-emphasis on the formative aspect).

7–1.5   Ground-Idea Analysis: Example From Sociolinguistics

Ground-Idea analysis may be illustrated with Lamb's (2014) monograph, which employs Halliday's (1976) sociolinguistic notion of *antilanguage* to cast doubt on a socio-theological paradigm, which was introduced in §6–3.4. This sees the Gospel and Letters ascribed to John in the New Testament not as Divine revelation, but as expressing the views and culture of a separate "Johannine Community"

(JComm) that is an "antisociety'. This view is taken as an assumed truth, needing no explanation. Lamb's argument is that the paradigm became accepted on rather shaky grounds and cannot be supported by sociolinguistic analysis of the text. We may see each of the three Ground-Idea elements as follows.

1. Lamb's '*world*', from which he obtains data, is composed of significations of material that he read in (a) publications that discuss the paradigm, (b) publications that introduce and develop the antilanguage paradigm and (c) excerpts from the Gospel and Letters. The data he abstracts from this world is meaningful in three main aspects, lingual, social and pistic, reflecting his intention to apply sociolinguistics to socio-theology. Apart from aspects on which these three most depend foundationally (formative, lingual and ethical), data that could be abstracted from most other aspects play little part.

2. The *rationalities* related to the focal aspects of sociolinguistic research are primarily lingual (e.g. about questions, adverbs and pronouns, and about antilanguage, including Halliday's (1976) re- and over-lexicalisation) and social (e.g. about interactivity, personal stance, shared knowledge and antisociety) (Lamb 2014, 100–1). Lamb's criticism of a "false assumption that there is a direct link between antilanguage and antisociety" (p. 140) expresses the irreducibility between the lingual and social aspects (§3–2.3). His discussion over the presumed form of relationship between antilanguage and antisociety expresses their inter-aspect dependency (§3–2.4.4). Since Lamb's concern is socio-theological, he also employs pistic rationality, e.g. that "ideological use of [the notion of] antilanguage" (p. 139) gives flawed arguments.

The rationality of data collection is also lingual, in interpreting what writers mean. Several other rationalities are employed in arguing his findings from the interpreted data—the analytic about distinctions and contradictions, the quantitative about "Not enough data" (p. 138), and the juridical in criticising too heavy reliance on antilanguage, which Halliday saw as a provisional proposal (pp. 117–9).

3. The third element, *wider meaningfulness*, draws attention to the often implicit pre-theoretical motivations that underlie the coming-into-being of the paradigm and reactions against it. They may perhaps be discerned in Lamb's discussion of the JComm paradigm, its rise and fall, in which he briefly presents arguments of authors, for and against. One must lift the foliage of the arguments to see the ground-motive soil in which the paradigm germinated, grew and might wither (see §6–3.6).

We may detect the influence of the Nature-grace ground-motive in the pro-antisociety authors seeking secular explanations for the Gospel and Letters instead of traditional revelation ideas and, in the reaction by other authors, back toward the sacred. The sacred-to-secular move might be seen in replacing religious communities with "intellectual schools" (Lamb, 9) and in such statements as "Martyn relates much of the action in the GJ not to the life of Jesus but rather to events in the life of the JComm" (p. 7). Moreover, the pro-JComm seminal author, Brown (1967), explicitly sets his ideas in context of Bultmann's demythologisation. The secular-to-sacred reaction may be seen in "a desire to defend the traditional apostolic authorship of the GJ" (Lamb, 15).

However, in many of Lamb's very brief summaries the sacred-secular dialectic is not easily discerned. In these, we may detect, rather, emphasis on different aspects that were previously overlooked in a Scholastic view dominated by the pistic aspect. A Dooyeweerdian view implies multiple explanations, from various aspects. Authors whom Lamb summarises emphasise the lingual, social, formative and juridical aspects especially, which enable, and are influenced by, the pistic functioning. Lamb's own argument covers all these more fully and also others, including the aesthetic aspect.

To see wider meaningfulness as a panoply of spheres of meaningfulness might be a useful alternative to seeing it as a ground-motive, especially if the dialectical ground-motives are problematic (§5–2.4). This is elaborated in §7–2.2.

> *Research opportunity: Ground-Idea analysis.* The above is only indicative; full techniques of Ground-Idea analysis need to be further developed.

7–1.6 Reflection

Dooyeweerd argues that any full philosophy—underpinning research—takes a position on the three transcendental problems, with a three-part Ground-Idea, of world diversity, unity and wider meaningfulness. Philosophies may be characterised by reference to the positions they take on these. The notion of Ground-Idea offers a way of deconstructing the relationship between research and philosophy, without destroying it.

With the three-part Ground-Idea, four triples have been introduced. Do they relate to each other? They are:

- Research content, activity and application (Chapter 1)—these are three main things to discuss about research, of which there might be more.
- Relationships of researcher to world, pre-theoretical to theoretical thinking and pre-theoretical to theoretical knowledge (Chapter 2)— these express subject, functioning and object (§4–3.9).
- Roles of philosophy in research, as approach, foundations and source of conceptual tools (Chapter 5)—these are three that I have found important; there may be more.
- Ground-Idea elements, world diversity, unity especially of rationalities, and wider totality of meaningfulness (Chapter 7)—the first two express the diversity and coherence discussed in Chapter 3, and the 'ocean' of meaningfulness (Chapter 4). The idea of origin of meaning expresses the fundamentally referential characteristic of meaning and some of the presuppositions held by society.

There seems to be no direct connection between the triples, except that origin of meaningfulness relates to philosophy-as-approach. How each triple relates to others has yet to be explored.

We will now discuss several issues that challenge research, continuing into Chapter 8.

7–2.   On Progress and Advance in Knowledge

Research presupposes advance in theoretical knowledge is a good thing. In PhDs, "originality" is demanded. But what is advance, progress or originality in knowledge? Accepting progress as the opening up of the potential of aspects (§4–3.8.3), we may understand research as contributing generic, reliance-worthy *understanding of aspects* to humanity's bodies of knowledge— about aspects as law-spheres and as modes of being, functioning, possibility, rationality and good (§4–3). How does such advance occur?

Traditionally it has been seen either as incremental improvement of the detail, accuracy or flexibility of theories or the entry of radical new ideas that replace older theories by something that explains more (such as Einstein's Theory of Relativity), which Kuhn (1962) calls "normal science" and "scientific revolutions" or "paradigm shifts" respectively. (See §8–2 for discussion of what paradigms are.)

7–2.1   Clarification Offered by the Notion of Ground-Idea

Dooyeweerd's notion of Ground-Idea can make sense of both types of advance, and perhaps ameliorate existing problems by basing both types in meaningfulness.

- In relation to world aspects, we may see advance as either a deepened understanding of aspects of reality already recognised (incremental) or as introducing new aspects previously overlooked (radical).
- In relation to rationalities, we may see advances as either better harmonisation of rationalities (incremental) or as introducing new rationalities (radical).
- In relation to wider meaningfulness, we may see advances as either suggesting more aspects of wider meaningfulness (incremental) or as moving away from dualistic and exclusivist attitudes in the field to pluralistic, more inclusivistic thinking, when the field begins to move away from its presupposition of a dialectical opposition towards multi-aspectual respect (radical).

For example, Klein & Myers' (1999) study of interpretive field studies shows most of these. Their paper, though about a research approach (and used as such elsewhere in this book), is itself research insofar as they surveyed the field of information systems research and added seven principles for interpretive research to its body of knowledge. Its world-aspect was primarily the formative, of how research was carried out, collecting data about actual interpretive research activities. It was both incremental, in deepening our understanding of interpretive studies, and radical, in crystallising principles that had previously only been tacit. In regard to its rationality, it was incremental that it drew out principles, by the lingual rationality of the hermeneutic cycle, the analytic rationality of generalising, and others. In relation to wider meaningfulness, it proved to be a radical shift, in that they suggested that principles could guide interpretive research. In this, Klein & Myers went against the grain of the Freedom pole of the Nature-Freedom ground-motive, which had dominated interpretive research, in suggesting something that might constrain such research: principles.

The widespread acclaim for the paper (cited nearly 10,000 times) shows that it resonates with the everyday experience of interpretive research: researchers had been floundering in a sea of "freedom" and yearned for principles by which their supposed freedom of interpretation could be meaningful and fruitful.

7–2.2   Accounts of Dialectic

Paradigm shifts often occur dialectically. Hegel's idea of dialectic offers one account of progress, which he believed could explain all development, of organisms, of plots in novels, of philosophical ideas and indeed of all reality from Matter to Spirit (Aquila 1985). It is development of philosophical ideas that interests us. A simple understanding of Hegel is that ideas advance by a cycle of thesis-antithesis-synthesis: an idea (thesis) becomes dominant, an opposing one (antithesis) arises, then they are merged (synthesis), which becomes dominant, and the cycles continue. What drives this is "contradiction": each thesis contains its own negation, which emerges as its antithesis.

Basden (1999) argues that this echoes Dooyeweerd's notion of how dialectical ground-motives generate worldviews, which offers a slightly better explanation, especially as it humanises it. Basden then suggests that Dooyeweerd's notion of aspects offers an even better explanation for such development. An aspect is accorded dominant importance (paradigm), gradually the problems of absolutising it become apparent as the importance of the other aspects asserts itself (since all aspects function in coherence), courageous thinkers begin to draw attention to one of these aspects, which attracts interest and investigation, and a new paradigm arises. Eventually this becomes dominant. Hegelian "contradiction" lies in all the initially ignored aspects, since no aspect can be isolated from others.

Thus advance is seen no longer as dialectical swings, but as a sequence of discovery of the importance of aspects to the field, one by one. This offers a more nuanced, fine-grain account of what actually happened in, for example, the environmental movement (Basden 1999), oriented to mutual respect instead of dialectical opposition. See §8–2 for a discussion about paradigms.

7–3.   Ground-Ideas as a Basis for Dialogue

Dooyeweerd believed his notion of Ground-Ideas might "pave the way for a real contact of thought among the various philosophical trends" (NC,I, 70, 526)—even those apparently incommensurable—because they make visible the deepest presuppositions. This is exactly what I found in the information systems field and discuss in Basden (2011a).

7–3.1 An Example: Positivist, Interpretivist and Socio-Critical Approaches

The supposedly incommensurable research approaches of Positivism, Interpretivism and Socio-criticalism may be integrated into a single understanding of research by Ground-Idea analysis. The following is a summary of Basden (2011a).

> *Note on terminology: critical.* Often, "critical" in the "critical approach" or "critical theory" can be confused with "critical" in philosophy or in practical life. So we use "socio-critical approach" here, which emphasises its interest in social structures.

As suggested in §5–2.4, the apparent incommensurability is based on presupposed polar opposition in the Nature-Freedom ground-motive, Positivism aligning with the Nature pole, Interpretivism with the Freedom pole. Socio-critical approaches try to bridge the two but presuppose the gulf they try to bridge, ending up in antinomy. A Ground-Idea analysis using aspects can take us further.

The *positivist approach*, in brief, aims to test hypotheses for 'truth' by empirical research, usually involving quantitative measures and statistical reasoning and often constructing predictive models. It presupposes (*origin of meaningfulness*) that reality operates by invariant, causal, largely mechanical laws, by analogy with the physical aspect, and it tries to minimise expressions of freedom in both researcher and researched world. From the *world*, it abstracts quantified 'facts' obtained by measurement or statistics. For *rationality*, it demands detachment and suppression of opinion, belief or ethics, and a reduction to logical-statistical rationality in order to minimise free variability. (TAM is not purely positivistic.)

The *interpretivist approach*, drawing on phenomenology, aims not to test hypotheses but to gain insight about what is meaningful in situations, and then harmonise the multiplicity of issues encountered. It welcomes opinions, as indicators of what is meaningful, and recognises these are shaped by *Weltanschauungen* (Checkland 1981). From the *world*, interpretive research abstracts idiographic interpretations, each distinguished from others by clearly articulating its detail and context ("social and historical background" (Klein & Myers 1999, 72)). Its *rationality* is aesthetic rather than logical, seeking harmony between detail and context (hermeneutic cycle), and usually lingual since most data is mediated via utterances. Interpretivism's *origin of meaningfulness* presupposition is the importance of beliefs, assumptions and *Weltanschauungen* (pistic aspect). Since the Nature-Freedom ground-motive sees these as expressions of freedom, they go unquestioned, so interpretivist research fails to properly understand or challenge social structures (the status quo), belief structures and norms (Hirschheim et al. 1995).

The *socio-critical approach* takes account of these and seeks to question prevailing assumptions. It presupposes that the situation in every discipline is dysfunctional, because of oppressive power structures. Its *world* consists of social structures to be critiqued and transformed. The main *rationality* is pistic, involving subversion of the status quo and apologetics in relation to socio-critical authors, whose writings are treated as revelatory: Myers & Klein's (2011) first principle of socio-critical research is adherence to an accepted socio-critical theory. They name Habermas, Foucault and Bourdieu, but I have argued that Dooyeweerd could be included (Basden 2002). The differences between variants complicates the picture with secondary aspects: formative for Foucault's power, lingual for Habermas' communicative action, juridical for Bourdieu's "violence", as well as ethical rationality for Myers & Klein's (2011) emphasis on self-critique (discussed in Basden (2011a)).

The wider *origin of meaningfulness* that motivates critique and transformation is a presupposition of 'wrongness', from which emancipation is sought (juridical aspect). How this is seen is dictated by the Nature-Freedom ground-motive: Emancipation is the solution to wrongness offered by that ground-motive (and causes paradox: §5–2.4). Other ground-motives might offer alternative solutions to oppression. The Nature-grace ground-motive might offer escape to a 'heaven', while the Creation-Fall-Redemption ground-motive might offer restitution and transformation.

Table 7.2 shows these aspects of the world, rationalities and origin of meaning that are most important to positivist (P), interpretivist (I) and socio-critical (C) approaches. C2 indicates secondary aspects of socio-critical.

7–3.2   Reflection

If we adopt Dooyeweerd's ground-motive, we can accept the simultaneous validity of these approaches so they may work together, each making its own unique contribution. Conflict may be replaced with cooperation. This analysis provides spaces where other approaches may be located, such as action research, which is included in the Ground-Idea analysis in Basden (2018a, 97–101).

> *Research opportunity: research approaches.* Apply this analysis to research approaches, "isms" or paradigms in any field, including to Burrell & Morgan's (1979) sociological paradigms.

This does not offer one single integrated approach. Rather, it offers a basis for dialogue among the approaches. My aspectual analysis might be over-simple (for example, §7–1.3 finds eight rationalities active in TAM, which took a positivist approach), and in each approach other aspects might be found important, but this does at least demonstrate the possibility of Dooyeweerd's notion of Ground-Idea in showing where dialogue is possible. (It also, Basden (2009) argues, overcomes an impracticality that some find in the socio-critical approach.)

Table 7.2 Main aspects of positivist (P), interpretivist (I) and socio-critical (C) approaches. Based on Basden (2011a) and Basden (2018a).

Aspect	World	Rationality	Origin of Meaning
Quantitative	P: quantified 'facts'	P: quantitative methods	
Spatial			
Kinematic			
Physical			P: mechanistic causality
Organic			
Psychical			
Analytic	I: distinct cases (interpretations of detail and context)	P: logical (detached observer)	
Formative		C2: power (Foucault)	
Lingual		I: hermeneutic C2: communicative (Habermas)	
Social	C: social structures		
Economic			
Aesthetic		I: harmonising (researcher as sense-maker)	
Juridical		C2: violence (Bourdieu)	C: 'wrongness' in structures, from which emancipation is sought
Ethical / Attitudinal		C2: self-critique (Myers & Klein)	
Pistic / Faith		C: subversion, apologetics	I: beliefs, *Weltanschauungen* (accepted without question)

7–4. Applications of Ground-Ideas in Research Projects

How the notion of Ground-Idea can be of practical use in planning research is discussed in Section 11–1. Here, a couple of general points are discussed.

7–4.1 *Ground-Ideas as Research Philosophy*

As discussed in Chapter 5, research is influenced by philosophy and researchers are expected to identify and justify the philosophical basis of their research. It is sometimes difficult, however, to identify precisely one extant philosophy that is suitable, either because their community tends to presume a philosophy without discussion or because no single philosophy suits their research. In the latter case, researchers, especially those undertaking PhD, are sometimes expected to give lip service to an accepted philosophy that is not really appropriate.

With Ground-Ideas, both these problems might be ameliorated. If Dooyeweerd is correct that all philosophies presuppose something about diversity, coherence and totality (origin) of meaningfulness, then it should be adequate if a researcher, instead of identifying one named philosophy, discusses how their research approaches diversity, coherence and totality directly.

For example, Walsham (2001, 66–74, 91) reports a case study into the behaviour of hardware support engineers in response to their company requiring them to work from home rather than office, and installing a computer system, Traveller, to facilitate communications. The experience of three engineers, G, K and N, are described, gleaned from in-depth interviews and observations. The research philosophy is Foucault's ideas on power-knowledge. The 'world' of this study is, ostensibly, the full experience of their working (hence every aspect is potentially relevant), but in fact focuses on how Traveller was used for surveillance and control (a Foucauldian theme, which emphasises the formative aspect). The findings are about power. While this is arguably appropriate for N and K, to describe G as "leveraging power over" (p. 91) the company radically distorts our picture of him. In fact, the exact opposite seems to be the case. From Walsham's account, G went beyond the call of duty, to give good service to customer and company, even carrying his own stock of spares (ethical aspect). Taking Foucault to define the totality of meaningfulness hides this from us; it is an inappropriate research philosophy here. A multi-aspectual origin of meaningfulness would be more appropriate. For further discussion, see Basden (2008a, 159–64).

Instead of adhering to one philosophy, with all its baggage, researchers might directly state what their research requires from each of the three Ground-Idea elements.

- Diversity (of world). Which focal aspects of the world are important in the research, and why. The "why" can be derived from the extant literature and its gaps. Several ways of analysing literature to find aspectual gaps are offered in §11–2. The selected focal aspects indicate which data collection methods are appropriate (Table 8.1).
- Coherence (of rationalities). Which aspectual rationalities it is important to apply to the data. As listed in §7–1.3, these include those of the following aspects: the focal aspects, those they depend on, aspects of the methods of data collection and analysis, and aspects of contribution.
- Totality (of wider meaningfulness). Which aspects are important in situating the research in the wider world, including those which the relevant paradigms find meaningful and those of major challenges in the field or in society. An example of the latter is climate change and threats to global biodiversity: physical and organic.

7–4.2 On Bias in Research

There are many sources of bias in research, which undermine the "on which it is reasonable to rely" (§1–2.1) of research findings. While some are well known, many are hidden.

From the realm of professional research, Sarniak (2015) finds four sources of bias arising in human respondents in interviewing (acquiescence, social desirability, habituation and sponsor bias) and five arising in the researcher (confirmation, culture, question-order, leading questions and halo effect). These occur in data collection or analysis, and Sarniak believes that bias can be minimised "if you know what to look for and how to manage it."

In their review of biomedical research with animals, Mullane & Williams (2013) find 253 types of bias and claim that bias is the rule, not the exception. They categorise them as bias by ignorance, by design (for example, designing an experiment to support rather than refute the hypothesis) and by misrepresentation.

Both Sarniak and Mullane & Williams mention the amorphous concept of culture, which can "amplify" research bias; example: competitiveness in the profession and desire for career-advancement.

These all exemplify less-visible types of bias, and Dooyeweerd's notion of Ground-Idea might be able to help us understand and manage them.

- World: Bias arises from the aspectual functioning of researcher and researched and from ignoring salient aspects during focal-aspect abstraction. The biases Sarniak mentions are mostly dysfunctions in various aspects (e.g. social desirability bias is partly ethical dysfunction).
- Rationality harmonisation: Bias arises from choice of rationalities employed, especially when tacit, and also in how they are harmonised; Mullane & Williams' study shows misapplication of rationalities (e.g. hypothesis-support is ethical-pistic dysfunction).
- Subsequent critique in relation to wider meaningfulness: Bias occurs in presuppositions by the research community of what is meaningful when it differs from the actual wide meaningfulness of the situation. It may also occur because of dialectical ground-motives, which blind research to half of reality (§5–2.4).

Research opportunity: bias in research. This initial suggestion may be developed into a model of research bias that includes both visible and invisible sources. See §11–7.3.6 for initial empirical study.

7–5. Conclusion

This chapter has introduced Dooyeweerd's notion of three-part Ground-Idea, which emerges from his transcendental critique of theoretical thought in Chapter 6. Every philosophy, he argues, concerns itself with and takes a stance on diversity, coherence and totality, and §7–1 has discussed and illustrated how they are manifested in research:

- *diversity of world/reality*, how we abstract aspects and set them asunder from each other;
- *unity or coherence of diversity*, and how we may obtain valid findings from this fragmented data by better understanding the multiple rationalities involved;
- *totality of meaning*, or *wider meaningfulness*, and its origin, as the context in which critique occurs and the motivations that drive the research.

This offers a systematic approach by which researchers can discuss how philosophy underpins their research. The subsequent sections discuss how this helps address several issues that challenge research:

- Advances in knowledge may be seen as opening up our understanding of aspects and, in both incremental and radical (paradigm-shift) advances, the three elements help us understand what is happening (§7–2).
- Dialogue between research approaches may be facilitated by Ground-Idea analysis, including between apparently incommensurable approaches (§7–3).
- The difficulty of identifying one extant philosophy to serve as a research project's philosophy may be ameliorated by discussing, instead, what the research presupposes about diversity (of world), coherence (of rationalities), and totality (wider meaningfulness) (§7–4.1).
- Hidden biases in research may be deconstructed by reference to how they arise from each of the three Ground-Idea elements (§7–4.2).

Chapter 8 continues to apply the notion of Ground-Idea, to discuss the differences between fields (sciences, disciplines), to understand discourses in a field, and to clarify Kuhn's notion of paradigm. That leads up to clarifying concepts and into Part III.

8   Fields of Research

Why is it that the methods of the physical sciences have not proven particularly successful in the social sciences? Nor vice versa? What is it proper to study in any field, and why? Research takes on a very different form and feel in different fields, from mathematics, through physics, chemistry, biology, and psychology, to linguistics, sociology, economics, art, jurisprudence, ethics and theology.

This chapter suggests that most such fields focus on single core aspects and fleshes this out with the notion of three-part Ground-Idea that was discussed in the previous chapter. There are also fields that are interested in more than one aspect, especially interdisciplinary fields.

("Field", "science", "discipline" are almost synonymous; see §1–2.2.)

In addition to fields as such, this chapter is also about how researchers can grasp what is going on in their fields and what broad contributions can and should be made. It discusses:

- understanding the core of the field;
- understanding paradigms;
- clarifying problematic concepts and ideas.

8–1.   Understanding Research Fields and Disciplines

What differentiates one field from another? Their theories and research methods differ; they have different journals, funding bodies, communities of thought and of practice. Their bodies of knowledge differ.

In most fields, arguments continue about their nature or identity. What should mathematics rightly cover? Or linguistics, economics or theology? Why does it seem wrong when one field encroaches on what is meaningful in another? Yet why is interdisciplinary research acceptable?

This section briefly reviews approaches to identifying the core of fields and then proposes a staged Dooyeweerdian understanding. First, by reference to the Ground-Idea elements of world and unifying rationalities, we assign single core aspects to fields, then recognise secondary aspects and multi-core fields, and then discuss wider meaningfulness, including research application, reference fields, inter-field relationships and interdisciplinarity.

8-1.1   Some Approaches

What actually do we mean by the identity of a field? On what basis is it valid to draw boundaries? What about relationships between fields, for example between linguistics and sociology, or between mathematics and economics or art? There are also practical questions, such as, how strictly should PhD research be constrained by the accepted interests of the department within which it has been registered?

In my own field of information systems (IS), many suggestions have been argued for understanding the identity of the field. The following is a summary of the discussion in Basden (2010a), which will translate across to other fields.

Some authors (identified in Basden (2010a)) have tried to compose definitions of the field's proper concerns, but agreement on these is rare and proposed definitions have seldom captured the excitement and diversity that should characterise the field. Some authors have tried to identify the intellectual core of the field. This might be indicated by identifying other disciplines to which reference is made by the field or those disciplines that make reference to our field. However, a true discipline or field cannot rely wholly on theories from other fields but should have its own unique theories. Some have examined terms used, while others try to define a field by the journals in which researchers tend to publish. Some distinguish a field by its research methods. Others try to plot nets of relationships among concepts used, or between authors. Using these methods is susceptible to editorial fashions and other imbalances of interest (for example a preponderance of managerial topics in the IS field). An alternative approach is to try to plot the history of the field (Hirschheim & Klein 2012).

Similar questions arise in the natural sciences; see Musgrave (1971).

Much discussion sees the identity of a field in a static way. At least in the IS field, much of it looks back at the past rather than discussing which future directions are possible and appropriate. There is little discussion of the responsibility of the IS field. These characteristics might arise from a deep substance presupposition (§4–3.3) and/or a subjectivist immanence-standpoint (§5–3). Basden (2010a) suggests that, instead of identity, we should consider dignity, destiny and responsibility of fields.

Much of the discussion presumes boundaries around fields, and so do many journal editors. Yet Midgley (2000) argues that it impossible to draw hard boundaries and that all boundaries must be permeable. So it is common to treat the IS field as a "socio-technical" combination of organisational studies and information technology. However, Lee (2004) argues that the notions and interests of technical, social and socio-technical systems are not enough, but (p. 13) "information itself is a rich phenomenon that deserves its own separate focus no less than either information technology or organizations." He poses the question, Where can we locate this rich phenomenon? Lee points hopefully and vaguely in the direction of hermeneutics and systems theory but does not develop the suggestion. Basden (2010a) suggests that Dooyeweerd offers a better understanding.

8-1.2   *Fields as Centred on Aspects*

From a Dooyeweerdian perspective, what Lee has done is to identify three of what we have called spheres of meaningfulness: the formative and social aspects for the socio-technical approach and the lingual in between them. The lingual is often taken for granted and seldom explicitly discussed (ironically despite the field's name!). Basden (2010a) argues that it is precisely this aspect that helps us identify the core of the information systems discipline, as dignity, destiny and responsibility.

The proposal here is first that, usually, *each field centres on one core aspect*. This is the aspect that it is usually most important to abstract from the world by theoretical thought in that science. It is the aspect that is the sphere of law that is relevant to that field, and the mode of being, functioning, possibility, rationality, good and knowledge (these are explained in §4–3). Some fields, such as physiology or sociolinguistics, have a couple of core aspects.

> Note on terminology: core and focal aspects. Earlier chapters use the term *focal aspect* for the main aspect(s) abstracted in research; this is very often the *core aspect* of the field but not always.

Table 8.1 suggests sciences (and a few disciplines) that centre on each aspect (columns 1, 2). Column 3 suggests typical main research questions relating to the core world aspect of each. Column 4 indicates research methods appropriate to fields of each aspect.

Some notes: (1) The idea of fields centring on aspects applies equally across all kinds of science and research, without denying their differences. Seemingly fundamental differences between mathematical, natural, social and societal sciences and humanities may be explained by the irreducibly different possibilities that laws of each aspect enables (§4–3.8.1). (2) It is the core aspect that most defines the *dignity* of the field (as its unique, meaningful contribution in the world) and its *destiny* (opening up the potential of that aspect). (3) The main *responsibility* of the field comes from the fundamental normativity (axiology) of its core aspect (§4–3.7). (4) *Cross-over fields* like physiology span more than one aspect. (5) Since aspects are ordered by dependency (§3–2.4.4), so sciences of later aspects depend on earlier ones to some extent (e.g. physics on mathematics).

The data collection part of a research method is determined mainly by the core world aspect(s) and the data analysis, by the rationality of these along with the rationality of aspects of analysis method, as illustrated in Chapter 7 in the fields of information systems and sociolinguistics. Aspectual analysis related to a field's core aspect can reveal interesting facets that might improve research.

Example: In Chapter 7, it was found that the main aspect in Davis' (1989) *Technology Acceptance Model* (TAM) was the formative, but that subsequent research revealed nearly every aspect to be relevant. But neither Davis

Table 8.1 Examples of sciences, issues and research methods

Aspect	Science / Discipline	Example Main Research Question	Typical research methods
Quant'ive	Arithmetic, Algebra, Statistics	Is every even integer the sum of two primes (Goldbach Conjecture)?	Deduction, Computation
Spatial	Geometry, Topology	Can an n-dimensional convex body admit an expansive homeomorphism? (Klee 1960)	Geometric proofs
Kinematic	Kinematics, Mechanics, Dynamics	How can we get linear motion from rotary motion?	Infinitesimal calculus
Physical	Quantum physics, Physics, Chemistry, Materials science	*Physiology* — What is the electric charge radius of the proton?	Laboratory experiment
Organic / Biotic	Life sciences, Biology, Ecology, Taxonomy, Surgery	How do cells determine what size to grow before dividing?	Experiments, Field studies, Dissection
Psychic / Sensitive	Psychology, Sensory sciences, Cognitive sciences	How does previous experience alter perception and behaviour?	Stimulus-response trials
Analytic	Logic, Analysis	What are the limits of understanding thinking as a form of computing?	Thought experiments, Logic, Cognitive methods
Formative	Design science, History, 'Sciences of the Artificial'	How to optimally cut a cake so that every recipient feels they have a fair piece?	Game playing, Puzzle-solving, Build + test
Lingual	Linguistics, Semiotics, Hermeneutics, Literature, Language studies, Information Systems	*Sociolinguistics* — How does grammaticalization function?	Text analysis, Discourse analysis
Social	Sociology, Organisational studies	Does social media make us lonely?	Surveys, Questionnaires, Interviews
Economic	Economics, Management science	Why is it that individuals or institutions in many countries hold only modest amounts of foreign equity?	Statistics, Model building, As social science

Aesthetic	Aesthetics, Art, Sport science, (Systems thinking?)	What is the line between art and non-art?	As social science + design, construction
Juridical	Jurisprudence, Political Science	How may we compare Indian and Iranian laws?	Review of cases and histories, Reflection on all aspects
Ethical / Attitudinal	Ethical theory	Why do many people pursue hedonistic lifestyles?	Attitude surveys, Reflection
Pistic / Faith	Theology, Some anthropology	What is the relationship between belief commitment, courage and motivation?	Reference to 'sacred' writings, Apologetics, Hermeneutics

nor the 1990s information systems community give the lingual aspect the prominence we might expect if Basden (2010a) is correct, that the core of the information systems field is the lingual aspect. This opens up questions to investigate. Is Basden (2010a) wrong? Is it that technology acceptance concerns information systems *use*, which is formative functioning (tool use)? Or is it explained by Lee's (2004) complaint that the theme of information (lingual aspect) had been overlooked. Indeed, Basden (2018a) argues that TAM should be augmented with a construct concerned with the lingual quality of information that an information system provides.

It is the irreducibility of aspectual meaning-kernels (§4–3.2) that places *boundaries* between fields, and inter-aspect coherence (§3–2.4) that makes them permeable. So, attempts to employ methods and rationalities from other aspects can either enrich a field or result in problems that confuse the operation of a field. The difference may be understood via the juridical aspect, of appropriateness: imposition by one scientific field of its rationalities or methods on another where they are inappropriate usually harms the research activity.

This provides a foundation for understanding mixed methods research (quantitative and qualitative), where the rationalities of quantitative and analytic (and lingual) aspects must be harmonised; see §11–7.

8–1.3   Secondary Aspects

Assigning aspects to fields is only a start, however. How do we account for the importance of the social and technical (formative) aspects to the IS field? Basden (2010a) argues that while the lingual aspect is the core, the neighbouring aspects, social and formative, are strong seconds, one foundationally depended on and the other antecipated (§3–2.4). The further neighbours, analytic and economic, are tertiary. This is depicted in Figure 8.1.

So, for example the following topics are relevant in the IS field and included in its research: communication (lingual), the structure and technology of

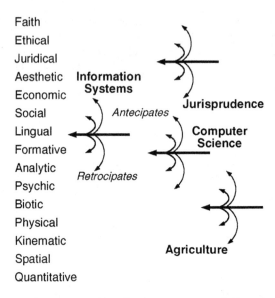

Faith
Ethical
Juridical
Aesthetic   **Information**
Economic   **Systems**
Social   *Antecipates*
Lingual
Formative
Analytic   *Retrocipates*
Psychic
Biotic
Physical
Kinematic
Spatial
Quantitative

Jurisprudence

**Computer
Science**

Agriculture

Figure 8.1 Aspects of interest to the information systems field, and others

information (formative), cultural conventions (social), data types (analytic), or information overload (economic).

Other fields, like jurisprudence (juridical) or agriculture (organic), may be treated similarly.

Some fields have two core aspects. To healthcare, the organic-biotic and ethical aspects are important and, if we include mental health, the psychic aspect too. The organic (and psychic) aspect provides the focus of attention for the day-to-day activity in the healthcare sector, while the ethical aspect provides the impetus and overall importance of it, and also its foundation in history—without it the Hippocratic Oath would long ago have been forgotten. Thus healthcare has two core aspects, and two sets of later and earlier neighbours.

Taking the organic core, healthcare depends foundationally on physico-chemical functioning, and hence much of the discourse is around chemical and physical issues, though always meaningful in the context of the organic or biotic (hence biochemistry and physiology of drugs, etc.). To the organic aspect, the psychic aspect is anticipated so that, in treating bodily ailments, mental issues cannot be ignored.

Taking the ethical core, healthcare depends crucially on the juridical aspect, and so it is no surprise that we find major legal issues within healthcare. Its sole antecipated aspect is the pistic, which, as discussed in §9–1.14, provides motivation for the ethical functioning of healthcare. It is relevant in several ways, such as motivating nations to build up their healthcare sectors and beliefs among populations that lead them to take healthcare for granted as a basic human right.

What is the difference between fields focusing on the same aspect, such as linguistics, information systems and literature (e.g. novels), all of which have the lingual aspect as their core? The differences may be understood by reference to secondary aspects. In information systems, the formative aspect of technology is more important as a medium for information than in the other two. In literature, the social, pistic and aesthetic aspects are important, because most such literature is intended to entertain and is about relationships, beliefs and commitments. In linguistics, the secondary aspects merely serve the core one.

In such ways, aspectual analysis of fields by world-aspect and rationalities can clarify what kinds of issues are relevant to the research and why. It builds up what Dooyeweerd calls an individuality structure for the field (§4–3.4). Examples may be found in Chapter 11.

8–1.4 *Wider Meaningfulness: Applications and Interdisciplinary Research*

There is a yet finer difference between fields. What is the difference, for instance, between linguistics and semiotics, between Islamic, Orthodox Jewish, Roman Catholic, Reformed, Evangelical and Pentecostal theologies? Though with closely overlapping concerns, such fields have different names, communities and journals. So far, we have taken account of diversity of abstracted world aspects and of harmonising these with rationalities to understand inter-field differences. It is wider meaningfulness, however, that might account for these finer differences, as expressed, for example, in the cultures within which these fields have arisen. Such cultures tend to differ slightly in their presuppositions of aspectual emphasis, for example Roman Catholic theology may be seen as giving more explicit attention to the aesthetic aspect, and Evangelical to the lingual.

Wider meaningfulness links with *research application*, in that it concerns the place and role of the research in the world. As suggested above, in the IS field, the economic and social aspects take tertiary and secondary roles in aspects abstracted from the world. Historically, however, they have had much more impact on the IS field than this would suggest, because they are primary application domains. Almost all IS research has presupposed an organisational context, and the majority of organisational issues researched have been expected, at least indirectly, to serve economic ends like efficiency, management or profit. Benbasat & Zmud (2003) believe this has distorted the field. Indeed, important applications of IS have been ignored, like computer games, scientific computing and geographic information systems (Basden 2018a, 163–4, 173–4, 198–9, 208–9) which have been neither taken into account in, nor served by, mainstream IS research.

However, research application also takes account of, and influences, which world aspects are abstracted and which rationalities are active. This is the reason for "multiple aspects" in some rationalities of the TAM example in §7–1.3.

Inter-field relationships are also expressions of wider meaningfulness. The IS field has many fields to which it makes reference, ranging from psychology to sociology and economics, from which it employs theories and taxonomies as ready-made conceptual tools (for example, Burrell & Morgan's (1979) sociological paradigm; c.f. §8–2.2). Moreover, once a field has developed its own theories—as part of its dignity and responsibility—other fields begin to reference it.

Inter-field relationships take different forms. Does studying how language use affects communities differ from studying how social factors affect language use? Or from the application of mathematics to economics or art, or studying the use of movement in art or, conversely, studying the beauty in mathematics? We may understand these by reference to inter-aspect dependency, analogy and simultaneity (§3–2.4). The effect of language use on communities arises from the foundational dependency of the social on the lingual aspect; the effect of social factors on language use arises from the retrocipatory impact of the social on the lingual aspect. The application of mathematics in other fields may be understood as transducing their meaningfulness into quantitative terms, which involves both analogy and dependency. Beauty in mathematics may be studied as inter-aspect analogy, but also that in actual reality that which functions in the quantitative also functions simultaneously in the aesthetic aspect.

In *interdisciplinary research* and practice, Boden (1999) distinguishes six types, ranging from "encyclopaedic" interdisciplinarity, such as in a university, where several disciplines are made available but individual researchers are not forced to cross discipline boundaries, to "integrated" interdisciplinarity, in which "some of the concepts and insights of one discipline contribute to the problems and theories of another—preferably in both directions" (p. 20), via intermediate types like "shared" interdisciplinarity, where researchers share a common goal. Full integrated interdisciplinarity is the most demanding: Researchers should understand what is meaningful in other fields—a complex of concepts, processes, relationships, normative implications, etc. We may deconstruct these using Dooyeweerd's notion of Ground-Idea. Obviously, how the world is meaningful to each partner must be understood by others, and the rationalities relevant to those, by which we combine them and reason about them. For full mutual understanding, however, the wider meaningfulness of each field must be sympathetically respected, for example as expressed in the culture around each field. This is often intuitive and tacit in nature, shared only indirectly by social activity (c.f. Nonaka & Takeuchi 1995). This can account for why, in interdisciplinary research, informal social activity, and indeed all hidden aspects of research activity discussed in Chapter 10, prove important. Dooyeweerd's notion of Ground-Idea might provide a structure with which interdisciplinary working might be guided. See Strijbos & Basden (2006) for fuller discussion, which celebrates the work of the Centre for Philosophy, Technology and Social Systems across a number of fields.

8–1.5   *Conclusions About Fields*

The notion of Ground-Idea, discussed in Chapter 7, helps us understand fields like information systems. Figure 8.2 summarises our discussions. On the left are the three elements of Ground-Ideas, with core aspects meaningful to the field, in the middle is the research leading to findings that are published, and on the right, the bodies of knowledge to which research contributes. Most of the issues mentioned earlier, such as data, definitions and dignity, are found in the diagram.

Our discussion has painted a big picture of research, in which fields are placed in relation to each other by their core aspects and inter-aspect relationships. It helps us understand why over-emphasis on non-core aspects (economic aspect of management, for instance) distorts the field. The question about constraining PhD research is, of course, partly to do with management and training in research skills, but it may be informed by comparing the aspects meaningful around the research topic with the aspects meaningful to the department.

I have found it can also help us understand other fields in which I might have less expertise. Our understanding of everyday experience, of aspectual kernel meaningfulness and of aspectual inter-relationships can furnish us with at least an initial understanding of what is meaningful in a field, and why it is meaningful in relation to other aspects, and thus other fields.

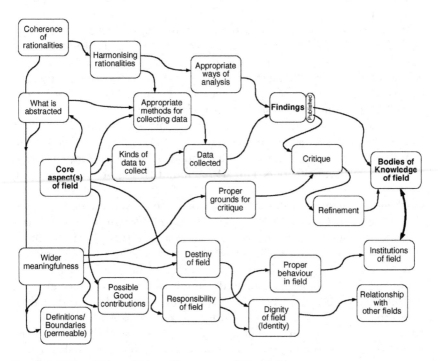

Figure 8.2 How Ground-Idea affects research in a field

Within every field, however, several paradigms will be operating, around which sundry discourses arise. The next section discusses the idea of paradigms.

8–2.   On Paradigms

Every field hosts several paradigms. Though the term 'paradigm' predates Kuhn, its present popularity originates with Kuhn's ground-breaking 1962 book *The Structure of Scientific Revolutions*. Influential in both academic and popular circles, it has transformed the philosophy of science and wider intellectual life.

8–2.1   *The Idea of Paradigm*

Kuhn (1962) proposes that science progresses not only through evolutionary development (which he calls "normal science"), but also through "paradigm shift", a revolutionary displacement of one paradigm by another ("scientific revolutions"). An example is the shift from Newtonian to Einsteinian mechanics. Within a decade, examples of paradigms were found in such diverse fields as history, philosophy, political science, anthropology, sociology, theology and even art (Eckberg & Hill 1979), suggesting that the idea crystallised what many had known intuitively. As discussed in §2–3.2, Kuhn's notion of paradigms evinces the non-neutrality of theoretical thought and discourse.

Normal science is science pursued by a community of scientists who share a paradigm—a consensus about how the world is to be understood, types of issues that are meaningful and how problems may be solved. A new paradigm allows new research questions to emerge and new theories to be generated. New paradigms are often introduced via exemplars, but might also be couched in symbolic generalisations or models (Kuhn 1971).

The paradigm idea is, unfortunately, ambiguous. For example, Burrell & Morgan's (1979) four "sociological paradigms" (§5–1.2) have been criticised for not being "true" paradigms in the Kuhnian sense, but rather epistemological approaches; Eckberg & Hill (1979) found 12 sets of "paradigms" in sociology, categorised in several ways, some by movements in philosophy like Phenomenology, others by ground-motive poles, yet others by general philosophical concepts. Masterman (1970) finds 21 different ways Kuhn uses the term; see Joneidy (2015) and Basden & Joneidy (2019) for discussion.

In response to criticism, Kuhn's (1971) *Second Thoughts* tries to clarify the notion by suggesting two broad uses of "paradigm", (a) as a global *disciplinary matrix*: "embracing all the shared commitments of a scientific group", "the entire constellation of beliefs, values, techniques, and so on shared by the members of a given community" (p. 175) and (b) as *exemplars*: "a particularly important sort of commitment" that shows how scientific problems are solved by the community, "and thus a subset of the first". Kuhn (1971) believes the second meaning is the more important, in need of philosophical attention. The community that shares a paradigm might be, for example, all physicists, or all solid-state physicists, down to those couple of dozen who are interested in a very specific problem.

Musgrave (1971), however, was "disappointed" with this, as a "pale reflection of the old, revolutionary Kuhn" (p. 296). I myself find Kuhn's *Second Thoughts* rather unnecessarily limited. Can we recover the richness and excitement of the idea, yet with less ambiguity?

8–2.2   *A Dooyeweerdian View: Paradigms as Meaningfulness*

Musgrave might inadvertently give a clue, when he asks rhetorically whether the "entire" constellation of beliefs should include beliefs about the Trinity, values about drug-taking or techniques of love-making. Obviously not! But why not? One answer is *meaningfulness*, as discussed in Chapter 4.

A paradigm may be seen as expressing what is meaningful to a community. Differentiating paradigms from each other might be by any of the three elements of the Ground-Idea of the underlying philosophy, since these express three roles meaningfulness plays in theoretical thought—by which aspects of the world are focal, how rationalities are harmonised, and/or by different wider meaningfulness. Section 11–3 contains several examples of new paradigms that have been generated by approaching fields with a Dooyeweerdian perspective. What has recently become known as "viewpoint diversity" may be understood and even navigated by reference to aspects.

Considering research content, different paradigms occur because they concern different spheres of meaningfulness in what the field is studying, and paradigm shifts, because new aspects are discovered to which attention should be given in the field's body of knowledge. For example, Einsteinian mechanics gives more respect to the kinematic aspect than does Newtonian.

We may understand the research activity within a paradigm as multi-aspectual functioning that targets the aspects of interest to the community (§4–3.8.2, §4–3.9; Chapter 10). Here is Kuhn's (1971, 1) statement of the working of paradigms, marked with the aspects that make each phrase meaningful:

A scientific community [soc] consists, in this view, of the practitioners [fmv] of a scientific specialty [anl]. Bound together [soc] by common elements in their education [lng] and apprenticeship [fmv], they see themselves [pis] and are seen by others [pis] as the men responsible [jur] for the pursuit of a set of shared goals [soc-fmv], including the training [fmv] of their successors [soc]. Such communities are characterized by the relative fullness [aes] of communication [lng] within the group [soc] and by the relative unanimity [soc-aes] of the group's judgment in professional matters [jur]. To a remarkable extent the members of a given community will have absorbed the same literature [lng] and drawn similar lessons [anl] from it. Because the attention of different communities is focused [anl] on different matters [distinct target aspects], professional communication [lng] across group lines [soc] is likely to be arduous [fmv-eco], often gives rise to misunderstanding [lng], and may, if pursued, isolate significant disagreement [soc].

We can see a wide range of aspects there; see Chapter 10 for deeper discussion.

The view that paradigms express meaningfulness might affirm, critique and enrich several of the contributions in Lakatos & Musgrave's (1970) collected discussion of Kuhn's idea by eminent thinkers. Kuhn's and Feyerabend's view that scientific activity involves more than reason alone echoes Dooyeweerd's contention that theoretical thought is not autonomous (§2–3, §6–3). Masterman mentions "meaning" repeatedly, as more than signification-meaning; the 21 significations of "paradigm" may be understood by aspectual analysis (Joneidy 2015; Basden & Joneidy 2019); for example, paradigm as "textbook" and "standard illustration" are part of the lingual aspect of paradigm functioning, and paradigm as "analogy" the aesthetic. Feyerabend's diversity might be a call for irreducibly distinct aspects (§3–2.3). Popper's criticism that paradigms cannot be falsified becomes irrelevant, once it is recognised that paradigms express what is meaningful rather than what is true (c.f. §6–4). Lakatos' argument that favourable evidence must be accumulated before Popperian falsification may be seen as recognising the process of discovering and delineating meaningfulness.

> *Research opportunity: paradigms.* This, and even Basden & Joneidy (2019), are only initial suggestions for how paradigms might be understood with Dooyeweerd. Fuller exploration is needed.

8–2.3   An Example: Linguistics and Sociolinguistics

Consider the development of paradigms in the fields of linguistics and sociolinguistics over the decades. If paradigms are concerned with different spheres of meaningfulness in the field, then this development might be understood as humanity's opening up or discovery of the diversity of the (everyday) reality of language use and activity (§4–3.8.3). If we see diversity in terms of Dooyeweerd's aspects, we can trace a clear pattern. This is not the place to argue this in detail, but only to give an indication.

To Frege, language is a vehicle to express logical reasoning, denoting things in the world and valid processes of reasoning about them, and the meaning of a sentence is the meaning of its parts ("compositionality"). He highlighted the difference between sense and reference—but struggled insofar as he could never properly define sense, the best he could do was link it to 'thoughts'.

Chomsky offers an almost opposite perspective, in recognising the human. Language is a (supervening) property of the state of a certain system that is found in all human minds/brains, which he called the language system. This gives an internal I-language, but he also recognised a social, external language, which impinges on I-language. I-language and linguistic competence are the only proper topic of study. This, however, severs language use from life and cannot account for tacit knowledge (Hymes 1972).

Piaget was concerned with development of language in children but offers a higher, cognitive, perspective, in which concepts are not just supervening labels for brain activity but should be treated as real.

Speech act theory (Austin, Searle) sees language as human action beyond the internal, so that utterances have a pragmatic as well as semantic meaning.

Conversation Analysis is interested in the structure of conversations, taking into account its semantic and pragmatic meanings and how this shapes social relationships. Discourse Analysis is interested in how the social context shapes language use. Critical Discourse Analysis is interested in the cyclical relationship, how each shapes the other, and how discourses relate to each other. Its social interest extends beyond this to societal structures, and especially those of power and oppression, and sometimes also self-correction through reflexivity. Feminist Poststructural Discourse Analysis (Baxter 2010) is interested more in diverse identities and transformation than oppression and emancipation, and recognises a wider range of factors, including playfulness and the body.

We may see this as an almost sequential opening up (§4–3.8.3) of our understanding of the role each aspect plays in language use (lingual activity) as a whole:

- Frege: analytic entities;
- Chomsky: psychic and formative foundation of the lingual;
- Piaget: analytic and formative functioning of language;
- Speech Act Theory: lingual and social functioning;
- Conversation Analysis: lingual antecipation of the social, with some interest in formative foundation of this;
- Discourse Analysis: social retrocipation onto the lingual;
- Critical Discourse Analysis: (a) both antecipatory and retrocipatory lingual-social relationships; (b) the juridical aspect (oppression) with some ethical aspect (self-correction);
- Feminist Poststructuralist Discourse Analysis: (a) the whole range of aspects, not just lingual-social and juridical, but also including aesthetic and organic (c.f. Basden's (2008a) characterisation of feminist thought as multi-aspectual; it is interesting that FPDA also eschews polar oppositions, in favour of seeing aspects, as advocated in §7–2.2); (b) the antecipatory and retrocipatory interplay among the entire range of aspects; (c) a particular interest in the pistic aspect, being that by which people define their identities and their overall meaningfulness.

Insofar as this brief analysis has any validity, several things may be noticed. (a) Seemingly incommensurable paradigms in a field might simply emphasise different spheres of meaningfulness that are all potentially relevant to the field (c.f. §7–3). (b) The earlier aspects were usually discussed before the later; this reflects, and might empirically support, the order of aspects, their dependency (§3–2.4) and aspectual opening (§4–3.8.3). (c) Some discourses arise from an interest in retrocipations, others in antecipations.

Chapter 11 provides examples of using Dooyeweerd to generate new paradigms, critique existing ones, and understand how discourses inter-relate. See §11–7.6 for a practical suggestion for Discourse Analysis.

8–3.   Concepts and Ideas in a Field

In every field, many important concepts or ideas are undefined or ambiguous. Strauss (2009, 11–13; 176ff.) usefully differentiates between concepts and ideas that transcend concepts, but our concern here is the ambiguity of either. Often, they are the foundational ideas, which those in the field take for granted, perhaps as part of the lifeworld of the field—the shared understanding or knowledge that forms a background to the field. Husserl (1954/1970) suggested that, for example, in the field of geometry, concepts like straightness are of this kind: How straight is straight?

Polanyi (1967) made the idea of tacit knowledge known, and Polanyi & Prosch (1975) suggest this comes from "indwelling" meaning (§4–3.10). In biology, for example,

> the contrast between sentience and insentience, between intelligence and its absence, were known before they were studied in science. These were common knowledge, and so were many details of living functions: hunger for food, the need to breathe, the processes of digestion, . . . Our prescientific knowledge of living things must therefore have arisen from acts of profound indwelling, comprehending the general panorama of biotic features—*and this remains the way these features are known today even by scientists.* // Biology must ultimately bear on life as life is known to the nonbiologist. Otherwise it has lost any claim to a specific subject matter.
>
> (pp. 140–1, emphasis in original)

The Dooyeweerdian understanding of Polanyi's "indwelling" as what I have called "ocean of meaningfulness" (§4–3.10), of intuition as the coherence of multi-aspectual knowing (§4–3.12), and of the meaning of terms as parcelling up 'pieces of meaningfulness' (§4–3.11), might help researchers firm up ambiguous concepts. Two ways of clarifying concepts are opened up. One is to understand the kernel meaningfulness of each aspect (see Chapter 9); for example, geometry, sentience, intelligence and life functions are meaningful in the spatial, psychic, analytic and organic aspects respectively, and scientific understanding of these is rooted in intuitive grasp of aspects.

The other way is to clearly separate out analogical from original meaning (§3–2.4.3); each aspect contains echoes of the others but operates by its own, not those others', laws.

Example: In quantum theory, the notion of information (*qubit*) has been useful, but it is not information in the original lingual sense but a lingual analogy in the physical. Recognising that this is an analogy reminds us not to expect lingual laws to apply but physical ones (e.g. the no-teleportation problem), which might dispel some of the confusion around quantum information.

Ways of clarifying concepts and ideas are elaborated and illustrated in Chapter 11, with the examples given, including:

- Understand the kernel meaningfulness of the primary aspect of the concept, in detail.
- Understand (types of) things as foundational enkaptic interlacements (§4–3.5).
- Identify antecipations and retrocipations among the aspects that make the concept meaningful.
- Discuss the entire aspectual individuality structure of the concept.
- Plot an aspectual 'story' of a sentence or situation.

8–4. Conclusion

This chapter has shown how Dooyeweerd can enlighten us about fields and their dignity, their cores and boundaries, about the nature of paradigms, and about how to clarify concepts and ideas. In all these, Dooyeweerd's notion of diverse meaningfulness and aspects has proven important. In this way a number of conundrums that trouble research might be resolved.

Our discussion, however, has been fairly broad—major sciences—and about paradigm as philosophical idea. It needs practical outworking. That is the role of Part III. Methods of addressing the issues discussed here are introduced in Chapter 11, based on actual experience.

Part III

Part III offers practical guidance for researchers using Dooyeweerd's ideas.

- Chapter 9 is an encyclopaedia of Dooyeweerd's suite of aspects, for reference during aspectual analysis.
- Chapter 10 examines the real-life activities of research from an aspectual perspective. It also suggests a practical way of critically engaging with extant thought without antagonism or acquiescence.
- Chapter 11 is a compendium of expertise using Dooyeweerd's philosophy in research, across a wide variety of fields. It finds that Dooyeweerd's philosophy has been used in at least six of the seven typical stages of research.

9   Dooyeweerd's Suite
of Aspects

Much has been said about Dooyeweerd's suite of aspects. Throughout Parts I and II, we have worked with an informal understanding of the kernel meaningfulness of each.

The purpose of this chapter is to provide an understanding of their kernels that can be used as a reference point by researchers. It is not primarily the purpose to argue philosophically for the kernel meaning of each aspect, though some indication of reasons for this interpretation are given. This entails (a) offering the opportunity to gain an intuitive grasp of the kernel meaningfulness, (b) providing a succinct characterisation that could be critiqued or referred to, and (c) providing some indications of why each aspect is understood in the way indicated, including some of Dooyeweerd's own discussions.

So each aspect's kernel meaningfulness will be discussed separately, but with reference to other aspects. Following this is a discussion of grouping of aspects and then of comparing Dooyeweerd's suite with others. Finally, an overview is given of reasons why Dooyeweerd's suite can be relied upon, but also a warning.

9–1.   Description of Each Aspect

This section is copyright ©The Dooyeweerd Pages, and used with permission.

The purpose of this section is to help readers develop their intuitive grasp of aspectual kernels, sufficient to be able to use and discuss them with some confidence. Each aspect has its own section, mainly drawn from Basden (2011b), which is best read almost as an essay on the aspect, despite its systematic, list-like format. The material is designed to be referred to and maintains a reasonably cross-cultural applicability, for example most of the good mentioned would be applauded as good in most cultures.

In each section, after a statement of kernel meaningfulness for the aspect, are:

- some ways this aspect is experienced in the pre-theoretical attitude, sometimes with additional notes;
- a list of the good possibility (§4–3.7) that this aspect introduces to reality but which is meaningless to earlier aspects, along with an indication of dysfunction that is meaningful in the aspect (in the first four aspects, dysfunction is meaningless);
- ways in which the aspect depends foundationally on earlier aspects (§3–2.4.4);

- some differences from earlier aspects, to clarify understanding (entries in brackets are differences from later aspects where this occasionally seems useful);
- a list of pages where Dooyeweerd discusses the aspect, which is useful for deeper analysis;
- sundry notes about and discussions of the aspect, which explain why the aspect is understood in this way;
- some analogies of this aspect in others (§4–2.4.3);
- common mistakes made, which confuse this aspect with others;
- how this aspect antecipates later aspects.

For each aspect, a diagram depicts the kernel meaningfulness of the aspect surrounded by a constellation of things, properties and/or functions meaningful in that aspect (§4–3.4, §4–3.8). Each diagram is best reflected on as a text. Items to the left take some meaningfulness from earlier aspects, and those to the right gain some meaningfulness from later aspects, with those in brackets on the boundary more meaningful in the neighbouring aspect. Since the quantitative and pistic aspects are terminal aspects, their diagrams are only half filled. Note: These constellations are only illustrative and by no means complete.

These are my own interpretations of what I think Dooyeweerd was getting at in each aspect, based on 25 years of using and reflecting on the aspects; others might disagree. The description of each aspect takes account of the principles for delineating them set out in Basden (2019) and summarised in §4–3.13.

9–1.1   *The Quantitative Aspect*

Kernel: Discrete quantity/amount ("numberness"). **Experienced as:** One, several and many, and comparisons of less and more.

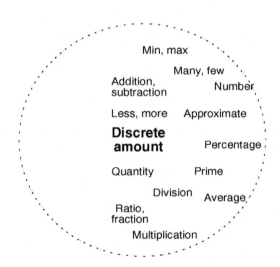

Figure 9.1 The quantitative aspect and some of its constellation

Good:

- Reliable amount and order: Each amount (numberness), other than infinity, always and in all situations retains the same quantitative meaning and differs from all others. 4-ness is always more than 3.9-ness and less than 4.1-ness. This is so fundamental that we usually take it for granted, yet functioning in all other aspects relies on this, so mathematics seems a foundational science.
- Ordering: The less-and-more relationship in the quantitative aspect provides us with a natural way of placing things in order: 1, 2, 3, . . .

Foundational Dependencies:

- None. But the possibility of quantity depends on the origin of meaning.

Differences From Neighbours: See Spatial.
Notes, Discussion: NC,II, 79–93

- Quantitative functioning feels like static property of having-an-amount.
- Number-of and 'numberness': 4 wheels on a car and 4 points on the compass—whereas the analytic aspect differentiates wheels from compass-points, and might see two 4s here, the quantitative aspect does not: there is always only one 4. It is not number-of-things that exists quantitatively, but what we might call 'numberness', quantity-as-such: 4-ness, 1-ness, 146-ness, 3/4-ness, 3.9-ness and so on.
- Dooyeweerd places continual emphasis on "unity and multiplicity", "the one and the many", stressing that quantity is *discrete*, not continuous. He sees ratios as relationships, whereas I see them also as amounts in their own right.

Analogies of This Aspect:

- "More beautiful, faithful, costly, understandable . . . " and correspondingly, "Less . . . ", and the suffixes "-er" and "-est" denote quantitative analogies in almost all other aspects.
- Equality is a quantitative analogy; beware!

Mistakes:

- The kernel is amount or quantity, not number, since number implies lingual symbols.
- Counting, though led by the quantitative aspect, also involves analytical functioning (distinguishing things to count) and lingual symbolisation.

Antecipations:

- Irrational numbers antecipate the spatial in that they become important only when spatial meaning is imported. Example: The square root of two has little meaning to purely quantitative thinking and cannot be discovered by purely quantitative processes of converging approximations.

- Differential functions anticipate the kinematic aspect (NC,II, 94).
- Zero and negative numbers might anticipate the economic aspect.

9–1.2   *The Spatial Aspect*

Kernel: Continuous extension (extendedness). **Experienced as:** Here, there, between, around, inside and outside, shape, proximity.

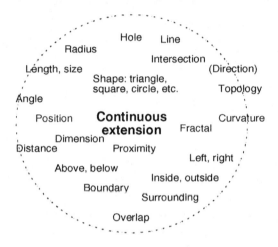

Figure 9.2 The spatial aspect and some of its constellation

Good:

- Simultaneity. Shapes, dimensions occur together.
- Continuity. Space, in its original meaningfulness, is smooth. This is why purely quantitative methods can never find irrational numbers.

Foundational Dependencies:

- Quantitative (reliable amount): Number of dimensions of a spatial world.

Differences From Neighbours:

- Quantitative is discrete; spatial is continuous.
- Quantitative gives sequential order; spatial allows simultaneity.
- (Spatial is static, kinematic is dynamic.)

Notes, Discussion: NC,II, 63–5, 85–96, 98–106

- Spatial functioning feels like static property.
- What is space? Kant argued space is an inherent subjective category (maybe because of the myriad of analogies?). Dooyeweerd argues there is real space and that space as subjective is psychic or analytic analogy of space.

Analogies of This Aspect:

- "Around 40 at the meeting" is a spatial analogy in the quantitative, meaning "approximately".
- Size, etc., of organisations: spatial analogy in the social. Length of paragraph: spatial in lingual.
- Spaces for thinking or discourse: spatial analogy in analytic, lingual.
- Boundaries of knowledge, jurisdiction, etc., are spatial analogies, as are inside and outside.
- Left- and right-wing politics seems like spatial (and organic) analogy in the juridical, but we need social convention to understand their implications.

Mistakes:

- "Extension" is extendedness, not processes of extension.
- Discrete points have no spatial existence (NC,II, 102). Either they are analytic things, when their distinction is emphasised, or quantitative, in the form (x,y).
- Space is not "filled up" by physical things (NC,II, 95).
- The relativistic stretching and curvature of 'space' discovered by Einstein refers not to space as such, but to a physical analogy of space (NC,II, 101).

Antecipations:

- Wiggly line might antecipate kinematic path or route.
- A sequence of snapshots, each individually a unique spatial universe, antecipates the kinematic; this is employed in cinematography and animation.

9–1.3   The Kinematic Aspect

Kernel: Movement. **Experienced as:** Going and flowing; forward and backward.

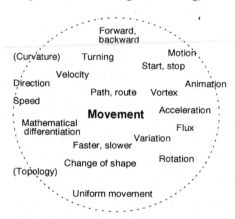

Figure 9.3 The kinematic aspect and some of its constellation

Good:

- The kinematic is the first aspect to introduce the possibility of *dynamic variation* or *change* to temporal reality (but see Discussion).

Foundational Dependencies:

- Depends on spatial continuity.

Differences From Neighbours:

- Kinematic is dynamic; spatial is static.
- Quantitative aspect is pure before-and-after with no simultaneity and the spatial aspect is pure simultaneity with no before-and-after, but the kinematic aspect merges before-and-after with simultaneity.
- (Constant, uniform movement is meaningful to kinematic, but meaningless to physical.)
- (Kinematic speeds can exceed that of light, physical cannot.)

Notes, Discussion: NC,II, 93–106

- The kinematic was the last aspect that Dooyeweerd delineated; initially he conflated the kinematic with the physical (NC,II, 98–99), but then antinomies convinced him it was different.
- Strauss (2009) takes the kernel meaningfulness of the kinematic aspect to be "constancy", and he moves change to the physical. However, this goes against intuition, which sees the kinematic as movement. From extensive references to how this is echoed in other aspects, it is clear that Dooyeweerd means *change or variability*.
- Acceleration, defined as force/mass and linked with a cause, is physical ("the physical concept of acceleration" (NC,II, 99)), but, defined as dV / dt (change in velocity, without regard to any cause), acceleration is kinematic. Uniform movement is a special case when dV / dt = 0, meaningful in kinematic but not physical (p. 99).

Analogies of This Aspect:

- The mathematical notion of *variable* (an amount that could 'change') anticipates the kinematic aspect analogically.
- (Inverse) Speed is a kinematic concept but it retrocipates the quantitative aspect, by an analogy that enables us to say "less" or "more". Velocity retrocipates spatial and quantitative.
- Movement of thought and social movements, involving commitment and belief, are kinematic analogies in the analytic and social-pistic.

Mistakes:

- Kinematic movement is not relative to a static background (example: bird flying across the sky); static background is neither necessary nor even meaningful. Assuming it reduces kinematic to spatial

(NC,II, 98). So does using Cartesian coordinates to think about movement; think about it via intrinsic curves instead.

- Zeno's paradox (p. 103) reduces kinematic to spatial.
- Originally Dooyeweerd used the term "motion", but this is not ideal (Kalsbeek 1975, 101) because, in conceiving of motion, we tend to think physically.

Antecipations:

- Movement is very important in physics, as dynamics, especially in Relativity Theory.

9–1.4   The Physical Aspect

Kernel: Energy. **Experienced as:** Matter, forces, energy, etc. (at microscopic, human and macroscopic spans)

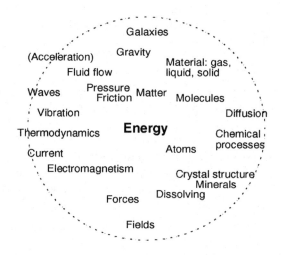

Figure 9.4 The physical aspect and some of its constellation

Good:

- Causality
- Resistance to causal change; momentum.
- Irreversibility
- Persistence—that physical change remains in place

Foundational Dependencies:

- Physical functioning requires movement and change (kinematic), space and reliable quantity.

Differences From Neighbours:

- Immaterial v. material.
- Physical has persistence and uni-directional time; kinematic has neither.
- From kinematic: Uniform movement is meaningless.
- From biotic: Boundary is meaningless (see Mistakes).
- Discrete space: This is a theoretical construct. If valid, it will occur because of physical discreteness of energy (quanta). Spatiality is still continuous.

Notes, Discussion: NC,II, 95, 99, 100, 101—patchy

- At the human and macroscopic spans, physical causality is deterministic (predictable from initial conditions); at the microscopic span it might not be.
- It is with the physical aspect that we first experience time as past-present-future.
- Whether chemistry should be incorporated in the physical aspect, as in Dooyeweerd, or separated, as in Bunge (1979), is a matter that still deserves discussion.

Analogies of This Aspect:

- Causality: repercussions. Hardness (of problems, personalities, etc.) is a physical analogy of resistance to being changed.

Mistakes:

- In the physical aspect there seems to be no such thing as an entity that is distinct from its environment. Rivers or hills merge into each other; electrons are smears. Physical laws do not stop at any boundary. Distinction is an analytic functioning for our convenience, rather than ontically physical.

Antecipations:

- Carbon chemistry, with its long-chain atoms, strongly antecipates life; without organic meaningfulness, it would remain a mere speculative curiosity.

9–1.5   *The Organic/Biotic Aspect*

Kernel: "Vital unity" and "organizing" (NC,II, 110); often seen as "life functions". **Experienced as:** Living healthily as organisms in an environment.

But what is "living"? It consists at least in the organism maintaining its equilibrium separately from the environment, with repair, and also the ability to reproduce after its kind.

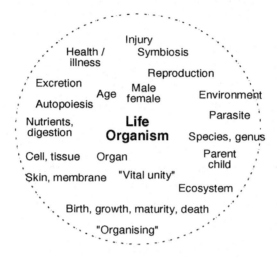

Figure 9.5 The organic/biotic aspect and some of its constellation

Good and Evil:

- The possibility of *organisms* that can *sustain themselves* within their *environment*, dependent on it but not wholly controlled by it, and *reproduce* after their own kind.
- Separateness (not discreteness) enters with the organic aspect.
- From the biotic aspect onwards, it is meaningful to talk of negative as well as positive: death, disease, poison, starvation, injury, etc.

Foundational Dependencies:

- On chemical processes, to form cellular materials. Example: Digestion depends on chemical reactions—but such chemical reactions can only rightly be called digestion if they serve to keep their organism alive.
- Cell processes depend on causality, forces, transport of chemicals, etc.

Differences From Neighbours:

- Organism's equilibrium state is not determined by the physical environment.
- Physical laws are those of fields, and extend to infinity; organic-biotic laws are those of the organism, relative to its distinct entity.
- The more we use a physical thing, the more it wears out and the weaker it gets; the more we use an organic thing (e.g. muscle), the more it builds and the stronger it gets.

Notes, Discussion: NC,II, 107–11

Dooyeweerd's discussion is brief and not entirely clear. He argues why life cannot be reduced to physical and chemical processes even though it depends on them, and argues against both vitalism and mechanistic views.

Analogies of This Aspect:

- Birth, growth, maturity, environment have clear analogical meaning for businesses (economic entities).
- Health is used analogically for good in many aspects.

Mistakes:

- Materialist reductionism assumes dependency implies reducibility.
- Vitalism treats life as a special substance or property (§4–3.3) added to matter, rather than an aspect. Hartmann makes the mistake of saying that life "transforms" matter (NC,II, 110–1 footnote).

Antecipations:

- Activity in a cell usually affects other cells in its proximity. But nerve cells have special properties: very long dendrites which are surrounded by a fatty sheath, so that activation in these cells finds its way to distant cells rather than diffusing to neighbours. What good this does cannot be understood from the biotic-organic aspect, but antecipates the psychic-sensitive aspect.

9–1.6   *The Psychic/Sensitive Aspect*

Kernel: Feeling, emotion. **Experienced as:** Sensing, responding and feeling (such that animals have, like fear, hunger).

Psychical functioning is both of the whole organism and also of the organs and cells (nervous system and neurons), which includes signal transmission, pattern-detection, pattern-recognition and memory.

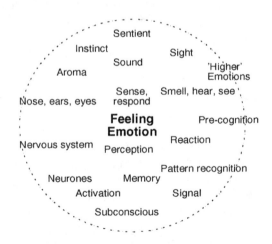

Figure 9.6 The psychic-sensitive aspect and some of its constellation

Good and Evil:

- This is the first aspect to introduce interactive engagement with the world (via senses and employing mental processes).
- Dysfunction: insensitivity, memory loss, etc.

Foundational Dependencies:

- Organic functions make the mental possible.
- The spatio-organic axon-dendron arrangement of neurones is the organic foundation of memory and recognition.
- Physical persistence (change in chemical composition) makes memory possible. Physical causation (electro-chemistry) makes signal-transmission possible.

Differences From Neighbours:

- Mental rather than bodily functions.
- Whereas organic-biotic organisms react passively to world (e.g. plant growing towards light), psychic-sensitive interaction is active.
- Organic functions operate by spatial proximity; psychic functions escape spatiality (e.g. neuronal signals to feet, hence the need for insulating sheaths).

Notes, Discussion: NC,II, 111–118

- Dooyeweerd does not discuss neuronal functioning, so the above is my own suggestion.
- Dooyeweerd's discussion of the psychic aspect: (a) why the kernel meaning is feeling rather than soul; (b) why psychic feeling cannot be set alongside volition and knowledge as *Erlebnisse* (Kant), which are trans-aspectual (c.f. §4–3.12).

Example Analogies:

- The 'feeling' of a meeting is usually social agreement with some attitude (ethical).

Mistakes:

- Usually, "I feel that . . ." is not psychic but analytic or pistic.
- Much of our feeling, e.g. of beauty or contentment, imports meaningfulness from later aspects, which are targets (§4–3.8.1) of the psychical feeling.

Antecipations:

- Psychic memory antecipates cognitive concept nets; pattern recognition antecipates focal attention.
- Post-animal feelings (such as beauty, insult) are psychic feeling targeting later aspects (aesthetic, ethical).

9–1.7   *The Analytical Aspect*

Kernel: Distinction: "setting apart what is given together" (NC,I, 39). **Experienced as:** Conceptualising, clarifying, categorising and cogitating. Conceptualising is of something meaningful in the world (c.f. interpretation-meaning, §4–1). We clarify that meaning, separating 'this' from 'that'. Categorising differentiates ways of being meaningful. Cogitating is thinking that involves these.

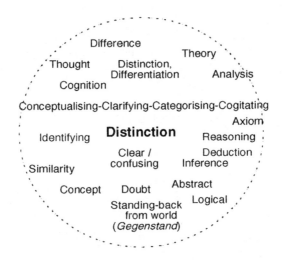

Figure 9.7 The analytic aspect and some of its constellation

Good and Evil:

- Ability to think independently of the world as given.
- This in turn allows imagination, fiction, even impossibilities (e.g. square circle).
- It also enables the *Gegenstand* attitude of **theoretical thought** (§2–1.1, §6–3.3) and the ability to distinguish aspects (§4–3.13).
- Enables 'conscious' awareness.
- Dysfunction: confusion.
- Evil: The independence from the world enabled by this aspect makes it easier for us to be arrogant, act selfishly and perpetrate or ignore injustice.

Foundational Dependencies:

- Depends on psychical functioning in nervous system. There can be no disembodied minds in this temporal reality.

Differences From Neighbours:

- Independence from world: The organic aspect enables distinct beings with dependence on the world. The psychic aspect enables interactive engagement with the world. The analytical aspect enables a degree of independence.

- Analytic mental activity is less bound to the senses than psychic is.
- Psychic pattern recognition (e.g. animals recognising mates) is not conceptualisation (NC,I, 39) (c.f. two streams in artificial intelligence: cognitive and neural nets).
- Psychic functioning is analog; analytic is digital.

Notes, Discussion: NC,II, 118–125

- Other names: Logical aspect.
- Dooyeweerd's discussion is mainly about relationships with other aspects—though his whole discussion of theoretical thought is an indirect discussion of this aspect: its *Gegenstand* requires analytic independence from world.
- Independence is not absolute autonomy. It operates by reference to aspects, e.g. thinking about square circles requires prior intuition of spatial meaningfulness.

Analogies of This Aspect:

- Analytic logic/reason has analogies in all aspects as their rationality (sense-making: "The reason I did this was . . ."); see §4–3.6.
- Clarity of text is analytic analogy in lingual. (Clarity of judgement is not analytic analogy but analytic functioning in the multi-aspectual activity of judging.)
- Aspectual distinction might be an analytic analogy on the entire suite of aspects.

Mistakes:

- "Distinction" refers not to social distinction or to animals recognising their mates (which is psychic pattern recognition), but to crisp concepts.

Antecipations:

- Imagination antecipates formative, lingual and aesthetic creativity.
- Ability to conceptualise antecipates formative power.

9–1.8 *The Formative Aspect*

Kernel: Formative power. **Experienced as:** Shaping, making, planning, achieving; innovation (NC,II, 198); goals, techniques, tools, technology. All kinds of things can be shaped: clay into pots, concepts into concept-structures, reasons into arguments, words into sentences, people into performers, social relationships into institutions, etc. Historical impact is formative.

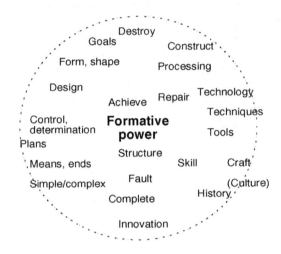

Figure 9.8 The formative aspect and some of its constellation

Good and Evil:

- Achievement and innovation; construction.
- The good of achievement and innovation can then occur in any target aspect.
- Through technology, technique and training, good in any targeted aspect can be amplified. So can evil.
- Dysfunction: laziness or destruction (not deconstruction).

Foundational Dependencies:

- Formative functioning depends on analytical functioning (conceptualising, etc.).

Differences From Neighbours:

- From analytic: doing rather than thinking.
- Construction versus deconstruction.
- While the analytic aspect distances us from the world, the formative aspect achieves things in the world and makes changes in the world; c.f. theory-practice duality.

Notes, Discussion: NC,II, 68–9, 192–217, 218–98

- Other names: Cultural, historical aspect (Dooyeweerd's names. History is the story of human formative power or achievement (NC,II, 193)—but "history" connotes the past. In Dutch the root of the word *culture* refers to human formative power (as in *agriculture*)—but, in English, "culture" is strongly social. Hence, here, "formative".

- Pages 192–217 discuss many other views and pages 218–98 link with other aspects, the history of humankind, and progress as humanity's "opening up" of aspects.
- De Raadt (2002) splits this into operational and historical aspects.

Analogies of This Aspect:

- Work is formative, with analogy in physical (kWh) and economic.
- Power is formative, with analogy in physical (watts) and in the juridical as oppressive power relationships.
- Aspectual structure might be a formative analogy of the entire suite of aspects.

Mistakes:

- Spiders building webs is not formative functioning, but by psychical instinct (NC,II, 198).

Antecipations:

- Much that we form—boundary stones, hieroglyphics, stories—has symbolic value, but this cannot be understood from the formative aspect. It anticipates the lingual aspect.
- Whereas our formative functioning leaves a trace in the world, its meaning is not clear; with lingual functioning, it can be much clearer.
- Formative creativity anticipates the aesthetic.

9–1.9   The Lingual Aspect

Kernel: Symbolic signification. **Experienced as:** Expressing, recording and reading/hearing. This can be by speech, text, pictures, gestures and even such things as boundary stones. The main aspect of signs, symbols, signification-meanings (§4–3.11.1), discussion and argument.

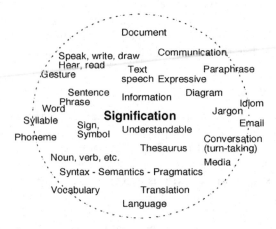

Figure 9.9 The lingual aspect and some of its constellation

Good and Evil:

- The lingual aspect is the first that enables externalisation of clearly intended (target) meanings, so they can persist and/or be shared with others.
- Dysfunction: deceit, obfuscation and equivocation.

Foundational Dependencies:

- Formative structuring is essential for lingual functioning: syntax. So is analytical conceptualising into distinct linguistic units.
- The precise signification-meaning of a symbol varies with historical (formative) context. It is the social aspect (antecipatory dependency), however, that determines whether it is at the right time and in the appropriate situation.

Differences From Neighbours:

- Structure v. its signification; syntax v. semantics.
- Formative internalises, lingual externalises. If we forget or die, our formed thoughts are lost; if written down, they can persist.
- However, making of artefacts (formative) can externalise attribution-meanings, but these are not as precise as lingual signification-meanings.

Notes, Discussion: NC,II, 221–7, 284–5

- Other names: Epistemic aspect (de Raadt 2002).
- Signification-meanings are objects generated by lingual function, targeting other aspects (§4–3.11).
- Dooyeweerd's discussion is rather brief, surprising for someone for whom meaning is so important.
- Dooyeweerd privileges neither recipient (reader, hearer) nor originator (writer, speaker), nor sign nor the signified, but sees them all as functioning in the 'ocean' of meaningfulness (§4–3.10). Many other thinkers (de Saussure, Peirce, Barthes) privilege one of them.

Analogies of This Aspect:

- 'Reading' a landscape is lingual analogy in the analytic aspect (§4–3.11.2, §11–4.3), quantum 'information' in the physical.
- Aspects as kinds of meaning: That each aspect is meaningful in a different way might be seen as an analogy of the lingual in the entire system of aspect; this is Strauss' (2013) view.

Mistakes:

- See analogies: 'reading' is not reading, etc.

Antecipations:

- Agreement about the signification of signs cannot easily be accounted for by the lingual aspect but requires the social. This is especially so for connotation, idiom, etc.
- Succinctness antecipates the economic, interest, the aesthetic, and truth the juridical aspects.

9–1.10   The Social Aspect

Kernel: "Social intercourse" (Dooyeweerd); "Company" (Stafleu 2005).
Experienced as: We, us and them; agreeing, appointing and associating. Agreeing implies shared action, belief, assumptions, etc. Associating implies treating others as like myself and submerging (though not obliterating) the *I* in the *we*. Association is either relationships or institutions, and implies roles (reader-writer, leader-follower, etc.), hence "appointing".

Communities and organisations are social wholes, formed of agreement and association, with more or less internal structure. Different types are led by different aspects (target aspect of social functioning), such as business (economic), the state (juridical) and the media (lingual).

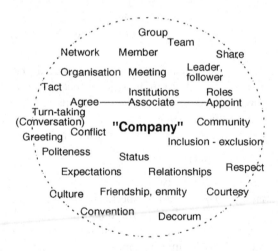

Figure 9.10 The social aspect and some of its constellation

Good and Evil:

- The social aspect enables working together. Especially with institutions, this *amplifies* the functioning and impact of individuals beyond their sum—whether for good or evil. The impact that is amplified is in a target aspect.

- Dysfunction: Aloofness, disrespect, rudeness, etc. (Disagreement is not necessarily a dysfunction.)

Foundational Dependencies:

- Without lingual externalisation of pieces of meaning, good social functioning would not be possible.
- On the formative; see Discussion.

Differences From Neighbours:

- Lingual is (inter-)individual; social is communal.

Notes, Discussion: NC,II, 141, 227–8

- Dooyeweerd's discussion of the kernel of the social aspect is surprisingly meagre, though he does have a lengthy discussion of social categories and institutions (NC,III, 565–624; Dooyeweerd 1986).
- He uses the term "intercourse", listing norms like "courtesy, good manners, tact, sociableness, fashion, and so on" (NC,II, 141 footnote) and "making a bow, giving a handshake, lifting one's hat, letting a superior precede" (pp. 227–8).
- How (European) times change! No longer do we lift hats. This shows the important part the formative (historical) aspect plays, but Dooyeweerd argues why social cannot be reduced to formative. His discussion of social institutions shows Dooyeweerd recognises much more than such norms.
- In his theory of social institutions, Dooyeweerd (1986) drew fundamental distinctions within the social aspect between inter-personal, intra-communal and inter-communal relationships. Class distinctions and power relationships are harmful in inter-personal and intra-communal relationships but may be valid in inter-communal.

Analogies of This Aspect:

- Relationship as a link between two concepts (e.g. in databases) is a social analogy in the formative aspect. That between two mathematical variables is a social analogy in the quantitative (also kinematic).
- Plant or animal "societies" is a social analogy in the organic aspect and in the psychic of interaction.
- (Inverse) The word "organisation" betrays its roots in (analogy with) the organic aspect.
- The relating of aspects: That each relates to others and each seems to have a distinct role might be an analogy of the social in the entire system of aspects.

Mistakes:

- Some social scientists tend to assume that all post-social functioning can be treated as mere sub-fields of sociology (NC,III, 157ff).
- Inter-individual activity is not always social; can be e.g. lingual.

Antecipations:

- Togetherness antecipates respect (juridical) and courtesy (ethical). Togetherness gains strength from self-giving and is undermined by selfishness (ethical aspect).
- Acting together to bring the good that is *shalom* (§4–3.7) requires transfer of "goods". These are resources; to understand this antecipates the economic aspect.

9–1.11 The Economic Aspect

Kernel: Frugality. **Experienced as:** Managing limited resources carefully, treating them as having value. Economic functioning is "the sparing or frugal mode of administering scarce goods, implying an alternative choice of their destination with regard to the satisfaction of different human needs" (NC,II, 66). This can be at level of individuals, organisations, societies and humanity as a whole. Resources can be of any type (here, words).

Figure 9.11 The economic aspect and some of its constellation

Good and Evil:

- Sustainable *shalom.*
- Frugality brings good, not only during scarcity, but also during plenty. This not only sustains future prosperity but also stimulates originality, responsibility and generosity.
- *Satisfaction* of needs is good economic functioning, not maximisation of capital (profits, income, owner value, GDP, etc.); cf. Simon (1956).

- Dysfunction: waste, squandering resources, leading to unsustainability, destitution.

Foundational Dependencies:

- Frugality can be individual, but its fuller form involves distribution of resources, which depends on social functioning. Economic needs-satisfaction in not primarily for individuals but for "us and them", including future needs.
- Economic functioning depends on formative (planning) and lingual (tokens of value).

Differences From Neighbours:

- Social is relating; economic is managing.
- The economic has some notion of limits and resources; the social lacks this.

Notes, Discussion: NC,II, 66–7, 122–7, 344–5, 360–2

- Most of Dooyeweerd's discussion is devoted to economy of thought, logic, language, aesthetics and law rather than 'the economy'.
- Currency (money) is only a quantitative measure of lingual tokens of value, and not itself value.
- Modern economics is distorted by a mechanistic view of the world (NC,II, 344).
- Growth (economic) is a retrocipatory analogy to the biotic aspect. That prosperity need not involve growth is discussed in Jackson (2009): ignoring the environmental 'limits to growth' undermines the foundations of future prosperity.
- Marx's error was to absolutise the economic aspect (NC,II, 293).

Analogies of This Aspect:

- "Value" is an economic term, but is often used analogically to refer to the kinds of good that each aspect brings, such as social value, aesthetic value. Similarly, "capital".
- The value of all aspects: That each aspect contributes some value to reality might be an analogy of the economic in the entire system of aspects.

Mistakes:

- Economic is not primarily to do with money or finance, nor to do with production, exchange and consumption. These are means to the end of frugality.
- Growth is organic analogy, so imposition of organic laws on the economy misdirects and harms it.
- Over-emphasising accounting (quantitative) or money (lingual symbol) distorts the economic aspect, leading to aesthetic dysfunction.

Antecipations:

- Economy of words is good in writing and especially poetry, but to understand why this is so requires the meaningfulness of the aesthetic aspect.
- Originality, responsibility and generosity, stimulated by frugality, are meaningful in the next three aspects.
- Successful economic functioning presupposes that (a) we balance different needs, (b) exchange is just, (c) generosity stimulates, (d) brokers operate in 'good faith'—antecipating the next four aspects.

9–1.12   The Aesthetic Aspect

Kernel: Harmony, delight. **Experienced as:** holism, orchestration, integration, rest, leisure, enjoying, playing, beautifying, humour and fun. Surprise and originality are aesthetic. The orchestra of daily life, a multitude of instruments, generates something harmonious, interesting and enjoyable—or not, as the case may be. "Whole is more than sum of parts."

Figure 9.12 The aesthetic aspect and some of its constellation

Good and Evil:

- Aesthetic aspect is the first that makes harmony and integration meaningful. In research: innovative harmony with extant knowledge.
- It makes delight (enjoyment, interest, fascination, fun, ecstasy, etc.) possible.
- Aesthetic dysfunction: tedium, repulsiveness, pretension, fragmentation, snobbery.
- See Seerveld's (2001, 175) table of aesthetic normativity.

Foundational Dependencies:

- The best aesthetic is frugal (economic), it "speaks" (lingual) and is crafted (formative), and is worse for excess and lazy execution.
- What is considered beauty is socially agreed.

Differences From Neighbours:

- Economic parsimony v. aesthetic play; necessity v. delight.
- Purely economic criteria in building generates ugliness and tedium (aesthetic dysfunction).

Notes, Discussion: NC,II, 66–7, 128, 139, 345–8

- The aesthetic aspect seems to cover two things: harmony and delight. Should it be split in two? Jones (2007) believes so, from his experience in sustainability, arguing that integration does not ensure beauty. Dooyeweerd emphasises harmony; Seerveld (2001), delight. Yet there is an intuitive link between the two.
- This has generated considerable discussion about Dooyeweerd's understanding of aesthetic meaningfulness in Reformational Philosophy (Seerveld 2001 and many others), suggesting perhaps that Dooyeweerd's view is not sustainable. An extensive collection of such discussions of the aesthetic aspect may be found at http://dooy.info/aesthetic.html.
- Maybe they combine as follows. Dooyeweerd asks, "What is beauty? What makes it possible?" and answers with "Harmony". A poem, film or piece of music with many threads that all interweave and come together is seen as finer or greater art.
- Seerveld (2001) argues that the kernel meaningfulness is "nuance", but is he over-emphasising links with the analytic aspect?
- Harmony is always urging us to see the whole. It is a close friend of Truth (NC,II, 347).

Analogies of This Aspect:

- Aesthetic harmonious "wholeness": organic health, organic ecosystem, social concord, formative integrality.
- Aesthetic rest: psychic relaxation, pistic sabbath.
- Harmony is not uniformity nor sameness; c.f. symphony.
- That each aspect coheres with others, in several ways, might be an analogy of aesthetic harmony in the entire system of aspects.

Mistakes:

- Harmony is not uniformity but the oneness of an orchestra or good team.
- Aesthetic is not confined to 'art' but pervades all of life. The aesthetic aspect is for everyone, not just the affluent, refined, clever,

educated. Artists have no special claim on it. The aesthetic aspect goes beyond art. "The beauty of nature," Dooyeweerd wrote (NC,II, 139), "is signified to those who are susceptible to aesthetic harmony, in the colours, the effect of light, the sounds, the spatial relations of nature etc." Mundane activities can be aesthetic.

Antecipations:

- "Only in justice must delight be sown; only by love should delight be watered; only in faith can true delight blossom" (Basden 2011b).
- Juridical depends on the sense of the whole that the aesthetic makes possible (NC,II, 135).
- Aesthetic can encourage the evils of unconcern, elitism and snobbery (juridical, ethical, pistic).

9–1.13 The Juridical Aspect

Kernel: Due. **Experienced as:** Appropriateness, responsibility and justice. We can experience this personally and socially as intuition of what is appropriate in situations, as debt (due to another), as rights and responsibilities, as legal proportionality, the actions of rewarding or punishing ("retribution" (NC,II, 129)), and as (un)fairness, oppression or emancipation.

Figure 9.13 The juridical aspect and some of its constellation

Good and Evil:

- The juridical aspect introduces the notion of appropriateness, of proportion, of right and wrong, of 'ought'.
- Juridical introduces (im)partiality, equality and fairness.
- Juridical dysfunction: partiality, inappropriateness, disproportion; injustice, oppression.

Foundational Dependencies:

- Depends on social agreement about what is appropriate, due or just for each kind of thing in its situation.
- Impartiality depends on aesthetic harmony: a "well-balanced harmony of a multiplicity of interests" (NC,II, 135).
- The use of precedent in legal judgments must harmonise with all previous judgments (though not necessarily agree).

Differences From Neighbours:

- Recreation (aesthetic) v. responsibility (juridical).

Notes, Discussion: NC,I, 29, 550, 553; NC,II, 67–70, 119–138, 181–185 and much in 290–411; NC,III discussion of the state

- Due: what is due or appropriate differs according to the type of thing (their aspectual profile, §4–3.4)—plant, animal, human. For humans what is due depends on roles (teacher, student, friend, parent). Due also varies according to situation.
- The misleading connotations of harshness and rigidity in *retribution*, Dooyeweerd argues (pp. 128–34), come from the pagan idea of revenge, the old Indian notion of *karma* and the old Chinese notion of *tao*, and that a richer meaning of retribution emerges with the Biblical notion of love.
- Justice is not justice unless it applies *to all*—not only to myself and people close to me, but also to people further away, the dead, past generations, future generations; to groups, roles, cultures; to animals, habitats: to all according to type. Hence its dependency on aesthetic harmony.
- So societal infrastructures of policy, law and enforcement have emerged, constructed by agreement (social aspect).
- Because of Dooyeweerd's roots in law and politics, his extensive study of the juridical aspect and especially his investigation of fundamentally different philosophies of law and of its manifestation in the institution of the state are worth taking seriously. But see Chaplin's criticism in §12–1.5.

Analogies of This Aspect:

- That aspectual law guides the temporal actualisation of reality might be an analogy of the juridical in the entire system of aspects (e.g. "law of gravity").

Mistakes:

- Right and wrong: Often confused with goodness (ethical).
- "Justice" is not just legal judgement, but the state of all things together being appropriate.

- "Retribution" is not revenge; see the Discussion.
- Fairness is juridical, but is often overplayed. Occasionally real justice feels unfair to individuals. Similarly equality.

Antecipations:

- That juridical functioning is better when tempered with love and mercy, and retribution guided by love is superior to revenge, antecipates the ethical aspect.

9–1.14 The Ethical Aspect

Kernel: Self-giving Love. **Experienced as:** Attitude of self-giving, generosity, openness (vulnerability), trust, willing sacrifice.

Figure 9.14 The ethical aspect and some of its constellation

Good and Evil:

- Full ethical functioning permeates reality with extra goodness, beyond the imperative of due, e.g. forgiveness.
- Self-giving can change attitudes in others, permeating communities or society, which benefits all, including the giver.
- Dysfunction: not hatred so much as selfishness, self-protection, advantage-taking, competitiveness, uncaringness, and so on, and these retrocipatively poison earlier aspects.
- In almost all cultures, those we call "truly good" are self-giving rather than selfish.

Dependencies:

- One can hardly claim love when one deprives others of justice.
- Like juridical functioning, ethical functioning is orientated towards the whole (aesthetic).

Differences From Neighbours:

- Law (juridical) v. love (ethical). (In Christian theology, law v. grace.) Rights v. mercy. Deserts v. generosity, mercy. Reward v. gift.
- Repaying good for good, evil for evil (juridical) ameliorates wrongs proportionately (zero-sum); repaying good for evil (ethical) increases the sum total of good in reality.
- Copyright (juridical) v. "copyleft", open source software (ethical).
- Self-giving vulnerability disarms hostility more effectively than laws or punishment do.
- Aesthetic and ethical functioning go beyond imperative, but whereas in aesthetic functioning, we ourselves benefit, in ethical the other benefits. *Agapè* rather than *eros* (NC,II, 153).

Notes, Discussion: NC,II, 141–60

- Also known as "moral aspect", "trothic aspect". I sometimes call it "attitudinal aspect" (because ethical functioning is not just overt acts of self-giving, so much as inner, oft-hidden attitude).
- Dooyeweerd (pp. 157–60) expresses the kernel meaningfulness of this aspect as "love". "Self-giving" is prefixed to it here, to differentiate it from self-centred desire.
- Notice the *paradox in the ethical aspect*: Giving with even the slightest hope that we ourselves will benefit (as in much social 'generosity') can become its opposite!
- Dooyeweerd argues that views of ethics by thinkers like Aristotle, Kant, Buber, Aalders and Brunner are controlled by dialectical presuppositions (§5–2.4) that make it difficult to keep morality separate from legality or faith (juridical, pistic), which is necessary (NC,II, 148). (However, does Dooyeweerd misinterpret Buber's distinction between I-thou and I-it, which I see as overcoming Heidegger's conflation of self-giving and self-formation?)

Analogies of This Aspect:

- Sharing goods is an ethical analogy in the economic; sharing stories is an ethical analogy in the lingual.
- Investment is an ethical analogy in economic functioning.

Mistakes:

- "Research ethics" is mainly juridical rather than ethical in the Dooyeweerdian sense.

Antecipations:

• What motivates self-giving? Never pushing itself, self-giving cannot be its own motivation; motivation is pistic.

9–1.15   The Pistic/Faith Aspect

Kernel: Faith, commitment. **Experienced as:** Belief, commitment, certainty, motivation, courage, ultimate meaningfulness, hope, morale.

Pistic ranges from that "immediate certainty which manifests itself . . . in practical life" (NC,II, 299) by which we live moment by moment (e.g. assuming chair will hold my weight), to firm ideological or religious belief for which people give their lives. Pistic is found at personal, group and societal levels as, for example, personal beliefs and the courage of those who stand alone; group beliefs and mindset (including *Weltanschauungen*); presuppositions that determine the direction in which theoretical thinking develops (§5–2).

Figure 9.15 The pistic aspect and some of its constellation

Good and Evil:

• Good: Courage, motivation, loyalty, hope, meaningfulness.
• Pistic enables the direction of society to be changed.
• Pistic functioning is profound and powerful in its retrociparory effects on all other functioning, bringing out both the best good and the worst evil.
• Dysfunction: Pride, hubris, narcissism (partly ethical), cowardice, disloyalty, despair, idolatry, meaninglessness.

Foundational Dependencies:

- Depends on good functioning in all aspects, for example the lingual (to exhort, praise), the social (together in a cause), but especially the juridical and ethical aspects.

Differences From Neighbours:

- Pistic commitment motivates ethical self-giving.
- Religious differences do not imply ethical differences.

Notes, Discussion: NC,II, 298–334

- Also known as "certitudinal aspect", "fiduciary aspect", "credal aspect" (which misleadingly connotes statements of faith).
- Faith is not *doxa* (Greek: hypothetical opinion) but is *pistis*, firm faith that is active certainty (pp. 303–5).
- Pistic functioning includes our ultimate identity—who we see ourselves to be and our ultimate meaningfulness—from which derives our life-meanings. Is this why identity politics runs deeper than justice politics?
- Dooyeweerd links pistic to our ability to transcend time (NC,II, 304).
- How faith relates to magic, totemism and myths: p. 312–8.
- Clouser (2005) differentiates religious from non-religious beliefs. Religious beliefs are *divinity beliefs* about what is ultimately self-dependent and on which all else depends; non-religious pistic functioning involves non-ultimate depending, e.g. assuming chair will take my weight.
- Dooyeweerd's entire *NC*, Volume I, may be seen as an argument that faith underlies all theoretical thought.
- In arguing the importance of faith in history (NC,II, 291–8), does Dooyeweerd place too much emphasis on Augustine's notion of struggle between *civitas Dei* and *civitas terrena*?
- Sadly, much of Dooyeweerd's discussion of this aspect seems occupied with defending his ideas against other Christian thinkers (who had attacked them). Ho-hum, the NGGM!

Analogies of This Aspect:

- Trust is pistic analogy in the ethical.

Mistakes:

- Assent to a creed is usually social, and only pistic if it expresses one's deepest faith-commitment.

Antecipations:

- None. Instead "this terminal aspect was destined to function as the opened window of time through which the light of God's eternity should shine into the whole temporal coherence of the world" (NC,II, 307). It is therefore the aspect of human functioning that welcomes Divine Revelation, or rejects it and welcomes a substitute.

9–2.   Grouping the Aspects?

Dooyeweerd is adamant that there are no *genus proxima* (NC,II, 14), no 'super-aspects' that group the aspects together. However, we often find it useful to group them according to what is meaningful to us at the time, for particular purposes. Indeed, Dooyeweerd himself occasionally does this, for example calling the first three the "mathematical aspects" (e.g. NC,II, 12).

Common groupings include:

- "physical" (including organic)—mental—social (5–4–6 aspects);
- mathematical—pre-human—cognitive—social—societal (3 aspects each)
- de Raadt (2002) groups aspects into character—civic—intellect.

The Good that a group offers is that of all its aspects, possibly with emphasis on one of the group. Be wary of grouping aspects. No one aspectual Good is *a priori* more important than any other.

9–3.   Comparison With Other Suites

Many thinkers have come up with other suites of aspects. Table 9.1 (in two parts) compares some with Dooyeweerd's suite.

Discussion of these may be found in "http://dooy.info/compare.asp.html" or Basden (2018a, 64–5).

Despite some combining or overlapping, three things stand out. (1) Most of the suites are subsets of Dooyeweerd's. (2) In most suites, the order is similar. This implies that Dooyeweerd's suite is at least a reasonable one to use. The way Dooyeweerd delineated aspects (§4–3.13), and his philosophical underpinning of them, makes it even more reasonable. (3) Some things seem to be multi-aspectual, e.g. being, functioning, risk, danger.

> *Research opportunity: suites of aspects.* The comparison of aspectual suites is based only on cursory reading in some cases and has not been subjected to peer review. Make it more rigorous by fuller discussion of each thinker's aspects in comparison with Dooyeweerd.

Table 9.1 Suites of aspects compared

Dooyeweerd Aspects	Maslow Needs	Checkland 'E's	Hartmann Strata	Bunge System Levels	Giddens Modalities	Habermas Action Types	Kierke-gaard Stages	Wilenius	Boulding	Roget Thesaurus	Encyc. Britannica
Quantitative										Abstract relations	Maths
Spatial										Space	
Kinematic										Space (motion)	
Physical			Inorganic	Physical Chemical				Physical	Mechanical	Matter	Matter Energy Earth
Organic/ Biotic	Biological		Organic	Biological				Organic	Creodic Reproductive Evolutionary Ecological		Life
Psychic/ Sensitive	Safety		Psychic					Mental Psychical	Cybernetic	Affection: personal	Life
Analytic	Enquiry	Efficacy							Human	Intellect	Logic Science Philosophy

Continued...

... *Continued*

Dooyeweerd Aspects	Maslow Needs	Checkland 'E's	Hartmann Strata	Bunge System Levels	Giddens Modalities	Habermas Action Types	Kierkegaard Stages	Wilenius	Boulding	Roget Thesaurus	Encyc. Britannica
Formative		Effectiveness	Historical	Technical	Power Domination	Instrumental					Technology
Lingual	Expression				Interpretive Signification	Communicative					Symbolism
Social	Affiliation Esteem		Supra-individual	Social		Strategic?		Social	Social	Affection: sympathetic	Society History
Economic		Efficiency			Resources						
Aesthetic	Aesthetic	Elegance				Dramaturgical	Aesthetic	Aesthetic	Social?		Art
Juridical					Norms Legitimation	Normatively regulated	Ethical (duty)	Truth	Social?	Affection: moral	Law Politics
Ethical/Attitudinal		Ethicality			Domination Moral sanction		Ethical (giving)	Ethics		Affection: moral	
Pistic/Faith	Transcendence Self-actualisation				Meaning	Discursive?	Religious	Religious belief	Transcendental	Affection: religion	Religion

9–4.   On Trusting Dooyeweerd's Suite

In discussing foundations of a field, any suite of aspects could in principle be employed that has irreducibly distinct kernels and for which inter-aspect relationships are understood, but Dooyeweerd's suite:

- has wider coverage than other suites, including mathematical, pre-human, cognitive, social and societal aspects (see §9–3);
- coheres (see §3–2.4);
- is geared to everyday ('real life') experience (see §3–2.1), rather than specific interests (e.g. Bunge's systems, Maslow's needs);
- takes into account 2,500 years of reflection across several cultures—including the Scholastic period, which some skip—so may be expected to apply in cross-cultural research (see §4–4.2);
- is grounded in a clear philosophical understanding of the nature of aspects (Chapter 4);
- has been subjected to the philosophical scrutiny of excluding antinomies (§4–3.13).

At this point in time, Dooyeweerd's suite of aspects seems to be the best suite available to us.

However, as Dooyeweerd warns us (NC,II, 556) no suite of aspects can ever claim to be a final truth. As Dooyeweerd says, "Theoretical thought has never finished its task"—especially not that of delineating the aspects. At any time, other aspects might be discovered, or existing aspects need to be split, merged or modified. However, as discussed in Basden (2008a, 2018a), attempts by others to alter Dooyeweerd's suite have not been entirely convincing. So, we may use Dooyeweerd's suite, but with caution and self-critique.

9–5.   Conclusion

This chapter presents an understanding of what is meaningful and good in each aspect. Full intuitive grasp of aspectual meaningfulness does not occur however just by reading, but by living reflectively within the aspects. This chapter can assist that living and reflection, especially during research.

It is intended for reference by the researcher and others during analysis of research data or texts, or the clarification of ideas or conceptual frameworks. The following chapters make much use of Dooyeweerd's aspects to understand the complex, multi-aspectual, human activity that is research (Chapter 10) and, through all stages of research, in dealing with research content (Chapter 11).

10 The Complex Activity
   of Research

This chapter is primarily about research activity, rather than content or application. As discussed in Chapter 2, the theoretical thinking that is the core of research cannot be separated from its everyday experience. Even mathematics, which some consider the purest, most analytical and most dispassionate form of research,

> involves more than just numbers and black boards but also politics, passion and dedication. It is no longer just a boring look at historical numbers and theories but a real life feel to the story behind the work.
> (Curtis & Tularam 2011, 267)

Shortly before that, Curtis & Tularam remark (p. 263),

> Little is known about what the real life aspects behind the numbers represents. There is also not much written on the passion, politics and real life but rather one notes instead numerous texts on higher level work with pages of lifeless numbers.

This chapter attempts to rectify that. Though the philosophical under-pinnings of research may be understood via Ground-Ideas, as discussed in Chapter 7, actually carrying out research is multi-aspectual functioning (§4–3.8.2), involving every aspect in coherence with all others. In research activity, we function in every aspect simultaneously, pre-human, individual, social and societal together. The aspects are irreducibly distinct and yet inher-ently inter-dependent and without fundamental conflict (§3–2). Each makes a distinct kind of Good possible (§4–3.7).

This chapter discusses each aspect, not only describing research activity, but also offering it as a criterion with which to guide and evaluate research. Since the analytical functioning of research has been discussed deeply in Part II, this chapter concentrates more on other aspects. In Section 10–3, the 'obvious' aspectual functioning in research activity is briefly discussed, but it is the non-obvious, hidden aspects of research that require most dis-cussion. This occurs in Section 10–4. Before that, Section 10–1 outlines an overall attitude and approach which I have found useful, and Section 10–2 introduces research as multi-aspectual functioning.

10–1. Overall Approach: "LACE"

In Chapter 5, I argued that Dooyeweerd's approach was not antagonistic nor acquiescent to mainstream philosophies but critically engaged therewith. Several times, "listen, affirm, critique, enrich" (acronym "LACE") has been mentioned. This is an approach I have deployed to engage with thought that is based on different research philosophies, approaches, ground-motives or standpoints from my own. I recount it here for any reader who, likewise, wishes to engage with thought that differs from their own in fundamental ways. It rests on the presupposition of a common 'ocean' of meaningfulness in which we all 'swim' (§4–3.10). Doubtless, other methods are available too.

10–1.1   The Elements of LACE

LACE is partly a technique and partly an attitude. Listening and affirming free us from antagonism, while critiquing and enriching free us from acquiescence, to engage fruitfully with different streams of thinking. The four elements are expressed as guidance.

- **Listen** to the ideas and discourses intently, to discern what is primarily meaningful at their core. Respect the diversity of meaningfulness, assisted by an intuitive grasp of Dooyeweerd's aspects (§4–3.13). In their own terms, concepts and values rather than my own, what were they trying, deep down, to achieve, and why—what is their motivation? This prepares us for both immanent and transcendental critiques (see §6–2).
- **Affirm**, as far as possible, what their discourse aims at by understanding from their perspective what they see as problematic in previous thought (which might be any elements of the underlying Ground-Idea). Refuse to get distracted by peripheral paraphernalia like connotative terminology. This is part of immanent critique (§6–2.1). The lenses through which researchers view the world can be identified by reference to Dooyeweerd's aspects and related by his understanding of inter-aspect relationships (§3–2.4). (Aligning lenses with ground-motive poles, as some Reformational philosophers do, I find less helpful, because it incites rejection.)
- **Critique** the way the other thought has developed, by exposing foundational presuppositions, and work out whether they prevent their ideas achieving what they hoped. This is part of immanent critique. Often, what has been proposed to fulfil their motivation has been constrained by an immanence-standpoint or dialectical ground-motive; refer to problems of these in §5–3.1, §5–2.4, especially absolutisation of aspects. Work out what is generally necessary to fulfil their motivation (transcendental critique, §6–3). I find that thinking in terms of meaningfulness is helpful here.
- **Enrich** their ideas. The transcendental critique prepares for this by clarifying what is important. I have found insights from Dooyeweerd's philosophy helpful, especially aspects that have been overlooked.

The process can reveal unexpected possibilities not currently discussed, including new paradigms. Listening and affirming are especially important when there is disagreement or even dislike.

Examples follow of LACE in action, with two of philosophy's roles, approaches (§5–1.2) and foundations (5–1.3). Though, from my experience in the field of information systems, they may be generalised for other fields.

10–1.2 Example of LACE With Information Systems Approaches

The discussion of apparently incommensurable approaches in §7–3.1, and at greater length in Basden (2011a), is actually an exercise in LACE; it should be read alongside what follows.

First, we *listened* to what was said about positivist, interpretivist and socio-critical approaches by their proponents and opponents, to understand what each tries to do and what motivates it. Using Dooyeweerd's notion of Ground-Idea (§7–1) and his suite of aspects, we identified how each approach understands the world, what rationalities each employs and the wider meaningfulness that is referred to by its community when critiquing research within the approach. Dooyeweerd's aspects not only helped separate out differently meaningful issues, but, taking aspectual normativity into account, *affirmed* them. See Table 7.2.

Critique was not of the approaches themselves but of the presumed incommensurability. As argued in §5–2.4, this arises from the Nature-Freedom ground-motive and leads to irresolvable paradox.

Reinterpreting the approaches from Dooyeweerd's pluralistic ground-motive offers two types of *enrichment*. One examines variants of the socio-critical approach (Habermas, Foucault, Bourdieu) by reference to secondary aspects. The apparent paradox of emancipation as both freedom and constraining norm is resolved when understood as of the juridical aspect (§7–3.1). The other incorporates other approaches within the same picture; Basden (2018a, 99–101) adds in action research.

Such an analysis of research approaches does four things. First, it shows that the approaches are not necessarily incommensurable; each might make its own unique contribution. Second, it provides spaces where other approaches may be located that need no longer to be squeezed into the main three, such as action research. Third, it replaces conflict with mutual appreciation and humility as part of the multi-aspectual activity that is research (see later). Fourth, it suggests that there may be a myriad of other research philosophies, each having a different combination of different aspects.

10–1.3 Examples of LACE With Foundations of Information Systems

Chapters 5 to 9 of Basden (2018a), which are summarised in §11–3.6, explore and sometimes suggest foundational frameworks for understanding the information systems field. They demonstrate various ways in which

Dooyeweerd's ideas can affirm, critique and enrich foundations. The use of LACE is exemplified in its Chapter 6, which formulates a foundational framework for understanding how humans use ICT (information and communication technology).

Listen

Seventeen discourses around ICT use were 'listened to' carefully by reading their literature and by being involved in them. Some are listed below. 'Listened to' were not only academic research literature and professional literature, but also everyday experience. The author's 'listening' occurred over a lifetime of being active in several discourses and activities, from the emergence of the topic in the 1970s to the present day.

The aim of listening is to find out what key issues are central in each discourse. This was informed by some portions of Dooyeweerd's philosophy explained in Section 4–3, such as the novel idea of subject-object, the distinction between law- and subject-object-sides, the multi-levelled understanding of things and of relationships, and the 'oceanic' view of meanings and meaningfulness. See Basden (2018a, 154–219) for details.

It is important to listen especially to minority discourses on the fringe of the field and, by reference to everyday experience, to detect missing discourses, because these can highlight overlooked aspects. Example: Computer games and home computing, in which the aesthetic aspect is important, are under-discussed.

Affirm

The key issues were affirmed by explicit reference to portions of Dooyeweerd's philosophy. For the 17 discourses listed in Basden (2018a, 211–2), different portions were found important, for example:

- 1, Ease of use and interactions with technology (human-computer interaction (HCI))—Aspects, Law-subject-object
- 2, Organizational issues in IS—Aspects, Theory of social institutions, Enkapsis
- 5, ICT in its Wider Environment—Theory of being, Aspects, Immanence Standpoint, Law-subject-object, Enkapsis
- 9, Information systems success—Aspectual normativity
- 14, Discourses on non-use of ICT, resistance—ICT as object within multi-aspectual human functioning; Everyday experience
- 15, Use of features of ICT, Affordance—Aspects, Law-subject-object
- 17, Applications and domains overlooked by the IS field—Target aspects, Meaningfulness of each aspect

Taken as a whole, Dooyeweerd's philosophy was able to affirm each and every discourse.

Critique

Each discourse was critiqued, especially by reference to overlooked aspects or to philosophic theories that take an immanence-standpoint and so get tangled up in its problems, listed in §5–3.1. Some discourses divorce meaningfulness from reality and, especially, ignore normativity. Some, such as that on affordance, struggle because they presuppose the subject-object relationship offered by Descartes or Heidegger. Some struggle with the multi-aspectual nature of reality, being overly reductionist or ignoring aspects. Lack of interest in certain issues (missing discourses) may be critiqued by reference to everyday experience.

Enrich

Dooyeweerd's philosophy enabled a conceptual framework to be sculpted that makes sense of all 17 discourses (an "Aspectual Engagements Framework" described in §11–3.6, in which engaging with interface and technology, with meaningful content and in life with ICT, are all seen as multi-aspectual subject-object and subject-subject functioning). This enabled many of the discourses to be reinterpreted. Not only were many overlooked aspects then offered to the various discourses, but, as discussed in Basden (2008a), separating issues into aspects revealed a third aspectual engagement (with meaningful content) which helped clarify confusions that had occurred when it had been conflated with the other two engagements. The metaphor of ocean of meaningfulness and the innate normativity of aspects proved especially helpful.

Chapters 5, 7, 8, and 9 of Basden (2018a) undertake a similar, though slightly different, exercise of LACE, with four other areas of concern, the nature of information and computers (including artificial intelligence), ICT features, societal issues and information systems development. Nearly 40 other discourses were listened to and enriched in these areas. The exercise resulted in over 100 specific suggestions for projects to enrich research in the IS field.

> *Research opportunity: rethinking foundations.* As far as I am aware, the above approach may be applied to any field, from mathematics, through the sciences and humanities, to theology, by listening to discourses and everyday experience for key issues, affirming by reference to portions of Dooyeweerd's philosophy and from these constructing foundational conceptual frameworks, critiquing by reference to failures of the immanence-standpoint and ground-motives, and enriching by reinterpreting the discourses by reference to the framework and other Dooyeweerdian ideas.

10–2. Research as Multi-Aspectual Functioning

Saunders et al. (2012), typical of books on research, has chapters on the:

- Business and management research, reflective diaries and the purpose of this book;

- Formulating and clarifying the research topic;
- Critically reviewing the literature;
- Understanding research philosophies and approaches;
- Formulating the research design;
- Negotiating access and research ethics;
- Selecting samples;
- Using secondary data;
- Collecting primary data through observation;
- Collecting primary data using semi-structured, in-depth and group interviews;
- Collecting primary data using questionnaires;
- Analysing quantitative data;
- Analysing qualitative data;
- Writing and presenting your project report.

This is a reasonably complete set for much research, though perhaps modified in the natural sciences, where data-collection is through experiment or field studies; in mathematics, where imagination, deduction, computer searches or thought experiments play important parts; and in conceptual research like philosophy, where argument is a major activity. In *Research Techniques in Organic Chemistry*, for example, Bates & Schaefer (1971) discuss only three things:

- reaction techniques;
- isolation techniques;
- structure determination techniques.

It was assumed then that all organic chemistry research consists of forming or analysing new compounds, so issues like clarifying research topic and negotiating access and research ethics did not warrant much discussion. In their Introduction, they mention use of literature, but only to find out if the compound of interest has already been studied.

Many texts on research treat it as a collection of *tasks* to be completed, as components of the overall research activity, either in sequence or in cycles. In this chapter, however, the activity of research is discussed from the point of view of its *aspects* rather than its component tasks or activities. This is for three reasons.

1. Aspects are cross-cutting concerns, which might permeate or apply to all tasks and component activities. This is especially so for the later aspects, though some of the middle aspects are those which qualify tasks mentioned above (see Table 10.1). The coherence of meaningfulness (§3–2.4) implies that we cannot justify what we are doing based on one aspect when we ignore, or function poorly in, others. Therefore, research activity is treated as full *multi-aspectual functioning* (§4–3.8.2), in line with its everyday quality (§2–6.2).

2. The tasks mentioned earlier are the obvious activities or aspects of research, whereas there are many hidden issues, such as the impact of competitiveness. These are seldom discussed in research texts, so they are discussed here. Whereas individual issues may be discussed, as isolated problems, they are seldom discussed in relation to each other. Seeing research as meaningful in each aspect helps us do this.

3. Such texts offer guidance for research. The reason for guidance is that there is a difference between success and failure, between good and poor research. This presupposes meaningful normativity. It is in relation to meaningful normativity that we may question the offered guidance, may evaluate or design research for success. But there is a plethora of issues to consider (see Table 10.1) that lead to success or failure, and most texts gloss over them. I have found Dooyeweerd's aspects can help me maintain a whole picture, reveal and affirm hidden issues, and provide a basis for questioning and modifying standard guidance. This is possible because Dooyeweerd's aspects (a) express reasonably well the entire diversity we are likely to encounter and (b) innately guide because of their normativity. I have used them, not to avoid failure as such, but to avoid overlooking and misunderstanding issues that might lead to failure.

Section 10–3 looks at the above, and other, activities through the lens of aspects. Being often discussed, little extra is said here, except to show them all as part of a wider aspectual picture of the whole everyday experience of research. Section 10–4 then discusses hidden aspects one by one.

10–3. The More Visible Aspects of Research Activity

If the central aim of research is to understand, involving theoretical thought, then its primary aspect is the analytic (what Dooyeweerd would call its qualifying aspect). In Chapter 6, three transcendental issues of theoretical thought were discussed, and the activity around each involves analytic functioning: (a) abstracting aspects of the world for study (the analytic *Gegenstand* relationship), (b) applying rationalities to collected data to generate new knowledge and (c) the community distinguishing meaningful from meaningless grounds for critiquing the research.

Dooyeweerd argues in NC,I that theoretical thought is inescapably religious in nature; hence it involves pistic functioning. This is part of his contention that theoretical thought must be understood as undertaken by the fully human person (§2–3.3), and my experience concurs: the real activity of research involves all aspects, alongside the analytic and pistic.

This may be first indicated by asking which aspect primarily makes each of the tasks meaningful, which are listed above for business and organic chemistry research; readers may add their own. These are shown in Column 2 of Table 10.1. Column 3 expands on this, to indicate many more issues, which are mentioned throughout this book, especially §5–2.4, §6–1.2, §6–3.3, §6–3.4, §6–3.5, §7–1.2, §11–6.4, and Table 3.1.

Table 10.1 The multi-aspectual activity of research

Aspect	As listed above	More research activity (examples)
Quantitative	Analysing quantitative data	Measurement; Statistics; Scale; Management evaluation
Spatial		Geographic distance between researchers
Kinematic		Movements of thought
Physical		Physical environment
Organic		Researcher health
Psychic		Sensory-motor activity of observation; Researcher mental health
Analytic	Clarifying research topic, Critically reviewing	Argument, Conceptualisation, Gegenstand Abstraction
Formative	Formulating research topic, Formulating research design; Reaction, Isolation, Structure-determination techniques	Innovation; Purpose; Planning, preparation; Modification (of plans or ideas); Techniques, tools, methods; Facilitation, Power
Lingual	Reflective diaries, . . . reviewing the literature, Using secondary data, Collecting primary data (interviews, questionnaires), Writing and presenting project report.	Writing, discussing, interviewing, recording; Dissemination
Social	Negotiating access	Researcher-researched relationship and co-construction of data; errors of collusion Team-working, networking, community; Reputation (also pistic); Professional bodies; Peer review; Consensus and conflict
Economic		Managing research resources (time, funds, skills, effort); Paper length limits, Patience (treated as a resource)
Aesthetic		Harmonizing rationalities; Situating research in scholarly context; Applicability; Taking time for reflection
Juridical	"Research ethics"	Accuracy, completeness; Honesty; Democracy
Ethical		Self-critique; Transparency, openness; Discussion of limitations
Pistic/Faith		Reliance on prior theory, assumptions, etc.; Presuppositions; Suspicion thereof; Working against denial

From Column 2, it appears that the standard texts on research methods cited at the start may be overly narrow in which aspects they discuss (though Saunders et al. (2012) do discuss some wider aspects in their text).

Good research will function well in all aspects, whereas dysfunction in any aspect might jeopardise the success of research, especially in the long term (the *Shalom Principle* §4–3.7). An awareness of how every aspect is important in research activity can guard against common errors, such as the economic emphasis on funding may be seen in its context, so that it no longer drives research in inappropriate ways and yet recognises its rightful place. Such an aspectual understanding of research activity might offer better criteria for evaluating the quality of research carried out in institutions; for example, which aspectual issues does the UK Research Excellence Framework recognise and which does it ignore?

> *Research opportunity: research methods.* Explore the multi-aspectual nature of research and research methods in each field.

However, for full success in research we must take account of the hidden aspects, on which some in Column 3 verge.

10–4. Some Less-Obvious Aspects of Research Activity

Much that is important in research activity is taken for granted, yet it either contributes to success of the research or jeopardises it. This section discusses what many people in my experience have been saying privately, piece by piece, and brings some of them together, categorised by aspect. The issues discussed are encountered in the everyday experience of research, but at every level, from the individual researcher to their group and institution, to society. It offers an exemplar (paradigm) for how readers might find it useful to discuss others they encounter.

The chapter opened with "politics, passion and dedication". For example, see Walden University's online article that covers various hidden issues (Walden 2010). Under the heading of "choosing the right topic", among the more obvious tips, they advise "make sure the topic will hold your interest", "develop a doable topic", "you can't change the world with one dissertation", "let yourself shift gears", "fine tune your topic based on input from others". Other tips include, for example, "don't waste your money", "leverage the power of a network", "don't be afraid to reach out", "persevere", "follow your passion and purpose", "reward yourself", "ask for help".

This raises questions, such as "Why is each important?" and "Are there others not mentioned in their lists?"

In answer, Dooyeweerd's suite of aspects offers itself, since it has wide coverage of the normativities found in everyday experience and the laws that express them (§4–3.7, Chapter 9). Examining each aspect helps not only to account for such issues but also, with imagination, to think of others. We will consider the pistic to social aspects separately and then the early aspects together. By starting with the pistic aspect, we will see the retrocipatory influence that later aspects have on earlier ones.

The discussions that follow contain few citations. This is partly because many come partly from my own observations over the past 50 years, and partly because the issues discussed are seldom discussed. I cannot claim full verity, because I have not carried out careful research about them, but I offer them as stimulants to further discussion and also to demonstrate how an aspectual view can bring out issues that might not usually be discussed.

Readers will find some Walden issues in what follows, but aspectual consideration of the rest is left to readers, as an exercise.

10–4.1   Less-Obvious Pistic Functioning in Research

There are several ways in which the pistic aspect is important in research, beyond the obvious ones mentioned earlier. Refer to §9–1.15.

One of these concerns the meaningfulness or value of doing research in general: What's the point? Having a positive view of this will motivate the researcher ("passion"), and a negative, demotivate. Motivation and a sense of meaningfulness, as a pistic issue, affects almost all other functioning. Pistic motivation refers not primarily to the purpose or aim, but to the wider issue of "What does this research contribute to, and is meaningful in, the body of knowledge?" or even "Why do I/we research?"

An important motivator is religious or ideological beliefs. Johannes Kepler's motivation for his astronomy research was:

> I was merely thinking God's thoughts after him. Since we astronomers are priests of the highest God in regard to the book of nature, it benefits us to be thoughtful, not of the glory of our minds, but rather, above all else, of the glory of God.

Similarly, much Marxist, Feminist and Queer research is motivated by ideology. Religious or ideological belief inspires the individual researcher with direction and perseverance. What motivates a society to take research in a particular direction is their 'ideology' as rooted in the prevailing ("religious") ground-motive (§5–2.3, §6–3.6).

Where such beliefs are declared openly, as both the socio-critical approach and Dooyeweerd demand, dialogue can be opened up (as long as religious/ideological beliefs are not imposed on research), but too often their effect is masked and dialogue closes down. This is especially so with the secularist view that pervades much society, robbing our bodies of knowledge of benefit from religious perspectives (§5–2.4). Dooyeweerd's notion of Ground-Idea was designed to assist in opening up such dialogue (§7–3).

Pistic functioning can take other forms, both personal and social, both positive and negative.

Commitment is pistic—but this takes several forms, directed to several things, for good or ill. It is pistic commitment to their research topic that keeps a researcher persevering until they find a solution. It is pistic commitment to quality of research that inspires them to persevere until they get something right. Yet it is also pistic commitment that makes a researcher stubborn, holding onto theories (beliefs) regardless of evidence to the contrary. The difference is found not in the pistic but the ethical aspect, of self-giving versus self-protection.

Loyalty is pistic—to colleagues, institution, topic and especially to the research project and to the good of society and world. Albert Einstein is reputed to have refused to follow a research idea because of the harm that might come from it. Loyalty is crucial in most research projects since, when a key person leaves, the project often fails. The 2014 British Research Excellence Framework encouraged poaching of researchers by institutions from each other, which, I believe, devastated much research activity, so the 2021 Framework has changed its rules to discourage poaching.

Idolatry is pistic, negatively. When researchers grumble about their institution (university?) treating itself as the highest good and themselves as mere pawns, idolatry might lie at the root—idolatry of the institution. "Politics" in research is often motivated by idolatry and undue commitment, usually tacitly held. More widely, society's idols have widespread deleterious impact on humanity's mandate to research (§1–2.1), for example the monetization of research is a societal idolatry centred on the economic aspect.

At the interface between the personal and social is courage: courage to try new things or follow new ideas that are not fashionable, or courage to withstand pressure from peers, institutions or society. However, there is a difference between courageously following a new good idea and being over-keen to undermine established ideas (an idolatry of criticality for its own sake). The difference between them is not explainable in the pistic aspect but from the ethical, in that true courage involves willingness to sacrifice rather than defend one's own.

Thus, in these ways, and others, the pistic aspect can be important in the activity of research, though it is seldom discussed as such. Its impact is mediated via its retrocipatory effect on our functioning in other aspects. The solution to problems therein is not to be found in those aspects but in the pistic. And conversely . . .

10–4.2   Less-Obvious Ethical Aspects in the Activity of Research

To my shame, I recall, after I had critiqued a paper, being told, "They were devastated by your criticism!" Critique should never devastate. By contrast, I recall a critique of one of my early papers, in which I had shown an immature grasp of the topic, which showed mercy and was encouraging—and as a result I worked hard to produce a good paper. Both were critiques that could inform the papers; they differed in the ethical aspect, which mandates an attitude of self-giving love, rather than indifference or selfishness. It is a crucial aspect of the culture of research, pervading it in many hidden ways, some of which are discussed here.

> *Note on terminology: ethicality.* To many, "ethical" means what *ought* to occur, which is juridical. Do Dooyeweerd, and here, "ethical" is about going beyond what is due; it is about goodness. Refer to §9–1.14.

The ethical aspect norms a *generous attitude* towards colleagues (and towards groups, institutions, society, world and topic) being willing to make sacrifices for the good of others. Fortunately, generosity is generally accepted in most research communities at least as an ideal. We are expected to share our findings and open ourselves to critique, so that refinement can occur. A strong research group should not seek primarily to win plaudits, but to gift good researchers to others, so all may flourish.

Trust is an ethical issue of self-giving, of willingness to be vulnerable. It is different from, though closely linked with, the pistic act of relying on and believing something.

> Without trust there can be only my truth, the truth of my personal life and its experiences, and so only subjectivism. I must trust others if my grasp of truth is to be more than a merely subjective whim; I must trust my culture if I am to learn which resonances to trust.
>
> (Puddefoot 1999, 70)

The best researchers rejoice as much in advances by others as by themselves. It is often the ethical aspect that governs how we respond to thinkers with different underlying beliefs to ours, either negatively as competitors or positively to engage meaningfully. *Scientific modesty* has long been recognised as a virtue—the willingness to consider oneself wrong, to question one's own ideas and approaches, and to be open to the unexpected, as in Klein & Myers' (1999) principle of dialogical research which calls researchers to be willing to revise ideas or even abandon those once held dear.

Modesty is a corollary of theoretical thought not being able to capture the full diversity and coherence of reality.

> Real scientific modesty, however, should begin with a clear distinction between theoretical abstractions and the integral structures of human experience. The attempt to reduce the latter to the former is no real scientific modesty. On the contrary, it testifies to a hidden *hybris*, which . . . identifies this theoretical construction with the whole of empirical reality.
>
> (NC,III, 26)

Unfortunately, in some fields, modesty and openness have been replaced by trying to impose or bolster one's own ideas. My experience of the social sciences has been of supporters of each theorist trying to defend rather than critique them, with the result that only external critique is offered—and ignored. Such attitudes spread throughout the community, as each begins to defend their own ideas. Socio-critical theory itself seems to me to lack much understanding of the ethical aspect, replacing it by its opposite, power (see §7–4.1).

A highly destructive hidden influence of ethical dysfunction is the *competitive attitude* that pervades the global research community: every person or institution follows their own self-interest. The belief that competitiveness is valid is not a truth but pistic commitment. Though competition in research can sometimes stimulate creativity, in being a motivation that overcomes laziness or sloppiness (negative formative functioning), when competitiveness is promoted without qualification, it tends to bring even greater harm. Deutsch's (2000) classic work on competitiveness and cooperation differentiates between constructive and destructive competition. Giving the example of tennis, "In constructive competition, winners see to it that losers are better off, or at least not worse off than they were before the competition." Research, however, is not sport, and does not always have winners and losers. Instead, a self-centred, self-defending, competitive attitude harms all parties, while a self-giving attitude (the social aspectual analogy of which is cooperation) brings benefit throughout the research community.

Modesty, openness, generosity, trust or their opposites pervade all other aspects of research activity, such as our style of writing, our social relations, and our attitude to funding, through retrociptating other aspectual functioning. Though Deutsch initially seems to try to reduce competitiveness to psychological factors, they are influenced by "substitutability", "attitudes" and "inducibility", which may be understood as social, ethical and juridical retrociptations on psychical functioning. A concrete example of this retrociptation is the considerable time and human effort wasted because of the competitive nature of funding systems. Of the 550 person-years' effort expended on grant applications in one funding round in Australia, only 21% were successful, implying that over 430 person-years were wasted (Herbert et al. 2013). In 2016 in the UK, only 12% of applications to the Economic and Social Science Research Council were successful.

This raises the question of whether there is a more appropriate means of procuring the benefits that research should bring (contributing to our bodies of knowledge). One answer comes from the pistic aspect—commitment to something of ultimate meaningfulness, augmented with a juridical norm of due.

10–4.3   *Less-Obvious Juridical Functioning in Research*

For the juridical aspect, refer to §9–1.13.

The mandate of research is to contribute theoretical understanding to humanity's bodies of knowledge. "Mandate" is a juridico-pistic word, pistic as a meaningfulness beyond us to which we commit ourselves, and juridical as a responsibility. The juridical aspect highlights responsibility to bodies of knowledge, which has already been implied in previous chapters ("on which it is reasonable to rely" is a juridical issue). It is why research bias (§7–4.2) is a problem, and why standard texts emphasise carefulness, studiousness, criticality and exhaustiveness in research activity. Such issues, widely recognised, are not discussed here, except for one point, below.

The juridical aspect also highlights other responsibilities: to world and society, to those being researched, to colleagues and employers, to family.

Responsibility to world and society requires awareness of how research, in both its content and activity, might affect the world and society. Society includes not just the society in which researchers function (usually affluent, liberal society), but also that of those studied. This calls for respect for their societal beliefs, attitudes and structures, not treat them as objects of curiosity, as some early anthropologists did (see §2–2.2). Anthropology has learned its lesson; social, psychological and biological sciences might yet need to do so. The latter concerns responsibility to animals, plants and ecosystems, and may be extended to responsibility for planet and climate change (see discussion of this in Basden (2018a, 169, 264–5, 290–2)).

Responsibility to individuals being researched is often seen in terms of "research ethics" and is why ethical approval is needed before empirical study can begin. Though widely recognised, what is hidden about this is that it is not of the ethical (attitudinal) aspect but the juridical: It focuses on issues like consent and the privacy of data.

Responsibility to colleagues and employers takes a similar form to that in most organisational life. Again, a widely recognised issue, its hidden side is when responsibility to institution becomes over-played and used as an excuse for dysfunction in other aspects; the institution has become an idol (§10–4.1), so is it time to de-emphasise its claim on our responsibilities?

What is perhaps less discussed is responsibility to family. In Western cultures, this is often reduced to work-life balance, but this obfuscates the issue. As such, and especially in an individualistic culture, the focus can subtly shift to finding sufficient entertainment and social activity for oneself, and it becomes self-centred (ethical dysfunction). Among researchers with families, however, it is a responsibility to others—spouses and children—who are affected by the pressures of research life on the researcher. For international students from cultures like sub-Saharan Africa, the Middle East and India, the family takes on more importance than it does in individualistic cultures, and looking after families takes up considerable time. This is time that the young, unattached individuals from Western cultures can spend on extra reading and paper-writing to deepen their research and build their *curricula vitae*, for better careers, but these are denied to those with family commitments. There are several juridical problems here:

- Is not this discrimination against researchers with family commitments, especially international students . . .
- . . . especially against women and even more so for single mothers?
- Is it not an injustice to children?

- Some colleagues have remarked, "A PhD demands sacrifice"—is it right to impose those sacrifices on spouse and children too?

There is also a concern about responsibility to our bodies of knowledge, especially in the fields of social science and the post-social fields.

- Far fewer contributions are made to our bodies of knowledge from those with family-centred perspectives on life and reality than from those with individualistic perspectives. Does not this result in a gross, pernicious and long-standing bias in bodies of knowledge towards individualism and away from families?

Does not this make entire bodies of knowledge in the social, economic, artistic and legal sciences suspect? It is not enough to merely study perspectives, as a distal object of study, but for perspectives to be effective, they must be indwelt by researchers (§2–2.2). In my view, we need to install juridical structures that encourage rather than discourage family-friendly PhDs, such as defining PhD programmes midway between full- and part-time, and also attitudinal and social structures too. A similar issue arises for those with dyslexia and Asperger's syndrome; see §10–4.7.

Harmonising these and other responsibilities requires good aesthetic functioning.

10–4.4   Less-Obvious Aesthetic Functioning in the Activity of Research

The harmony of rationalities at the core of research involves aesthetic functioning; it has been discussed in §6–3.4 and §7–1.3. Here, other aesthetic issues are discussed. Research should be satisfying for all, enjoyable, interesting, exciting and exhibit a holism or harmony; refer to §9–1.12. There is a thrill in discovery and in developing new ideas. These things are seldom discussed but make a large difference to the efficiency and quality of research.

However, in seeking excitement, it is tempting to forget responsibility and generosity; the aesthetic aspect of research should itself harmonise with other aspects. Research is more satisfying when its various components, elements and even aspects exhibit a harmony among them that is more than just necessary for functional purposes, and even more so when it exhibits harmony with the world outside itself as discussed in Chapter 2.

Dysfunction in the aesthetic aspect tends to fragment research and make it less satisfying for at least some. This ranges from fragmented rationalities to attitudes like intellectual elitism. Intellectual elitism is partly pistic (elevated view of oneself) and ethical (self-centredness) but may be seen primarily as a kind of snobbery, which undermines the harmony of research in an entire field.

The widely cited paper, Klein & Myers (1999), which was discussed in §7–2.1, exemplifies multi-layered harmony. It fulfils a need (principles for what had been ad hoc). It links each principle with research and literature that illustrate it. It harmonises with philosophy (the hermeneutic cycle). It also harmonises with what is of central importance to researchers' actual experience, in that its principles encourage and challenge the very attitude of researchers. It is extremely well written, with each part linked with the rest and necessary to the overall theme. Aesthetics are enhanced when one is economic rather than wasteful; part of the satisfaction of Klein & Myers' (1999) paper is that it does not waste words. The aesthetic aspect depends on the economic.

10–4.5   *Less-Obvious Economic Functioning in Research*

Many economic issues in research are obvious. The following contains some examples of how we might think about hidden issues that are meaningful in the economic aspect. Refer to §9–1.11.

Frugality, often seen as to be avoided, is seen by Dooyeweerd as the beneficial kernel meaningfulness of the economic aspect—as long as it is not contaminated with the juridical dysfunction of unjust deprivation. The economic aspect often brings good in other aspects by retro- and antecipation. It stimulates creativity and innovation (aesthetic, formative). Being forced by editors to reduce word-count usually improves papers (lingual).

Research budgets are an obvious economic issue; less obvious is budget inflation in grant applications, which deprives other projects of funding. It may be driven by (a) fear of running out of resources and (b) all too often, our worth as researchers is 'measured' by managers in terms of how much funding we seek and attract, and, as a result, funding is sought for activities that are not fully necessary for research. We can understand the harm these cause, not from the economic aspect, but from the ethical and pistic respectively.

Patience is sometimes treated as a resource that runs out—but is it? Is it not rather like a muscle that is exercised and becomes stronger with use? An answer may be found in the ethical aspect: When thinking of our own patience, treat it as a muscle and just remain patient, but when thinking of the other's patience, treat it like a limited resource and do not over-tax it.

10–4.6   *Less-Obvious Social Functioning in Research*

Issues like the social nature of peer review, cliques, jealousies and the relationship of researchers to their families are often complained about privately but seldom discussed openly and seriously, yet their impact on research can be significant. These are the hidden social functioning of research; refer to §9–1.10.

Peer review, though many try to make it dispassionate, tends to involve networks of colleagues, which exert unseen bias on which research is supported or disseminated, as do cliques in conferences and groupthink in committees. Personal rivalries or jealousies can prevent research coming to light or bearing fruit. Conversely, good personal relationships can encourage people to good ideas and quality research.

It is common to view such issues through the lenses of either power or psychology. Power distorts the picture (see §7–4.1) and psychology cannot make the fine distinctions necessary. Rather than trying to understand social issues via other aspects (formative-ethical or psychic), it is better to understand them directly as social issues. Dooyeweerd (1986) developed a theory of social institutions, for which he differentiated types, the differences between which might help in understanding some hidden social aspects of research, especially concerning power relationships.

He differentiated intracommunal, intercommunal and interpersonal relationships, exhibited in research, respectively, in the need to make a cohesive team (and hence often a formal structure), in the interests of the various external stakeholders, and in the social friendships of participants. In intercommunal and interpersonal relationships, power relationships are inappropriate. They are valid only in intracommunal relationships, that is within a true social institution in which relationships of "authority and subordination" (Kalsbeek 1975, 199–200) pertain. Whereas, under the Nature-Freedom ground-motive, authority and subordination are seen as limiting freedom, to Dooyeweerd they are enabling and should have no negative connotation, because they are tempered by the juridical and ethical aspects.

The issue of *family-friendly PhDs*, introduced above, is not just a juridical issue but also a social one. It is a difference in cultural expectations and in taken-for-granted agreements about what is important in each community; it is about respect. Part of the solution is juridical, and even pistic (vision of what is important) but part is social: to respect the culture in which families are important and install social structures for support of families as a whole, alongside policy changes.

10–4.7 Less-Obvious Lingual, Formative and Analytic Functioning in Research

Much of the lingual (§9–1.9), formative (§9–1.8) and analytic (§9–1.7) aspects of research activity are well discussed (see Column 2 in Table 10.1), so only a few points are picked out here, as exemplars.

Though universities provide guidance on how to read academic literature and to write papers, the *ability* to do these is taken for granted. Yet those with dyslexia and Asperger's syndrome, for instance, have difficulty with these; this is a hidden lingual issue. Such people find it difficult to properly understand what others are saying or writing, because some dyslexics find the words themselves difficult while Aspergics find they cannot sift information in the way neurotypicals do, but must first take every detail into account before gradually working out what is important. In speaking and writing, some dyslexics find they cannot express their ideas properly, while some Aspergics write too much detail because they do not understand what others expect of them. This results in what they say in conversation, and what they write in papers or funding proposals, being rejected and ignored.

The impact on research is not unlike those from researchers having family responsibilities, who are less able to read widely and publish than those without. Similar juridical issues arise: discrimination and robbing our bodies of knowledge of the contributions of the unique and important perspectives that such people might bring (§10–4.3).

Several lingual dysfunctions are seldom discussed or taken into account, and hence remain hidden. Example: Deceit is a lingual issue that is seldom discussed. While deliberate falsehood is rare, equivocation, etc., occurs more often than most expect; the researcher wants to get a message across and spins what is said towards that aim.

Today, most research is carried out in discrete *research projects*, with a defined purpose, aims and objectives, against which their outcomes are judged. This is a hidden assumption that is meaningful in the formative aspect, but it often has overriding importance. That the formative is not the primary aspect to guide research should enable us to question this assumption. There are several implications. (1) Research may also be carried out as an on-going process, not just in projects, as in the early days of science (but then it relied on having the leisure afforded by wealth). Today, officially, on-going research is among the duties of academic faculty, but other pressures today often prevent it, and management tends to measure research effectiveness by amount of project funding. (2) While projects benefit from planning, plans of research projects should always be open to modification because research, by its nature, is a search or exploration of what is not yet known, rather than some goal to achieve. Much research takes unexpected directions and some comes up with unexpected results. (3) Since the primary mandate of research is meaningful in the analytic aspect (finding out to yield theoretical knowledge), the convention that research projects state an aim might not be appropriate because aims are formative-aspect concepts. Instead, it may be preferable for research projects to be defined by a main research question that the research seeks to answer.

10–4.8   *The Early Aspectual Functioning in Research*

Consider the following. The kinematic aspect tells us that research is dynamic and we should beware of treating it statically. The spatial aspect reminds us of areas of study—but also that participants in research projects might be scattered across the globe. The quantitative aspect is used, not only to keep count of things, but often to measure things like researcher worth (§10–4.5) or usefulness (§3–5.2).

The role of the early aspects in research activity is often hidden in two ways. One is that early aspects of the concrete research activity are often taken for granted, except when problems occur. Spatial distance might hinder collaboration. The concrete physical aspect of research includes electric power and bearing the weight of heavy equipment. The concrete organic aspect of research includes health of researchers and participants. The concrete psychic aspect concerns not only seeing, hearing and motor activity, which is obvious especially in the natural sciences, but mental health of researchers and their families.

The other way is that early aspects are often hidden in analogies in later aspects. "Area of study" is a spatial analogy in the analytic, connoting extendedness. The physical aspect offers notions of causality and force, for which analogies exist in every aspect, as aspectual repercussion. Organic analogies include health and growth of research. Analogies can stimulate fresh ideas but, as mentioned in §3–2.4.3, they are dangerous if we let the laws of the analogous aspect encroach too far on our reasoning.

Measurement also depends on analogy. Whenever it is meaningful to say "more" or "less" of a property (e.g. worth, usefulness), we can transduce it into the quantitative aspect. But, again, we must not allow quantitative laws to encroach too far.

Though some of these early-aspect issues appear trivial or obvious, what aspectual analysis of research activity does is to give them a place in our thoughts so that we can ensure they are not forgotten and are treated properly.

10–5.   A Case Study: Activities in a Knowledge Project

Though Dooyeweerd's philosophy has been used in the activities of research, as discussed in the next chapter, no overall study has yet been made of this. However, Gareth Jones (Jones & Basden 2004; Jones 2007) discusses extensively his use of Dooyeweerd's philosophy in the activities of developing knowledge based systems (KBS). This is an example of design research.

KBSs, when used and run, advise or stimulate human users in thinking about their situations. In Jones' (2007) case, the situations were sustainability policy in a local authority in the United Kingdom, for which he built nine KBSs.

Jones sees a KBS as a 'theory', since the knowledge encapsulated within it is intended to be generally applicable and that on which it is reasonable to rely. Therefore, development of KBSs is not unlike research, in that it involves gathering knowledge of a topic, analysing it to determine the relevant generic knowledge and then expressing that knowledge. A major difference between research and KBS development is that the generic knowledge in a KBS must be precisely enough known to be a kind of computer program.

This section discusses Jones' experience using Dooyeweerd to guide his activity. His working in a new paradigm is discussed in §11–3.3, his method of knowledge elicitation, which resembles data collection, is discussed in §11–6.6, and his suggestions for refining Dooyeweerd's philosophy are discussed in §11–4.5 and §9–1.12.

Jones (2007) discusses his experience of using Dooyeweerd's philosophy in ten activities of the development process, comparing them with two published methods. Most are relevant for research, in that, for example, the KBS itself equates to the findings of the research, the knowledge elicited, to the data collected and some literature, and the researcher to the KBS developer.

Managing stakeholder commitment (identifying stakeholders who need to involved or considered, eliciting their concerns, and gaining commitment, taking account of tacit commitments). In research: supervisors, colleagues, others in the field, those who or which might be affected by application of findings—maybe replace "stakeholders" by "authors" (§11–8.1). Jones used aspects to identify possible stakeholders, those to whom the KBS is meaningful in some way) and their commitments (e.g. "to develop policy", formative; "to protect ecological systems", juridical-organic-psychical). He used the "normative" aspects to explore explicit and tacit stakeholder commitments and promote consensus around not only project goals but also the use of Dooyeweerd in the project. Using Dooyeweerd's aspects, he identified commitments that are usually hidden, (a) because they transcend management and business issues, such as social justice, ecological protection; (b) because they are tacit, such as declaring all hidden agendas to promote trust.

Conceptualising problematic processes (that could be supported by the KBS). In research: properly understanding the realities of the potential situations to which research findings are to be applied ("everyday experience": §2–6.1), including aspects hidden by differences of expertise and culture. With two experts, Jones investigated four multi-aspectual subject-object relations between developer, users and the artefact, separating out what challenges each by aspect. Aspectual analysis, teasing out ambiguous statements, revealed 20 issues (a "Very thorough analysis" (p. 170)).

Identifying potential KBS uses. In research: specific potential applications and contributions. Stakeholders often cannot clearly identify what the KBS should do. Jones considered potential uses of the KBS in clarifying, forming and referring (analytic, formative, lingual functioning with the KBS as prior object, §4–3.9) in relation to the 20 issues.

Choosing a set of feasible and beneficial uses. Evaluating the benefit and feasibility of each potential use, and then selecting therefrom, developing a prototype KBS, testing it with participants. In research: analysing the actual kinds of benefit that application might bring, given the capabilities of researchers and available source data. Jones used the normativity inherent in each aspect to clarify kinds of benefit; those uses with greatest diversity of aspectual benefits were expected to deliver greatest opening potential. Many unanticipated benefits were unearthed. Feasibility was also assessed by aspect, such as capability of development team (formative), ability of stakeholders to work as a team (social)—several of which are discussed in §10–4. The expertise in sustainability was obscure so it was decided to see if Dooyeweerd's aspects could be used in knowledge elicitation to clarify relevant knowledge; see below.

Identifying stakeholders. Four kinds of stakeholder: developers and users of sustainability policy, developers and users of KBS. In research, three kinds: researchers, those who apply the findings and those affected thereby. In each kind, Jones used aspects to differentiate stakeholder types (e.g. social aspect, respectively: KBS team, community groups, departments, citizens). Using Dooyeweerd's notion of enkapsis and theory of social institutions (§4–3.5), he identified numerous stakeholder associations. The breadth of aspects of Dooyeweerd's suite ensures that commonly overlooked stakeholders were included, such as plants, animals, charities (organic, psychic, ethical).

Eliciting knowledge (from which to construct the KBS). In research: both the ideas in the literature and the data collected (abstracted) from situations, from which findings are inferred. The knowledge elicitation method, from both literary sources and interviewing experts, "needed to handle the diversity and complexity of the normative activity of sustainable UDP policy development" (p. 215) and thus be non-reductive. Dooyeweerd's suite of aspects fulfilled this requirement, based on the Dooyeweerdian-Clouserian understanding of abstraction (§6–3.2) along with the normative direction that aspects give (§4–3.7). Jones found this elicited tacit and deep knowledge as well as explicit.

Handling antithetical knowledge. Most knowledge that experts hold expresses the prevailing worldviews (§5–2.1), which can be antithetical to the knowledge required for sustainability. In research: the best research takes a critical attitude to prevailing presuppositions, without acquiescence or antagonism. Jones shows how both can be avoided by an understanding of aspectual normativity, instead of either rejection or mere 'balancing'. Jones' example is free-market economics which, he argues, undermines sustainability by encouraging waste and exploitation, going against the economic aspectual norm of frugality.

Choosing inference goals (the main meaningful inferences the KBS will make about the user's situation, each time it is run). In research: research questions and final theoretical findings. Jones suggests using aspects directly as inference goals (examples in the housing KBS: "The Council's commitment and vision promotes sustainable housing development", pistic; "The Council identifies all important sustainability issues", analytic). Experts found this provided "an appropriate measure of sustainability" that was easy to understand and a window onto the knowledge base. Research questions can be usefully clarified and refined by orientation to aspects.

Crafting texts (questions, results, etc. displayed by the KBS when it is run). In research: questions in questionnaires and during interviews. These should be understandable and not misleading. Jones discusses ten issues, in most of which he found that aspects and inter-aspect analogies (§3–2.4.3) helped compose the text. For example, he considered each aspect of the effectiveness of text (e.g. psychic visibility, analytic differentiation of what is important to convey, aesthetic integration of texts into wider context). Standardising verbs by aspect (e.g. "identify" for analytic verb) helped to simplify and clarify wording. Feedback from the experts showed this approach to have worked very well. See §11–6.1 for questionnaire design.

Amending the prototype system. During trials of the prototype KBSs, users made comments, which were analysed to improve them. In research: responses to unexpected difficulties that demand the research be rethought. Jones used Dooyeweerd's aspects to separate out kinds of problem or improvement, such as concerning calculations (quantitative) or helping users make important decisions (analytic). Doing this helped identify not only improvements but also the root causes of problems.

Common to all these is that his Dooyeweerdian approach proved easy to apply, rapid, and comprehensive in coverage, lending clarity, and able to uncover possibilities that are not usually considered. The portions of Dooyeweerd's philosophy that Jones found most useful are the suite of aspects, subject-object relationships, functioning (especially intentionality), and enkapsis. Dooyeweerd's idea of qualifying and founding functions (§4–3.4) was not particularly helpful.

This was an impressive piece of work, which shows the immense power that Dooyeweerd's philosophy offers, in practice, when wielded by someone who understands it well. In Jones' research, Dooyeweerd pervaded everything, both the management of research activities and the undertaking of those activities in detail. There was commitment to Dooyeweerd as whole view, just as there is in socio-critical research, to Foucault, Bourdieu, etc. Jones may be seen as empirically testing Dooyeweerd's philosophy in this role. In Chapter 11, the role of Dooyeweerd in individual stages of research is discussed.

10–6. Conclusions

This chapter offers insights into the carrying out of research. It began with the general challenge of how to engage with thought based on a different approach, of which Dooyeweerd's is an example (LACE: listen, affirm, critique, enrich). Most of the rest of the chapter has been devoted to discussing aspects of the everyday experience of research activity, treated as multi-aspectual functioning. It finishes with a discussion of a case study using Dooyeweerd to guide activities similar to those found in research.

Treating research as multi-aspectual functioning and as everyday experience has painted a rich but understandable picture of the plethora of issues that inhabit research activity, which helps clarify in what ways each issue is important. Some issues (e.g. mandate) are meaningful in a couple of aspects.

Relationships among issues may be understood as inter-aspect dependency and analogy.

The picture is made possible because each aspect offers a space of meaningfulness in which issues may be placed. That aspects pertain, whether or not they are recognised and discussed, reveals hidden issues alongside those already widely discussed. This impels us to carefully consider every aspect.

With each aspect defining a different norm, the issues are no longer just descriptive; they offer guidance. Each aspectual norm is important for good research, and if there is dysfunction in any aspect then the quality, effectiveness or efficiency of research might suffer. This has allowed us to consider some issues quite starkly—such as family-friendly research. Research ethics has been extended beyond the normal juridical issues of privacy and consent into attitudes and responsibility towards many things. Being aware of how each aspect impacts on others gives pointers to increasing the efficiency and effectiveness of research.

In this way, the complex activity that is research may be more effectively managed and carried out, as the case study demonstrates. The discussion has interwoven all levels—the individual researcher, the group, the institution and society—just as they are interwoven in real life.

This chapter offers general practical guidance for carrying out research. Though it does not list all issues, it demonstrates how issues may be recognised, clarified, affirmed as important and linked with others, by reference to Dooyeweerd's aspects. Researchers will encounter many others in the everyday experience that is research and, with this approach, might better consider the importance of each.

Chapter 11 offers specific guidance on some of the more visible activities of research, by discussing experience of using Dooyeweerd's philosophy at each stage.

11 Experience of Research Using Dooyeweerd

This chapter reflects on actual experience of employing Dooyeweerd's philosophy in research. It draws on the adventures that a range of researchers have had with Dooyeweerd's philosophy in several fields, from a variety of countries and cultures in the Middle East, Africa, Europe, America, Australasia and Asia.

If the mandate of research is to help build bodies of theoretical knowledge that is generally applicable and on which it is reasonable to rely (§1–2.1), then what might be called a Dooyeweerdian approach to achieving this, as has been set out in the previous chapters, might be summarised as follows:

- Given that we consider research content, activity and application together rather than separately,
- and that research content is abstracted from the fullness of reality that we have called "everyday experience" (Chapter 2), which is meaningful diversity and coherence (Chapters 3 and 4), (and we may provisionally take Dooyeweerd's delineation of 15 aspects as set out in Chapter 9 as expressions thereof),
- and given that researchers are full human beings, so research activity has its own multi-aspectual everyday experience beyond the formal and logical, including hidden aspects (§2–6.2; Chapter 10), which together contribute to overall success (*shalom*: §4–3.7) of research,
- and given Dooyeweerd's approach of making meaningfulness the ground for all being (functioning), good and knowing (§4–3), so that ontology, methodology, axiology and epistemology intermingle (§5–1.1),
- and given that all philosophy and theoretical thinking is inescapably non-neutral (§2–3), being governed by ground-motives and standpoints of a religious character (Chapter 5), so that none may be considered

absolute truth (§6–1), though there is a truth or reality of which we may hope to gain some understanding (§6–4),

- and given that all theoretical thought involves *Gegenstand* focus on certain aspects of the world, by which data is abstracted, and to this data we apply multiple rationalities in order to generate findings as new knowledge to submit to the bodies of knowledge, and that the harmonising of those rationalities is our responsibility (§6–3, §7–1),
- and given that our findings are critiqued and refined by a community by reference to wider meaningfulness and its presupposed origin (§6–3.5),
- and given Dooyeweerd's notion of Ground-Idea as a basis for critically understanding research philosophies, seeing fields and paradigms as centred on certain aspects, and encouraging dialogue between ideas (Chapters 7, 8),

then we are in a position to review how Dooyeweerd's philosophy has actually been employed in research.

Section 11–1 outlines how Dooyeweerd's philosophy might be useful at each stage of research. Section 11–2 reflects on experience of using Dooyeweerd to provide overviews of the researcher's field and help in making sense of literature in the field. Section 11–3 discusses adventures with Dooyeweerd among paradigms and conceptual frameworks and Section 11–4, among concepts and ideas. Section 11–5 discusses the selection and justification of research methods. Section 11–6 discusses experience of using Dooyeweerd in data collection. Section 11–7 reviews experience of using Dooyeweerd in analysis of data that generates findings. Section 11–8 discusses a couple of gaps in the current experience.

11–1. Stages of Research Using Dooyeweerd

Each stage of a research project can benefit from Dooyeweerdian thought in different ways. Table 11.1 indicates which main portions of Dooyeweerd's philosophy might be useful at each stage (Column 1). Column 2 shows which elements of Dooyeweerd's notion of Ground-Idea (Chapter 7) are most relevant (W: world, R: rationalities, O: origin of meaningfulness). Column 3 sets out how understanding of, and reference to, Dooyeweerd's notions of ground-motives, immanence-standpoint and aspects can assist researchers at that stage (Chapters 4, 5).

Research opportunity: research stages. These suggestions arise from observation, as included in this chapter. They require working out with critical discussion and refinement.

Table 11.1 Dooyeweerd's philosophy in each stage of research

Research stage	Gl	Useful portions of Dooyeweerd's philosophy
Introduction: Clarifying, justifying the topic and the main research question	W O	**Ground-motives:** Can reveal root of dialectical conflicts so as to avoid taking sides. **Aspects:** Understanding aspect kernels can reveal major gaps in field and clarify meaningfulness of the topic in its field to situate, clarify and justify the main research question.
Literature Review: Selecting and analysing literature, finding gaps	W O	**Immanence Standpoint:** Can reveal presuppositions as root of problems in fields, and of narrowing of focus. **Aspects:** Can help understand what motivates discourses in field and identify missing discourses and gaps in literature that need researching.
Conceptual Framework: Choosing, justifying paradigm and preparing CF for the research	R	**Immanence standpoint:** Moving from presupposition of existence to meaningfulness, towards everyday conception of things. **Aspects:** Kernel meaningfulness and inter-aspect relationships can clarify what is really important; Suite of aspects help prevent overlooking issues; Helps maintain axiology.
Research Methods: Choosing, justifying approach/methods to use in research	W R	**Aspects:** Aspectual rationalities can clarify reasoning and validity of methods, along with aspects of world. **Ground-motives:** To see beyond apparent incommensurability.
Data collection and preparation	R	**Aspects:** Data collection guided by aspects can ensure richer picture. Aspectual interpretation can reveal full range of meaningfulness in data ready for analysis, especially overlooked issues, by separating out confused issues.
Discussion: Analysing data to obtain findings to submit to the bodies of knowledge	R O	**Aspects:** Meaning-kernels systematise reasoning; Quantitative and qualitative aspectual analysis help to uncover hidden issues, classify issues and recognise values.
Conclusion: Overview, limitations, contributions, future work	W O	**Ground-motives:** Can help set the findings within extant ground-motives without adopting them. **Aspects:** Aspectual analysis of what is meaningful to community might help situate findings more generally and practically.

11–2.   Understanding the Discourses and Literature of a Field With Dooyeweerd

The first two stages, introduction and literature review, provide an understanding of the field of research. Though each field might be defined by core aspects, as discussed in Chapter 8, to gain an overview of a field (including when writing research proposals) researchers must understand the diversity of discourses that range across the field and how they cohere around the topic to be researched. This is also useful at the conclusion of the research, when discussing contributions the research might make.

The importance of diversity and coherence is the second of Dooyeweerd's starting-points, discussed in Chapter 3. This leads us to the importance of his third starting-point of meaningfulness, discussed in Chapter 4. The discourses each revolve around something its participants find meaningful, and the entire panoply of discourses, which forms a context for research, itself exists and occurs in the 'ocean' of meaningfulness (§4–3.10).

Dooyeweerd's first starting-point, of respecting everyday experience (Chapter 2), raises two questions. How well does the literature address itself to the full reality of the field? And in what ways has the development of discourses to date been influenced by the everyday functioning (lifeworld) of the research community, especially in commitments, attitudes and responsibility?

It is with these starting-points that those who have adventured with Dooyeweerd's philosophy have found ways of gaining an understanding of the discourses in a field to fit them into a coherent picture, encourage inter-discourse dialogue, and find gaps that might make new research meaningful. Eriksson offers a method based on ground-motives (§11–2.1). Joneidy offers a method for systematic study of seminal papers (§11–2.2), which would be useful in a literature review. Breems has developed a method for acquiring an intuitive, immediate overview of the discourses in a field, which can be useful, when research starts, to reveal the gaps that any proposed research might fill (§11–2.4). Between them (§11–2.3) sit a couple of examples of how to make sense of diverse collections of papers.

11–2.1 Methods Involving Ground-Motives

As discussed in Section 5–2.4, Eriksson (2003) used Dooyeweerd's idea of ground-motives to reveal the roots of the conflicts among systems thinking approaches, to show there is space for multi-modal systems thinking (MMST, §11–3.2). Eriksson shows how extant approaches adhere to poles of the Nature-Freedom ground-motive and argues that MMST escapes this and can thus take better account of the richness of social reality.

Such an exercise gives a useful broad-brush overview of a field and its discourses, especially as a similar history may be found in many fields because of the malign influence of a dialectical ground-motive (§5–2.4). Hartley finds similarly in mathematics; see §11–3.1.

A ground-motive analysis is, however, seldom sufficient to fully justify a particular piece of research. A richer picture of the discourses in a field emerges when we use Dooyeweerd's aspects, as discussed in the remainder of this section.

11–2.2 Joneidy's Analysis of Seminal Papers

From time to time seminal papers emerge, which begin new discourses that might introduce new paradigms or variants thereof. How may we judge their contribution and fit them into an overall picture? How can we understand the relationships among them? How should we think about those that are not yet widely recognised?

Joneidy (2015) carried out an investigation of discourses around information systems use, analysing seven seminal papers. By an aspectual analysis method of excerpts from the papers, which is described in §11–7.2, he revealed what motivated the publication of each paper, in terms of aspects that made their motivation meaningful.

He found that in most papers two aspects are important in their motivation. Comparing the aspect-pairs across the papers can throw light on the discourse structure of the field. Unique pairs indicate a validly distinct paradigm (§8–2.2) and discourse, even if the paper is not widely cited. Sharing one aspect might indicate overlapping interests, and thus potential for immediate mutual understanding and dialogue. Sharing both aspects suggests papers are in the same discourse. Missing aspects might indicate discourses yet to emerge. Acknowledging aspectual diversity can encourage mutual respect among authors, paving the way to dialogue.

Joneidy has applied this technique in the fields of information systems use and healthcare informatics (Joneidy & Basden 2018; Joneidy & Burke 2018). A similar analysis is described in §11–4.4. He believes such analysis can facilitate assessing how the field is progressing, inspiring new researchers and structuring textbooks. It might also offer a systematic method for the literature analysis stages in research.

11–2.3   *Understanding Collections of Papers*

A decade before I discovered Dooyeweerd, I was involved in the fields of artificial intelligence, knowledge representation and computer cognition. In 2008, I joined Maria Kutar in a discussion of cognitive models, which resulted in an edited collection of 17 papers under the title *Advances in Cognitive Systems* (Nefti & Gray 2010). Maria and I contributed the final chapter, about which we believed,

> A final chapter of a collection like this, however, should not just review the others but should, if possible, suggest new and interesting ways forward that are, perhaps unknowingly, already implied in the other chapters.
>
> (Basden & Kutar 2010, 466)

The collection revealed such diversity that it was difficult to find a useful theme from within the two traditionally accepted paradigms of cognition as thinking (Descartes) or as interaction with the world (Heidegger). This dialectic had been well rehearsed for decades and tended to divide rather than unite. We opted for a third approach, based on Dooyeweerd's aspects, which bridges both and might bring the chapters together.

To achieve this, we identified the key issues that interest each chapter and, then, which aspects most made that issue meaningful, usually a pair of aspects for each chapter. For example, Chapter 7 is about strategic versus

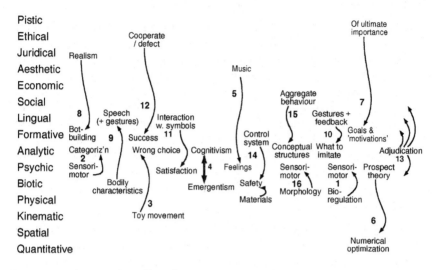

Figure 11.1 Aspectual profiles of cognitive modelling papers
Based on Figure 1 in Basden & Kutar (2010).

tactical choices in organism motivation, which seemed to us to be meaningful in the pistic (ultimate importance) versus formative (goals) aspects respectively. Figure 11.1 shows these aspects for the chapters (numbered).

This offers an overview of both topics and aspects that make them meaningful. It reveals both the diversity of the collection, in that nearly every aspect is featured in at least one paper, and its coherence, around the aspects most relevant to cognition itself, the psychic to lingual. This approach was able to bring Cartesian and Heideggerian perspectives together in one understanding.

I undertook a similar exercise in the field of built environment, contributing the final chapter to *Future Challenges in Evaluating and Managing Sustainable Development in the Built Environment* (Brandon et al. 2017). This collection of 19 papers emerged from a workshop in honour of Peter Brandon. Again there was considerable diversity, because we had been asked to "think outside the box", ranging from the role of carbon in sustainable development to smart cities, digital technologies, value-oriented stakeholder engagement, sustainability in practice, construction contracts, the role of time, and Peter's own chapter, "Initiative and Obsolescence in Sustainable Development".

My chapter (Basden 2017) sought to construct a coherent picture of the "outside the box" diversity from within the multi-aspectual paradigm of sustainability (§11–3.3), as well as suggest a way ahead. This approach let us see all the activities as multi-aspectual functioning. As above, aspects allowed us not just to feel the diversity but also to understand it. Unlike the field of cognition, where coherence was around some central aspects, here it was the whole "coherence of meaning" of all aspects, which underlies the entire reality of built environments.

11–2.4   *More Complex Inter-Discourse Analysis*

The above two examples yield overviews of discourses. Nick Breems developed a method that offers more complex understanding of the interests and capabilities of discourses. The primary reason for his research (Breems 2014) was to test Basden's (2008a) framework for understanding information technology/systems (IT, IS) use, as three multi-aspectual human engagements (see §11–3.6.3), but what interests us here is that, in doing so, he developed a method for (a) understanding complex problems and (b) understanding why extant discourses had not adequately addressed that problem. Breems' work led to the Aspectual Engagements Framework discussed in Basden (2018a), summarised in §11–3.6.3.

11–2.4.1   *Breems' Study*

Whereas a theory might be tested by falsification, a framework (or paradigm; see §8–2.2) must be tested for utility instead. Breems decided to investigate how well the framework could cast light on the challenging problem of computer procrastination—when faced with an arduous task, we take "just a few minutes" to check social media or play a game, and this extends to several wasted hours, so we end up feeling guilty!

By introspection of his everyday experience of playing the Yahtzee computer game, he identified aspects that make each of the three engagements (§11–3.6.3) meaningful; examples: spatial proximity in the user interface, aesthetic attractiveness of tempting content, and waste of time in life (economic). Potentially, this gives 3-times-15 (45) sets of aspectual issues. He similarly analysed, by aspect and engagement, five discourses that might be expected to throw light on computer procrastination—psychology, human-computer interaction (HCI), technology acceptance, non-work-related internet use (NWRIU) and problematic internet use (PIU). For his method, see §11–7.4 and Breems & Basden (2014).

For his empirical study and for each discourse, he charted the results as "heatmap diagrams", 3-by-15 arrays of cells, in which the shade, darkness or colour indicates how important a discourse finds the corresponding aspect of the corresponding engagement. The result is shown in Figure 11.2.

Breems' analysis shows (a) the different interests of the five discourses (for instance, psychology is concerned only with human life, HCI is concerned only with engaging with interface, TAM is concerned with both, but fewer aspects are important); (b) that some restrict themselves to one or two engagements and others to certain aspects; (c) that none of the discourses are adequate to address the full meaningful complexity of the problem of computer procrastination (right-hand heatmap) . . . (d) not even if the interests of the five discourses were amalgamated; (e) and that this might explain why the problem has not received the attention it should.

Breems' method is discussed more fully in Breems (2014) and Breems & Basden (2014). It offers a systematic approach to understanding diversity of discourses in a field as a whole, enabling comparisons of patterns of

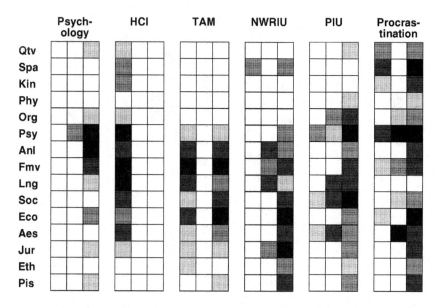

Figure 11.2 What is meaningful in computer procrastination and five relevant discourses

meaningful factors to be made both between discourses and with everyday experience.

> *Research opportunity: computer procrastination.* Breems' empirical study of computer procrastination was by introspection. Use the Aspectual Engagements Framework to make a more precise empirical study of computer procrastination—and other complex problems.

11–2.4.2   Basden's Study

Breems' method was used by Basden (2018a) to gain perspective on 17 discourses around IT use (see §11–3.6.3), which is shown in Figure 11.3. For full explanation and discussion of this, see Basden (2018a, 209–12).

Briefly, this reveals the following about the research area that is IT use.

The field is unbalanced, with only two discourses interested in engaging with interface and technology, and only three seriously interested in engagement with meaningful content. In 11 of the 17 discourses, aspectual issues appear mostly in the right-hand column, which expresses engagement in life with IT. The lack of interest in the other two engagements is worrying. Might this suggest the need for a substantial change in direction in the field? The growing interest in 'materiality' and affordance (#15) might indicate awareness of this, and Dooyeweerd's philosophy can affirm, critique and enrich them (see Chapters 6 and 7 in Basden (2018a)).

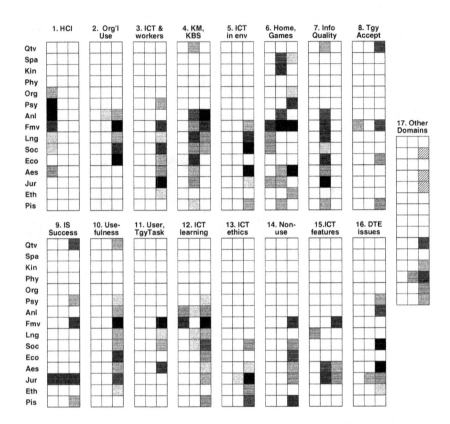

Figure 11.3 Aspectual engagement heatmaps for 17 discourses in IS use

Likewise, certain aspects are given much more attention than others—the formative and juridical, especially—and many aspects are ignored. For example, there is little discussion of the ethical aspect in the field, as self-giving love, and maybe even presupposing its dysfunction (self-interest), which might account for problems in social media. Underrated aspects suggest new avenues of research that might be fruitful. We might critique each discourse by pointing to its limited ranges of aspects and suggest that considering other aspects might enrich it. We might examine whether reductions of ignored aspects to favoured aspects have occurred in a discourse; for example, of ethical to juridical aspect when thinking about "ethics".

One discourse, "6. Home, Games", finds more aspects meaningful than others do and recognises the importance of all three engagements. This perhaps is not surprising, since home computing and computer gaming are closer to everyday life than are most of the other use topics, which are from a professional context. Frissen (2000, 73) argues that "knowledge of the dynamics of everyday life is indispensable to understanding the processes of acceptance of ICTs"; this aspectual analysis reveals that his call seems to have gone unheard.

11–2.4.3   Reflection on Heatmaps

This approach offers a principled way of gaining an overview on diversity, because it can investigate and express complex patterns of aspects in a way the human visual system finds it easy to process.

Shading is, of course, not as precise as the length of a bar or a number, so such a display is useful where degrees rather than precise counts are to be shown, especially those arising from intuitive judgments, as in Breems' and Basden's studies. Their judgment of how important each aspect of each engagement was within a discourse arose from their reading of papers within it, noticing the frequency with which issues meaningful in each aspect were mentioned; Joneidy's method above is more systematic.

> *Research opportunity: discourses in a field.* Undertake similar analyses in other fields.

11–3.   Conceptual Frameworks: Dooyeweerdian Adventures Among Paradigms

Research is carried out with reference to a conceptual framework and within a paradigm. Usually, these are selected from extant alternatives, perhaps with modification, and Dooyeweerd can help critique them, to inform the selection. Sometimes, either or both might be constructed anew, and Dooyeweerd is especially good for that, because of his radically different standpoint. This section looks at experience of using Dooyeweerd's philosophy to critique paradigms, generate new paradigms and formulate conceptual frameworks, demonstrating several different approaches that readers might generalise for their own fields.

11–3.1   Critique of Paradigms in Statistics

Hartley (2008) identifies four paradigms for statistical inference—direct and indirect frequentism (DF, IF), and objective and subjective Bayesianism (OB, SB). He argues that these paradigms influence both the statistical procedures used and how the results thereof are interpreted. He then employs Dooyeweerd's conception of the Humanistic Nature-Freedom dialectic (§5–2.2; NC (I, 148–206)) and other Dooyeweerdian thought to appraise the paradigms.

He argues that DF is controlled by the Nature pole, which leads it into unjustifiable objectivism and speculative attempts to arrive at truth by purely mathematical means. The 'religious' (§5–2.3) adherence to the Nature pole hides several problems, as may be seen in the following. DF takes the standard statistical 95% confidence interval (CI) as an interval that, once calculated, contains the targeted unknown quantity (the "parameter," such as a population mean) with 95% probability. First, the 95% is a purely social convention (a hidden social rationality, §7–1.3). Second, the DF position tends to obscure the meaningfulness of the aspect of the world being statistically analysed (physical, biological, psychological, social, etc.) by encouraging us to ignore expert opinion about those aspects in favour of mathematical determination. Third, its common interpretation of the CI as the probability that the CI contains the parameter is unwarranted under quantitative rationality, because the CI is actually a single member of an infinite set of CIs (one CI per experiment, in an infinite series of hypothetical experiments), 95% of which should contain the parameter.

The IF analyst calculates roughly the same statistical results as does DF, but interprets those results merely as informal "evidence" to be combined loosely—rather than mechanistically—with whatever other information happens to be available about the parameter. This is expressed in "That's up to you. Statistical calculations provide the p-value. You have to interpret it" (Motulsky, cited by Hartley 2008, 32). Expert opinion would be accepted without question, regardless of the possibility that experts can be mistaken or biased. Because of 'religious' adherence to the Freedom pole, IF offers no basis for interpretation other than subjectivity.

Dooyeweerd offers aspectual meaningfulness and law as such a trans-subjective but non-mechanistic basis.

Both OB and SB recognise the pertinence of beliefs and seek to update pre-analytic beliefs ("priors") about parameters using modelled data. OB seeks to remove all human freedom and judgment from this updating, by insisting that priors must be formed solely using mathematical principles such as "maximum entropy" or "non-informativity" (Hartley 2008, 47). SB forms priors from whatever background information is available, including experts' opinions, and expresses the priors as pre-analytic degrees of belief of an individual or community.

Hartley claims that IF, DF and OB all exhibit problems of dialectical ground-motives discussed in §5–2.4. He suggests, however, that (a) SB need not be subjectiv*ist*, (b) SB may be situated and enriched with Dooyeweerd's multi-aspectual ground-motive and (c) most statistical procedures of the other three paradigms (though not their interpretations) may be incorporated therein. The incorporation is facilitated not only by virtue of the mathematics shared by all the paradigms, but also by the ways in which, under some conditions, frequentist and OB results approximate SB results.

Dooyeweerd would suggest that statistical inference should synthesise the rationalities, properties and laws of the quantitative aspect, the pistic aspect (beliefs) and the focal aspect(s) of the research (physical, organic, social, etc.), respecting the sovereignty and the mutual dependence of the various aspects of human experience. Hartley argues that SB, taken non-reductively, can achieve this.

11–3.2 *Paradigms and Frameworks in Systems Thinking*

As discussed by Eriksson (2003) (§5–2.4), the three standard paradigms of systems thinking, known as hard, soft and critical systems thinking, exhibit flaws. Hard systems thinking is rigid, soft systems thinking though less rigid ignores normativity and critical systems thinking too narrowly fixes on norms of emancipation or power and ignores everyday experience. In response, two new paradigms of systems thinking have emerged from the Reformational perspective and a modification of soft systems thinking.

Multi-modal systems thinking (de Raadt 1991) criticises soft systems thinking for being nihilistic and critical systems thinking for presupposing the dogma of the autonomy of theoretical thought (§2–1.2) and thus unable to provide normative guidance. It holds that God has provided the universe with laws that govern it, and de Raadt employs a modified version of Dooyeweerd's suite of aspects to provide a conceptual tool for practical analysis of those laws. This is why it is called "multi-modal".

Disclosive systems thinking (Strijbos 2006) is similar, but emphasises disclosure. Using more of Dooyeweerd's understanding of reality (§4–3), it offers four principles: (1) Intrinsic normativity. Humans keep producing new things, which discloses new possibilities. (2) Simultaneous realization of norms led by a qualifying norm. Norms are multifarious, and all should be actualised together, recognising the correlation between law and reality. Strijbos links this with God. (3) Disclosure is multi-actor activity. Justice must be done to the responsibilities of all actors. (4) Critical awareness of the socio-cultural context. As in critical systems thinking, social structures should be questioned, but in addition there must be critical awareness that norms are not merely socially constructed.

Strijbos' DST is rather abstract. Goede et al. (2011) suggest making it more usable with Dooyeweerd's aspects providing the norms that, beyond social construction, open up possibilities and need to be simultaneously realized (*shalom*, §4–3.7).

The "appreciative critique" of Checkland's (1981) Soft Systems Methodology (SSM) by Mirijamdotter & Bergvall-Kåreborn (2006) applies Dooyeweerd's ideas to critically affirm and enrich several of its key notions, drawing on their empirical studies. SSM's idea of rich picture may be seen as multi-aspectual analysis of the functioning of a situation. Its evaluation criteria ("E's") clearly relate to distinct aspects (see Table 10.1). Its Design and Comparing phase may be guided by aspects, to pose meaningful questions. Aspects also offer excellent performance indicators for SSM's Conceptual Activity System. Bergvall-Kåreborn (2006) discusses the utility of Dooyeweerd's notion of qualifying aspect (§4–3.4) to the model-building phase, especially in the process of unfolding rationalities in defining problems and proposing improvements, and in clarifying and broadening the *Weltanschauungen* of participants. Basden & Wood-Harper (2006) enrich SSM's CATWOE analysis with aspects and other portions of Dooyeweerd's philosophy. The wide applicability of Dooyeweerd's aspects is not surprising, given that SSM aims to help us understand, evaluate and intervene beneficially and holistically in human activity systems taken as everyday experience.

11–3.3   A Multi-Aspectual Paradigm in Sustainability

Sustainability involves many factors that could undermine it indirectly. To understand and evaluate sustainability is very challenging. Brandon &

Lombardi (2005) introduce a new paradigm for evaluating sustainability in the built environment, by which the plethora of factors and their intertwinement may be understood.

They use Dooyeweerd's aspects, treating sustainability as a version of multi-aspectual *shalom* (§4–3.7). Thus, for example, the organic aspect concerns sustainability of life and health, the physical aspect concerns such issues as climate change, the formative aspect concerns technology, the economic aspect concerns resource depletion, the juridical aspect, legal infrastructure, and the pistic aspect, prevailing beliefs in society, for instance about whether GDP or future generations are the more important. Humanity's functioning in these juridical and pistic aspects affect how we function in the organic aspect.

Brandon & Lombardi offer a paradigm at the macro level (Kuhn's (1971) 'disciplinary matrix'). Veronica de Raadt's (2002) *Ethics and Sustainable Community Design* offers one at the micro level (Kuhn's exemplar).

Guided likewise by a version of the *Shalom Principle*, de Raadt recognises that for a community to be sustainable over the long term, many issues need attention. She discusses the normative issues in the community, opening up ethics, belief and science in particular. Drawing on the writings of Churchman and von Bertalanffy, who called for a humane science, she suggests that Dooyeweerd's aspects can offer a solution. She develops the *multi-modal systems approach*, in which multi-aspectual functioning (§4–3.8.2) is the norm for all social activities (family, church, school, sports, etc.), and which emphasises links between aspects. Links can be beneficial or detrimental for sustainability and form a network with several loops, including self-reinforcing loops (a systems notion).

Interviewing residents in a village in crisis in northern Sweden, de Raadt built a picture of aspectual loops that characterise the community. Identifying detrimental links and loops (§3–4) can assist community planning and perhaps propose community redesign with the aim of generating as many positive loops as possible. As de Raadt makes clear, use of this paradigm is susceptible to prior commitments, so these should be clearly identified when presenting results, as she does (p. 147); c.f. §10–4.1.

While Brandon & Lombardi focus on the built environment and de Raadt on community activities, Gunton et al. (2017) work within the multi-aspectual paradigm to propose a framework for valuing ecological sustainability, the Ecosystems Valuing Framework (EVF). The Ecosystems Services (ESS) idea was introduced in the 1990s as a way to raise strategic thinking above merely financial issues when thinking about, for example, whether woodland should be felled in order to build houses, by recognising the services that such things give to people. This, however, downplays that which has little direct, immediate benefit to human beings. The EVF is based on Dooyeweerd's aspects, as spheres of meaningfulness and law that transcend humanity and in which all temporal reality exists and occurs, and which define value that may not be reduced to human needs or desires. This escapes the anthropocentric nature of ESS, widens the range of issues considered and offers a better classification.

An initial test of this paradigm's quality might be offered by Gareth Jones' research, who constructed knowledge based systems to guide local authorities in developing sustainable policy. Jones (2007) did so within the multi-aspectual paradigm of sustainability. A screenshot of his knowledge base for environmental protection is shown in Figure 11.6, in §11–6.6, where his knowledge elicitation method is described. Others, e.g. housing, were more complex.

Four policy practitioners were asked to examine the content of the knowledge bases constructed within the multi-aspectual paradigm. All agreed that it was "insightful", "comprehensive", "exhaustive" and "generic" (Jones 2007, 371). Jones continues,

> Furthermore, no sustainability issue identified over the duration of the project failed to relate to this aspectual framework for understanding. The benefit of this aspectual suite is that it appears to provide high-level coverage of all relevant sustainability dimensions and a framework within which other indices might nest.

He also discusses the benefit Dooyeweerd offered to the *process* of sustainability policy development and evaluation, especially with aspects, analogies and normativity. The dimensions of sustainability process had been poorly understood, and the practitioners found this an "excellent way of understanding the process of sustainability" and a means of "gaining real insight into this complex process" (p. 372). See §10–5 and §11–6.6 for further details.

11–3.4 *A New Paradigm of the State and Civil Society*

Dooyeweerd extensively discusses the state, using especially his notion of multi-aspectual individuality structures and enkaptic relationships (§4–3.4, §4–3.5), which could be seen as a then-new paradigm of the state. Chaplin (2011) discusses this in the context of more recent developments, to yield the beginnings of conceptual framework that avoids "narrow focus on institutions as opposed to behavior or processes" and might be summarised as "power in service of justice" (pp. 161–2). Chaplin's goal in engaging with Dooyeweerd is to use his work to contribute to a clarified and enhanced account of contemporary concepts of "the state" and "civil society".

He discusses the identity of the state in terms of the structural principle of juridical qualifying and formative-historical founding functions, in which all other aspects also play important supportive roles. His discussion of the just state is largely in terms of institutional spheres of sovereignty in society, each defined aspectually, which can determine the state's own sphere of authority in relation to other spheres and judge (justly) between claims made by other spheres. Chaplin discusses absolutism and democracy, and presents Dooyeweerd's idea of legal pluralism as "original and fruitful" (p. 210), then he questions Dooyeweerd's belief that the tension between the two cannot be resolved by appeal to the structural principle of the state (p. 216). The relationship between state and nation, family, church, economy/industry, etc. must be informed by the mutual irreducibility of the aspectual norms by which each is led, leading to discussions of issues like worker participation in industry. Chaplin discusses Dooyeweerd's views on civil society and Christian pluralism by reference to an extra-Dooyeweerdian categorisation, civil society as protective, integrative and transformative. (See also §12–1.5.)

Chaplin's critical discussion of Dooyeweerd seems to me of enormous importance in the 21st-century political scene, though his intention seems to be less the development of a full conceptual framework and more an argument for the distinctiveness of Dooyeweerd's ideas. For instance, in his comparison of Dooyeweerd's with Walzer's similar ideas about spheres of justice, Chaplin's intent is to "bring the distinctiveness of Dooyeweerd's position into sharper relief" (p. 158) rather than establishing fruitful points of contact.

This echoes my own intention a decade ago in Basden (2008a), discussed in §11–3.6. Chaplin's and my own attempts might indicate a norm for introducing Dooyeweerd into a field: We must first work out in some detail for ourselves how Dooyeweerd fits into the field and, having done that, work to affirm, critique and enrich extant thought (§10–1), which in my case occurs in the later Basden (2018a).

11–3.5 New Paradigm in Knowledge Management and Tacit Knowledge

Tacit knowledge is an important issue in organisational knowledge management, but there is much confusion and fruitless debate. Polanyi (1967) highlighted the idea ("We know more than we can tell"), which was recognised as a challenge in knowledge elicitation. Then organisations, when trying to capitalise on knowledge 'within' them, encountered the problem that knowledge that people hold individually is not known more widely in the organisation as a whole ("tacit knowledge in organisations" (Baumard 1999)) and sought ways to explicate it. Nonaka & Takeuchi (1995) proposed the seminal SECI model (socialization, externalization, combination, internalization) with which to do so. Polanyian purists, however, argue that true tacit knowledge can never be explicated.

Alex Kimani (2017) drew on Basden's (2008a) model of multi-aspectual ways of knowing (§4–3.12) to critique, understand and situate six approaches to tacit knowledge found in the literature, finding they relate to the psychic, formative, social, economic, juridical and pistic aspects. His empirical study of tacit knowledge in a small business, guided by this multi-aspectual paradigm, revealed every aspect from psychic onwards to be present in tacit knowledge, in spoken and unspoken motivations, within statements made by interviewees, and in the functioning that is the making of the statements. From this, he constructed a model of tacit knowledge in organisations, which incorporates both individual and collective knowledge. He sees it as an aspectual version of SECI.

11–3.6 New Paradigms and Frameworks in the Information Systems Field

My 50 years' experience in information technology and information systems (IT/IS) has been in five areas of concern to the field:

- computer programming (and design and testing) and development of information systems, multimedia and websites;
- design and facilitation of information technology features: algorithms, data structures, user interface devices, including virtual reality, languages in which to express knowledge;
- use of information systems and technology, including computer gaming;
- the impact of IT on society and vice versa, sustainable and righteous living, and technological progress;
- artificial intelligence and the nature of information, computers, etc.

These are seen as different areas and seldom discussed together. Each area developed their own paradigms, which I found could seldom, if ever, allow us to understand everyday practice adequately. As elaborated in the prefaces to Basden (2008a) and Basden (2018a), during a dozen years in professional life, I had begun to think of new ways in which reality might be approached, understood, studied and guided.

That was before I met Dooyeweerd. The paradigms and approaches I had met in various areas had seemed, to my intuition, insufficient or distorting, but I did not understand why. I suppressed my intuitions until I found Dooyeweerd gave philosophical voice and validity to them. Upon discovering Dooyeweerd's philosophy, it gradually dawned on me that most of these paradigms and areas could be understood from a Dooyeweerdian perspective, alongside others, especially since he had an everyday, diversity-oriented perspective, expressed via his aspects, which I learned to use as a conceptual tool.

I did not want to force a Dooyeweerdian view on them, nor promote his philosophy as superior to others, but a decade later I understood how each of the ideas might be situated in a wider picture painted by Dooyeweerd. Basden (2008a) was an attempt to recount that, with a Dooyeweerdian framework for understanding each of the five areas, to try to show the distinctiveness and value of Dooyeweerd's ideas. Over the next decade I sought engagement between Dooyeweerd's ideas with extant ideas, paradigms and theories in each of the five areas. Indeed, I was often forced to do so in order to properly teach or supervise my students! Basden (2018a) expresses some of that engagement and discusses how each of the (now updated) Dooyeweerdian frameworks for understanding might affirm, critique and enrich around 50 discourses in these areas.

Each of the frameworks is both a different paradigm in Kuhn's (1971) macro sense of disciplinary matrix and a generator of new ones in his micro sense of exemplars (§8–2.1). I will explain each in turn, since reference is made to some of them from elsewhere in the book. Readers might like to generalise what I did to other fields.

For each, portions of Dooyeweerd's philosophy are mentioned, most of which are explained in Chapter 4.

11–3.6.1   ISD: Information Systems Development, Including Programming

See Basden (2008a's chapter VI, 2018a's chapter 9). The problems in the field of ISD revolve around the dialectic between control and freedom (Nature-Freedom ground-motive, §5–2.2) in programming, around errors and failures, and in both its silo mentality in academia and compartmentalisation in practice, with a shirking of genuine responsibility.

I reconceived ISD as four intertwined responsibilities, with four associated activities, each of which is multi-aspectual. I argue that agile development might be an intuitive attempt to recognise multiple aspects of the multi-aspectual activity and responsibility of ISD, and that other approaches may be understood as emphasising certain aspects. The important portions of Dooyeweerd's philosophy here are normativity of aspects, coherence of aspects and enkaptic interlacement of the responsibilities/activities.

This was recast as a master's course, *Key Issues in Information Systems Development*, in which I simply went through every aspect of each of the four responsibilities. It proved very popular with students, especially mature students with experience.

11–3.6.2   IT Features

See Basden (2008a's chapter VII, 2018a's chapter 7). Features are those things that IT users encounter, such as well-designed menus, which delight them, or inaccurate algorithms, which annoy them. This is now called "materiality of IT" and has given rise to the topic of affordance. Features enable or hinder users from accomplishing information-related tasks and activities and are often inappropriately designed, not only because development processes are flawed, but also because the languages for design and implementation do not recognise a full range of aspects and force developers to implement facilities meaningful in one aspect in terms of another (reductionism). This issue of appropriateness takes several forms.

ICT features are understood via the Dooyeweerdian subject-object relationship, its multi-aspectual nature and its corresponding multi-aspectual normativity. Thereby, the topics of affordance and appropriateness are integrated, and their diversity of kinds of each may be addressed.

11–3.6.3   IT/IS Use

See Basden (2008a's chapter IV, 2018a's chapter 6). What challenges the area of IT/IS use is isolation of discourses. Drawing on work by Breems and Joneidy (§11–2), I identified discourses, or lack thereof, around 17 areas of concern. While some discourses interact, many keep separate (especially ethics), some are ignored, and in particular there has been a tendency of the IS field to isolate itself from the 'technical' issues of computer science or programming. In this light, the socio-technical approach should be welcome but, as discussed in §8–1, it misses out the core aspect of information systems, namely information content. No overall framework for understanding IT/IS use had emerged that can address all 17 concerns.

What Basden (2018a) calls the *Aspectual Engagements Framework* conceives IT/IS use as three multi-aspectual human engagements, based around Dooyeweerd's notions of aspects, coherence, normativity and enkaptic relationships.

- EIT: engaging with interface and technology (examples: navigating menus, kinematic-analytic; battery failure, physical);
- EMC: engaging with meaningful content (examples: fighting a dragon in a dungeon game, formative; nurse responding to information on patient's record, ethical);
- ELI: engaging in life with IT, especially concerning benefits and harm (examples: information more easily available, economic; bullying on social media, ethical-juridical).

Normativity ("ethics", axiology) is built-in. The three are seen as enkaptically entwined, and all three are multi-aspectual.

This implies that to understand IT/IS use fully, we must take into account up to 15 sets of meaningful issues per engagement: 45 sets. No wonder most research into IT/IS use ignores many factors, as shown in Figure 11.3! Basden (2018a) discusses how each of the 17 discourses may be affirmed, critiqued or enriched when seen with this framework.

11–3.6.4   IT and Society

See Basden (2008a's chapter VIII, 2018a's chapter 8). The area concerned with IT and society is fragmented, with frequent ideological conflicts and little overall understanding of what is going on. Individual and societal issues are treated differently. The guidance received by governments, the IT industry, etc. from experts is suspect. What is the role of IT in society: to grow 'the economy', to 'emancipate' workers, or what? What is technological progress? What is the impact of widespread use of IT on society and planet?

Dooyeweerd's aspects allow us to consider individual, societal and also pre-human aspects together, with multi-aspectual inherent normativity. Widespread use is seen as aspectual repercussions multiplied by the social aspects, and the juridical, ethical and pistic aspects are seen as forming society's structures, which affect individual and organisational activity. The role of IT is lingual, which facilitates various targeted aspects, including both economic and juridical. Progress is seen as opening up of aspects (§4–3.8.3).

In addition, Dooyeweerd's notion of correlative enkapsis and *Umwelt* may be called on to understand how society relates to its denizens, and to other *Umwelten* like the economy and the Internet (§4–3.5). Links are made with Structuration Theory.

11–3.6.5   Nature of Information and Computers

See Basden (2008a's chapter V, 2018a's chapter 5). Fruitless debates continue over the artificial intelligence question, "Computer = Human?" There is no clear idea of what information actually is, nor documents nor computers, nor even programs.

Dooyeweerd's notion of being as multi-aspectual meaningfulness (§4–3.3) helps cut through this. We may understand information, computers and documents as multi-aspectual beings; see §11–4.3. The intransigence of AI debates may be accounted for by reference to the three dialectical ground-motives (§5–2.2, §5–2.3), so a new understanding, based on aspectual functioning, allows both Yes and No answers to the AI question. Programs also may be viewed as virtual law-sides that govern virtual worlds—and as performance art as well.

11–3.7   Broadening Paradigms in Engineering

Ribiero et al. (2017) uses Dooyeweerd's philosophy to argue for a more holistic model to guide the development of smart grids, in which renewable energy sources are integrated. In a paper aimed at engineers, they review the challenges of electricity supply, mentioning diverse factors, many of which are from everyday experience of both providers and potential 'consumers', including intermittency of supply, the incorporation of small-scale genera-tors, changes to the economic infrastructure, rural living and resistance by utilities. They end up with a model comprising three factors, "technical", "economic", and "social and ethical". They employ Dooyeweerd's aspects early on in the paper, to motivate readers to consider wider factors than just technical and economic.

I wondered why they did not employ Dooyeweerd's aspects more boldly, to generate their conceptual model, as the rest of this section might suggest. Their technical and economic factors are meaningful in the formative and economic aspects, as well as the physical (intermittency of wind, sun), but their "social and ethical" factor combines and conflates the social, aesthetic, juridical, ethical and pistic aspects. Though examples of each are mentioned throughout the paper, showing an awareness of them by the researchers, did they lose an opportunity to highlight the distinct importance and repercus-sions of each (§4–3.8)? For example, the pistic aspect of belief in, or resis-tance to, renewable energy is especially important because it retrocipatorily impacts all other decisions (§3–2.4.5).

It may be, however, that the authors felt they could not expect their audi-ence to take more than half a step towards a more holistic approach. Might this indicate a possible challenge to encouraging researchers and others to take Dooyeweerd's ideas seriously? Perhaps we need to be wisely bold and boldly wise.

11–3.8 Reflection

In adventuring among paradigms with Dooyeweerd's philosophy, a variety of researchers have critiqued, affirmed and enriched several fields, and some new conceptual frameworks or models have emerged from doing so. Enrichment has been either of existing paradigms, such as of systems theory, by reinterpreting more richly, or of whole fields, by suggesting new paradigms, especially in those of sustainability, knowledge management and information systems. Some of the paradigms are Kuhnian disciplinary matrices, others are exemplars (§8–2.1).

Most adventurers have employed Dooyeweerd's aspects to separate out tangled issues, clarify confusions, reinterpret some in richer ways, or to suggest new norms or meaningful ways of seeing situations that had been overlooked. The innate normativity and multi-aspectual coherence of aspects has imparted a fuller and more responsible feel to some of the paradigms. Along with this, other Dooyeweerdian notions have sometimes been found useful, especially in Basden's thought: Dooyeweerd's interesting subject-object idea, enkapsis and meaningfulness-grounded being.

Critique has been given sometimes by drawing attention to missing aspects and sometimes by viewing inter-paradigm oppositions in the light of dialectical ground-motives.

The challenge now is to widen the range of fields in which Dooyeweerd is brought to bear. Extending Dooyeweerd's ideas to fields like linguistics, economics and perhaps some of the humanities might follow similar lines as above. Extending to the natural sciences and mathematics, however, might be different, because they would seem to focus on a narrower range of aspects, as discussed in §11–8.3. Dooyeweerd did discuss some of these fields in the mid-20th century, with arguments that showed the potential therein, but his approach was mainly critique rather than affirmation or enrichment. Critique is marginally useful to a field, for example in halting folly, but enrichment is much more useful, opening doors to new avenues and adventures.

11–4. Conceptual Frameworks: Clarifying Concepts and Ideas

At several stages of research, but especially while formulating conceptual frameworks, concepts and ideas need to be clarified. This section discusses a few ways in which this has been accomplished using Dooyeweerd's philosophy.

As irreducibly distinct spheres of meaningfulness (§3–2.3), it is no surprise that Dooyeweerd's aspects offer an excellent basis for sound categorisation and classification (§4–3.2). They are also useful for differentiating ways in which a concept or idea is meaningful, understanding how the aspects relate to each other therein and sharpening up concepts by reference to the kernel meaningfulness of aspects.

11–4.1   Understanding a 'Simple' Concept: Diagrams

In diagrammatology the notion of diagram itself is not well understood but is based on our intuition. In *Wikipedia*, a diagram is "a symbolic representation of information according to some visualization technique", and visualization is "any technique for creating images, diagrams or animations to communicate a message". There is a circularity here. The *Wikipedia* page lists well over 100 types of diagram. As far as I know, no practical but philosophically sound basis exists for differentiating such a wide range of diagram types.

Fathulla (2007) employed Dooyeweerd's aspects to understand the nature of diagrams, as "Symbolic Spatial Mapping". It is symbolic insofar as it necessarily functions in the lingual aspect of signifying chosen pieces of meaningfulness (§4–3.11.1). It is spatial insofar as what carries this signification is spatial in its primary functioning, e.g. lines and shapes. This offers a basis for differentiating diagrams from photographs, for example, in which signification, if there is any, is carried by colour (psychic functioning), and art, in which it is carried by aesthetic functioning.

There is a mapping between the spatial and lingual, which defines the type of diagram, and Fathulla examines the mapping rules in detail for several types, not only box-and-arrows diagrams and bar charts, but less-discussed types like (geographic) maps and contours. A diagram's signification-meanings target yet another aspect, for instance quantitative and analytic for bar charts (amount, comparison), and spatial, formative and analytic for maps. Note: Maps involve the spatial aspect twice, as a foundation for visual psychic functioning and as target aspect.

This approach, based on aspectual irreducibility and coherence (§3–2), avoids circular definitions and allows us in principle to understand what makes each type of diagram work.

> *Research opportunity: diagrams.* Apply Fathulla's Symbolic Spatial Mapping to the 100 types listed in *Wikipedia*.

11–4.2   Exploring a More Complex Concept: Idolatry

The failure of many e-government projects may be laid at the door of idolatry, suggests both Heeks (2006) and Gauld & Goldfinch (2006). Both use the notion without much discussion, so Subrahmanian Krishnan-Harihara wanted to research this. He employs a characterisation of idolatry in Goudzwaard's (1984) essay, *Idols of Our Time*, which was written in response to what he felt was idolatry in Dutch politics of the time, of technology, of economism, of nationalism and of defence.

Idolatry is a dysfunction in the pistic aspect. Goudzwaard (1984) gives ten 'stages' in the development of an idolatry. It was written, Goudzwaard told him, as an intuitive response, and he later wrote a more rationalised version. Krishnan-Harihara decided to use the intuitive version because it is richer, more harmonious and closer to Goudzwaard's everyday experience of concern, and hence a better basis for understanding such complex phenomena (§2–6.3).

Idolatry begins when, metaphorically, "people sever something from their immediate environment, refashion it and erect it on its own feet in a special place". Krishnan-Harihara developed this idea into a substantial model of how idolatry operates to undermine e-government projects. For example, the idea of government is severed from its historical and social context and refashioned as ICT-enabled 'transformational government'. It occupies a special place in government thinking, often given a separate department. Just as worshippers "kneel before" the idol, so e-government receives adulation, and they see it "as a thing that has life in itself" by letting it determine its own course of development. Just as worshippers "bring sacrifices", much is sacrificed to install e-government, and the poor become increasingly disenfranchised. The full analysis can be found in Krishnan-Harihara & Basden (2009).

Aspectual dysfunction presupposes aspectual good (§4–3.7). So there is also a positive possibility of being committed to good rather than serving an idol. Krishnan-Harihara & Basden (2010) argues that each stage of idolatry has a positive counterpart, which is possible if a non-idolatrous attitude is maintained. Pistic functioning, good or bad, influences behaviour in all other aspects retrocipatorily, and the authors bring in Dooyeweerd's aspects to consider this.

This is an exemplar of how one of Dooyeweerd's aspects can be developed as the core idea of a research project, without ignoring other aspects. Basden (2018a, 295–6, 2008a, 329–32) contains detailed discussion of this work.

11–4.3 Multi-Aspectual Concepts: Information, Documents

What is *information*? Several parallel discussions are extant. Floridi (2004) presented 18 'open problems' for the philosophy of information, such as the dynamics of information, how data acquires meaning and whether there is information in reality without life. In parallel, Checkland & Holwell (1998) and others ask how information differs from data and knowledge (knowledge, not as knowing, but as that which encyclopaedias, newsfeeds or archives hold). Shannon (1948) tried to reduce information to patterns of digital bits. Most of these discussions presuppose information as a substance (§4–3.3) usually generated by a process (data becomes information, information becomes knowledge). Yet questions about the presupposition are beginning to emerge, for example in Tuomi's (1999) "iconoclastic argument" that "the often-assumed hierarchy from data to knowledge is actually inverse: knowledge must exist before information can be formulated and before data can be measured to form information." See Basden (2018a, 123–35) for an outline of the discussions.

Basden (2008a, 2018a) suggests that Dooyeweerd can throw light on the nature of information by seeing information (and data, knowledge, etc.) as aspectual beings of one whole that informs. Information is the multi-aspectual object generated by lingual functioning to signify (that is, to carry signification-meaning). Its medium might be paper, stone, human gestures or digital technology, and its language might be German, a computer language, data protocol or mathematical or diagrammatic notation, but these make no difference to its nature as information, because such variations occur in earlier aspects, on which the lingual functioning depends foundationally (§3–2.4.4) but cannot be reduced thereto. Media describes the physical and organic foundational aspects of information and language, the analytic and formative (vocabulary and syntax). The visual or bit pattern is information's foundational psychic aspect.

In this understanding, data is information is knowledge simultaneously and Checkland-Holwell meets Tuomi, and both can welcome Shannon. Almost all of Floridi's Open Problems can be addressed, though that possibility has yet to be subjected to critique. See Basden (2018a, 127–35) for a more detailed discussion of these, as well as how data mining can be understood.

> *Research opportunity: information.* Investigate in detail how Floridi's open problems for the philosophy of information may be addressed. See http://dooy.info/ext/floridi.html for initial ideas.

In similar vein, what are *documents*? Basden & Burke (2004) set out similar problems that beset conventional views of documents—likewise often seeking an understanding that presupposes substance and process—as well as other problems about writer and reader, context, history and literary works. Since the 1930s debate has raged about whether, for example, stones in museums or animals in zoos are documents, and on what basis we may decide.

Basden & Burke argue for seeing documents as enkaptically bound aspectual beings, with a full structure of individuality (§4–3.4) involving nearly all aspects, of medium (physical aspect), marks (psychic aspect), signs or symbols (analytic), syntactic structures (formative) and content that is argument, story, instructions and so on (lingual aspect), as well as material components (organic aspect), agreement on what words might mean (social aspect), economic aspect of parsimony, aesthetic aspect of harmony and nuance, juridical aspect of due to author, reader and topic (e.g. accuracy), ethical aspect of generosity and pistic aspect of incompatibilities in cultural worldviews between author and reader. A document is all of these.

Dooyeweerd's philosophy, and especially as developed into the model of meanings outlined in §4–3.11, allows us to address questions that include the following:

1. Discussions of what is, and is not, a document which began in the 1930s and continue today. Much confusion arises from aspectual analogies (metaphors) of the lingual in other aspects, and the meaning-oriented special role of the lingual aspect that links it to meaningfulness. A photograph of a stone may be a document, insofar as its purpose is to communicate or record, but if its main purpose is aesthetic,

it is a 'document' (metaphorically). We read a book (lingual functioning of signification-meaning), but we 'read' a landscape (analytic functioning of interpretation-meaning). Similarly most works of art are not documents but 'documents'. However, since the aesthetic aspect is post-lingual, there is usually some intentional communication in the artwork, whether explicit or hidden, and hence there is a genuine document-ness in many works of art.

2. The role of author and reader (problems raised by Gadamer and Ricoeur) may be seen in terms of lingual functioning with the document as object, prior object to reader, generated object to author (§4–3.9). Social context, culture and assumptions may be seen as social and pistic aspects of the document and its object-functioning as two aspects of a wider shared 'ocean' of meaningfulness.

3. Changes in a document (torn pages, margin notes (NC,III, 3)) may be seen as changes in various aspects that do not undermine the document's functioning as lingual prior object.

4. Literary works may be understood in terms of lingual and post-lingual aspects taken together, and their variants as changes meaningful in the post-lingual aspects, especially the aesthetic, facilitated foundationally by changes meaningful in the lingual aspect (inter-aspect dependency, §3–2.4.4.

What has bedevilled discourses around both information and documents is the immanence-standpoint (§5–3.1) in philosophy, which separates meaning from reality (c.f. §4–2) and hinders theoretical understanding of things as encountered in the reality of everyday experience.

11–4.4 *Complex Notions Incorporating Antecipations and Retrocipations*

A concept like trust is even more complex that those of information and documents. Trust is important in business, information technology and the Internet, in religion, philosophy and throughout everyday life, taking widely different forms in each—and yet is still recognisable as trust.

Stephen McGibbon, with a background in several of these fields, took on the challenge of understanding trust, using Dooyeweerd's philosophy to do so. McGibbon (2018) analyses a wide literature and concludes that trust is highly complex, involving almost every aspect, but is qualified by the ethical aspect (voluntary vulnerability). (Most would think trust is pistically qualified.)

McGibbon found not only that the simple single-aspect understanding was inappropriate, but also that the simple idea of individuality structure (a qualifying aspect relating to foundational aspects and those it anteci-pates, §4–3.5) was not adequate to understand complex issues like trust. He needed a way to do justice to what each author says about trust, and separate out their ideas in a way that is minimally dependent on his subjective assessments, which may be communicated to others and also back to himself when he returns to earlier interpretations. By a process described in §11–7.5, he arrived at a method that involves triples, not just pairs, of aspects ("cipation triples"). On reassessing the trust literatures in this way, he was able to obtain a fuller, more reliable picture of what authors believe to be meaningful about trust, which he could defend. He summarised this in a cell diagram shown in Figure 11.4.

Figure 11.4 What is meaningful about trust: authors by aspect

Such a plot can reveal several things about trust. (a) Almost every author conceives trust as intensely multi-aspectual, even though they might be regarded as focusing on one issue. (b) Most functioning is post-organic. (c) The kinematic aspect is mentioned only once. (d) Since the articles are in date order, we can see development. After Baier, the ethical aspect has been more recognised, and the juridical slightly less. (e) Lingual and aesthetic aspects are recognised more at the start and end than in the middle period. This confirms empirically his philosophical arguments (McGibbon 2018) that trust is ethically qualified.

Such an analysis offers a way to understand complex notions like trust in a way that takes account of a variety of communities of thought and practice and their historical development. It also offers a useful overview of literature, not unlike that of Joneidy (§11–2.2), but it took much longer than his did.

11–4.5   Contributing Ideas to Philosophy

Little has been discussed in this book about research that contributes to philosophic thought. In this section so far, we have used Dooyeweerd's philosophy to help clarify ideas, like Introna & Ilharco (2004) used Heidegger's philosophy to understand screens (§5–1.3). Now we reverse this, letting ideas from research contribute to philosophy. For example, McGibbon's idea of cipation triples might enrich the Dooyeweerdian understanding of things.

Breems (2017) makes what might be a more fundamental suggestion. Dooyeweerd's understanding of the subject-object relationship seems to allow only humans to function as subject in the post-psychical aspects, but how do we understand a computer program, especially one which incorporates artificial intelligence? For example, GPS software might "find a route" taking account of traffic restrictions; is it not thereby functioning as subject in the kinematic, analytic and juridical aspects? What about avatars in computer games, which are highly intelligent?

Basden (2008a) argued that the computer is still functioning only as object, even though in complex ways, in that it requires humans to program it, start it and feed it information, even though perhaps indirectly. Breems (2017) argues this is unsatisfactory and, while recognising the necessity of such human functioning, suggests a philosophic notion of *subject-by-proxy*. In this mode, the computer program functions as though subject in any aspect(s) even while dependent on humans. He shows how useful this idea can be in thinking about programmer responsibility. I now agree with Breems against Basden! It can help us understand the activity of such things as institutions.

11–5.   Using Dooyeweerd to Discuss Research Methods

Researchers must argue for their choice of research approach and of methods used for data collection and analysis, in order to allow others to critically evaluate whether it is reasonable to rely on their findings. The appropriateness of research methods can be aligned with aspects (Table 8.1), but actual experience of using Dooyeweerd during this stage is sparse.

This lack is what McGibbon (2018) struggled with in his research on trust. Every epistemological approach depends, itself, on trust, and so already takes a stance on what trust is—and hence will distort its study of trust. Recognising that "every piece of research is unique and calls for a unique methodology" (Crotty 1998, 14), he devised his own methodology rather than adopt an existing one. He argues that he needed a research philosophy that is able to:

- accommodate multiple epistemologies, even if incommensurable,
- contextualise the differences between them,
- accommodate their different norms for validity of findings,
- provide taxonomic consistency, which implies a common ontological basis, and
- fulfil all the normal conditions for generating new knowledge.

He argues that Dooyeweerd's philosophy can achieve all these. He refers to Basden (2002), which presents Dooyeweerd among the critical theorists, who argue for the ideological (Dooyeweerd: "religious") basis of knowledge, and to Basden (2011a), which shows how Dooyeweerd can bring incommensurable approaches together.

Basden (2011a) does not actually use Dooyeweerd to select research approaches, but does show we can use Dooyeweerd's notion of three-part Ground-Idea (§7–1) along with Dooyeweerd's suite of aspects, to situate apparently incommensurable approaches within a wider picture. In doing so, this at least exonerates Dooyeweerd's philosophy as a useful alternative approach to the traditional dialectical approaches, such as the positivist, interpretivist and socio-critical approaches. Basden's study is described in §7–3.1.

Using Ground-Idea elements linked to aspects, as in that study, could potentially be used to review, critique and select, and maybe even construct, a research approach that is suited to research, especially research for which no conventional philosophy fits well (§7–4.1).

Regarding methods for data collection and analysis, I have not yet found any concrete experience of using Dooyeweerd to *select* or formulate, and *justify*, these. This may be because it is only recently that experience using Dooyeweerd for collecting and analysing data has become broad enough to give us authoritative views on what might and might not be suitable. That recent experience, of using Dooyeweerd to inform *actual methods* of collecting and analysing research data, is discussed in the next two sections. They present quite a variety of methods. From now on, therefore, the experience presented below might be referred to when choosing and justifying research methods.

11–6.   Data Collection With Dooyeweerd

The main experience of using Dooyeweerd in collecting research data is by interviews in the social sciences, seeking to understand what is meaningful to people being researched. This section discusses two methods of interviewing and one of designing questionnaires, using Dooyeweerd's aspects. Observation research and research in the natural sciences are discussed later (§11–8), though more speculatively.

When data is collected about human behaviour, whether at psychological, social or societal levels, every aspect is potentially relevant in principle and intertwined with all the others (§3–2.4), since humans function as subject in all aspects. So, no aspect can be ignored, *a priori*. Unless the remit of a study has been deliberately constrained, we should normally seek data from every aspect in research involving humans. This is so whether the data comes via observations, questionnaires, interviews or written or other material. Even in psychology, where the focus is psychical or cognitive, the retrocipatory impact of later aspects is acknowledged in psychologies of belief, art, and in, for example, in Maslow's psychological theory of motivation and Vygotsky's psychology of art.

11–6.1   Using Aspects to Design Questionnaires

There are two main ways in which questionnaires can obtain data from all aspects. One is to invite "any other comments"—but that is haphazard. The other is to design the questions asked to cover each aspect.

One of my master's students, Aisha Abuelma'atti, tried this in a questionnaire for users of multimedia in several art galleries and museums (Abuelma'atti 2007). She posed 12 Likert scale questions, each of which expresses the kernel meaningfulness of an aspect from psychic to pistic, with five of them inviting open comment. Her questions are shown below. They were designed with the following criteria in mind: maintaining interest, number and order of questions, getting lost or confused, layout, making clear what to do and the wider context in which the questionnaire is posed. The last is an open (non-aspectual) question.

1. Overall, how satisfied are you with your use of this multimedia system? (psychic)
2. Did you come away with clear or confused information? If very clear or confused, please briefly explain why this was. (analytic)
3. Did you get what you wanted of the multimedia system? (formative)
4. To what extent did the multimedia communicate well with you and give you the feeling that it understood you and you understood it? (lingual)
5. Was there anything about this multimedia that was socially inappropriate? Please give an example. (social)
6. To what extent did you feel the multimedia was efficient or wasteful? Please give an example. (economic)
7. Did you enjoy using the system? (aesthetic)
8. Did you get the feeling that the whole system was harmonious and held together well, or not? (aesthetic)
9. Did the system give what you felt is due to you? (juridical)

10. Did you feel that the multimedia system served your interest or its own interest? What made you feel so? (ethical)
11. Was there anything that either disturbed or supported your basic belief? (pistic)
12. To what extent would you have preferred a human being standing for information rather than an information system? Why? (no aspect)

She discusses several benefits and challenges of using aspects to design questionnaires, including comments from two multimedia experts. Dooyeweerd's suite of aspects was easy to learn and use, put evaluation into sharper focus and helped the researcher to understand more deeply the complex issues around multimedia systems. It surfaced many repercussions and revealed gaps in her earlier attempts to formulate a questionnaire. She found that Dooyeweerd's order of aspects (§3–2.4.5) provides a sequence of questions that feels natural, beginning with how the respondent feels. In addition to evaluation, the aspects could help with design (of multimedia systems).

The main challenge was that it led to a questionnaire that omitted detail, which is essential to design, but the aspectual approach would be a good entry point. The breadth of meaningfulness of each aspect meant some respondents asked, "What do you mean?" when asked some questions, especially around the ethical aspect—but the answers as a whole gave useful information about it.

> *Research opportunity: questionnaire design.* There is a need to explore the use of Dooyeweerd's aspects in questionnaire design more widely and in more depth. For example, might each aspectual question then lead to more detailed ones in interactive questionnaires?

11–6.2   MAKE: Multi-Aspectual Knowledge Elicitation

Disciplines involve knowledge, some that can be articulated and shared and some that is tacit and not easily shared. Eliciting knowledge of a discipline involves "holistic . . . appreciation of things in their totality: Polanyi refers to this as an 'indwelling'" (Yates-Mercer & Bawden 2002, 22), in which details and particulars are seen in wider contexts.

Knowledge is "multifaceted" (Kakabadse et al. 2001, 141); facets of a jewel cut across each other at angles that are given by the nature of the material itself, and yet relate to each other. So with knowledge. It is not enough to elicit the main parameters, but, as Jacob & Ebrahimpur (2001, 78) express it, "One needs to have as broad a knowledge base as possible. It is the outer parameters that one must have knowledge about." Multiple facets and outer parameters are especially important in interdisciplinary fields. Therefore, two things are needed: (a) How do we identify all the facets and outer parameters of the knowledge, and especially those that are often overlooked? (b) How do we relate disparate facets to each other?

Various methods have been employed, which are discussed in Winfield & Basden (2006), such as cognitive mapping (Eden 1988), Soft Systems Methodology (SSM) (Checkland 1981) and Strategic Assumptions Surfacing and Testing (SAST) (Mason & Mitroff 1981). Though these have been developed through the decades, they do not fully satisfy the needs. Cognitive mapping encourages the expression of relationships but focuses on detail and offers no way of finding "outer parameters". SSM can find some "outer parameters" with its emphasis on multiple perspectives, but finds conflict difficult and can suffer from groupthink. SAST makes conflict into a virtue that forces differences (facets) into the open, but it is often too threatening to allow those who are sensitive (e.g. those with Asperger's syndrome) to express their knowledge fully (Attwood 2001).

Mike Winfield (Winfield 2000; Winfield et al. 1996) developed the *Multi-Aspectual Knowledge Elicitation* (MAKE) method, which seems to fulfil the needs above, in encouraging "outer parameters" and overlooked facets and assumptions to surface and the expression of relationships without an adversarial approach. It is based on Dooyeweerd's aspects. Facets are aspects, which inherently relate (inter-aspect coherence, §3–2.4), and the totality of aspects (§4–3.1) can disclose outer parameters. Since there is no inherent conflict among aspects (§3–2.4.2), surfacing assumptions need not depend on an adversarial approach. So Winfield developed the following method.

Typically, a MAKE interview involves an interviewer and a participant who has expertise in the topic and lasts around one hour. The interviewer guides the participant in explaining their expertise with non-leading questions. Winfield devised seven steps to guide it:

1. Introduction (e.g. obtain statement of requirements, or use some other entry point) and explain the kernel meanings of aspects, using an aspectual template, which is often placed on the table.
2. Identify a few important aspects; for a veterinary practice, this might be organic-biotic and economic.
3. Focus on one of these aspects and specify any laws, axioms, data, definitions and constraints that apply to the domain.
4. Identify as many concepts as possible that lie in this aspect. (Note: May need to check the concepts at a later stage for which aspect makes them meaningful.)
5. Apply low-level abstraction to each concept, which needs, or is thought to need, exploring. Eventually, concepts will emerge that are not meaningful in existing aspects, so the participant is asked which aspect makes them meaningful.
6. Repeat steps 3–6 as necessary.
7. Use the aspectual template to identify any new aspects, which may apply to the concepts specified and build bridges between concepts and aspects, and return to step 3.

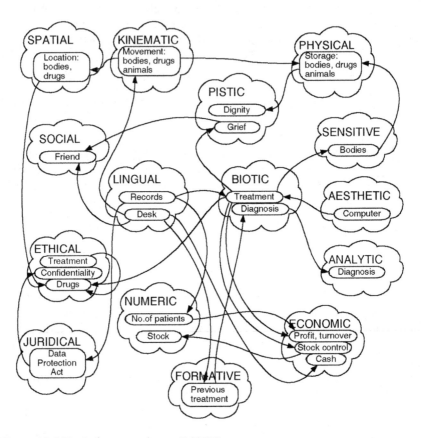

Figure 11.5 Typical aspectual map (MAKE)

The participants are in charge of identifying aspects that make their concepts meaningful, not the interviewer, who avoids leading questions. Useful prompts are "Why?", "When is this not meaningful?" and "What else?" As Winfield's discussions proceeded, he would draw an *aspectual map* expressing the concepts that emerge, their relationships and the aspects that make them meaningful, and check it with the participant. Figure 11.5 shows a simple example.

Winfield applied this to six case studies (tree planting, sustainability, veterinary practice, Islamic food laws, youth advice and management of a local housing business unit). Some of his students were involved as interviewers.

Several capabilities of MAKE are discussed by Winfield (2000) and Winfield & Basden (2006) and summarised in §11–6.4.

11–6.3   MAIT: Multi-Aspectual Interview Technique

The motivation behind Suzanne Kane's research, from which the Multi-Aspectual Interview Technique (MAIT) emerged, was to explore why mature students return to education (Kane 2006). MAIT was based on MAKE and operates in a similar way, but is future-oriented, exploring hopes, fears and aspirations, etc. rather than knowledge accumulated from past experience. MAIT offers an approach for supportive interviewing, to help interviewees express what is meaningful to them.

The participants in Kane's study were seeking to acquire skills with information technology (IT), some returning directly to higher education (university) and others to further education (college, which prepares them for university). Both were interviewed in the context of their everyday lives. Whereas some interviewees are used to being interviewed and thinking conceptually, many are not. The interview situation can be perceived as threatening, especially for those from less privileged backgrounds. So there is a need for supportive interviewing techniques that help interviewees to express what they really believe, know or feel, and the rich nuances therein.

Sixteen university and thirteen college students were interviewed, using Dooyeweerd's aspects. Various measures were taken to put the interviewees at ease, then the interview process followed steps not unlike those in MAKE above, including explaining Dooyeweerd's aspects, with a list thereof offered, so the interviewee could be in charge of interpreting what they said. As discussed in §11–6.4, whereas a MAKE-like interview sufficed for some students, others preferred to go through the aspects, one-by-one in any order. Towards the end, the interviewer prompts the interviewee on aspects not yet mentioned, but without pressure to respond.

11–6.4   Practical Reflections on MAKE and MAIT

Both Winfield (2000) and Kane (2006) discuss implications for the practice of interviewing using MAKE and MAIT.

1. On conceptual ability. Whereas Winfield's interviewees were all comfortable when thinking about concepts and relationships, Kane found that whereas university students were likewise, college students were less comfortable. They responded better to different approaches during the interview. Interviewees comfortable with conceptual thinking could offer issues related to aspects or could be asked, "To which aspect does [that issue] refer?" From such issues and aspects, visual maps were built up. By contrast, the college students were happier when asked to simply go through the aspects one by one and speak about each in turn, in any order they wished. This *seems* more directive, but it allayed fears the interviewees might have had about misunderstanding or not doing things 'correctly'. The college students preferred verbal transcripts to diagrams.

2. Ease of learning. MAKE and MAIT both seemed easy to learn by the interviewees, and even by potential interviewers, some of whom were Winfield's students. The fact that most interviewees were 'ordinary people', rather than academics, and could readily wield Dooyeweerd's aspects, is interesting, supporting Dooyeweerd's claim that the kernel meanings of the aspects are grasped by the intuition rather than by theoretical thought (§4–3.13), a claim that has been supported by Lombardi (2001) and Gunton et al. (2017). Whereas those comfortable with conceptual thought were happy

with a list of aspect names and conceptual keywords, the college students responded better to what Kane called *aspectually informed statements*, with more personal wording. Example: Instead of "If the answer relates to 'role in society' you may wish to reference this social aspect along with others" (conceptual), Kane used, "When I ask you about your 'role in society' I will link your answer to this social aspect" (more active and personal). With this, the interviewees quickly focused on the meanings rather than on the names of the aspects.

3. Emerging knowledge. Because of the innate coherence of aspects (§3–2.4), it is natural to move between aspects, so that concepts emerge that belong to different aspects, along with relationships both within and across aspects. In most cases a variety of aspects appeared quickly and easily. In MAKE at least 13 out of the 15 aspects were identified by the end. In MAIT, most of the 29 students gave information about every aspect from the psychic-sensitive to the pistic without any prompting, and all but one did so when prompted by the interviewer. In MAIT, all interviewees were invited to speak of issues without reference to aspects; only four students did so. These findings confirm that, in education and the professions at least, Dooyeweerd's aspects are meaningful to both conceptual and non-conceptual thinkers, and that Dooyeweerd's suite of aspects is complete enough for practical interviewing.

4. Everyday issues. Both MAKE and MAIT encourage the elicitation of everyday experience. Analysis of the interview transcripts in MAIT showed over three times as many everyday issues emerged as professional or theoretical issues (297 to 88). Unlike Ybema et al. (2009), who believe it is necessary to first focus on the extraordinary in everyday life, use of Dooyeweerd's aspects allows interviewees to focus on the ordinary. Unlike Ganguly (2002), who tries to rouse interest in the everyday by reference to the salacious, aspects enable focus on the wholesome.

5. Hidden issues and tacit knowledge. Both MAKE and MAIT proved very adept and efficient at eliciting tacit knowledge, but at different levels.

MAKE elicited whole swathes of an overlooked aspect that is taken for granted—the "outer parameters" alongside main ones. It can be used for making *Weltanschauungen* visible, but has the advantage over SSM of stimulating participants to look beyond the perspectives held by the group. MAKE has several advantages over SAST. Not requiring a group setting, it does not depend as heavily as SAST does on the quality of dialogue and is inherently non-adversarial. The participant is stimulated not by other individuals but by the suite of aspects that transcends all, which results in greater openness and less tendency to defend positions. Unlike both, MAKE helps to evoke multiple perspectives within a single individual, because it focuses not on the 'who' but on the 'why'.

MAIT elicited details, many of which were hidden. They can be hidden, usually unwittingly, by the researcher and by the interviewee. The range of issues sought can be limited by the researcher's theory, attitude, assumptions or what interests them. This can be ameliorated by encouraging the interviewee to consider every aspect, since each provides a space in which the often-unseen issues can be present alongside more visible ones. MAIT is thus sensitive to the unexpected. On the other hand, issues might be hidden by assumptions made by the interviewee about what the researcher would find interesting, by embarrassment, defensiveness, fear of ridicule, limitations in linguistic resources, or the general difficulty in expressing what is tacitly held can (Stommel & Willis 2004; Mooney et al. 2014). Some are addressed by aspectual analysis, in Section 11–7. Kane found the others could be addressed during the interview by going through all the aspects in turn.

Both allow hidden issues to be revealed more quickly than the 'slow-motion' approach of Baer (2008) or the lengthy ethnographic processes advocated by Paxton (2012).

6. Multiple participants and interdisciplinarity. MAKE can be undertaken with several participants, their maps being shared. This offers richer understanding and mutual respect, because each can see the meaningfulness of the other ideas and thus the rationality of each (§4–3.6). It separates real differences from those created by different naming conventions. Focusing on aspects de-emphasises differences of personality or organisational role, so conflict is reduced, and the views of non-dominant participants is more readily accepted. This helps to promote interdisciplinary communication.

7. Acceptability. Participants in both MAKE and MAIT expressed appreciation at the end for the way the aspects had opened their awareness. Comments given at the end showed the students had come not only to grasp the kernel meanings but to value them: "It makes you realise you're on track." "It gets you thinking." This does, of course, depend on the researcher's attitude, in that it is possible to use the aspects in a dominant way. Though Kane's (2006) study engaged only 29 interviewees and Winfield's (2000) only eight, and further study is recommended, it shows that the "voice" of the interviewee can readily be heard (Paxton 2012).

8. Interpretation of aspects. Because the introduction to the aspects is usually brief, interviewees will often have an incomplete understanding of their meaning. Mild misunderstanding does not seem to matter, however, because both interviewer and interviewee operate with intuitive rather than precise understandings, and in many cases when the interviewee is asked to explain, their choice of aspect has seemed justified. The main reason for using Dooyeweerd's aspects is to encourage interviewees to open up and express things that are often taken for granted.

Research opportunity: hidden issues. Empirical test of both methods, for example to investigate quality of hidden issues obtained, has yet to be undertaken.

Both Winfield and Kane found that the intuitive nature of aspects facilitated understanding and conversation and that presenting aspects to the interviewees gives them responsibility and freedom in interpreting aspectual meaning.

11–6.5   *Philosophical Reflections on MAKE and MAIT*

A number of philosophical reflections on both MAKE and MAIT may be made.

Both MAKE and especially MAIT treat text and context as both in the same 'ocean of meaningfulness'. There is no need to recouple them (§4–3.11.2), so the hermeneutic cycle becomes an attitude rather than a sequential iteration between them.

What is often called "co-construction of data" is no construction process but an intuitive sharing of meaningfulness in the same ocean by interviewer and participant.

Interviewing is challenged by barriers of culture, class, background and power. In MAKE and MAIT, researcher and interviewee are both subject to the same set of aspects (§4–3.10); neither party has authority in relation to them, so their use does not constitute a power relationship. Since the intuitive grasp of aspectual meaningfulness transcends culture, shared understanding across cultures or through barriers of class and background is possible (§4–4.2), without romanticisation of class identities, if attention is directed to the wide range of everyday issues beyond class. In such ways, MAIT especially proved to be emancipatory. Abuelma'atti's aspectual questionnaire also seemed to reach across cultures.

It might be objected that it is the researcher who provides the suite of aspects. That must be taken into account, but the fact that the aspects are all ones which ordinary people can grasp intuitively mitigates against this.

Some suggest that using a ready-made suite of aspects might inhibit the interview or distort the content that emerges, but this does not seem to be the case. Surprisingly, MAKE and MAIT seems to liberate and empower the participants, promoting individual awareness and encouraging them to say things that they felt slightly uncomfortable or embarrassed about. We attribute this to the fact that the aspects constitute a framework that the participant can 'hold onto' because it transcends their situation.

> *Research opportunity: Grounded Theory.* It might be that some version of MAKE or MAIT can contribute to Grounded Theory (Glaser & Strauss 1967). Explore this. The aspects are *not* prior categories (which GT tries to avoid) but rather wide spaces of meaningfulness in which things may be brought to light.

11–6.6   *Eliciting Detailed Expertise*

As discussed in §10–5, knowledge elicitation resembles research, and Gareth Jones (2007) employed an aspectual approach to eliciting knowledge for knowledge based systems (KBS) that encapsulate principled knowledge about the development of policies for sustainable urban futures. This is highly complex, interdisciplinary knowledge. He defines a systematic method for knowledge elicitation, which might be of use in some research.

Jones conceptualises the activities in question, elicits detailed and contextual knowledge and develops a provisional knowledge base, testing it with experts in the field of sustainable policy. Each of these stages has several steps during which aspects are considered one-by-one (pp. 221–3). With this method, Jones constructed nine knowledge bases of varying degrees of complexity, for assessing sustainability in housing (two), transport, social progress, environmental protection, employment, minerals, development control and town centres. Figure 11.6 shows a screenshot of one of the simpler ones, on environmental protection policy, where boxes signify propositions about a planning situation and lines, the inference relationships between them, both elicited from experts.

Knowledge bases require knowledge in the form of precisely defined "If-Then" inferences, which were communicated by experts or derived from what they said. To achieve this, Jones sought to elicit the laws of each aspect, backed up by knowledge of relevant entities. He found that the notions of qualifying and founding aspects were not useful for this, but that a fully multi-aspectual approach was required. The experts confirmed the comprehensive nature of the expertise Jones elicited when they ran his KBSs; the

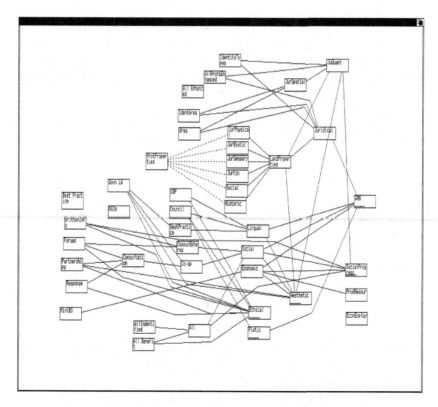

Figure 11.6 Knowledge base on environmental protection policy

KBSs raised questions about issues which the experts had not thought about and which previously would not have been considered.

11–7. Using Dooyeweerd in Data Analysis

Dooyeweerd's philosophy has been used to analyse both data collected in open interviews that have not been guided by Dooyeweerd's aspects and texts. It has proven adept at deriving findings from data by a process that has become known as *aspectual analysis*.

Aspectual analysis employs Dooyeweerd's aspects to reveal what is meaningful in written or spoken material. It brings all three of Dooyeweerd's starting-points to bear on data analysis—the source's everyday experience and the cohering diversity of what is meaningful to them (Chapters 2, 3, 4)—and this imparts a different tone to analysis, which has proven particularly useful in interpretive research and interdisciplinary situations in practice. It can take several forms, as discussed in the following subsections.

In many research cultures, quantitative and qualitative are seen as distinct methods, though *mixed methods research* has become popular. From a Dooyeweerdian perspective, the distinction is not fundamental, since both alike are abstractions away from reality, and mixing them is commonplace.

Though what is presented here is aspectual analysis of interview transcripts and texts in various literatures, it can be used more widely. It can be used to analyse data from observation, field studies and experiments, especially when contextual data is also collected (§11–8). It can even be used during conversations, as a continual intuitive awareness of which aspects are being mentioned and which are not. The following, however, are drawn from the experience of some of my erstwhile research students, and others, many in the field of information systems use. Note: Most aspectual interpretations here are those of other researchers and might differ from my own.

11–7.1 Simple Aspectual Analysis

The utterances in an interview may be analysed using Dooyeweerd's aspects in order to disclose what was meaningful to the interviewee. The following examples are selected from Kane's (2006) study of student aspirations.

- "Committed to going to university" (pistic aspect);
- "Ethical is part of my character, to give back when I take" (ethical aspect);
- "Respect is necessary and the responsibility is to learn" (juridical aspect);
- "I want to balance my life toward fulfilment" (aesthetic aspect);
- "Wants to make some money in IT" (economic aspect);
- "Able to speak out more in a group of mature students; feels more confident" (lingual, social aspect);
- "Student is still the same person, but being at college is helping the student to progress" (formative aspect);

- "Distinctions about qualifications for work, you can't get the job without the qualifications" (analytic aspect);
- "Always wanted . . ." (sensitive aspect).

We may notice several things.

First, aspectual analysis can reveal issues that might ordinarily be overlooked during analysis. For example, in a study of aspiration, whereas "Wants to make some money in IT" is obviously selectable as data to analyse, "give back when I take" might be ignored as a mere aside. To discipline oneself to assign aspects to utterances overcomes the analyst's bias towards certain aspects.

Second, aspectual analysis can help fulfil Klein & Myers' (1999) principles of recognising bias brought by the researcher and in the participants, which they noted are less often discussed. Aspectual analysis encourages discussing which aspects are overlooked in a study.

Third, such analysis demonstrates the nuanced complexity of aspiration. Aspiration, often treated as a simple, unitary notion, is inherently multi-aspectual, meaningful in a myriad of ways. Finding meaningfulness in all aspects stimulates the analyst to reflect more deeply on the phenomenon being studied. After the analysis from which the above is taken, Kane reflected on the role each aspect plays in aspiration; for example the formative aspect is about individual achievement, the social is about aspirations linked with family, and so on.

11–7.2 Finding Hidden Meanings: What Motivated Seminal Papers

What aspectual analysis does is to distinguish units of meaningfulness. These might be found not only in whole utterances, but also in phrases therein. Sina Joneidy took this line when he analysed the motivations behind seminal papers in the fields of information systems use (Joneidy 2015; Joneidy & Basden 2018) and health informatics (Joneidy & Burke 2018); see also §11–2.2.

Most seminal papers are motivated by highlighting previously overlooked issues, but motivations are sometimes not easily made explicit. Joneidy developed a reasonably systematic method for investigating motivations using Dooyeweerd's aspects, because motivation is closely linked with meaningfulness. Motivation is of course pistic functioning, but what motivates authors is its target aspect(s) (§4–3.9)—something meaningful to the field that had not previously been given due attention.

11–7.2.1 The Method

Joneidy would select excerpts from papers that indicate the wider meaningfulness of the paper. Most occur in the abstract, introduction and conclusion, but he would then scan the rest of the paper for others.

Motivation might be explicitly stated, as in "The purpose of this research is to pursue better measures for predicting and explaining use". But indicators of motivation are often implicit. They may be detected from several things. One is statements about what has been lacking or normatively askew in previous thought, such as "given contradictory results in past studies . . . our focused reconceptualization of the construct should enable more informed research". Another is the use of normatively loaded linguistic devices that tell the reader that what follows is likely to be important, such as "simple adoption of EHRs *does not necessarily* improve the quality of care" (Classen & Bates 2011, emphasis added). In this way, both semantic and pragmatic meanings are considered as indicators of wider meaningfulness.

Such excerpts were analysed to investigate which aspect(s) best accounted for what made each phrase meaningful or important. For example "pursue better measures" is a quantitative motivation, "contradictory" and "focused reconceptualization" are analytic motivation, and "improve the quality of care" is ethical and economic motivation.

11–7.2.2   Results

As with Kane, assigning aspects to pieces of text exerts a discipline that reveals meanings that might otherwise be overlooked.

In most papers, a pair of aspects seemed important. Where the pair is unique, because of the irreducible distinction between aspects, this was taken to indicate a genuinely new area of concern, perhaps a distinct paradigm, around which a coherent discourse subsequently develops. For example, Classen & Bates' paper is about the paradigm known as Meaningful Use, which concerns itself with benefit (economic and ethical aspect) and distinguishes itself from those discourses concerned with conceptualisation or measurement. This might reveal *why* new paradigms arise, to augment the usual discussions of *how*.

Where a pair of aspects is shared, this is taken to indicate that the papers are addressing the same general issue and together indicate the same paradigm, even though they might make different contributions in other ways. Where one aspect is shared between two pairs, the shared aspect might be meaningful in different ways (different parts of its constellation). Example: The economic aspect (§9–1.11) was important in one paper as productivity and in another as benefits. Such analysis reveals subtle differences and similarities that are often overlooked.

New avenues for discussion might be opened up, in at least two ways. Absent aspects might predict discourses or seminal papers yet to emerge. Considering inter-aspect dependency (§3–2.4.4) can help identify how papers and their discourses might relate to each other. Example: Joneidy found distinct discourses around beneficial use (ethical, economic aspects) and full use of IT features (lingual, formative); since former aspects depend foundationally on the latter, dialogue between the two discourses would be salient.

Not only might Joneidy's method be useful in examining papers and discourses, it might be useful during the literature review phase of research. It might also be useful in research into historical sources, because the past and present both share the same surrounding, prior meaningfulness (law-side), even though the fact-side might be different.

11–7.2.3   Challenges

Joneidy & Basden (2018) reflect on challenges of using Dooyeweerd's aspects. (1) Sometimes, issues that are meaningful in one aspect could have been meaningful in others, so judgment is required. This is to be expected because of the multi-aspectual nature of all things and activities (§4–3.3, §4–3.8.2). (2) Differences of culture between author and analyst causes problems, especially when the aspect that makes an utterance meaningful is not immediately obvious but is revealed only by understanding subtleties in the use of words. However, if Dooyeweerd is correct that all share the same spheres of meaningfulness, then at least some cross-cultural understanding is expected (§4–3.11.1, §4–4.2). (3) On the other hand, when author and analyst are apparently from a similar background, real subtleties or nuances in meaning can be overlooked because of assumptions by either party. Assumptions may be surfaced using Dooyeweerd's aspects, as found earlier in MAKE and MAIT. (4) An inexperienced analyst might initially employ a simplified reading of aspects but, after a short time, understanding of the meaning of aspects can become intuitive. Even then, two analysts might have different views. This was ameliorated by examining not just the semantic definition of terms, but also what the writer was trying to achieve. (5) The theoretical analyst begins to treat the aspects as a tool rather than as something within which they dwell; this might distort understanding and assignment of aspects. (6) It can be difficult for analysts to explain the often subtle reasons why they have assigned one aspect rather than others. This is especially challenging when trying to share with those who know little or nothing about aspects, such as in mainstream media.

11–7.3   Researching Everyday Down-to-Earth Issues

Down-to-earth issues are issues that are meaningful in the everyday experience of those being studied. For example, (un)helpfulness of support staff is important to users of IT 'on the ground', whereas *high-level issues*, like cost, technological prowess or power relations, are of interest to management, IT suppliers and academics respectively but less directly meaningful to users. High-level issues dominate in most academic and professional literature, and down-to-earth issues are often mentioned only in passing.

However, researching down-to-earth issues is challenging, because down-to-earth issues are extremely numerous, variable and often hidden. Nevertheless, three studies have developed a way to study down-to-earth issues using aspectual analysis. They are all in the field of information technology (IT) use, but the methods they developed can be applied more generally.

11–7.3.1   The First Study

Hawa Ahmad wished to unearth the down-to-earth issues that users of information technology (IT) encounter (Ahmad 2013; Ahmad & Basden 2013). Unlike Winfield and Kane, Ahmad did not use aspects while interviewing but only to analyse what was said.

She undertook qualitative analysis of transcripts of open interviews, using standard coding methods, to organise unstructured data, and then interpreted these using Dooyeweerd's aspects in order to identify which aspects make each phrase or utterance in the interview meaningful. She assumed each text might be meaningful by multiple aspects, not just one primary aspect. Example:

Question: If you have more things to do at one time, how do you handle the pressure?
Answer: I know I have work to complete [*Formative*] and it is my responsibility [*Juridical*] so I'll do it. I will do it by priority [*Analytic*], which one needs to be completed first [*Juridical*]. Then at a later stage I will do the rest [*Formative*].

Each aspect reveals a down-to-earth issue in the life/work of the interviewee.

In addition, meaningful issues might be deduced with the help of aspects by those who know the context, such as the background reasons for prioritizing tasks. Ahmad deduced an aesthetic aspect (prioritizing helps completeness and work enjoyment) and a social aspect (prioritizing helps other staff). Aspectual analysis very readily reveals multiple meanings, not just between different participants as Klein & Myers (1999) stress, but also within each participant.

Ahmad's (2013) approach helps uncover *indirect issues* that affect the quality of information systems use but which are not recognised in the literature, because often the utterances that refer to them do not refer directly to the system that is being studied. For example, one interviewee mentioned transport (p. 154): If there is a problem, they arrive late and upset and then cannot properly focus on their tasks (which uses the system), and until they arrive others have to cover for them and might not know their use of the system so well. Aspectual analysis helps the analyst not only take such issues seriously, but forces the analyst to reflect on why they are important to the interviewee: a juridical-psychical-social-formative-ethical complex behind the kinematic of transport.

Ahmad undertook a similar aspectual analysis of issues mentioned in academic literature, which showed that the literature is biased towards certain aspects and away from others; see also §11–7.3.6.

11–7.3.2   The Second and Third Studies

Ahmad's down-to-earth approach was used in two other research projects to explore everyday issues. They confirmed its power but also developed it in important ways.

Ghadah Khojah studied down-to-earth issues in use of electronic health records (Khojah 2013, 2018). Her analysis of health informatics literature shows there was a need to *reveal* down-to-earth issues (as distinct from high-level ones), to *uncover* hidden issues and to find a way to *classify* them. She argues that standard conceptual frameworks like Actor-Network Theory do not facilitate all three, but Dooyeweerd's aspects promise to do so. So she employed Ahmad's down-to-earth approach, interviewing healthcare workers (nurses, physicians, clerks, etc.) in four hospitals in the Kingdom of Saudi Arabia. Excerpts from the interview transcripts were analysed aspectually to find what was meaningful in both questions and answers (see below for explanation of Q, A, X). Example:

Questions: When do you check the file? [Q, formative, process] Where do you keep the patient files? [Q, spatial]
Answer: Well, sometimes I have it on my counter [A, spatial] because I try to get these things done [X, formative] before the doctor round [X, economic: time limit] and all that mess [X, economic, time-wasting]; the file check begins before the doctors' round [A, economic].

This gave her what she called *"aspectual issues"* (e.g. time limit because of doctor), which are issues that are meaningful in one (main) aspect of the life/work of the interviewee. These were collected together by aspect, to give a base of data for quantitative and qualitative analysis of what healthcare workers find meaningful about working with health records. Like Ahmad, she sometimes deduced issues, but far less often.

Opeoluwa Aiyenitaju interviewed teachers in three primary schools in the UK to study their down-to-earth experience of using IT in classrooms (Aiyenitaju 2018; Aiyenitaju & Basden 2017). She argues that extant frameworks are not adequate to handle the *diversity* and *depth* in everyday, down-to-earth issues teachers face, but that Dooyeweerd is. Early interviews showed the importance of teachers' *values*, so she also studied values by aspectually analysing value-statements made by teachers, to reveal a richer mix of types of values (in many aspects) than is conventionally discussed (§4–3.7).

Using a similar method to that of Khojah, Aiyenitaju undertook aspectual analysis of excerpts to obtain aspectual issues, to form a similar base of data. She learned an important lesson: At first she analysed the *words* used, but then realised it was important to analyse the *broader meaning* of each utterance, so redid her analysis.

These two studies differ from Ahmad's in two important ways. First, both distinguished direct answers to interviewer questions from *extra, spontaneously volunteered information*, perhaps as opinions or stories. It was expected that whereas direct answers to interviewer questions would be about issues meaningful to interviewers, the extra information would better express what is meaningful in the life and work of the interviewee; see §11–7.3.5 for confirmation of this. In the excerpt from one of Khojah's interviews above, "Q" indicates an aspect of a question, "A" of a direct answer and "X" of extra volunteered information. Second, whereas Ahmad had undertaken qualitative coding *before* aspectual analysis, Khojah and Aiyenitaju performed it *after* aspectual analysis. This is discussed later.

11–7.3.3   *Quantitative and Qualitative Analyses*

Khojah and Aiyenitaju analysed their aspectual issues quantitatively and qualitatively in several ways. First, they simply counted issues per aspect, to yield an *aspectual profile* of what interviewees found meaningful (in health-care and teaching), usefully depicted as a bar chart. Figure 11.7 shows Khojah's results for the relative importance of each aspect in everyday work with healthcare records.

It can be seen that formative, lingual and juridical issues are the most meaningful (most aspectual issues; most often mentioned) with economic and analytic running up. Biotic-organic, quantitative, aesthetic and ethical are least meaningful.

Aspectual profiles immediately prompt the question, "Why?" Why are biotic-organic issues not mentioned by healthcare interviewees devoted to health? Khojah suggests that in discussing healthcare records (not patients), health issues are taken for granted. So might ethical issues be. Such

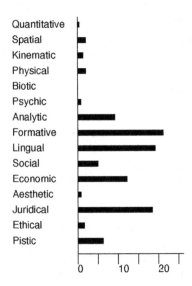

Figure 11.7 Aspectual profile: relative importance of each aspect (%) in work with healthcare record

possibilities might stimulate directed research, which might uncover hidden down-to-earth issues in the culture among healthcare workers.

Why are formative, lingual and juridical most meaningful? Emphasis on the juridical, lingual and formative aspects might be expected in any profession, characterised by legal duties, dissemination and achieving defined objects, but examination of the actual down-to-earth aspectual issues finds differently. Khojah undertook a qualitative coding of issues in each aspect separately and found that juridical issues cluster around Proper Working, Proper Documentation, Nurse Responsibility, Accessibility, Other Staff Responsibility and Proper Patient Care—issues of appropriateness and down-to-earth responsibilities rather than of formal legality or policy.

11–7.3.4 *Comparative Analyses*

Both Khojah and Aiyenitaju used their collected data of aspectual issues to investigate differences between cohorts. Khojah studied differences between hospitals, between users of paper and electronic records, between nurses and other healthcare workers, and between nationalities. Aiyenitaju studied differences between schools, genders and school years. Figure 11.8 shows the aspectual profiles for Aiyenitaju's three schools.

In comparing aspectual profiles, it is advisable to look at overall patterns, not precise quantities. This shows that School A had more emphasis on the formative and economic aspects than had Schools B and C, and less on the social, while School C has the smoothest, flattest profile, with no dominant aspect.

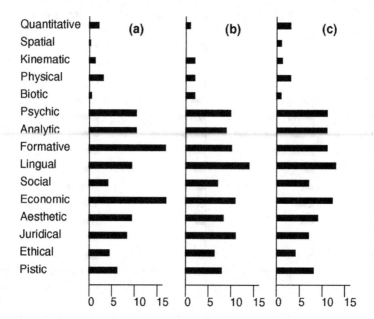

Figure 11.8 Aspectual profiles for three primary schools using IT

As with single profiles, we may ask "Why?" Why might schools differ on which aspects are important? Relating the different profiles to the different situations and histories of the three schools revealed several interesting points for discussion.

11–7.3.5   *The Value of Extra, Volunteered Information*

Both Khojah and Aiyenitaju separated direct answers (A) to interviewer questions (Q) from *extra, spontaneously volunteered information* (X), expecting A to be influenced by the interests of the researcher and X to better reveal what is meaningful to the interviewees. Aiyenitaju generated aspectual profiles of her Q, A and X; see Figure 11.9.

This confirms their expectations. It shows that whereas the researcher (via their questions) was particularly interested in the formative aspect, and this was reflected in the direct answers, the extra volunteered information shows no emphasis on this aspect but is more evenly spread across all aspects. It is also interesting that in both answers and extra information the economic aspect of daily resources emerged as important despite the researcher's relative lack of interest therein.

This implies that in all open-interview research, stripping away the direct answers to questions and working only with volunteered information might provide a more accurate understanding of what is meaningful to the interviewees. Examining the aspectual profile of the questions and direct answers might reveal the nature and extent of researcher effect.

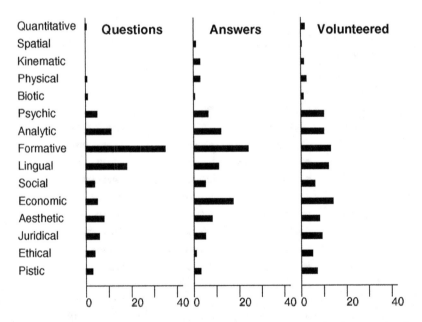

Figure 11.9 Aspectual profiles for questions, direct answers and volunteered information from teachers

11–7.3.6   *The Literature Versus Everyday Experience*

Khojah aspectually analysed the down-to-earth issues mentioned in the academic health records literature and compared the aspectual profile this yielded with that of the healthcare workers; see Figure 11.10.

Both workers and literature find the formative and juridical issues particularly important, and neither place much emphasis on ethical or aesthetic issues (nor on those of the early aspects). What is interesting, however, is that the literature places more emphasis on economic and social issues and much less on lingual and pistic than do healthcare workers. We may ask "Why?" to direct further research.

Qualitative analysis reveals even more difference. Though both literature and healthcare personnel found the juridical aspect meaningful, qualitative coding of both sets reveals different kinds of juridical issues. To health care workers, the top three juridical issues were Proper Working, Proper Documentation and Responsibility (nurse, others). These were completely absent from the literature analysed, the top three concerns of which were Patient Safety, Medical Error and Appropriateness (of system, to staff).

This strikingly shows bias in academic literature and the theoretical thought on which it is based (§2–3.2) away from everyday experience. Academic literature is consequently a poor guide to what is important in healthcare. Ahmad found similarly, as did Aiyenitaju in her study of teachers' values.

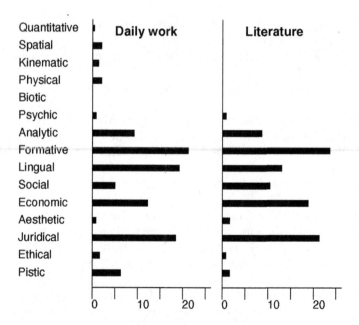

Figure 11.10 Aspectual profiles: relative importance of each aspect (%) for (a) healthcare workers and (b) health record literature

More generally, this provides empirical support for Dooyeweerd's original contention that theoretical thought is not neutral and theoretical bodies of knowledge are not 'truth' (§2–3, §2–4, §6–4, §7–4.2).

> *Research opportunity: non-neutrality of theoretical thought.* Extend Khojah's comparison with more literature, and in other fields. Aspectual analysis of literature in each field compared with down-to-earth issues of everyday experience might provide extensive empirical support or otherwise of Dooyeweerd's transcendental argument.

11–7.3.7   *Reflection on Aspectual Analysis of Down-to-Earth Issues*

It is customarily expected that down-to-earth issues of everyday experience are too profuse and contingent to be seriously studied as a whole. That expectation arises from presupposing either autonomous subjectivity or reductionist objectivity, but Dooyeweerd's understanding of diverse, coherent meaningfulness offers a philosophically sound basis for studying the plethora of issues, and Ahmad, Khojah and Aiyenitaju have developed methods for doing so. We may note the following.

1. *Revealing* of down-to-earth issues occurs primarily during aspectual interpretation of texts, which separates out aspectual issues. Revealing is possible because every phrase interviewees utter is meaningful in some way (§4–3.11.1), and Dooyeweerd offers a suite of aspects to help the analyst.

2. *Quantitative aspectual analysis* offers an overview of what is meaningful to a cohort, while *qualitative aspectual analysis* opens up some of the detail. Both work together. Focus on aspectual meaningfulness thus assists *mixed methods research*.

3. The *diversity* of aspectual issues can be handled well because of the irreducible distinctness of aspects (§3–2.3). Both Aiyenitaju and Khojah found early aspects are less frequently mentioned. Mostly their role is merely as foundational support for later aspects, though issues like movement of records with patients from one hospital location to another are directly meaningful.

4. *Values* may be studied in their diversity because of the innate normativity of aspects (§4–3.7).

5. *Uncovering* hidden down-to-earth issues, and exploring their *depth*, is stimulated by asking questions raised by aspectual profiles and by examining aspectual issues qualitatively. Uncovering is possible because every aspect is meaningful in the situations being studied, and hiddenness results from overlooking aspects.

6. *Classifying* down-to-earth issues is made possible because Dooyeweerd's suite of aspects offers a ready-made, philosophically sound basis for classifying issues (§4–3.2). Ahmad used aspectual classification after undertaking standard qualitative coding, but it makes sense to reverse this, as Khojah

and Aiyenitaju did and perform aspectual classification first. This is because qualitative coding, though it can reflect what seems relevant in the fact-side situations being studied, it also reflects the analyst's subjective selection of aspects of interest. All qualitative coding presupposes a basis for distinguishing ways of being meaningful (aspects), so why not capitalise on one of the best attempts so far to delineate those aspects (§9–4)?

7. Challenges in aspectual analysis. Khojah (2018) discusses a number of challenges she met in aspectual analysis.

a) Aspectual interpretation can sometimes be ambiguous. For most phrases only one aspect could be assigned, but in some, two aspects were possible. "Focusing more on patient care" could be formative and/or juridical. Which aspect prompted the utterance can sometimes be judged from surrounding text.

b) Different analysts might assign different aspects because they have different intuitive grasps of aspectual meaningfulness.

Research opportunity: aspectual interpretation. To investigate how aspects are interpreted differently, present the same interview transcripts to several analysts who all understand Dooyeweerd's aspects and compare the aspectual issues they come up with.

c) Researcher experience of the studied situation (Khojah had already worked in healthcare) can often yield more nuanced interpretations, closer to what is meaningful to interviewees, but it might also distort, because of the cultural assumptions. Aspectual analysis can ameliorate this by seeking pragmatic as well as semantic meanings and by considering all aspects in order to spotlight unspoken assumptions.

11–7.4 Complex Quantitative Comparisons

Bar charts are useful for simple comparison of a few aspectual profiles. However, Nick Breems needed to make a more extensive quantitative comparison between discourses in a field compared with each other and with everyday experience. The actual comparison is described in Section 11–2.4; this section describes his method of analysis.

The topic Breems studied was computer procrastination, which had never been adequately discussed in the literature, and he wanted to (a) understand why this was and (b) find a way to adequately study it and similar complex problems. As mentioned earlier, in the conceptual framework for his research, Breems used Basden's (2008a) initial framework for understanding IT use, which later became the Aspectual Engagements Framework of Basden (2018a) (§11–3.6.3). It sees IT use as three human engagements, each of which exhibits all 15 aspects in principle; this gives at least 45 spaces for discussion of factors that are meaningful!

Breems looked for major themes that occupy the discourses in each of five research areas, which might find computer procrastination relevant, and identified aspects that made each theme meaningful. For example, the HCI (Human-Computer Interaction) field might study response times to stimuli on screen, and Breems would count this as of the psychic aspect of engagement with the interface. He also empirically investigated the 45 aspects of the three engagements in the everyday experience of computer procrastination, by introspection while playing the Yahtzee computer game. For example, that the game is tantalizingly close, on the screen, to where he would be working (e.g. writing a report), counted as a spatial aspect of engaging with the interface. See Breems & Basden (2014) for the full analysis.

Breems created a useful visual device for comparing what is meaningful to discourses and in everyday experience, the heatmap diagram, shown in Figure 11.2. This reveals that none of the research areas that might be expected to understand computer procrastination can do so because, for each one, at least some aspects or engagements that are important in the everyday experience of computer procrastination are of little interest. His method of analysing and displaying the interests of discourses was adopted by Basden (2018a) when analysing 17 discourses in the field of IT use (*ibid.*, 209–12).

11–7.5   Complex Qualitative Comparisons

Stephen McGibbon wanted to investigate trust. As discussed in §11–4.4, trust is an extremely complex issue, discussed in many fields in different ways, yet always recognisable as trust. To do justice to such a myriad of meaningfulness and, at the same time, to its coherence as trust is a challenge for any research and a good test of the capability of Dooyeweerdian philosophy.

For this, he needed a method of analysing a wide range of literature to find out what each author finds meaningful about trust. He arrived at a complex picture that gives useful findings that are reasonably reliable and can be communicated and defended. See Figure 11.4.

Such a complex analysis was an uncharted territory with Dooyeweerd's philosophy, so McGibbon had to find his own ways, including recognising and retreating from dead-ends. McGibbon (2018) describes the adventure in detail; the following is a summary.

1. He first tried identifying primary aspectual functioning of trust mentioned by each author, counting the frequency of occurrence and displaying the results by various means (bar chart, radar diagram, pie chart, etc.) to see if this could provide insight into the differences and similarities among authors. This proved unsatisfactory for several reasons. (a) Fifteen aspects proved not rich enough when taken singly. (b) When he returned later, these could not remind him of his earlier thought processes. (c) It could not communicate well to others; and attempts to do so deteriorated into discussions of his subjective interpretations and counts. (d) If a certain aspect had zero count on the first interpretation, he found that, when he re-read the author,

he could invariably find occurrences of that aspect—which cast doubt on his interpretations.

2. He noticed that, when trying to remember or justify earlier interpretations, he would be referring to antecipations and retrocipations of aspects, which he called "cipations". So, instead of single aspectual meaningfulness, he began looking at cipation pairs. Such cipations themselves function in various aspects and form *cipation triples*. This was more successful and allowed him even to understand poetry from a different era in aspectual terms.

> Example: "It [mercy] droppeth as the gentle rain from heaven" in Portia's speech in Shakespeare's *Merchant of Venice*. "Gentle" (ethical) retrocipates "rainfall" (physical). The meaningfulness of ethical-physical gentle rain is that it waters plants to refresh and bring life: organic-biotic aspect. This yields the cipation triple ((ethical, physical), organic) as part of Portia's understanding of mercy.

This begins to open up some of the structure of individuality beyond the qualifying aspect and those on which it depends into something more like a network of aspectual relationships. It affords the richness McGibbon needed to understand what authors were meaning in their various utterances on trust. He found also that it communicated the meaning to others more easily and with less criticism of his subjective interpretations, and that it was easier to remember what he had meant when he returned to the interpretation later. It also offers a way of differentiating what authors meant when they used similar wording, but in non-precise ways. Example: "emotional aspect of trust" is psychic to one author and juridical-pistic to another.

3. On analysing Portia's whole speech in this way, phrase by phrase, he discovered that aspects present themselves in three distinct ways:

- "wherein doth sit" is direct spatial functioning;
- "earthly power" is spatial-formative antecipation;
- "upon the place beneath" is ethical-spatial retrocipation.

4. This allowed McGibbon to analyse the literature on trust in a way on which it is more reasonable to rely (§1–2.1) than on his subjective interpretations, but without seeking 'objective truth'. He then proceeded to identify which aspects were important to each author, and he summarised this in the cell diagram shown in Figure 11.4. What such a diagram reveals is discussed in §11–4.4.

In finding several aspects that make each utterance meaningful follows what Joneidy, Khojah and Aiyenitaju did, but McGibbon makes it more systematic and defendable. Where they might assign multiple aspects to an utterance, McGibbon seeks to understand the relationships between those aspects in terms of Dooyeweerdian theory of cipations. While all four necessarily employ their intuitive grasp of aspectual kernels, McGibbon perhaps reins this in somewhat, and he found he could remember each aspectual decision and communicate it better. Questions about his method still remain, but it offers a usefully systematic approach, to be developed further.

11–7.6   Overview

What has been described is research that has been actually carried out using Dooyeweerd's aspects in data analysis. It shows a progression, in which each discovered something more and each can be applied in different situations. Whereas all but two are analysis of interview transcripts, most methods can be applied to any texts.

- Joneidy, McGibbon and Breems apply aspectual analysis to literature while the others apply it to interview transcripts.
- Kane's assignment of a main aspect to each utterance or text is the simplest version and the easiest to learn, and it useful for finding what is meaningful to interviewees.
- Joneidy did something similar with phrases, to find motivations as aspects in which papers are meaningful in their wider context, but used methods to reveal implicit meaningfulness.
- Ahmad used aspects to reveal down-to-earth issues, as distinct from the "high-level" issues that dominate the literature, by finding multiple aspects meaningful in excerpts of text. Ahmad shows how to attach Dooyeweerd to conventional research methods, after qualitative coding. She recognises the difference between direct and deduced meaningfulness in texts.
- Khojah and Aiyenitaju separate out voluntarily offered extra information from that given in response to questions, as a way to understand the nature of researcher bias and to reduce it.
- Moreover, they apply aspectual analysis before qualitative coding, using the latter within each aspect. This makes it easier to undertake cohort comparisons.
- Aspectual analysis allows quantitative aspectual profiles to be built up, which can give overall pictures of profiles of interest followed by qualitative aspectual analysis of detail.
- Breems offers a way to facilitate comparisons of complex issues, for which extant discourses are not adequate.
- McGibbon explores ways of doing justice to extremely complex issues like trust. He works out more fully than most do the complexity of Dooyeweerd's notion of individuality structures (§4–3.4) by cipation triples that form a network of inter-aspect relationships.

This wealth of experience could be useful in many fields. I will discuss just one example, Discourse Analysis, which was briefly discussed in §8–2.3. Wooffitt (2005) remarks that Discourse Analysis lacks formal methodological procedures, and it might be that the methods above can fill this gap.

If Discourse Analysis may be seen as adding the social aspect to the lingual in text analysis, Dooyeweerd would welcome this, as recognising more of the multi-aspectual 'ocean' of meaningfulness (§4–3.10), in which our lingual functioning of generating and receiving signification-meanings (§4–3.11) 'swims'. He would however urge Discourse Analysis, and sociolinguistics in general, to be bolder and recognise other aspects beyond the social. This is, perhaps, what Feminist Poststructural Discourse Analysis tries to do (§8–2.3).

As such, the above methods, which attempt to give equal respect to every aspect of the human activity in which the analysed text is generated, could therefore make a signal contribution to methods of Discourse Analysis. In Dooyeweerd there is no micro-macro, individual-social dichotomy, but all are merely manifestations of the different aspects of the coherence of meaningfulness, so this would reinterpret Critical Discourse Analysis.

> *Research opportunity: text and discourse analysis.* Using the above ideas, formulate, develop, test and refine versions of Multi-Aspectual Discourse Analysis.

11–8. Extending These Ideas: New Adventures Awaited

Referring to Table 11.1, we can see that Dooyeweerd has been used in four out the seven stages of research and in limited ways in two others. There are gaps. I know of no cases where Dooyeweerd's philosophy has actually been used to clarify or justify the main research question or to discuss limitations and contributions of the research. Even in those stages where his ideas have been used, much territory still awaits exploration. For example, use of Dooyeweerd in data collection has been to design questionnaires and guide interviews, but not during observation, field studies or experimentation. His ideas have not been applied practically in the natural sciences and only once in mathematics. This section, therefore, discusses the possibility of using Dooyeweerd's philosophy in some of these areas. Such discussion is, of course, based on speculation rather than direct experience, but I trust that it might stimulate some exploration of these areas.

Section 11–8.1 discusses how Dooyeweerd's philosophy might be used at the start and end of research. Section 11–8.2 discusses using Dooyeweerd in observation (including, perhaps, field studies and experimentation) rather than interviews or questionnaires. Section 11–8.3 discusses possibilities of using aspects in the natural and mathematical sciences.

11–8.1   *Using Dooyeweerd at Beginning and End of Research*

To start the research requires an understanding of the field, so that the proposed research will fit in appropriately. Dooyeweerd has not been directly used for this, but two pieces of research might offer relevant methods.

As discussed in §10–5, Jones (2007) used Dooyeweerd to guide his knowledge based systems development, a couple of the stages of which resemble early stages in research. He used aspects to identify stakeholders and their interests, as well as the kinds of processes to which the system would be relevant. This might be used in research with "stakeholders" replaced or augmented by "authors" and "processes" by "areas of concern".

Section 11–2 outlines ways of overviewing discourses in a field. Basden & Kutar (2010) can provide a useful quick overview of which aspects might be of most and least interest among a small selection of papers in a field. Breems' (2014) heatmap diagrams provide a better overview, showing precise gaps, but require more extensive reading. Joneidy's (2015) method provides the most precise investigation.

> *Research opportunity: research planning.* Explore and develop aspectual analysis methods based on these suggestions for research planning: making a good initial overview of fields and clarifying and justifying the topic and main research question of research, and writing research proposals.

In the concluding phases of research, such aspectual analyses can assist discussion of its contributions to theory. The normative structure of Dooyeweerd's aspects can assist this, especially when discussing contributions to practice. Dooyeweerd's notion of Ground-Idea and the totality of meaningfulness that are the aspects might be useful to refer to when discussing limitations of the research.

> *Research opportunity: research conclusions.* Explore and develop methods, based on Ground-Ideas, for systematising discussion of limitations and contributions of research.

11–8.2   Using Dooyeweerd in Observation

Observing behaviour differs from interviewing or even analysing written texts in one fundamental way. The meaningfulness that is studied is not delivered via lingual signification-meanings generated by participants (interviewees or other writers), but by researcher-generated interpretation-meanings (see §4–1, §4–3.11 for the difference). Analysis of signification-meanings has been covered in Section 11–7, but analysis of interpretation-meanings is discussed here. The discussion is short and somewhat speculative because there has not, as far as I am aware, been any major work exploring the potential of Dooyeweerd's philosophy to assist these.

Saunders et al. (2012) offer a typical approach to observation research, differentiating between participant and structured observation, suggesting methods for each, and discussing problems of observer error, bias and effect. In participant observation, the researcher is immersed as part of the situation and might or might not hide their identity as researcher. In structured observation, the researcher maintains a distance from those observed, imposing their own list of meaningful criteria for observation, which is usually structured.

From a Dooyeweerdian perspective, the difference is less marked because the researcher is never fully detached, yet there is always some *Gegenstand* attitude (§2–2, §6–3.2). Both participant and structured observation seek to discover what is meaningful in the behaviour observed, observing fellow 'swimmers' in the 'ocean of meaningfulness' (§4–3.10). What is important, in both types, is sensitivity to the entire range of aspects, as ways in which behaviour can be meaningful, whether human or pre-human behaviour.

The participant observer may employ aspects to overcome their own bias towards certain issues and be sensitive to all—perhaps in ways discussed in §11–6 and §11–7. The structured observer may use aspects to ensure that the criteria they plan to observe include every aspect, rather than merely those that happen to interest them. An example of a recording sheet for observing behaviour in a group discussion (Saunders et al. 2012, 360) has the following, and I assign aspects:

- "Taking initiative"—formative;
- "Brainstorming"—psychic, analytic;
- "Offering positive ideas"—ethical, formative;
- "Drawing in others"—social, ethical;
- "Being responsive to others"—pistic, ethical;
- "Harmonising"—aesthetic;
- "Challenging"—juridical;
- "Being obstructive"—ethical dysfunction;
- "Clarifying/summarising"—analytic;
- "Performing group roles"—social.

Almost every aspect from psychic onwards is there—suggesting a reasonably wide coverage of what is important in real-life group discussion. This is not surprising since the sheet seems to have been developed in response to long experience, which Dooyeweerd holds to involve every aspect. If we wish to critique and improve the sheet we might ask: (a) Where are the lingual and economic aspects? (b) Why is only one aspect dysfunction explicitly mentioned?

> *Research opportunity: observation research.* Dooyeweerdian ideas are yet to be developed in both participant and structured observation.

11–8.3   Using Dooyeweerd in Natural and Mathematical Sciences

Discussion in this chapter so far has been about studying human behaviour, but the natural sciences study the behaviour of animals, plants and material and the mathematical sciences, the 'behaviour' of quantities, etc., in order to better understand the laws of the relevant aspects. How might Dooyeweerd's ideas help research in the natural sciences and mathematics? Experience is sparse, so the following is a brief, initial reflection, the aim of which is to stimulate readers into innovatively thinking about other possibilities.

Given that humans can function as subject in all aspects, most of the above methods have stressed the importance of considering every aspect. Since material functions as subject only in the first four aspects (§4–3.9), it might seem that only physical, kinematic, spatial and quantitative laws apply, and so the other 11 aspects are irrelevant to research content in the physical sciences. (For plant and animal sciences, the latest aspects are the organic-biotic and psychic respectively.)

That view is over-simple. Not only are research *activity* and application still multi-aspectual (see §4–4.2, Chapter 10), but natural science and mathematical research *content* is too. For example, Satherley (2011) argues, with reference to chemistry, that all things function in all aspects, even though some of this functioning is as object, involved in some other subject's functioning. So material like water molecules or planets can function as object in all 11 other aspects. Such object-aspects affect their physical subject functioning by retrocipatory influence. He offers, as example, the behaviour of water molecules and lipids that is governed not by physical laws but by organic ones, and is not found in the non-living world.

Even chemical processes that are found there might operate differently because of conditions that can only be explained from the perspective of later aspects. Physico-chemical behaviour is retrocipatorily influenced by the organic-biotic behaviour of the plant or animal. Chemistry, therefore, takes that which is meaningful in the organic-biotic aspect into account. Moreover, the plant behaviour might in turn be affected by human behaviour; for example whether the plant is in a garden or is being forced for sale in a continuously lit hothouse.

This is recognised, of course, but it may be made more systematic with an awareness of aspects. Satherley uses Dooyeweerd to clarify concepts and arguments. This is why research carried out by pharmaceutical companies is rightly viewed with suspicion unless their laboratory tests adequately match conditions in bodies, and moreover bodies in everyday life rather than the laboratory.

However, Satherley's main research in chemistry seems to make no reference to Dooyeweerd. It remains to be discovered how, if at all, Dooyeweerd can be relevant there.

Similarly, in mathematics, as discussed in §6–1.1, mathematical theories have to take into account their potential application context. The content of mathematical theories, especially their interpretation, is also influenced by research activity, especially the pistic aspect of beliefs and assumptions held by the community. This has been shown to be so in statistics by Hartley (2008), who employs Dooyeweerd's exploration of the Nature-Freedom ground-motive (§5–2.2, §5–2.4) to cast light on four paradigms in statistics: direct and indirect frequentism, objective and subjective Bayesianism (see §11–3.1). He argues that adhering to the nature and freedom poles constrain both the statistical procedures used and their interpretation. See §11–3.1 for his paradigm critique.

He presupposes, and slightly argues, the embeddedness of statistical analysis in everyday life and openness to the realities of research, which of course fits comfortably with Dooyeweerd's starting-points. In discussing statistical thresholds used in decision making (Hartley 2008, 88), he argues that decision makers must account for "economic, social, moral and biological" properties and laws, rather than only quantified degrees of beliefs. He also mentions a number of aspects that are important in undertaking statistical analysis, suggesting multi-aspectual functioning. For example, various steps may help the analyst reduce distortion while forming subjective priors (p. 91): eliciting knowledge from experts (juridical) individually and in groups (social), rewording questions (lingual), and seeking experts who do not stand to benefit from research conclusions (ethical). (This is of course verging on research activity.) See Hartley (2008) for further discussion.

These and other ideas need to be developed in order to, at least, ascertain just how useful Dooyeweerd might be in research content in the early-aspect sciences and, then, to forge good Dooyeweerdian methodological and conceptual tools for such research equivalent to those described for human research in this chapter.

11–9. Conclusion

Dooyeweerd's philosophy is relatively new among researchers. This chapter has discussed examples of how Dooyeweerd's philosophy has been used as an approach, as foundation for conceptual frameworks, and as a source of conceptual tools or methods for data collection and analysis—the three roles of research discussed in §5–1. The examples have been drawn from a number of researchers who have used Dooyeweerd across several fields, including my own.

Dooyeweerd's aspects have been the most widely used portion of his thought. This is not surprising since they embody and express the diversity and coherence of meaningfulness encountered in the everyday experience that is actual reality, the world we are trying to understand. Aspects have been used to compose questionnaires, guide interviews, form categories, analyse data, reveal issues that have been overlooked, critique paradigms, create new paradigms and frameworks for understanding, open doors to new avenues of research, clarify concepts like information, do justice to the nuanced complexity of ideas like trust, focus and open up ideas like idolatry, provide bases for comparing what is meaningful in extant discourses, compare them with empirical experience, gain overviews in diverse collections of papers, and, throughout all these, maintain a normative element in research.

Other portions of Dooyeweerd's thought have been used less. Dooyeweerd's idea of dialectical ground-motives has been useful in critiquing the state of a field by revealing the roots of conflicts and oppositions that hinder dialogue. Dooyeweerd's understanding of subject-object relationships, functioning, qualifying aspects and enkapsis have been useful in several places alongside aspects.

Dooyeweerd's philosophy has proven adept and efficient in four main stages of research, to gain an overview of fields, literature and paradigms, to understand paradigms and generate new, rich conceptual frameworks, to collect data and analyse data to yield findings. There are gaps, as discussed in Section 11–8.

What are the limitations and problems of using Dooyeweerd in research? Some challenges have been discussed (§11–2.4.3, §11–7.2.3, §11–7.3.7, §11–6.4). The subjective understanding of aspect kernels can sometimes affect interpretation of data, but with judicious research design the effect of this can be reduced (see the comment in §11–6.4). However, it is too early to properly discuss limitations until wider experience is gained. We need adventures with Dooyeweerd in observational and experimental research and in a wider range of fields, especially in the natural sciences. We need adventures in the initial and final stages of research.

Nevertheless, the adventures that have taken place so far with Dooyeweerd's philosophy have opened up considerable territory in research, which should enable and encourage further adventures. The discussions in this chapter should provide exemplars that can be adapted. Chapter 9 has been included in order to help researchers develop their intuitive grasp of aspectual kernels. Part IV concludes our discussion.

Part IV

Part IV calls researchers to join the adventures with Dooyeweerd's philosophy in research.

- Chapter 12 assembles criticisms of Dooyeweerd's philosophy, so that researchers will use Dooyeweerd's philosophy with their eyes open.
- Chapter 13 concludes our discussion, by summarising the contributions Dooyeweerd can make to research content, activity and application, examining the situation of research today and the coverage of Dooyeweerd's philosophy, and suggesting a way forward.

12 Criticisms of Dooyeweerd

Dooyeweerd welcomed criticism. In this chapter, I have assembled as many criticisms of Dooyeweerd's ideas as I can find, in order that readers may undertake their own critique and begin to employ Dooyeweerd's philosophy with their eyes open.

The criticisms that I have been able to find are patchy, with considerably more in some areas than in others. Many are not of good quality, some boiling down to "I don't like Dooyeweerd", "I don't agree" or "His thought is not complete"; most such are omitted. Many of the criticisms from his fellow Christians are of this kind, and one often detects the influence of the Nature-grace ground-motive (§5–2.2). This chapter reviews some of the more philosophically or practically substantial critiques, which are relevant to using Dooyeweerd in research. They are presented more or less in the order in which portions of Dooyeweerd's thought are introduced in this book.

To fully understand and address them requires philosophical discourse beyond the scope of this book, but since some readers might wish to undertake this, this chapter provides some pointers.

12–1. Criticisms of Dooyeweerd's Ideas

12–1.1 Critiques of Dooyeweerd's Approach to Everyday Experience

Hart (1985, 152) points out that Dooyeweerd did not clearly differentiate pre-theoretical thought from pre-theoretical experience, nor from knowledge and even cognitive activities. "As a result, he seldom examined naive thought as *thought*, that is, as conceptual in nature", and did not clarify the relationship between the object of pre-theoretical thought and the *Gegenstand* of theoretical analysis.

I too have felt this ambiguity in Dooyeweerd's thought. So what I have presented in Chapter 2 is the way I have been able to make sense of these parts of Dooyeweerd's ideas in the light of two decades of using Dooyeweerd in research. Moreover, I have tended to treating pre-theoretical thinking as analytic functioning within the multi-aspectual functioning that is everyday experience, with subjects, objects and target aspects (§4–3.8, §4–3.9). How faithful my interpretation is to Dooyeweerd's original writing and, more importantly, to what Dooyeweerd was trying to express and achieve, must be debated elsewhere.

12–1.2 Critiques of Dooyeweerd's View of Non-Neutrality or Non-Autonomy of Theoretical Thought

When in the 1930s Dooyeweerd first published his idea that theoretical thought is not autonomous, several criticisms were offered. These and more recent ones are summarised by Choi (2000, 47–52). Some just dogmatically rejected Dooyeweerd's idea, and those are ignored here. More nuanced are Geertsema's (2000) criticisms. Two criticisms (pp. 64–5), concerning Dooyeweerd's uses of theological ideas need not concern us here. The one that does (p. 93) relates to Dooyeweerd's emphasis on the human heart in his transcendental critique of theoretical thought, which Geertsema argues is not necessary; all that is necessary is Dooyeweerd's more fundamental idea that the human thinker and the fully human nature of thinking are taken into account. This is the line I have taken in Chapter 6.

12–1.3 Critiques of Dooyeweerd's Approach to Diversity and Coherence

I am not aware of any critiques of Dooyeweerd's ideas of diversity and coherence (Chapter 3), though there have been many discussions about his suite of aspects; see later.

12–1.4 Critiques of Dooyeweerd's Idea of Meaning(fulness)

According to Choi (2000, 103), van Loon (1994), a Humanist thinker, seems to agree with Dooyeweerd's idea of meaningfulness in reality, but this is not developed.

I am aware of only one critique of Dooyeweerd's notion of meaningfulness as such (as prior, surrounding and pervading, with diverse and coherent aspects), made by Plantinga (1958/2006). Most of his criticisms arise from misunderstanding Dooyeweerd and confusing signification-meaning with meaningfulness. The useful points he raises include: Is Dooyeweerd's statement that meaning has the character of referring a mere truism? (But is Dooyeweerd merely pointing out a transcendental implication of meaning, §4–3.1?) Did Dooyeweerd's expression in NC imply too much separation between meaning and being? (I see Dooyeweerd as integrating them.) Did Dooyeweerd tie substance ideas too closely to the Form-Matter groundmotive? Plantinga finds Dooyeweerd to be suggesting that a substance-idea makes everyday subject-object impossible, and I too find Dooyeweerd's argument there problematic, but am not convinced by Plantinga either. Few of Plantinga's criticisms undermine the use of Dooyeweerd in research. A full discussion of Plantinga's critique may be found at "dooy.info/ext/ plantinga.ctq.html".

A different critique is that Dooyeweerd, in writing so much about meaning, was overly influenced by the Linguistic Turn in philosophy. Strauss (2013) suggests that, when trying to express the fundamentals of created reality, Dooyeweerd moved from his earlier metaphor of organic coherence toward one of linguistic meaning and that Dooyeweerd's interest in meaning arises from (over-)extending the lingual aspect to the whole of reality. This may also be seen occurring in the Linguistic Turn. On the other hand, Zuidervaart (2016, 15) believes the opposite, that Dooyeweerd did not take sufficient account of the Linguistic Turn.

I wonder whether it is not that Dooyeweerd was overly or underly influenced by the Linguistic Turn, but rather that he was already thinking about meaning as central (in the way I have presented in Chapter 4) at a time when Phenomenological and Linguistic Turn thinkers had also been discussing meaning. There is a difference in direction that is hidden from us until we differentiate the types of meaning as in §4–1. Whereas they started with attribution-, interpretation- and signification-meanings and found themselves moving towards meaningfulness, Dooyeweerd began with meaningfulness and, moving towards a fresh understanding of these types of meaning, he then met the thinkers en route. Perhaps he found some of their insights useful.

Instead of seeing all meaning as merely an extension of the lingual aspect, we may reverse this. Meaning(fulness) is cosmic and coherent, and the lingual aspect bears a special 'role' or 'responsibility' among the aspects of enabling us, when we function lingually, to externalise explicit 'pieces' of prior, surrounding meaningfulness. In this way, 'pieces of meaningfulness' can be made objects of study and shared with others with some clarity; see §4–3.11 and Basden (2019).

12–1.5 Critiques of Dooyeweerd's Notion of Being, including the State

Choi (2000, 47–52) outlines some criticisms of Dooyeweerd's notion of being, but most turn out to be dogmatic disagreements which simply reject Dooyeweerd's ideas, so are of little value here.

Dooyeweerd's ideas of enkapsis have been criticised, e.g. Basden (2008a, 2018a), but the thrust of the criticism is that it is an unfinished theory; enkapsis is otherwise very useful.

Dooyeweerd extensively discusses the being of the state. Chaplin (2011) criticises some parts of this, especially Dooyeweerd's understanding of politics; see also §11–3.4. Dooyeweerd gives insufficient importance to the part played by popular social movements (p. 214) and oppositional movements (p. 302) rather than established political parties, and Dooyeweerd's principles can in fact yield proposals contrary to Dooyeweerd's views (Chaplin 2011, 216). Chaplin finds some of Dooyeweerd's proposals interesting but "undeveloped and ambiguous" (p. 225). Might some of Dooyeweerd's more detailed prescriptions near his own field of expertise (politics, jurisprudence) owe their origin more to his cultural context (Dutch, Calvinist, in an era shocked by the horrors of Nazism and Communism) than to the principles he derives?

12–1.6   Critiques of Dooyeweerd's Idea of Good and Evil

I know of no critiques of this.

12–1.7   Critiques of Dooyeweerd's Idea of Aspectual Functioning

I know of no criticisms here, except that my introduction of the notion of targets of aspectual functioning (§4–3.9) might be seen as a criticism. Dooyeweerd does discuss intentionality and "logical object-side", which might refer to the target of analytic subject-functioning, but does not make these clear.

12–1.8   Critiques of Dooyeweerd's View of History and Progress

Dooyeweerd's theory of progress and history has two main themes: aspectual opening (§4–3.8.3) and differentiation of societal structures.

Aspectual opening, which is the more relevant to research, has received some criticism. Klapwijk (1987, 123) criticises Dooyeweerd's idea of progress as too close to German idealist metaphysics and having "romantic-organismic, progressivistic and universal-historical connotations," "that in one way or another eventuates, as it turns out, in modern *Western* culture" (emphasis in original), rather than as truly emerging from his main thought. This is a little unfair, because Dooyeweerd distanced himself from such a view, but the gradient of this part of his thought seems always towards Western modernity, in that it so happens that it is in that culture where aspects have most been opened up. This criticism does not undermine Dooyeweerd's basic idea, but it does warn us to question whether *how* they have been opened up might be dysfunctional.

The idea of societal differentiation has attracted several criticisms, some of which are discussed by Choi (2000, 35–9). That Dooyeweerd's idea of progress is too uncritical of Western society (Klapwijk 1987) might also be because in that society, institutions are differentiated from each other, compared with "primitive" societies. Choi cites Griffioen, for example, suggesting that "primitive", "undifferentiated" cultures can be as rich as "developed" ones. Dooyeweerd emphasises the formative ("historical": §9–1.8) aspect in progress, but McIntire suggests that progress and culture are more multi-aspectual than formative, as does Geertsema. McIntire (1985) believes Dooyeweerd conflates the problem of unity and diversity with that of time—but that might be seen as a philosophical insight of Dooyeweerd's rather than a deficiency.

12–1.9   Critiques of Dooyeweerd's View of Ground-Motives

Choi (2000) gives a very useful review of a number of thinkers who have criticised Dooyeweerd's understanding of the three dialectical ground-motives. Most find the notion of ground-motives as such useful. Ignoring some theological rather than philosophical disagreements with Dooyeweerd, most of the reviewed criticisms are that Dooyeweerd's dialectical view is over-simple and too antithetical, that other factors also come into play, and that actual philosophers in the Greek, Scholastic and Humanistic eras have more complex or nuanced views than Dooyeweerd allows.

(It is interesting, however, how *seldom* Dooyeweerd is criticised for mis-understanding any of the 100 philosophers he examined. Curiously, he did not cover American Pragmatism.)

Choi's own critique is based on his attempt to apply the ground-motive idea to Korean thought, and this gives it some authority. He finds Dooyeweerd's idea fits that non-Western culture, in being able to account for deep problems in its major streams of thought, that it can take seriously its Shamanist, Confucian, Buddhist and Christian roots, but that ground-motives need not be dialectical to generate deep problems.

These are probably valid criticisms, which imply that the strongly dialectical view must be toned down. Indeed, Dooyeweerd's own account, especially in Dooyeweerd (1979), shows more nuance. (It may be that the various ground-motives might in fact arise from elevation and grouping together of groups of aspects; see §5–3.3.)

Dooyeweerd's dialectical view may be seen as a useful broad-brush that helps to account for why some philosophical schools always talk past each other or seek to undermine each other. Basden (1999) argues that Dooyeweerd's idea of dialectical ground-motives, while preferable to Hegel's antithesis, is not nuanced enough to truly understand movements in a field. He finds an explanation based on the elevation of aspects provides a more apt account (this might facilitate Choi's analyses).

12–1.10   Critiques of Dooyeweerd's Idea of
the Immanence-Standpoint

Dooyeweerd opposes the immanence-standpoint to his transcendence standpoint. According to Choi (2000, 103), van Loon (1994) suggests this is too antithetical, excluding other options; he suggests a third standpoint of "intransparency". Choi, however, argues that van Loon did not fully understand Dooyeweerd and his "intransparency" is little more than relativism.

Clouser (2005) does suggest a third standpoint, what he calls Eastern, in which the entire temporal creation is part of the Divine (§5–3.2), and that another 11 are possible. This does not undermine Dooyeweerd's insight, which is important for research, that the immanence-standpoint has led to a number of deep problems for philosophy, which are listed in §5–3.1, but it might need widening to incorporate Eastern thought.

12–1.11   Critiques of Dooyeweerd's Transcendental Critiques of Theoretical Thought

Choi (2000) summarises three critical responses to Dooyeweerd's publication of his first way of critique (Dooyeweerd 1935), which were partly responsible for Dooyeweerd developing his second transcendental critique, which this book uses.

Some of the criticisms of the second critique arise from the tortuous style of its exposition that Dooyeweerd offers in Volume I. Most of the critics fail to recognise that Dooyeweerd applied the same critique not only to philosophy in Volume I but also to sciences in Volume III. My presentation in Chapter 6 is an attempt to clarify it, taking both into account, in a way that I trust Dooyeweerd intended and would have approved in relation to research, had he been alive today. It is an interpretation in which I have been informed by some of the criticisms. The following criticisms are of Dooyeweerd's original rendering, not my reinterpretation that is presented in Chapter 6 and has yet to be fully discussed.

Hart (1985, 152) points out that Dooyeweerd never questioned his own belief that theoretical thought is fundamentally different from pre-theoretical. (I believe Dooyeweerd was justified in this, since he took it as a starting-point, Chapter 2.) Hart finds a discrepancy here, in that while "As theory, philosophy is bound to the antithetical attitude of abstraction," philosophy "is occupied with coherence and even totality, the opposite of abstraction." (Is it not possible, however, to take an abstractive attitude when concerning oneself with coherence?)

Hart points out that whereas Dooyeweerd validly proved that theoretical thought rests on extra-theoretical (pre-theoretical) foundations, he had not necessarily shown that these foundations are religious. Hart makes a suggestion that seems to me a mere recapitulation to the status quo in philosophy, of presupposing the self-sufficiency of theoretical thought. However, I wonder whether Hart has misread Dooyeweerd here, in that, if theoretical thought is grounded in meaningfulness (§6–3.7) and if meaningfulness it tied up with our religious functioning (§4–3.1), then Dooyeweerd has indeed shown the religious root of theoretical thought. Clouser's (2005) version of Dooyeweerd's transcendental critique clearly shows the foundations are religious.

Even if Hart's criticisms are valid, he concludes (p. 153), "These problems, however, do not negate or even undermine the chief positive insights which I have noted Dooyeweerd has to offer."

Strauss (1984) offers eight detailed criticisms of Dooyeweerd's transcendental critique, as logical contradictions when we take Dooyeweerd's statements with a strict interpretation. Geertsema (2000) also raises some similar criticisms. Dooyeweerd's response, summarised by Strauss, was that whereas Strauss was using contradiction (intra-aspect), he was using antinomy (inter aspect). Unfortunately, this sidestepped rather than addressed Strauss' logic-based criticisms. So Strauss himself suggests some resolutions. If I understand

Strauss aright, my interpretation of Dooyeweerd in Chapter 6 incorporates some of Strauss' suggestions, of which two seem relevant here.

First, Dooyeweerd's notion of *Gegenstand* refers to two oppositions, of thinker from thought-about and of the focal aspect from its coherence with other aspects (§6–3.3), but Dooyeweerd blurs the distinction.

Second, whereas §6–3.3 speaks of aspects of the world, Dooyeweerd expresses it as "opposition of the non-logical aspects to the logical aspect of meaning" (NC,I, 18, 45), adding "It is from this very opposition that the theoretical problem is born." Does Dooyeweerd's critique not apply to analysis of the analytic (logical) aspect itself (theory about theory)? Might not the analytic aspect itself be the focal aspect? Since Dooyeweerd later allows for theory of theory (NC,I, 40n) (I find Dooyeweerd's reasoning opaque there), Strauss finds an important contradiction. However, finding weakness in Strauss, Geertsema expands this, suggesting that we need to understand the subject-functioning that is one type of abstraction, and the disruption of coherence that is the other type, and that the analytic aspect is like any other as a possible *Gegenstand*.

That is the view taken in §6–3.3. With Geertsema, it emphasises the pre-theoretical basis and fully human activity of theoretical thought and differentiates between what I have called target aspects and the aspect of functioning (§4–3.9). It replaces the restrictive "non-logical aspects" with "aspects of the world", which includes the analytical.

Clouser's (2005) suggestion of a halfway "lower abstraction" between pre-theoretical and theoretical attitudes might also address some of Strauss' criticisms and is adopted here.

Finally, Dooyeweerd's critique might not be absolutely transcendental, perhaps depending on an aspectual view of reality or a double-separation *Gegenstand* (see §6–3.3). However, "transcendental" critique is never absolute, but always relative to one's starting-points. If we respect everyday experience, then we cannot escape an aspectual view, and if we respect diversity and coherence, we probably find double-separation unavoidable in theoretical thought.

12–1.12 Critiques of Dooyeweerd's Idea of Antithesis Between Christian and Non-Christian Thought

Dooyeweerd was influenced by Augustine's absolute antithesis between *civitas Dei* and *civitas terrena*, to emphasise the fundamental difference between his ("Christian") and mainstream ("non-Christian") philosophies. Yet Dooyeweerd also recognised that by what Christian doctrine calls common grace, "non-Christian" philosophy delivers genuine insight that should be respected. Some thinkers who followed Dooyeweerd have taken the first but downplayed the second, to adopt an extremely antithetical stance. While some of Dooyeweerd's writings seem to exude this, I do not find this in most. Dooyeweerd positively appreciates many mainstream philosophers, e.g. Kant, Rickert, Husserl, Heidegger (NC,II, 443, 275, 475, 22). Dooyeweerd's critical exposing of presuppositions was not to bring about opposition but to facilitate genuine dialogue, especially between Christian and non-Christian views. It is for this reason I have written this book and advocate LACE in §10–1.

12–1.13 Critiques of Dooyeweerd's Aspects

There has been little critique of Dooyeweerd's notion of aspects as such, as irreducibly distinct yet coherent kernels of meaningfulness, as spheres of aspectual law. However, Dooyeweerd's suite of aspects has been widely discussed, in ways too voluminous to detail here. Most critics accept most of Dooyeweerd's suite and criticise individual aspects. Some thinkers add more aspects (Stafleu (2005) wants to add a political aspect (Basden 2005) and De Raadt (1997) adds about five aspects). Some disagree over specific aspects, such as kinematic (Strauss 2009), social (Stafleu 2005) and especially the aesthetic (Seerveld 1985; Stafleu 2003). Zuidervaart (1995) makes a useful critique of Dooyeweerd's treatment of the arts, comparing and contrasting it with Heidegger's.

Such debate is healthy, answering Dooyeweerd's call (NC,II, 556) for continual critical reappraisal of his, and every, suite of aspects, and contributing to a Special Theory of Modal Spheres (§4–3.13).

Those are philosophical criticisms. I am aware of three main practical criticisms of Dooyeweerd's aspects (which might feed into philosophical understanding).

One is confusion. Aspects often present themselves in different manifestations simultaneously in a situation, and this can be confusing. See §11–7.3.2 for an example of three economic aspects. This is another reason I differentiate between aspectual functioning and targets (§4–3.9), even though Dooyeweerd did not discuss the latter.

A second is genericity. My colleague, Frances Bell, valued Dooyeweerd's aspects but, on seeing how information systems students used them in their projects, she commented that aspects tend to give analyses that are too broad, without detail. Broad analyses give useful overviews of fields and paradigms (§11–3) and of expertise (§11–6.2), but there is a need for something more detailed too. In fact, aspects can be used for more detailed analyses (§11–7), but this raises the third problem.

The third is the challenge of subjectivity of interpretation of the meaningfulness of Dooyeweerd's aspects, especially during research. See Joneidy's discussion of this in §11–7.2.3. Insofar as Dooyeweerd is correct, our theoretical understanding of aspectual meaningfulness will always be 'subjective'—not primarily because of personal interests or any supposed autonomy of the thinker, but more fundamentally because we are trying to understand, in aspects, what enables us to understand (§4–3.10): how can fish understand the ocean (§4–3.13)?

This, however, does not imply zero trust in our interpretations, because (a) our very living furnishes us with pre-theoretical intuition of aspectual meaningfulness; (b) the three elements of Ground-Ideas can help separate out relevant issues; (c) Dooyeweerd worked out his General Theory of Modal Spheres with care (§4–3.13); (d) the order of aspects is not subjectively constructed; (e) Dooyeweerd's suite of aspects was always tied to the full diverse reality of pre-theoretical experience rather than to theoretical systems (Bunge, Hartmann) or particular themes (Maslow). It thus has a cross-cultural validity (§4–4.2), which has been valued by many from different cultural backgrounds (§5–4.3).

More practically, in much research, the use of aspects is primarily to help clarify tangled issues, as in MAKE and MAIT (§11–6), so some differences in interpretation need not undermine the research, as long as they are consistent and reasonably in line with Dooyeweerd's carefully worked out suite. Moreover, it may be that the subjectivity of analysts' use of aspects is less than that which occurs during standard qualitative coding. Khojah (2018) discusses the impact of the researcher's prior experience on interpretation (§11–7.3.7); an intuitive awareness of aspects can help reveal more clearly the elements of that experience. Further, McGibbon (2018), to minimise the impact of his subjective assessments on his findings, employs aspectual cipations (§11–4.4, §11–7.5).

12–2. Reflection

The above criticisms of Dooyeweerd's philosophy are ones that I have encountered, many from Choi (2000), plus some of my own. There are doubtless others, and readers should assemble their own collections.

The impression I have is that some of Dooyeweerd's thought that is most criticised is not foundational but rather comes from accretions that are influenced by his own cultural background, with some arising from an attempt to defend his ideas against initial criticism from fellow Reformational thinkers and various Christian thinkers. Some of his more foundational ideas seem to have received less criticism.

Almost all of the criticisms above have arisen from philosophical theorists. What is needed is critique of Dooyeweerd by those who have actually used his philosophy in the real, everyday life of research or more widely. Is it not only once we use something that we most fully understand it? The next, final, chapter urges readers to join the adventure of applying Dooyeweerd's philosophy in research.

13 Summary and Conclusions

To look back on adventures with Dooyeweerd's philosophy in research, both mine and others', has been a joy and brings some amazement. This book has recounted what has happened during those adventures over the past 30 years (especially in Chapter 11) and also reflected on what it is about Dooyeweerd's philosophy that has been so fruitful. Both the actual experience and the reflections have proven to be richer and more extensive than I had expected when I began to write.

The book has been about research in general, in a range of fields of research. It is my hope that it will help other researchers to begin their own adventures with Dooyeweerd's philosophy and forge ahead over the next 30 years, helping to ensure good quality research that contributes to humanity's bodies of knowledge in significant ways.

13-1. Summary of Contributions to Research

There are two main reasons why Dooyeweerd's philosophy has been useful in research, as demonstrated in Part III: (a) it is well tuned to the fullness of reality, that was introduced in Part I as "pre-theoretical everyday experience" in its diversity and coherence of meaningfulness, and (b) it offers sound foundations, as discussed in Part II. This is because Dooyeweerd adopted an unconventional standpoint and ground-motive, as discussed in Chapter 5, which encourages radically different perspectives that bring new things to light. The message of this Part IV is a call for researchers to use, critique and refine Dooyeweerd's philosophy.

13-1.1 Overall Benefits

We have seen how Dooyeweerd's philosophy can bring benefits for each stage in research.

- It can provide a clear picture of the fields of our research, as discussed in §8–1 and §11–3, which is useful at the beginning of research.
- It can make sense of the cacophony of ideas and discourses, and do so with some rigour, as discussed in §7–3 and §11–2, which can be useful when reviewing literature.

- Innovative conceptual frameworks and tools can be formulated, as discussed in §5–1, §8–3, §11–3 and §11–4.
- It offers a new perspective on research philosophy, (a) keeping axiology integrated with ontology and epistemology, so encouraging respect not only for diversity but for responsibility too, as discussed in §4–4.1, and (b) providing a sound basis, in Dooyeweerd's notion of Ground-Idea (§7–1), for critiquing extant philosophies and research approaches. Specifically, it enables us to see through apparent incommensurabilities to a wider picture and frees researchers from having to select from among philosophies that do not entirely suit their research (§7–4.1).
- It likewise frees researchers to construct their own methodologies if necessary, providing the philosophically sound foundation on which to do so (§11–5).
- It opens up new approaches to data collection, especially using questionnaires and interviews, which have encouraged participants to give voice to tacit knowledge or issues they might feel are too trivial or embarrassing to mention (§2–6.3, §11–6).
- It offers an efficient approach to analysing collected data—whether from interviews or texts—that can reveal the "down-to-earth" issues of people's complex realities, uncover hidden issues, including a diversity of motivations or values, and then manage the plethora of issues that emerge, by providing philosophically sound, broad categorisations prior to conventional quantitative and qualitative analyses (§11–7).

There are still gaps in the portfolio that need filling, which are discussed in §11–8, but in the psychological, design and social sciences, researchers have demonstrated that Dooyeweerd can help fulfil the mandate of research to contribute to humanity's bodies of knowledge, good quality generic (theoretical) understanding on which it is reasonable to rely.

13–1.2   Contributions to Research Content

Chapter 2 offers a reorienting perspective on research, which makes all fields more open to the diversity of everyday experience, avoiding reductionism. It argues that theoretical knowledge (theories) and thinking are situated within, and depend on, the pre-theoretical (i.e. intuition, tacit knowledge).

Chapter 3 opens up an understanding of the diversity and coherence both *of* research topics, as those of fields, and *within* them, as those of concepts, ideas, etc. It introduces Dooyeweerd's suite of irreducibly distinct yet interconnected aspects as a conceptual tool with which researchers may approach this diversity; the suite is given fuller shape in Chapter 9.

Dooyeweerd's aspects offer spaces for exploring meanings and foundations for classifying. The irreducible distinctness of aspects helps the researcher avoid overlooking issues and the inter-aspect relationships of non-conflict, dependency and analogy (§3–2.4) helps them understand the coherence of what is being researched.

Chapter 4 provides the foundation for a clearer understanding of the concepts that we study and form in research and how to understand the meaningfulness of each. Things and activities (behaviours) are seen as multi-aspectual; viewing them from one aspect restricts our research to a narrow understanding.

This is especially true when studying people because their subject-functioning (§4–3.9) embraces all aspects (§4–3.8.2), but it is also true in the natural and mathematical sciences where, even though the range of subject aspects is more limited, the full range of aspects might be meaningful as object-functioning.

Rationalities and possibilities differ radically in each aspect, as do what is good and evil (axiology) and ways of knowing (epistemology). All is rooted, ultimately, in meaningfulness as an 'ocean' in which both researcher and researched 'swim'. This shared fundamental meaningfulness gives the hope of cross-cultural understanding (§4–4.2) and of reducing or at least understanding and managing research bias (§7–4.2, §11–7.3.5).

Examples are given in Chapter 11 of how these meaningfulness-based understandings clarify concepts and assist in data collection and analysis.

Chapter 5 opens up the religious root of theoretical thought and all that comes from it, as exhibited especially in dialectical ground-motives, which result in narrowing the viewpoint, and in the immanence-standpoint, which has hindered theoretical thought (and therefore research) in understanding everyday experience, how entities appear and function therein, and in taking meaningfulness seriously. Awareness of this instils the intellectual humility that is so necessary for good research. Dooyeweerd offers ways of crossing research boundaries with mutual respect.

Chapter 6 offers a philosophical understanding of the realities of theoretical thought, posing three transcendental questions (some but not all of which are addressed by other philosophers like Kant, Husserl, Foucault and Bhaskar). Doing so offers a fresh approach to truth, as neither Realist nor Anti-Realist, neither modern nor postmodern. With his three transcendental questions, Dooyeweerd developed the notion of three-part Ground-Idea (Chapter 7) with which several problems may be addressed:

- Is data only from sensory inputs; what about research instruments?
- What is progress and advance in knowledge, especially in the light of dialectic and paradigm shifts?
- How can apparently incommensurable perspectives respect and dialogue with each other?
- What happens if one's research does not quite fit accepted research philosophies?
- How may we reduce bias in research?

Using Dooyeweerd's notion of three-part Ground-Idea, Chapter 8 offers ways to overcome confusion around fields, discourses, paradigms, and concepts and ideas. This encourages mutual respect without encroachment and undergirds interdisciplinary research. The twin problems of boundaries between fields being too rigidly drawn and fields encroaching on each other may be ameliorated by replacing the idea of boundary with that of meaningful core, focusing on the responsibility implied by each aspect defining a unique meaningfulness, good and possibility (§4–3). Mutual isolation among discourses may be transformed into inter-discourse dialogue by aspectual analysis of what motivates their emergence and of what interests each. This also offers a way to test claims about the seminality of papers. Examples of doing this are found in §11–2.

Dooyeweerd's idea also addresses the confusion surrounding Kuhn's notion of paradigm; almost all views of what paradigms are may be subsumed under the idea that paradigms are expressions of what is aspectually meaningful to a community (§8–2).

Chapter 9 offers, for reference, a systematic understanding of each aspect, the good (and harm) it makes possible and its relationships with others and provides pointers to further study, especially in Dooyeweerd's writings. It also offers a reasoned justification for using Dooyeweerd's suite of aspects, to which researchers might refer.

Chapter 10, though mainly about research activity, indicates how that activity can affect research content and especially its quality.

Chapter 11 assembles actual experience of how Dooyeweerd's philosophy has been used in most of the stages of research. First, it shows how overviews of fields and their literature have been obtained in several ways, by separating out issues using aspectual analysis. Given in many fields a need for new paradigms and conceptual frameworks, it discusses examples of critique of paradigms, the generation of new paradigms, and formulation of conceptual frameworks. It then discusses the clarification of concepts and ideas, from simple to complex.

In discussing methods of data collection and analysis, Chapter 11 draws attention to tacit knowledge in expertise and to unspoken life aspirations, etc. It offers hope that, instead of focusing on the usual 'high-level' issues that are of interest to management or academics, which fill academic literature, it is possible to be sensitive to the host of 'down-to-earth' issues that are of interest to people living/working 'on the ground', to reveal, uncover and classify them. It offers a systematic way to reveal, measure and understand researcher bias, by separating out direct answers to interview questions from extra volunteered information and analysing both by aspect.

13–1.3 Contributions to Research Activity

Chapter 1 introduces research as a highly complex but delightful human, responsible activity. It suggests that we do not try to define research in terms of its tasks or activities, but in terms of its mandate that should govern research activity, content and application alike.

Chapter 2 urges us to treat research activity not just as a formal, planned, controllable process, nor even as that as an ideal, but as rightly having an everyday character, with the researcher treated not as detached observer but as a participant in the world being researched.

Chapter 3 offers foundational reflections on the diversity and coherence of this research activity, which we develop more fully in Chapter 10. Chapter 10 is the foremost chapter concerned with research activity. Its LACE (listen, affirm, critique, enrich) approach seeks to overcome fruitless conflicts and encourage mutual respect between researchers with different perspectives. Each aspect of research activity is discussed, drawing attention to a host of issues that are usually overlooked.

Chapter 4 develops the holistic mandate for research, situating it within the 'ocean of meaningfulness' that enables all reality to be and occur, including the activity of research. From experience gained, which is recounted throughout Chapter 11, the idea of oceanic meaningfulness seems to be a sound philosophical foundation for participatory research and for the possibility of cross-cultural research. It also offers a philosophical basis for the validity of the multi-aspectual approach taken in Chapter 10.

Chapter 5 opens up the deleterious impact of dialectical religious ground-motives and the immanence-standpoint in research activity, especially in fuelling fruitless battles and mutual disdain. Dooyeweerd offers an escape from this, which situates apparently incommensurable approaches within a wider picture, all making valid contributions, which can be understood by reference to aspects as illustrated in §11–2, in a way that can open up dialogue, which is discussed in §7–3.

Chapter 6 reminds us why the core activity of research, which is the generation of theoretical knowledge along with subsequent critique and refinement thereof, is not neutral or autonomous, but guided by pre-theoretical ("religious") presuppositions, which influence our pre-theoretical research choices.

Chapter 7 not only discusses dialogue between perspectives, but also offers fresh insights into advance in knowledge, in both "normal" and "revolutionary" science, as defined by Kuhn (1962), and into bias in research.

Fields, and discourses among them, too often operate in isolation from each other. Chapter 8 provides a foundation for, and encourages, mutual respect among fields, based on the idea that each field has core aspects that make it meaningful, so more fruitful dialogue between fields may be facilitated. This is especially important in interdisciplinary research.

The systematic presentation of each of Dooyeweerd's aspects in Chapter 9 should help in (a) developing the researcher's intuitive grasp thereof, (b) undertaking aspectual analysis, and (c) making, and justifying, aspectual distinctions in research planning.

Chapter 11 presents actual experience of research activity guided by Dooyeweerd's philosophy, including:

- gaining an overview of the research field by critiquing paradigms using ground-motives and/or identifying what is meaningful using aspects;
- reviewing literature by aspectual analysis, especially to identify gaps;
- developing conceptual frameworks for research;

- clarifying concepts and ideas;
- developing a bespoke research method;
- data collection using questionnaires, interviews and secondary literature;
- data analysis, both quantitative and qualitative, leading to findings.

13–1.4 *Contributions to Research Application*

Chapter 1 sets research in the context of bodies of knowledge and the wider world, with the mandate and possibility of advancing the understanding in one and benefit in the other. Responsibility pervades research. Chapter 2 develops this theme by drawing attention to the meaningfulness in the everyday experience of the wider world and provides a philosophical foundation for doing so.

Chapter 3 discusses the plethora of repercussions that applying research brings, most of them hidden, indirect, unexpected, and some long term. It discusses both the coherence of research with the wider world and the incorporation of findings into bodies of knowledge, which is further developed in Chapter 6.

Chapter 4 offers research application a way to avoid reductionism, and introduces the *Shalom Principle* by which we attend to the diversity of repercussions of research as meaningful aspects, both direct and indirect.

A problem of applying research is that findings emerge from within paradigms and discourse communities in which certain presuppositions and assumptions hold sway that might be inappropriate in the application context. Chapter 5 looks at these presuppositions—worldviews, ground-motives and standpoints. Though affecting mainly research activity and content, the problems that dialectical ground-motives (§5–2) and the immanence-standpoint (§5–3) generate in philosophy and our ways of understanding the world also pervade the application of research in the world (and the way it contributes to bodies of knowledge), because they are the "absolutely central mainspring of human society" (Dooyeweerd 1979, 9). They force us into opposing camps (e.g. Capitalism v. Socialism), denigrate everyday reality, sideline meaningfulness, and narrow our perspectives down to one, or a few, favoured aspects.

Dooyeweerd offers a new idea on how research can bring benefit into the world, not by dialectical opposition or narrow focus but by radical perspectives of multi-aspectual respect, especially in attending to aspects often overlooked or derided.

Chapter 6 discusses the process of critique and refinement of research findings, which informs their use as foundation for further work and for their reliance-worthiness. This is developed in Chapter 7.

Chapter 8, via its aspectual view of disciplines as centring on a core aspect while attending also to neighbouring and other relevant aspects, offers us a basis to transform the competition between institutions in society into teamwork for the benefit of the world.

The systematic presentation of each of Dooyeweerd's aspects in Chapter 9 should help those who apply research to develop an intuitive grasp of their irreducible meaning-kernels, so that they may more cleanly and soundly separate out issues and also distinct normativities. Chapter 10 uses Dooyeweerd's aspects to open up some less-discussed issues of the application context of research.

The methods of data collection and analysis presented in Chapter 11 can be directly applied in real-world contexts, especially to uncover tacit knowledge, unspoken hopes and fears, and hidden down-to-earth issues. The ability to reveal, uncover and classify down-to-earth issues meaningful to people 'on the ground', including their values, as distinct from high-level issues meaningful to management, academics, politicians, etc., should be able to make the output of research more relevant in application.

13–2.   The Changing World of Research

The world of research has changed since Dooyeweerd's time. Then, research was undertaken mostly by an intellectually trained elite (though in Scotland, the Netherlands and a few other countries, the 'ordinary' was respected and the working person was expected to be a thinker); now a much wider range of people undertake research, some of whom have less experience in critical thinking. This is partly why I have sometimes explained what some seasoned thinkers might think was obvious, and I have tried to interpret Dooyeweerd's transcendental understanding of the nature of theoretical thought in terms that I hope most researchers can understand.

Then, society acknowledged the value of allowing space for reflective thinking; now, all researchers are pressured by the absolutisation of values of managerialism and the economy, and time spent on leisured reflection is viewed with suspicion. I doubt that those halcyon days will return. This is one of the reasons I have stressed the multi-aspectual nature of research activity (Chapter 10), so that even in a pressured environment researchers can ensure their research is sound and fulfilling. Wearne (2011, 8) applauds several authors who, aware of these issues and Dooyeweerd's philosophy, have contributed to debate that does not directly fulfil the requirements of their management. It is also why I chose to think of research, not primarily in terms of projects that deliver end-products or published findings, but in terms of its mandate to contribute generic knowledge to humanity's bodies of knowledge on which it is reasonable to rely (§1–2.1), and thereby bring benefit into the world. The meaningfulness of research need not be squeezed out by pressure.

Compared with Dooyeweerd's time, the range and number of papers that a researcher has to read has ballooned. It is difficult to keep up and still have time to reflect. Chapter 11 shows how Dooyeweerd's philosophy can assist the understanding of papers, his ground-motives can initially situate papers and paradigms, and his aspects can help to immanently understand what their authors are saying and how it might be relevant.

Then, the edifice of Western philosophy was taken as our main philosophical context; now there is much greater awareness of the rest of the world. Then, the main major global issue in the minds of most thinkers was the terror unleashed by Nazism and Stalinism and perhaps concerns about colonialism; now, environmental destruction is (in my view) the main global issue, setting the context for all the others, so the overall impetus of philosophical thinking and research is changing. I believe that Dooyeweerd's idea of meaningfulness that transcends humanity (§4–1, §4–3.11) can equip researchers with philosophical ideas to meet this challenge (§11–3.3).

This is one of the reasons I chose to begin the book with Dooyeweerd's starting-points of pre-theoretical everyday experience and its diversity and the commonality of meaningfulness, rather than with the nature of thinking or philosophy as such.

Then, the European versions of the Christian religion (Roman Catholic, Protestant) still exerted major influences, even among intellectuals who tried to oppose them; now the beliefs of society are very different. So Dooyeweerd's transcendental and immanent explorations of the religious root of theoretical thought are even more important now than they were then, giving us a sound basis for critically questioning long-held assumptions about religion.

I hope that this book will help translate Dooyeweerd's ideas into this new era. If Dooyeweerd is correct, then every era and every culture 'swims' in the same 'ocean' of meaningfulness (§4–4.2), even if each era works it out in different ways, so the translation should not be difficult—as the experience in Chapter 11 suggests. We can only know whether Dooyeweerd's ideas can meet the challenges to come by trying them out, seriously and widely.

On the positive side, there is much wider access to Dooyeweerd's ideas than there was 30 or even 20 years ago, especially in the English language. Dooyeweerd-aware researchers and university teachers are now spread through all continents and cultures, including Korea and Malaysia, the Middle East, Africa, Australasia, South America, North America and Europe.

13–3. Coverage of Dooyeweerd's Philosophy

The fields from which examples have been drawn in this book include agriculture, anthropology, biology, chemistry, cognition, computer procrastination, diagrammatology, discourse analysis, documentation, e-government, education, electrical engineering, finance, government policy on research, healthcare, healthcare records, history, information science, information systems, information systems development, information systems use, knowledge management, knowledge representation, Korean culture, mathematics, philosophy of trust, physics, politics, psychology, quantum theory, sociolinguistics, sociology, software development, statistics, sustainability, sustainability policy, theology and trust. If we see each field as centring on core aspects (§8–1), we can see that nearly every aspect is represented there.

If we refer to Table 11.1, we find that the utility of Dooyeweerd's philosophy has been demonstrated well in four, and partly in another two, of the seven typical stages of research. As discussed in §11–8, there are still gaps to fill, especially in using Dooyeweerd at the beginning and end of research and in discussing alternative research methods. Dooyeweerd's philosophy has still to be applied to several data collection methods, including observation, field studies, experiments and thought experiments. Whereas in interviews and questionnaires, a major benefit of Dooyeweerd's philosophy comes from uncovering hidden issues, in these, the benefit might be rather in the clarification of concepts. This comes from clearer delineation of kernel meaningfulness and inter-aspect relationships, as discussed in §11–8.3, §11–4 and §8–3.

The potential of Dooyeweerd's philosophy in the natural and mathematical sciences has yet to be explored. While the diversity of meaningfulness is still likely to prove important, even though less than in the social sciences, what is likely to be more important here is this clarification afforded by clear delineation of aspect kernels and inter-dependency, as for example Satherley (2011) does in the field of chemistry (§11–8.3), arguing for chemical emergence as well as emergence of life. Section 8–3 suggests a useful clarification in quantum theory. Chapter 9's presentation of aspects is designed to assist this.

In the social, human and interdisciplinary fields, Dooyeweerd's philosophy has been demonstrated to be beneficial in both detail and overview in Chapter 11, but more work is needed to establish methods and the limits and potential of the benefits.

Three dozen suggestions have been made of opportunities for research that could be carried out. Over a hundred more specific ones are offered in the field of information systems in Basden (2018a).

13–4. The Adventure Is Just Beginning

Dooyeweerd's ideas have only just begun to be properly tried in mainstream research—even though he called for this in 1955 (NC,I, vii):

> I am strongly convinced that for the fruitful working out of this philosophy, in a genuinely scientific manner, there is needed a staff of fellow-labourers who would be in a position independently to think through its basic ideas in the special scientific fields.

Some ask whether Dooyeweerd is a solution looking for a problem. Some of the problems in research for which I have found Dooyeweerd to be a solution have been more felt than recognised beforehand. Sometimes researchers continue in their work feeling a little uneasy, and it is only when someone offers a "solution" that a deeper problem is brought to light, is recognised and begins to be discussed. I have found that Dooyeweerd as a "solution" has helped me recognise some deeper problems, both in my own field of information systems and in research in general, including the inappropriate ways research treats everyday experience, the way the rich diversity that is experienced in everyday life is narrowed down or even denigrated, the fragmentation of fields, approaches and paradigms (so that those working in them either ignore or talk past each other), the separation of meaningfulness, values and normativity from explanation, and a presumption that theorising offers absolute authority when increasingly this is being questioned. Without Dooyeweerd, I would have felt these problems but never recognised them.

The adventures with Dooyeweerd's philosophy in research, discussed in this book, have been exciting. Discovering Dooyeweerd's philosophy, and especially his aspects, has had a huge impact on my research, that of my students, and some of my colleagues. (It has also revolutionised my teaching and my outlook on life.) I believe his impact can only grow, as others discover how transformatively useful Dooyeweerd can be. My hope is that this book will help researchers to begin this adventure for themselves in their own fields, while always maintaining a critical and self-reflective stance.

If anyone asks me where to begin, my advice is: with Dooyeweerd's aspects, as I did (see Preface). It has been my experience that those who begin with Dooyeweerd's aspects find their way of thinking fruitfully transformed, whereas those who begin with the themes of ground-motives or structures of individuality—themes beloved by many colleagues in Reformational Philosophy—have so far tended to remain in the realms of philosophical questions or abstract overviews and top-level approaches. This is another reason why I deliberately began this book with Dooyeweerd's three starting-points of everyday experience, cohering diversity and meaningfulness, rather than, as some have done, with his ground-motives and his Christian roots. My second piece of advice, to Christian thinkers, is: There is no need to emphasise the supposed difference between Christian and non-Christian thought; are we not all living and even 'swimming' in the same Creational order?

I will rejoice if this book, or any other, (a) stimulates researchers to seriously explore Dooyeweerd as a research philosophy for their approaches, foundations and sources of conceptual tools, and (b) encourages more of my Reformational colleagues to emerge from discussing philosophy and use his ideas more courageously in mainstream research.

I wish everyone well in their adventures.

References

Abuelma'atti A. 2007. *A Philosophical Underpinned Evaluation Strategy for Multimedia*. Masters of Science Dissertation, University of Salford, Salford, UK. Available from the author of this book on request.

Adam A. 1998. *Artificial Knowing: Gender and the Thinking Machine*. Routledge, London, UK.

Ahmad H. 2013. *Down-to-Earth Issues in the Mandatory Use of Information Systems*. PhD Thesis, University of Salford, Salford, UK.

Ahmad H, Basden A. 2013. Down-to-earth issues in information system use. Proceedings of the Pacific Area Conference on Information Systems (PACIS). Paper 191. Jeju Island, Korea.

Aiyenitaju OT. 2018. *Understanding Classroom Issues Encountered by Teachers: The Application of Dooyeweerd's Philosophy*. PhD Thesis, University of Salford, Salford, UK.

Aiyenitaju OT, Basden A. 2017. ICT in the classroom: A study of diverse aspects. UK Academy for Information Systems (UKAIS) Annual Conference, 4–5 April, University of Oxford, UK.

Aquila RE. 1985. Predication and Hegel's metaphysics. Pp. 67–84 in M Inwood (Ed.) *Hegel*. Oxford University Press, Oxford, UK.

Attwood T. 2001. *Asperger's Syndrome: A Guide for Parents and Professionals*. Jessica Kingsley Publishers, London, UK.

Baer LD. 2008. Misunderstandings about student transitions to university: A slow-motion dialogue between staff and students. *Journal of Geography in Higher Education*, 32(2), May, 303–20.

Basden A. 1999. Engines of dialectic. *Philosophia Reformata*, 64(1), 15–36.

Basden A. 2002. The critical theory of Herman Dooyeweerd? *Journal of Information Technology*, 17, 257–69.

Basden A. 2005. Brief comments on Stafleu's proposal for a new political aspect. *Philosophia Reformata*, 70(1), 70–5.

Basden A. 2008a. *Philosophical Frameworks for Understanding Information Systems*. IGI Global Hershey, PA, USA.

Basden A. 2008b. Engaging with and enriching humanist thought: The case of information systems. *Philosophia Reformata*, 73(2), 132–53.

Basden A. 2009. Practically critical: Making the critical approach more useful. Pp. 41–65 in C Brooke (Ed.) *Critical Management Perspectives on Information Systems*. Elsevier, Oxford, UK.

Basden A. 2010a. On using spheres of meaning to define and dignify the IS discipline. *International Journal of Information Management*, 30, 13–20.

Basden A. 2010b. Towards lifeworld-orientated information systems development. pp. 41–65 in H Isomaki, S Pekkola (Eds.) *Reframing Humans in Information Systems Development*. Springer, London, UK.

Basden A. 2011a. Enabling a Kleinian integration of interpretivist and critical-social IS research: The contribution of Dooyeweerd's philosophy. *European Journal of Information Systems*, 20, 477–89.

Basden A. 2011b. A Presentation of Herman Dooyeweerd's aspects of temporal reality. *International Journal of Multi-Aspectual Practice*, 1(1). http://dooy.info/papers/ijmap/issue1/Basden-Aspects.docx.

Basden A. 2017. Suggestions for future sustainability: Philosophical and practical. Pp. 319–43 in P Brandon, P Lombardi, G Shen (Eds.) *Future Challenges in Evaluating and Managing Sustainable Development in the Built Environment*. John Wiley & Sons, Chichester, UK.

Basden A. 2018a. *Foundations of Information Systems: Research and Practice*. Routledge, London, UK.

Basden A. 2018b. A Dooyeweerdian critique of systems thinking. Pp. 37–50 in C Boshuijzen-vanBurken, DM Haftor (Eds.) *Reason, Faith and Practice in Our Common Home: Festschrift for Dr. Sytse Strijbos*. Rozenburg Publishers, Amsterdam, Netherlands.

Basden A. 2019. Dooyeweerd's understanding of meaning (1): Some main themes. *Philosophia Reformata*, 84(1), 1–32.

Basden A, Burke M. 2004. Towards a philosophical understanding of documentation: A Dooyeweerdian framework. *Journal of Documentation*, 60(4).

Basden A, Joneidy S. 2019. Dooyeweerd's understanding of meaning (2): Some implications. *Philosophia Reformata*, 84(2), 1–32.

Basden A, Kutar M. 2010. Diversity in cognitive models. Pp. 465–82 in S Nefti, JO Gray (Eds.) *Advances in Cognitive Systems*. The Institution of Engineering and Technology, London, UK.

Basden A, Wood-Harper AT. 2006. A philosophical discussion of the Root definition in soft systems thinking: An enrichment of CATWOE. *Systems Research and Behavioral Science*, 23, 61–87.

Bates JP, Schaefer RB. 1971. *Research Techniques in Organic Chemistry*. Prentice-Hall, Englewood Cliffs, NJ, USA.

Baudrillard J. 1977/2007. *Forget Foucault*, tr. N Dufresne. Semiotext, Los Angeles, CA, USA.

Baumard P. 1999. *Tacit Knowledge in Organisations*, Sage Publications Ltd, London, UK.

Baxter J. 2010. Discourse analytic approaches to text and talk. Pp. 117–37 in L Litosseliti (Ed.) *Research Methods in Linguistics*. Continuum, London, UK.

Benbasat I, Zmud RW. 2003. The identity crisis within the IS discipline: Defining and communicating the discipline's core principles. *MIS Quarterly*, 27(2), 183–94.

Berger P, Luckmann T. 1967. *The Social Construction of Reality: A Treatise in the Sociology of Knowledge*. Penguin Books, London, UK.

Bergson H. 1908. *L'evolution Creatrice*. F. Alcan, Paris, France.

Bergson H. 1911/1998. *Creative Evolution*, tr. A Mitchell. Dover Publications, Mineola, NY, USA.

Bergvall-Kåreborn B. 2006. Reflecting on the use of the concept of qualifying function in system design. Pp. 39–62 in S Strijbos, A Basden (Eds.) *In Search of an Integrative Vision for Technology: Interdisciplinary Studies in Information Systems*. Springer, London, UK.

Bhaskar RA. 1975/2008. *A Realist Theory of Science*, 2nd edition. Verso, London, UK.

Bhaskar RA. 2012. *Reflections On Meta-Reality: Transcendence, Emancipation and Everyday Life: A Philosophy for the Present*. Routledge, Abingdon, UK.

Black S, Harman M. 2006. *Aspect Oriented Software Development: Towards a Philosophical Basis*. Technical Report TR-06-01, Department of Computer Science, King's College London, UK.

Boden MA. 1999. What is interdisciplinarity? Pp. 13–24 in R Cunningham (Ed.) *Interdisciplinarity and the Organisation of Knowledge in Europe*. Office for Official Publications of the European Communities, Luxembourg.

Bohm D, Peat FD. 1987. *Science, Order and Creativity*. Bantam Books, New York, USA.

Bordo MD, Redish A, Rockoff H. 2015. Why didn't Canada have a banking crisis in 2008 (or in 1930, or 1907, or . . .)? *The Economic History Review*, 68(1), 218–43.

Bourdieu P. 1977. *Outline of a Theory of Practice*, tr. R Nice. Cambridge University Press, Cambridge, UK.

Bourdieu P. 1990. *The Logic of Practice*. Polity Press, Cambridge, UK.

Brandon PS, Basden A, Hamilton I, Stockley J. 1988. *Expert Systems: The Strategic Planning of Construction Projects*. The Royal Institution of Chartered Surveyors, London, UK.

Brandon PS, Lombardi P. 2005. *Evaluating Sustainable Development in the Built Environment*. Blackwell Science, Oxford, UK.

Brandon PS, Lombardi P, Shen G. (Eds.). 2017. *Future Challenges in Evaluating and Managing Sustainable Development in the Built Environment*. John Wiley & Sons, Chichester, UK.

Breems N. 2014. *The Human Use of Computers Framework: Assessment Using the Computer Procrastination Problem*. PhD Thesis, University of Salford, Salford, UK.

Breems N. 2017. Subject-by-proxy: A tool for reasoning about programmer responsibility in artificial agents. *Ethicomp*, 5–8 June, De Montfort University, UK.

Breems N, Basden A. 2014. Understanding of computers and procrastination: A philosophical approach. *Computers in Human Behavior*, 31(2014), 211–23.

Brown RE. 1967. The kerygma of the gospel according to John: The Johannine view of Jesus in modern studies. *Interpretation*, 21(4), 387–400.

Bunge M. 1977. *Treatise on Basic Philosophy, Vol. 3: Ontology 1: The Furniture of the World*. Reidal, Boston, USA.

Bunge M. 1979. *Treatise on Basic Philosophy, Vol. 4: Ontology 2: A World of Systems*. Reidal, Boston, USA.

Burrell B, Morgan G. 1979. *Sociological Paradigms and Organisational Analysis*. Heinemann, London, UK.

Calomiris CW, Haber SH. 2014. *Fragile by Design: The Political Origins of Banking Crises & Scarce Credit*. Princeton University Press, Princeton, NJ, USA.

Chaplin J. 2011. *Herman Dooyeweerd: Christian Philosopher of the State and Civil Society*. University of Notre Dame Press, Notre Dame, IN, USA.

Checkland PB. 1981. *Systems Thinking, Systems Practice*. John Wiley & Sons, Chichester, UK.

Checkland PB, Holwell S. 1998. *Information, Systems and Information Systems: Making Sense of the Field*. John Wiley & Sons, Chichester, UK.

Chesterton GK. 1908. *Orthodoxy*. The Bodley Head, London, UK.

Choi Y-J. 2000. *Dialogue and Antithesis: A Philosophical Study of the Significance of Herman Dooyeweerd's Transcendental Critique*. Thesis, Potchefstroomse Universiteit, S. Africa.

Classen DC, Bates DW. 2011. Finding the meaning in meaningful use. *New England Journal of Medicine*, 365(9), 855–8.

Cliteur PB. 1983. Een inleiding tot de filosofie en rechtstheorie van Herman Dooyeweerd. *Radix*, 9, 198–213.

Clouser R. 2005. *The Myth of Religious Neutrality: An Essay on the Hidden Role of Religious Belief in Theories*. University of Notre Dame Press, Notre Dame, IN, USA.

Collins JC, Porras JI. 1998. *Built to Last: Successful Habits of Visionary Companies*. Century, London, UK.

Confluence Media. 2012. *The Two Dimensions of Being a Detached Observer*. https://confluencemedia.wordpress.com/2012/10/08/the-two-dimensions-of-being-a-detached-observer/ accessed 3 October 2018.

Crotty MJ. 1998. *The Foundations of Social Research: Meaning and Perspective in the Research Process*. Sage Publications Ltd, Thousand Oaks, CA, USA.

Curtis M, Tularam GA. 2011. The importance of numbers and the need to study primes: The prime questions. *Journal of Mathematics and Statistics*, 7(4), 262–9.

Dahlbom B, Mathiassen L. 1993. *Computers in Context: The Philosophy and Practice of System Design*. Blackwell, Oxford, UK.

Davis FD. 1989. Perceived usefulness, perceived ease of use, and user acceptance of information technology. *MIS Quarterly*, 13(3), 319–40.

De Certeau M. 1984. *The Practice of Everyday Life*, tr. S Rendall. University of California Press, Berkeley, USA.

DeLone WH, McLean ER. 1992. Information systems success: The quest for the dependent variable. *Information Systems Research*, 3(1), 60–95.

Demares B, Wolfe CT. 2017. The organism as reality or as fiction: Buffon and beyond. *History and Philosophy of the Life Sciences*, 39(2), 2.

De Raadt JDR. 1991. *Information and Managerial Wisdom*. Paradigm Publications, Idaho, USA.

De Raadt JDR. 1997. A sketch for humane operational research in a technological society. *Systems Practice*, 10(4), 421–41.

De Raadt VD. 2002. *Ethics and Sustainable Community Design*. Universal Publishers, USA. www.uPUBLISH.com/books/deraadt3.htm. ISBN 1-58442-603-4.

Deutsch M. 2000. Cooperation and competition. Pp. 21–40 in M Deutsch, PT Coleman (Eds.) *The Handbook of Conflict Resolution: Theory and Practice*. Jossey-Bass Publishers, San Francisco, USA.

Dewey J. 1938/1991. *Logic: The Theory of Inquiry*. Holt, Rinehart and Winston, New York, USA.

Dooyeweerd H. 1935. *De Wijsbegeerte der Wetsidee*, 3 vols. Amsterdam H.J., Paris, France.

Dooyeweerd H. 1947. Introduction to a transcendental criticism of philosophic thought. *Evangelical Quarterly*, 19(1), January, 42–51.

Dooyeweerd H. 1955. *A New Critique of Theoretical Thought*, vols. 1–4, Paideia Press (1975 edition), Jordan Station, ON, Canada.

Dooyeweerd H. 1979. *Roots of Western Culture: Pagan, Secular and Christian Options*. Wedge Publishing Company, Toronto, Canada.

Dooyeweerd H. 1986. *A Christian Theory of Social Institutions*, tr. M Verbrugge (Ed.), *The Herman Dooyeweerd Foundation*. La Jolla, CA, USA.

Dooyeweerd H. 1997. *Essays in Legal, Social and Political Philosophy.* The Edwin Mellen Press, Lewiston, NY, USA.

Dooyeweerd H. 1999. *In the Twilight of Western Thought: Studies in the Pretended Autonomy of Philosophical Thought.* The Edwin Mellen Press, New York, USA.

Dutreuil S. 2014. What good are abstract and what-if models? Lessons from the Gaïa hypothesis. *History and Philosophy of the Life Sciences*, 36(1), 16–41.

Eckberg DL, Hill L, Jr. 1979. The paradigm concept and sociology: A critical review. *American Sociological Review*, 44, December, 925–37.

Eden C. 1988. Cognitive mapping. *European Journal of Operational Research*, 36, 1–13.

Eriksson DM. 2001. Multi-modal investigation of a business process and information system redesign: A post-implementation case study. *Systems Research and Behavioral Science*, 18, 181–96.

Eriksson DM. 2003. Identification of normative sources for systems thinking: Inquiry into religious ground-motives for systems thinking paradigms. *Systems Research and Behavioral Science*, 20(6), 475–87.

Fathulla K. 2007. *Symbolic Spatial Mapping.* PhD Thesis, University of Salford, Salford, UK.

Feynman R, Leighton R, Sands M. 1964. *The Feynman Lectures on Physics.* California Institute of Technology, Pasadena, CA, USA.

Fishbein M, Ajzen I. 1975. *Belief, Attitude, Intention and Behaviour: An Introduction to Theory and Research.* Addison-Wesley, Reading, MA, USA.

Floridi L. 2004. Open problems in the philosophy of information. *Metaphilosophy*, 35(4), 554–82.

Foucault M. 1977. *Discipline and Punish.* Pantheon Books, New York City, USA.

Frissen VAJ. 2000. ITSs in the rush hour of life. *Information Society*, 16(1), 65–75.

Ganguly K. 2002. Everyday life. *Cultural Critique*, 52, 1–9.

Gauld R, Goldfinch S. 2006. *Dangerous Enthusiasms: E-Government, Computer Failure and Information System Development.* Otago University Press, New Zealand.

Geertsema HG. 1992. *He Menselijk Karakter van ons Kennen* (The Human Character of our Knowing). Buijten en Schipperheign, The Netherlands.

Geertsema HG. 2000. Dooyeweerd's transcendental critique: Transforming it Hermeneutically. Pp. 83–108 in DFM Strauss, M Botting (Eds.) *Contemporary Reflections on the Philosophy of Herman Dooyeweerd*, The Edwin Mellen Press, New York, USA.

Geertsema HG. 2002. Which causality? Whose explanation? *Philosophia Reformata*, 67(2), 173–85.

Glaser BG, Strauss AL. 1967. *The Discovery of Grounded Theory: Strategies for Qualitative Research.* Aldine de Gruyter, New York, USA.

Goede R, Basden A, Ingram R. 2011. Disclosing disclosive systems thinking: Towards a methodology. Pp. 29–40 in J van der Stoep, S Strijbos (Eds.) *From Technology Transfer to Intercultural Development.* Rozenberg Publishers, Amsterdam, Netherlands (ISBN 978 90 361 029 0), and African Sun Media, Bloemfontein, South Africa (ISBN 978 1 9202383 28 2).

Goudzwaard B. 1984. *Idols of Our Time.* Inter-Varsity Press, Downers Grove, IL, USA.

Gunton RM, van Asperen E, Basden A, Bookless D, Araya Y, Hanson DR, Goddard MA, Otieno G, Jones GO. 2017. Beyond ecosystem services: Valuing the invaluable. *Trends in Ecology and Evolution*, 32(4), 249–57.

Habermas J. 1972. *Knowledge and Human Interests*, tr. JJ Shapiro. Heinemann, London, UK.

Habermas J. 1986. *The Theory of Communicative Action: Volume One: Reason and the Rationalization of Society*, tr. T McCarthy. Polity Press, Cambridge, UK.

Habermas J. 1987. *The Theory of Communicative Action: Volume Two: The Critique of Functionalist Reason*, tr. T McCarthy. Polity Press, Cambridge, UK.

Habermas J. 2002. *Religion and Rationality: Essays on Reason, God and Modernity*. Polity Press, Cambridge, UK.

Halliday MAK. 1976. Anti-languages. *American Anthropologist*, 78, 570–84.

Hart H. 1985. Dooyeweerd's *Gegenstand* theory of theory. Pp. 143–66 in CT McIntire (Ed.) *The Legacy of Herman Dooyeweerd: Reflections on Critical Philosophy in the Christian Tradition*. University Press of America, Lanham, NY, USA.

Hartley AM. 2008. *Christian and Humanist Foundations for Statistical Inference*. Resource Publications, Wipf & Stock, Eugene, OR, USA.

Hartmann N. 1952. *The New Ways of Ontology*. Chicago University Press, Chicago.

Heeks R. 2006. *Implementing and Managing eGovernment*. Sage Publications Ltd, London, UK.

Heidegger M. 1927/1962. *Being and Time*, tr. J MacQuarrie, E Robinson. Harper & Row, New York, USA.

Heidegger M. 1971. *Poetry, Language and Thought*, tr. A Hofstadter. HarperCollins, New York, USA.

Heidegger M. 1972. The end of philosophy and the task of thinking. Pp. 55–73 in M Heidegger (Ed.) *On Time and Being*. HarperCollins, New York, USA.

Heidegger M. 1977. *The Question Concerning Technology and Other Essays*. HarperCollins, New York, USA.

Henderson RD. 1994. *Illuminating Law: The Construction of Herman Dooyeweerd's Philosophy*. Free University, Amsterdam, Netherlands.

Herbert DL, Barnett AG, Clarke P, Graves N. 2013. On the time spent preparing grant proposals: An observational study of Australian researchers. *BMJ Open*. http://bmjopen.bmj.com/content/3/5/e002800 accessed 22 May 2018.

Hicks JR. 1967. Monetary theory and history: An attempt at a perspective. Pp. 155–73 in JR Hicks (Ed.) *Critical Essays in Monetary Theory*. Clarendon Press, Oxford, UK.

Hirschheim R, Klein HK. 2012. A glorious and not-so-short history of the information systems field. *Journal of the Association for Information Systems*, 13(4), 188–235.

Hirschheim R, Klein HK, Lyytinen K. 1995. *Information Systems Development and Data Modelling: Conceptual and Philosophical Foundations*. Cambridge University Press, Cambridge, UK.

Husserl E. 1913/1950. *Ideen zu einer reinen Phänomenologie und phänomenologischen Philosophie*. Felix Meiner Verlag, Germany.

Husserl E. 1954/1970. *The Crisis of European Sciences and Transcendental Phenomenology*, tr. D Carr. Northwestern University Press, Evanston, IL.

Hymes D. 1972. Review of *Noam Chomsky* by John Lyons and Frank Kermode. *Language*, 48(2), 416–27.

Introna LD, Ilharco FM. 2004. Phenomenology, screens and the world: A journey with Husserl and Heidegger into phenomenology. Pp. 56–102 in J Mingers, L Willcocks (Eds.) *Social Theory and Philosophy for Information Systems*. John Wiley & Sons, Chichester, UK.

Jackson MC. 1991. *Systems Methodology for the Management Sciences.* Plenum Press, New York and London, UK.

Jackson T. 2009. *Prosperity without Growth: Economics for a Finite Planet.* Earthscan, London, UK.

Jacob M, Ebrahimpur G. 2001. Experience vs. expertise: The role of implicit understanding of knowledge in determining the nature of knowledge transfer in two companies. *Journal of Intellectual Capital,* 2(1), 74–88.

James W. 1907. *Pragmatism: A New Name for Some Old Ways of Thinking.* Longmans, Green and Co., New York, USA.

Jochemsen H. 2006. Normative practices as an intermediate between theoretical ethics and morality. *Philosophia Reformata,* 71(1), 96–112.

Johansson P, Hall L, Sikström S, Tarning B, Lind A. 2006. How something can be said about telling more than we can know: On choice blindness and introspection. *Consciousness and Cognition,* 15, 673–92.

Joneidy S. 2015. *Making Sense of the Information Systems Use Field.* PhD Thesis, University of Salford, Salford, UK.

Joneidy S, Basden A. 2018. Exploring diversity in a field: An application of Dooyeweerd's philosophy. *Philosophia Reformata,* 83(2), 102–29.

Joneidy S, Burke ME. 2018. Applying Dooyeweerd's aspects to understand Meaningful Use in electronic health records. *Health Information and Library Journal,* 36(2), 134–52.

Jones GO. 2007. *Dooyeweerdian Philosophy, Knowledge Based Systems and Sustainability.* PhD Thesis, University of Salford, Salford, UK.

Jones GO, Basden A. 2004. Using Dooyeweerd's philosophy to guide the process of stakeholder engagement in ISD. Pp. 1–19 in MJ de Vries, B Bergvall-Kåreborn, S Strijbos (Eds.) *Interdisciplinarity and the Integration of Knowledge: Proc. 10th Annual Working Conference of CPTS,* 19–24 April: CPTS'2004. Centre for Philosophy, Technology and Social Systems, Amersfoort Netherlands; ISBN 90-807718-3-X.

Kakabadse NK, Kouzmin A, Kakabadse A. 2001. From tacit knowledge to knowledge management: Leveraging invisible assets. *Knowledge and Process Management,* 8(3), 137–54.

Kalsbeek L. 1975. *Contours of a Christian Philosophy,* Wedge Publishing Company, Toronto, Canada.

Kane SC. 2006. *Multi-Aspectual Interview Technique (MAIT).* Doctoral Thesis, University of Salford, Salford, UK.

Kant I. 1790/1987. *Critique of Judgment,* tr. WS Pluhar. Hackett Publishing Company, Indianapolis, IN, USA.

Kelty CM. 2018. Robot life: Simulation and participation in the study of evolution and social behavior. *History and Philosophy of the Life Sciences,* 40(1), Article 16.

Khojah GM. 2013. A new approach to the transition from paper to electronic medical records. Pp. 277–83 in D Stacey, J Solé-Casais, H Gamboa (Eds.), *Healthinf 2013: Proceedings of the International Conference on Health Informatics,* 11–14 February. Barcelona, Spain.

Khojah GM. 2018. *Using Dooyeweerd's Aspects to Understand Down-to-Earth Issues in Use of Medical Records.* PhD Thesis, University of Salford, Salford, UK.

Kimani AG. 2017. *A New Framework for Defining, Identifying and Explicating Tacit Knowledge: Qualitative Research Using Aspectual Analysis on SMEs.* PhD Thesis, University of Salford, Salford, UK.

Klapwijk J. 1987. Reformational philosophy on the boundary between the past and the future. *Philosophia Reformata,* 52, 101–34.

Klapwijk J. 2008. *Purpose in the Living World: Creation and Emergent Evolution*, tr. & ed. H Cook. Cambridge University Press, Cambridge, UK.

Klee V. 1960. *Unsolved Problems in Intuitive Geometry*. University of Washington, Seattle, WA, USA.

Klein HK, Myers MD. 1999. A set of principles for conducting and evaluating interpretive field Studies in information systems. *MIS Quarterly*, 23(1), 67–93.

Knight F. 1924/2009. The limitations of scientific method in economics. Pp. 97ff. in F Knight (Ed.) *The Ethics of Competition*. Alfred Knopf, New York, USA.

Kottak C. 2006. *Mirror for Humanity*. McGraw-Hill, New York, USA.

Krishnan-Harihara S, Basden A. 2009. Understanding failures in e-government: Idolatry as a lens. In A. Basden, D Eriksson, A Strijbos (Eds.) *The Problem of System Improvement: Proceedings of the 13th and 14th Annual Working Conference of the CPTS*. Centre for Philosophy, Technology and Social Systems, ISBN: 978-90-807718-6-4.

Krishnan-Harihara S, Basden A. 2010. Is idolatry a suitable tool to test e-government? Pp. 107–25 in R Goede, L Grobler, DE Haftor (Eds.) *Interdisciplinary Research for Practices of Social Change: Proc. 16th Annual Working Conference of the Centre for Philosophy, Technology and Social Systems (CPTS)*, 13–16 April. Centre for Philosophy, Technology and Social Systems, Maarssen, Netherlands; BZ Repro, Haaksbergen, Netherlands. ISBN/EAN: 978-90-807718-8-8.

Kuhn TS. 1962/1996. *The Structure of Scientific Revolutions*. University Chicago Press, Chicago, USA.

Kuhn TS. 1971. Second thoughts on paradigms. In F Suppe (Ed.) *The Structure of Scientific Theories*. Illinois University Press, Urbana, USA.

Lakatos I, Musgrave A (Eds.). 1970. *Criticism and the Growth of Knowledge*, Cambridge University Press, Cambridge, UK.

Lamb DA. 2014. *Text, Context and the Johannine Community: A Sociolinguistic Analysis of the Johannine Writings*. Bloomsbury T&T Clark, London, UK.

Lazarsfeld PF, Reitz JG. 1970. *Toward a Theory of Applied Sociology*. Technical Report, Bureau of Applied Social Research, Columbia University, New York, USA.

Lee AS. 1999. Rigor and relevance in MIS research: Beyond the approach of positivism alone. *MIS Quarterly*, 23(1), 29–34.

Lee AS. 2004. Thinking about social theory and philosophy in information systems. Pp. 1–26 in J Mingers, LP Willcocks (Eds.) *Social Theory and Philosophy for Information Systems*. John Wiley & Sons, Chichester, UK.

Levi AW. 1975. Philosophy, history of Western. Pp. 247–75 in *Encyclopaedia Britannica*, vol. 14. Encyclopaedia Britannica, Chicago, USA.

Lombardi PL. 2001. Responsibilities towards the coming generations: Forming a new creed. *Urban Design Studies*, 7, 89–102.

Lyon D. 2007. *Surveillance Studies*. Polity Press, Cambridge, UK.

Lyotard J-F. 1984. *The Postmodern Condition: A Report on Knowledge*. Manchester University Press, Manchester, UK.

Maddy P. 2007. *Second Philosophy: A Naturalistic Method*. Oxford University Press, Oxford, UK.

Maddy P. 2009. An interview with Penelope Maddy, March 2009, University of California, Irvine. *The Dualist*, 15, Spring.

Malina BJ. 1985. The Gospel of John in sociolinguistic perspective. In *48th Colloquy of the Center for Hermeneutical Studies*. Center for Hermeneutical Studies, Berkley, CA, USA.

Malinowski B. 1922. *Argonauts of the Western Pacific*. Routledge, London, UK.

322 References

Marcel P. 2013a. *The Christian Philosophy of Herman Dooyeweerd: I. The Transcendental Critique of Theoretical Thought.* WordBridge Publishing, Aalten, The Netherlands.

Marcel P. 2013b. *The Christian Philosophy of Herman Dooyeweerd: II. The General Theory of the Law-Spheres.* WordBridge Publishing, Aalten, The Netherlands.

Marshall P. 1984. *Thine Is the Kingdom: A Biblical Perspective on the Nature of Government and Politics Today.* Marshall Morgan and Scott, Basingstoke, UK.

Maslow A. 1943. A theory of human motivation. *Psychological Review,* 50, 370–96.

Mason RO, Mitroff II. 1981. *Challenging Strategic Planning Assumptions.* Wiley, New York, USA.

Masterman M. 1970. The nature of a paradigm. Pp. 59–89 in I Lakatos, A Musgrave (Eds.) *Criticism and the Growth of Knowledge,* Cambridge University Press, Cambridge, UK.

McGibbon S. 2018. *Towards an Aspectual Conception of Trust.* PhD Thesis, University of Salford, Salford, UK.

McIntire CT. 1985. *The Legacy of Herman Dooyeweerd: Reflections on Critical Philosophy in the Christian Tradition.* University Press of America, Lanham, MD, USA.

Merleau-Ponty M. 1962. *Phenomenology of Perception,* tr. C Smith. Routledge & Kegan-Paul, London, UK.

Midgley G. 2000. *Systemic Intervention: Philosophy, Methodology and Practice.* Kluwer & Plenum, New York, USA.

Mingers J, Willcocks LP. (Eds.). 2004. *Social Theory and Philosophy for Information Systems.* John Wiley & Sons, Chichester, UK.

Mirijamdotter A, Bergvall-Kåreborn B. 2006. An appreciative critique and refinement of Checkland's Soft Systems Methodology. Pp. 79–102 in Strijbos & Basden (2006).

Mooney L, Knox D, Schacht C. 2014. *Understanding Social Problems.* Cengage Learning, Boston, MA, USA.

Moran D. 2000. *Introduction to Phenomenology.* Routledge, London, UK.

Mullane K, Williams M. 2013. *Bias in Research: The Rule Rather Than the Exception? Editor's Update, Elsevier Comment,* Posted on 17 September. www.elsevier.com/editors-update/story/publishing-ethics/bias-in-research-the-rule-rather-than-the-exception accessed 14 September 2018.

Musgrave AE. 1971. Kuhn's second thoughts. *British Journal for the Philosophy of Science,* 22, 287–97

Myers MD, Klein HK. 2011. A set of principles for conducting critical research in information systems. *MIS Quarterly,* 35(1), 17–36.

NC. See Dooyeweerd H. 1955.

Nefti S, Gray JO (Eds.). 2010. *Advances in Cognitive Systems.* The Institution of Engineering and Technology, London, UK.

Nisbett RE, Wilson TDC. 1977. Telling more than we can know: Verbal reports on mental processes. *Psychological Review,* 84(3), 231–59.

Nonaka I, Takeuchi H. 1995. *The Knowledge Creating Company.* Oxford University Press, Oxford, UK.

OECD. 2018. *Global Material Resources Outlook to 2060: Economic Drivers and Environmental Consequences.* Organisation for Economic Co-Operation and Development (OECD). www.oecd.org/environment/global-material-resources-outlook-to-2060-9789264307452-en.htm accessed 24 October 2018.

Open Science Collaboration (OSC). 2015. Estimating the reproducibility of psychological science. *Science*, 349(6251), 943–50. DOI: 10.1126/science.aac4716

Paxton M. 2012. Student voice as a methodological issue in academic literacies research. *Higher Education Research & Development*, 31(3), 381–91.

Peirce CS. 1878. How to make your ideas clear. *Popular Science Monthly*, 12, 286–302.

Pike KL. 1954/1967. *Language in Relation to a Unified Theory of Structure in Human Behavior*, 2nd edition. Mouton, The Hague, Netherlands.

Plantinga A. 1958/2006. Dooyeweerd on meaning and being. *Myodicy*, 27, 10–15, originally *The Reformed Journal*.

Pilling D. 2018. *The Growth Delusion: Wealth, Poverty and the Well-Being of Nations*. Crown & Archetype, Penguin Random House, London, UK.

Polanyi M. 1962/1974. *Personal Knowledge: Towards a Post-Critical Philosophy*. University of Chicago Press, Chicago, USA.

Polanyi M. 1967. *The Tacit Dimension*, Routledge and Kegan Paul, London UK.

Polanyi M, Prosch H. 1975. *Meaning*. University of Chicago Press, Chicago, USA.

Puddefoot JC. 1999. The trust relationship. *Tradition and Discovery: The Polanyi Society Periodical*, 26(3), 62–70.

Reason P. 2006. Choice and quality in action research practice. *Journal of Management Inquiry*, 15(2), 187–203.

Ribiero PF, de Souza ACZ, Banatto BD. 2017. Reflections about the philosophy of technology in the emerging smart power systems. *Ninth Annual IEEE Green Technologies Conference*, 195–202. DOI: 10.1109/GreenTech.2017.35

Ricoeur P. 1974. *Existence and Hermeneutics*. Pp. 3–24 in D. Ihde (Ed.) *The Conflict of Interpretations: Essays in Hermeneutics*, tr. K McLaughlin, Northwestern University Press, Evanston, USA.

Roethlisberger FJ, Dickson WJ. 1939. *Management and the Worker: An Account of a Research Program Conducted by the Western Electric Company, Hawthorne Works, Chicago*. Harvard University Press, Cambridge, MA, USA.

Romme G. 2016. *The Quest for Professionalism: The Case of Management and Entrepreneurship*. Oxford University Press, Oxford, UK.

Russell CA. 2000. *Michael Faraday: Physics and Faith*, ed. O Gingerich (Oxford Portraits in Science Series). Oxford University Press, New York, USA.

Ryle G. 1949. *The Concept of Mind*. Penguin, London, UK.

Sacks O. 1973. *Awakenings*. Duckworth, London, UK.

Sarniak R. 2015. 9 types of research bias and how to avoid them. *Quirks*, Article 20150825-2, Published August 2015, www.quirks.com/articles/9-types-of-research-bias-and-how-to-avoid-them accessed 14 September 2018.

Satherley J. 2011. Emergence in the inorganic world. *Philosophia Reformata*, 76(1), 32–49.

Saunders M, Lewis P, Thornhill A. 2012. *Research Methods for Business Students*, 6th edition. Pearson, Harlow, UK.

Schutz A, Luckmann T. 1973/1989. *The Structures of the Life-World, Volumes I, II*. Northwestern University Press, Evanston, IL, USA.

Searle A. 2005. The Tolsdorff trials in Traunstein: Public and judicial attitudes to the *Wehrmacht* in the Federal Republic 1954–60. *German History*, 23(1), 50–78.

Seerveld C. 1985. Dooyeweerd's legacy for aesthetics: Modal law theory. Pp. 41–80 in CT McIntire (Ed.) *The Legacy of Herman Dooyeweerd: Reflections on Critical Philosophy in the Christian Tradition*. University Press of America, Lanham, MD, USA.

Seerveld C. 2001. Christian aesthetic bread for the world. *Philosophia Reformata*, 66(2), 155–76.

Shannon CE. 1948. A mathematical theory of communication. *Bell System Technical Journal*, 27(3,4), 379–423, 623–66.

Shklar JN. 1986. Squaring the hermeneutic circle. *Social Research*, 71(3), 657–8.

Shortliffe EH. 1976. *Computer Based Medical Consultation: MYCIN*. Elsevier, New York, USA.

Simon HA. 1956. Rational choice and the structure of the environment. *Psychological Review*, 63(2), 129–38.

Stafleu MD. 2003. On aesthetically qualified characters and their mutual interlacements. *Philosophia Reformata*, 68(2), 137–47.

Stafleu MD. 2005. On the character of social communities: The state and the public domain. *Philosophia Reformata*, 69(2), 125–39.

Stanford. 2013a. *The Meaning of Life*. Stanford Encyclopedia of Philosophy, updated 3 June 2013.

Stanford. 2013b. *Theories of Meaning*. Stanford Encyclopedia of Philosophy, updated 3 June 2013.

Stanford. 2016. *On Value*. Stanford Encyclopedia of Philosophy, updated 28 July 2016.

Stommel M, Willis C. 2004. *Clinical Research: Concepts and Principles for Advanced Practice Nurses*. Lippincott, Williams and Wilkins, Philadelphia, PA, USA.

Strauss DFM. 1984. An analysis of the structure of analysis (The Gegenstand-relation in discussion). *Philosophia Reformata*, 49, 35–56.

Strauss DFM. 2009. *Philosophy, Discipline of the Disciplines*. Paideia Press, Grand Rapids, Michigan, USA.

Strauss DFM. 2013. Understanding the *Linguistic Turn* and the *Quest for Meaning*: Historical perspectives and systematic considerations. *South African Journal of Philosophy*, 32(1), 90–107.

Strijbos S. 2006. Towards a disclosive systems thinking. Pp. 235–56 in Strijbos & Basden (2006).

Strijbos S, Basden A (Eds.). 2006. *In Search of an Integrative Vision of Technology: Interdisciplinary Studies in Information Systems*. Springer, New York, USA.

Suppe F. 1972. What's wrong with the received view on the structure of scientific theories? *Philosophy of Science*, 39(1), 1–19.

Terry DJ, Gallois C, McCamisk M. 1993. *The Theory of Reasoned Action: Its Application to Aids-Preventative Behavior*. Psychology Press, Hove, UK.

Tuomi I. 1999. Data is more than knowledge: Implications of the reversed hierarchy for knowledge management and organizational memory. Pp. 147–55 in *Hawaii International Conference on Systems Sciences, Proceedings from the Thirty-Second HICSS*. IEEE Computer Society Press, Los Alamitos, CA, USA.

Vallone L. 2018. *Big and Small: A Cultural History of Extraordinary Bodies*. Yale University Press, New Haven, CT, USA.

van der Hoeven J. 1978. In memory of Herman Dooyeweerd: Meaning, time and law. *Philosophia Reformata*, 130–43.

van Loon JFG. 1994. Dooyeweerd en gesprek en filosofie [Dooyeweerd in dialogue with philosophy]. Pp. 95–113 in *Dooyeweerd Herdacht: Dooyeweerd Commemorated: Lectures held at the Dooyeweerd-Symposium at the Free University of Amsterdam, Friday, November 18 1994, de Bruijn*. VU Press, Amsterdam, The Netherlands.

Verburg ME. 2015. *Herman Dooyeweerd: The Life and Work of a Christian Philosopher*. Paideia Press, Jordan Station, ON, Canada.

Verkerk MJ, Hoogland J, van der Stoep J, de Vries MJ. 2015. *Philosophy of Technology: An Introduction for Technology and Business Students*. Routledge, London, UK.

Vollenhoven DHTh. 1950. *Geschiedenis der Wijsbegeerte. I. Inleiding en geschiedenis der Griekse wijsbegeerte voor Plato en Aristotles*. Wever, Franeker, The Netherlands.

Walden. 2010. *7 Research Challenges (And How to Overcome Them)*. Walden University. www.waldenu.edu/connect/newsroom/publications/articles/2010/01-research-challenges accessed 17 September 2018.

Walsham G. 2001. *Making a World of Difference: IT in a Global Context*. John Wiley & Sons, Chichester, UK.

Wand Y, Weber R. 1995. On the deep structure of information systems. *Information Systems Journal*, 5, 203–24.

Wearne BC. 2011. Jacob Klapwijk's invitation: Come to the party: Introduction by guest editor. *Philosophia Reformata*, 6(1), 1–10.

Webster. 1971. *Webster's Third New International Dictionary of the English Language, Unabridged*. G. & C. Merriam & Co., Springfield, MA, USA.

Wenger E. 1998. *Communities of Practice: Learning, Meaning and Identity*. Cambridge University Press, Cambridge, UK.

White PA. 1987. Causal report accuracy: Retrospect and prospect. *Journal of Experimental Social Psychology*, 23(4), 311–15.

Wilson FA. 1997. The truth is out there: The search for emancipatory principles in information systems design. *Information Technology and People*, 10(3), 187–204.

Winch P. 1958. *The Idea of a Social Science and its Relation to Philosophy*. Routledge and Kegan Paul, London, UK.

Winfield MJ. 2000. *Multi-Aspectual Knowledge Elicitation*. PhD Thesis, University of Salford, Salford, UK.

Winfield MJ, Basden A. 2006. Elicitation of highly interdisciplinary knowledge. Pp. 63–78 in S Strijbos, A Basden (Eds.) *In Search of an Integrated Vision for Technology: Interdisciplinary Studies in Information Systems*. Springer, London, UK.

Winfield MJ, Basden A, Cresswell I. 1996. Knowledge elicitation using a multi-modal approach. *World Futures*, 47, 93–101.

Witte J. (Ed.). 1986. *A Christian Theory of Social Institutions*. The Herman Dooyeweerd Foundation, La Jolla, CA, USA.

Wooffitt R. 2005. *Conversation Analysis and Discourse Analysis: A Comparative Critical Introduction*. Sage Publications Ltd, London, UK.

Yates-Mercer P, Bawden D. 2002. Managing the paradox: The valuation of knowledge and knowledge management. *Journal of Information Science*, 28(1), 19–29.

Ybema S, Kamsteeg F. 2009. Making the familiar strange: A case for disengaged organizational ethnography. Chapter 5 in S Ybema, D Yanow, H Wiels, F Kamsteeg (Eds.) *Organizational Ethnography: Studying the Complexities of Everyday Life*, Sage Publications Ltd, London, UK.

Yousafzai SY, Foxall GR, Pallister JG. 2007. Technology acceptance: A meta-analysis of the TAM: Part 1. *Journal of Modelling in Management*, 2(3), 251–80.

Zuidervaart L. 1995. Fantastic things: Critical notes toward a social ontology of the arts. *Philosophia Reformata*, 60(1), 37–54.

Zuidervaart L. 2016. *Religion, Truth and Social Transformation: Essays in Reformational Philosophy*. McGill-Queen's University Press, Montreal, Canada.

Index

Note: Page numbers for tables are in **bold** and those for figures are in *italics*. Underlined references indicate key material. Section numbers are preceded by §️ and indicate that the entire section is relevant to the entry.

Printed in the United States
by Baker & Taylor Publisher Services